# COURTS, REGULATORS, AND THE SCRUTINY OF ECONOMIC EVIDENCE

# Courts, Regulators, and the Scrutiny of Economic Evidence

*Comparative Perspectives*

DESPOINA MANTZARI

OXFORD
UNIVERSITY PRESS

OXFORD
UNIVERSITY PRESS

Great Clarendon Street, Oxford, OX2 6DP,
United Kingdom

Oxford University Press is a department of the University of Oxford.
It furthers the University's objective of excellence in research, scholarship,
and education by publishing worldwide. Oxford is a registered trade mark of
Oxford University Press in the UK and in certain other countries



First Edition published in 2022



Published in the United States of America by Oxford University Press
198 Madison Avenue, New York, NY 10016, United States of America

British Library Cataloguing in Publication Data
Data available

Library of Congress Control Number: 2022940358

ISBN 978–0–19–885160–8

DOI: 10.1093/oso/9780198851608.001.0001

Printed and bound in the UK by
TJ Books Limited

# Preface and Acknowledgements

One of the principal motives when embarking on this book was to shed light on the challenges expert economic evidence and analysis present for judicial review in a neighbouring field to that of competition law, the field of utility regulation, which has been largely underexplored by both competition law and administrative law scholars. It soon became clear that although there is a significant body of doctrinal analysis on judicial review of regulatory agencies' decisions, there is very little research that has sought to systematically examine the interaction of both regulators and courts with economic evidence. This book aims to address this gap in the literature by engaging deeply with economics and exploring for the first time their impact on the exercise of regulatory discretion and judicial review in two common law jurisdictions: the US and the UK. It represents a profoundly comparative and interdisciplinary endeavour. This is not out of methodological ambition. It is rather that the issue of adjudicating economic evidence in regulatory disputes is a complex one. It depends in part on normative arguments about which institutions in the regulatory state (courts or regulators) should have primary interpretive authority over defining economically informed concepts upon which our enjoyment of essential services depends. It also requires an understanding of how judicial and other institutions respond to the demands of judicial review of economic evidence, how they perceive their role in the regulatory enterprise, and how their role evolves over time. It is essentially about regulatory and judicial discretion, its constraints, and limits at the intersection of two distinct 'rationalities': legal and economic. To answer these questions the book combines theoretical, doctrinal, comparative, and empirical analysis. It aspires to stimulate and encourage a productive dialogue between lawyers and economists, who have tended to talk past each other despite facing common interpretive challenges.

The work started life as a doctoral research project at University College London (UCL), Faculty of Laws. Given its origins, primarily thanks go to my inspiring supervisor Professor Ioannis Lianos. To Professor Lianos I owe enormous gratitude for his guidance, immense support, and advice he has provided throughout my academic life. I have been extremely lucky to have had such an open-minded supervisor who gave me the liberty to explore different research avenues. I am also grateful to Professor Richard Rawlings, my second supervisor, for his thoughtful comments on the administrative law aspects of the book and his steady guidance. While writing this work I benefited from a research stay at UC Berkeley Boalt Hall School of Law. To my supervisor at UC Berkeley, Professor Martin Shapiro, I am grateful for courageously introducing me to the world of political science. I should also acknowledge and thank Valentine Korah, Emeritus Professor of Competition Law at UCL for her kind mentorship all these years. My examiners, Professor Pierre Larouche and Professor Tony Prosser, provided helpful feedback and much-appreciated encouragement to develop the original thesis into a monograph. I would also like to thank the UCL Faculty of Laws for a period of post-maternity sabbatical leave that proved instrumental for completing the manuscript. The editorial team at Oxford University Press has been excellent throughout the way.

The manuscript benefited from insightful comments from Peter Freeman CBE (QC), Chairman at the UK Competition Appeal Tribunal, and suggestions for improvement from five anonymous referees. I have also benefited enormously from the intellectual stimulation of my colleagues at UCL and elsewhere. I would like to thank Maria Ioannidou, Andriani Kalintiri, Pablo Ibáñez Colomo, Niamh Dunne, Damien Geradin, Amber Darr, Andrew McLean, Javier Tapia, Philipp Hacker, Florence Thépot, Saskia Lavrijssen, Ioannis Kokkoris, Chris Hilson, and Dimitrios Kyritsis for reading drafts of this work and for their thoughtful comments. I would also like to thank my economists-friends for our many discussions over the years and in particular Germain Gaudin, Minyan Zhu, and Anna Rita Bennato. The following people also made important clarifications in conversation or correspondence: Honourable Judge Ginsburg, President of the DC Circuit Court of Appeals of the US; Sir Nicholas Forwood QC, formerly judge at the EU General Court; Dr Peter Davis, former executive member of the UK Competition Commission; Stephen Littlechild, fellow, Judge Business School, University of Cambridge; Catherine Waddams, emeritus professor in Norwich Business School and member of the Centre for Competition Policy; Amelia Fletcher CBE, professor of competition policy at Norwich Business School and deputy director at the Centre for Competition Policy; Morten Hviid, professor of law at the University of East Anglia and founding member of the Centre for Competition Policy; Chris Decker, research fellow at Oxford University; Professor Pietro Crocioni, currently economist at DG Competition; Howard Shelanski, professor of law at Georgetown University; and Cristina Caffarra, senior consultant to Charles River Associates.

Portions of this work were introduced to various audiences over the last years: the UCL Centre for Law, Economics and Society, the UCL Laws Lunchtime Research Seminar Series (2019), the ECPR Standing Group for Regulatory Governance Conference (2018), the Institute of Advanced Legal Studies Evening Guest Seminar (2018), Tilburg University (2018), the University of Reading (2017), Oxford University, Centre for Socio-Legal Studies (2017), Society of Legal Scholars (2017), the UK IVR Annual Conference (2017), Humboldt University (2016), and the Centre for Competition Policy at the University of East Anglia (2014). I benefited greatly from feedback at each.

I received major research support funding from the UK Arts and Humanities Research Council. The UCL Faculty of Laws also provided me with various grants to conduct research for this study and to present my work in conferences, including a Major Award. In 2016, I was awarded a British Academy/Leverhulme Small Research Grant to develop the empirical dimension of this work, which is included in Chapter 4. I am grateful for the Academy's support and indebted to all the interviewees at the UK regulatory agencies who set aside their valuable time to assist with this project. I would also like to thank Dr Francesca Pia Vantaggiato for her excellent research assistance with the empirical aspects of the work.

Most of all I am grateful to my parents, Gerassimos and Stella and to my brother Ioannis. Without their love, humour, encouragement, and support all these years, this book would never have been attempted, let alone completed. Lastly, this journey would not have been the same without the unconditional love of my husband Panos and our daughter Stella. To them, the light of my life, this book is dedicated.

# Contents

# List of Figures

# List of Tables

# Table of Cases

## UNITED KINGDOM

## EUROPEAN UNION

## NEW ZEALAND

## UNITED STATES

# Table of Legislation

**Regulations**

**Other Rules**



## INTERNATIONAL INSTRUMENTS



## NEW ZEALAND



## UNITED STATES

**Legislation**

**Orders and Rules**

# 1
# Introduction

## 1.1 Scope and Aims

Undeniably professional experts and expertise have shaped much of our modern regulatory society. From the regulation of hazardous waste to the monitoring of assisted reproduction and from the supervision of financial markets to the regulation of utilities, experts sitting in independent regulatory agencies have been delegated enormous discretionary powers to address and defend the legitimacy of policy decisions. Whether interpreted as an effort to 'depoliticise public issues'[1] or more generally as a manifestation of the 'knowledge society'[2] we live in, expert knowledge is here to stay.

This larger trend of appealing to expertise in the decision-making process of regulatory agencies can be contrasted with the generalisation characterising much of the judiciary. We tend to think that independence and impartiality are the defining characteristics of the judiciary, and we forget that generalisation is also an important, yet understated feature. Surely specialised courts (charged with the resolution of a specific type of disputes) and specialist courts (comprised of professional and lay members) exist in several countries,[3] but still the judiciary largely remains the domain of the generalist judge. Martin Shapiro has rightly pointed out that 'to the extent that (courts) specialise, they lose the one quality that clearly distinguishes them from administrative lawmakers'.[4] Yet, those last generalists left in a specialised world are the final arbiters of expert regulatory judgments.[5] And although in the wake of the mass privatisations programmes scholars reserved a rather modest role for courts in the regulatory state, the surge in the number of legal battles between the regulators and the regulated demonstrates otherwise: that courts have in fact become one of its central actors.[6] This is not only the case in the US, which is notorious for its 'regulation through litigation'[7] mode of governance. In the last twenty years or so, several western European countries, such as the UK, have also experienced an enhancement of the role of courts, and other types of adjudicative body, in the regulatory process.

[1] Dorothy Nelkin, 'The Political Impact of Technical Expertise' (1975) 5(1) Soc Stud Sci 35, 36.

[2] See Peter Drucker, *The Age of Discontinuity—Guidelines to our Changing Society* (Harper & Row 1969).

[3] See, eg, in the UK, the Competition Appeal Tribunal (CAT); in Belgium, the Conseil de la Concurrence; in Chile, the Tribunal de Defensa de la Libre Competencia (TDLC); in Australia, the Australia Competition Tribunal (ACT); and in Canada the Competition Tribunal, all charged with the resolution of competition law disputes. In France, see the Conseil d'Etat charged with the resolution of administrative law disputes; in the US the Court of Appeals for the Federal Circuit charged with the resolution of disputes involving patent laws.

[4] See Martin Shapiro, *The Supreme Court and Administrative Agencies* (Free Press 1968) 53.

[5] See Diane Wood, 'Generalist Judges in a Specialised World' (1997) 50 SMU L Rev 1755, 1756.

[6] See Julia Black and Peter Muchlinski, 'Introduction' in Julia Black, Peter Muchlinski, and Paul Walker (eds), *Commercial Regulation and Judicial Review* (Hart 1998) 1.

[7] See Kip W Viscusi (ed), *Regulation through Litigation* (Brookings Institution Press 2002). See further Robert A Kagan, *Adversarial Legalism: The American Way of Law* (Harvard Univ Press 2003).

*Courts, Regulators, and the Scrutiny of Economic Evidence*. Despoina Mantzari, Oxford University Press.
 DOI: 10.1093/oso/9780198851608.003.0001

What factors might account for the judiciary's growing involvement in regulating the regulators? The answer is found in both institutional and substantive developments taken place since the early nineties. On the institutional front, the number of actors involved in the production and application of the law has increased tremendously in the EU Member States following the EU-driven liberalisation and market integration efforts. The liberalisation directives in areas such as telecommunications and energy provided for the establishment of National Regulatory Authorities (NRAs) to administer regulation[8] and institutionalised in certain areas a 'triangular relationship' between the Commission, the NRAs, and national courts.[9] At the same time, the directives established 'network agencies', namely the Body of European Regulators for Electronic Communications (BEREC)[10] in electronic communications and the Agency for the Cooperation of Energy Regulators (ACER)[11] in energy regulation to develop best practices that could be shared among the NRA members in cooperation with the European Commission. The upshot of these developments has been that national bodies, supranational bodies, 'network agencies', as well as private actors now interact in what has become an institutionally fragmented regulatory process.[12] As a result of such institutional complexity, rich incentives are presented to prospective litigants to challenge regulatory decisions before national, European, and even the Strasbourg Court.

On the substantive front, broader constitutional and jurisprudential developments in several EU Member States have created new grounds for the review of regulators' decisions. Prominent amongst these is the UK, which enjoys a 'multi-streamed jurisdiction',[13] a term employed to denote that judicial review encompasses not only common law principles, but also relevant applications of retained EU law and of the European Convention on Human Rights (ECHR).[14] At the same time, the establishment of a specialist tribunal, the Competition Appeal Tribunal (CAT), possessing both statutory review jurisdiction (similar to common law judicial review) and statutory appeal jurisdiction (where it engages with the factual merits of the case) represents a new, attractive venue to challenge regulatory decisions.

Courts' empowerment in the realm of regulation has inevitably required judges to routinely adjudicate disputes where several types (eg scientific, forensic) and forms (eg quantitative, qualitative, statistical, econometrical) of evidence are involved. What the book is particularly interested in exploring is the interaction of judges (and regulators)

[8] See, eg, Commission Directive 90/388/EEC of 28 June 1990 on competition in the markets for telecommunications services [1990] OJ L192/10, Art 7.

[9] See Pierre Larouche and Maartje de Visser, 'The Triangular Relationship between the Commission, NRAs and National Courts Revisited' (2006) 64 Communications & Strategies 125.

[10] Regulation (EC) 1211/2009 of the European Parliament and of the Council of 25 November 2009 establishing the Body of European Regulators for Electronic Communications (BEREC) and the Office [2009] OJ L337/1 (BEREC Regulation).

[11] Regulation (EC) 713/2009 of the European Parliament and of the Council Establishing an Agency for the Cooperation of Energy Regulators [2009] OJ L211/1 (ACER Regulation).

[12] See Javier Tapia and Despoina Mantzari, 'The Regulation/Competition Interaction' in Damien Geradin and Ioannis Lianos (eds), *Handbook on European Competition Law—Substantive Aspects* (Edward Elgar 2013) ch 14.

[13] Richard Rawlings, 'Modelling Judicial Review' (2008) 61 Current Leg Probl 95, 96.

[14] See, eg, *Peter Marcic v Thames Water Utilities Ltd* [2002] EWCA Civ 65 and *Marcic v Thames Water Utilities Ltd* [2003] UKHL 66.

with economic evidence and the challenges this raises for the error-correction function of judicial review.

To keep the discussion focused, the book examines appeals from utility regulators in two common law jurisdictions: the United Kingdom[15] and the United States of America (on the federal level). The choice of these comparator jurisdictions is owing to the significant institutional differences that exist between the two with regard to the procedures available for the review of economic evidence—differences of such magnitude and scale that permit, as we shall see throughout the book, the observation of a rich set of factors that affect the judicial scrutiny of economic evidence. The scope of the book now comes into greater focus: it is concerned with appeals from the sector-specific regulators of communications (Office of Communications, OFCOM),[16] energy (Office of Gas and Electricity Markets, OFGEM), and water (Office of Water Services, OFWAT) in the UK and from the federal regulators of communications (Federal Communications Commission, FCC) and energy (Federal Energy Regulatory Commission, FERC) in the US.[17] The work of the Competition and Markets Authority (CMA) in the UK with respect to utility regulation is also discussed. In terms of positive analysis, the study focuses on post-privatisation developments in the sectors of telecommunications, gas, electricity, and water regulation in the UK, and on post-liberalisation developments in the markets for gas and electricity and in the local telecommunications market in the US.

Economic evidence as understood in this work encompasses theories, methods, and tools used by the discipline of economics (mostly neoclassical, industrial organisation economics) with the aim to advance normative claims on matters of regulatory policy. It does not include economic analysis employed to measure the costs and benefits of different policy options (ie cost–benefit analysis), which, notwithstanding its relevance to the regulatory state, it nonetheless has a different logic to industrial organisation economics. Competition law scholars may be quick to note that courts' interaction with economic evidence has already been explored in their field.[18] This may be true for competition law, but the present endeavour aims to shed light on the manifestation and adjudication of economic evidence in the closely neighbouring and underexplored realm of utility regulation. In fact, a systematic analysis

[15] Technically speaking, the 'United Kingdom' refers collectively to the three legal systems of England and Wales, Scotland, and Northern Ireland. When dealing with UK materials the book will be assuming the England and Wales jurisdiction unless otherwise stated.

[16] But only with respect to the regulation of telecommunications.

[17] The US lacks a federal regulator for water. This is because the provision of water and wastewater services is handled at the local level with public water utilities serving almost 80 per cent of the population. Federal oversight is limited to environmental regulation including water safety standards and is undertaken by the Environmental Protection Agency.

[18] See, eg, Michael R Baye and Joshua D Wright, 'Is Antitrust Too Complicated for Generalist Judges? The Impact of Economic Complexity and Judicial Training on Appeals' (2011) 54 J L Econ 1; Claus-Dieter Ehlerman and Mel Marquis (eds), *European Competition Law Annual 2009: The Evaluation of Evidence and its Judicial Review in Competition Cases* (Hart 2011); Ioannis Lianos, '"Judging Economists": Economic Expertise in Competition Law Litigation: A European View' in Ioannis Lianos and Ioannis Kokkoris (eds), *The Reform of EC Competition Law: New Challenges* (Kluwer Law International 2010) ch 10; Anne-Lise Sibony, *Le Juge et le Raisonnement Économique en Droit de la Concurrence* (LGDJ 2008); Christopher Bellamy, 'An EU Competition Court: the Continuing Debate' in Ioannis Lianos and Ioannis Kokkoris (eds), *The Reform of EC Competition Law: New Challenges* (Kluwer Law International 2010) ch 3.

of the interaction of both sectoral regulators and courts with economic evidence is missing from existing legal scholarship. This is despite the enormous societal impact of utility regulation and the important role of economists within regulatory authorities. For instance, if one takes a closer look at the 'outputs' of regulatory authorities she will soon quickly realise that the discipline of economics has become the most important source of wisdom since the liberalisation of the essential services of energy, telecoms, and water. Because the competitive transformation of such services was accompanied by considerable rules concerning, amongst other matters, access to networks and price regulation, expert economists sitting in independent regulatory agencies were called to bring their own esoteric knowledge and tools to bear on regulatory decision-making. This is not only the case in the US where the appointment of world-class economists to the chairmanship of federal regulatory agencies was first documented.[19] Economists also surged as important institutional actors in the UK privatisation process[20] by directing the newly created 'Ofdogs',[21] that is, the non-ministerial governmental departments that were established during the Thatcher era to control the privatised monopolies. Today, several high impact regulatory decisions, not solely concerned with the promotion of economic efficiency, but also with equity considerations are informed by economic evidence and analysis.

The pervasiveness of economic evidence in regulatory outputs gives rise to an uncomfortable question: how can appellate courts staffed with generalist judges feel confident in reviewing such decisions? This question becomes even more pressing if we think that judicial review serves, amongst others,[22] as a key error-correction device, that is, a mechanism for ensuring the soundness and accuracy of regulatory decisions.[23] Assuming, therefore, that judicial review can minimise erroneous regulatory decisions, does the increased amount of economic evidence that is presented in regulatory disputes challenge the error-correction function of judicial review? To put it otherwise, what are the limits of judicial review of economic evidence in appeals from utility regulators in the US and the UK? And how should such limits be addressed from an institutional design perspective?

The question is highly topical. From distant Australia to South America and from Asia to the UK, several jurisdictions have been focusing their attention on the review mechanisms of regulatory decisions in the utility sector, as evidenced by several high-profile policy reforms.[24] The loose strands of the ongoing academic and policy debate

[19] For example, Alfred Kahn was appointed in 1974 to the chairmanship of the New York Public Service Commission, which was responsible for the regulation of electric, telephone, gas, and water companies and later on under President Carter to the CAB. For an analysis see, Thomas K McCraw, *Prophets of Regulation* (Harvard Univ Press 1984) ch 7.

[20] Notable economists served as DG's. See, eg, Sir Bryan Carsberg who was the first DG of OFTEL or Professor Sir Steven Littlechild who served as Director General of Electricity Supply from 1989 to 1998 and Sir Ian Byatt who served as the UK Director for Water Regulator from 1989 to 2000.

[21] Carol Harlow and Richard Rawlings, *Law and Administration* (3rd edn, CUP 2009).

[22] To this effect see Harlow and Rawlings (n 21) 669. See further Martin Shapiro, 'Appeal' (1980) 14 L Soc Rev 629.

[23] See, eg, Steven Shavell, 'The Appeals Process as a Means for Error Correction' (1995) 24 J Leg Stud 379; Chad M Oldfather, 'Error Correction' (2010) 85 Ind LJ 49.

[24] In Australia, see Standing Council on Energy and Resources (SCER), 'Review of the Limited Merits Review Regime' (July 2012). In the UK, see Department for Business, Innovation and Skills (DBIS), 'Streamlining Regulatory and Competition Appeals: Consultation on Options for Reform' 19 June 2013, available at: https://assets.publishing.service.gov.uk/government/uploads/system/uploads/attachment_

on regulatory appeals seem to revolve around two issues. The first issue may be dubbed 'jurisprudential' and concerns the appropriate scope of review of regulatory decisions. Couched in the familiar language of 'judicial deference' versus 'non-deference' the scope of review encompasses questions concerning the standard of review (eg correctness, reasonableness) and the intensity thereof. The second one may be dubbed 'institutional' and broadly relates to the optimal institutional response to the pervasiveness of economic evidence in regulatory decisions. For instance, should such decisions be reviewed by courts of general jurisdiction or by specialist adjudicatory bodies composed of professional judges and lay members with a background in economics?

Such issues are not new in the broader competition law and regulation and public law scholarship. An abundance of literature explores the appropriate scope of review of administrative action,[25] while the policy debate on the optimal institutional response to regulatory agencies' expertise in regulatory matters traces back to the very rise of the New Deal regulatory state.[26] But the challenges posed by economic evidence bring these age-old questions into new light. How does the increasing reliance of regulators on economic inputs in the regulatory state affect the legal outputs of regulation and transform administrative discretion and judicial review? What is the extent of judicial scrutiny of economic evidence and of the judiciary's corresponding deference to the regulatory agencies' decisions? Does—and—should economic evidence change the process, standard, and intensity of judicial review? And on a broader level, with the ever-increasing recourse to expert economic evidence and analysis, what is the fit with older conceptions of the court-regulatory agency in the US and the UK? Although there is a significant body of doctrinal analysis on judicial review of regulatory agencies' decisions in these two jurisdictions, there is very little research that has sought to systematically examine the interaction of courts and regulators with economic evidence. This book aims to address this gap in the literature by engaging deeply with economics and exploring for the first time their impact on the exercise of regulatory discretion and judicial review. In doing so it adopts a mixed methods approach, which combines theoretical and doctrinal analysis with an empirical perspective. This is crucial as there has never been an empirical analysis of the influence and integration of economic evidence in the regulatory decision-making process.

In this context, the aim of this book is threefold. First, it seeks to open the 'black box' of the regulatory decision-making process and explore the influence of economic evidence and analysis on the discretionary assessments of economic regulators

data/file/229758/bis-13-876-regulatory-and-competition-appeals-revised.pdf accessed 6 June 2022. In September 2020, John Penrose MP was commissioned by the UK Chancellor of the Exchequer and the Secretary of State for Business, Energy and Industrial Strategy to write an independent report on how the UK's approach to competition and consumer issues could be improved. The report was published in February 2021, see 'Power to the People: Independent Report on Competition Policy' available at: <https://www.gov.uk/government/publications/power-to-the-people-independent-report-on-competition-policy> accessed 6 June 2022. See also Navroz Dubash and Bronwen Morgan (eds), *The Rise of the Regulatory State of the South: Infrastructure and Development in Emerging Economies* (OUP 2013).

[25] The literature is vast. See amongst others: Stanley De Smith and others, *De Smith, Woolf and Jowell's Principles of Judicial Review* (Sweet & Maxwell 1999); James Landis, *The Administrative Process* (Yale Univ Press 1938); Stephen Breyer, 'Judicial Review of Questions of Law and Policy' (1986) 38 Admin L Rev 363; Paul Daly, 'Deference on Questions of Law' (2011) 74 Modern L Rev 694.

[26] For a discussion see further, Peter Cane, *Administrative Tribunals and Adjudication* (Hart 2010) 48–57.

(Chapter 4). Secondly, it seeks to identify and critique the limits of judicial scrutiny of economic evidence by exploring in a systematic manner the way economic evidence is scrutinised in both generalist courts (ie US federal courts, UK High Court) and specialist courts, where generalist judges and economists lay members, share the bench (ie UK Competition Appeal Tribunal) (Chapters 5 and 6). Finally, after delineating how positive law has so far responded to the challenges posed by economic evidence, the book engages in a normative debate on the appropriate scope of judicial review in an era of regulatory economics and the optimal institutional response to the pervasiveness of economic evidence in economic regulation (Chapters 7 and 8).

Before we proceed to the next section, we need to pause here for a minute for a brief albeit crucial terminological clarification of what we mean when we refer to 'judicial review' in this comparative work. This clarification is significant because although the US and the UK share a basic, long-lived understanding of judicial review as the scrutiny by the judicial branch of administrative action, its nature and characteristic functions differ significantly in these two jurisdictions. Judicial review, as understood in the US, allows the judge to consider the merits of the case. In the UK, however, a distinction exists between appeal and review that is not found in the US. Appeal is understood to be concerned with the merits of the case and further entails the power to substitute the decision for that of the primary decision-maker. Moreover, appeal rights are statutory, meaning that the courts have no inherent appellate jurisdiction. Review, on the other hand, is concerned not with the merits of the decision, but with its 'validity'. Unlike appeal, it is not based on a statute, but on an inherent jurisdiction within the superior courts. As already mentioned, the UK's specialist CAT enjoys appellate and review jurisdictions over certain regulatory decisions, which are created and defined by legislation. The CAT's statutory appeal jurisdiction, in particular, is of great importance as the legislative provision of appeal rights on the merits clearly encourages, as we shall see in Chapter 6, the Tribunal to assess the economic evidence that arises in regulatory disputes. To avoid terminological confusion, when discussing the assessment of economic evidence under the CAT's appellate jurisdiction the term 'judicial scrutiny' will be used, rather than 'judicial review'.

## 1.2 The Error-correction Function of Judicial Review

While we could all agree that reviewing for error is one of the prime institutional functions of appellate courts and tribunals, we could find ourselves disagreeing on the function's scope, application, and purpose. The reason why there is little uniform conception of what 'error correction' entails, is perhaps due to our inability to determine or agree upon what should qualify as 'error'. The formalists would suggest that the role of appellate courts is merely to consider whether the agency has erred in its determination of what legal standard applies to the dispute before it. Or in its application of a legal standard to the facts in the case before it. But even when adopting the legal formalism's simplistic account of error correction, it still provides little guidance for assessing whether regulatory discretionary assessments made were the 'correct' ones. This is because in many areas where regulatory authorities are required to exercise discretionary powers, legal rules may provide little guidance and there may be no obviously 'correct' way to proceed. As we shall see in Chapter 4, regulatory implementation often entails matters of significant complexity, requiring consideration of diverse, disparate, and often conflicting interests. But it is not only the multifactorial and 'polycentric', as we shall see later in the book, nature of regulatory decisions that renders elusive courts' insistence upon 'correct' decisions. It is, additionally, the contested nature of economic evidence as a source of wisdom that rarely throws up obvious solutions when implementing the statutory regime. These features of regulatory decision-making process have been acknowledged by the courts. As we shall see in Chapter 6, both the CMA and the CAT, despite being specialist adjudicative bodies, able to subject the regulators' assessments to a 'profound and rigorous scrutiny'[27] they do not perceive their institutional function as examining whether the regulators' discretionary assessments are the 'correct' ones, but whether the approach adopted was the 'wrong' approach.[28] They will not strike down any error in reasoning, but only errors of 'sufficient importance' to vitiate discretionary assessments in whole or in part.[29] There are several reasons informing this deferential standard of review, relating mainly to *institutional capacity* and *institutional legitimacy* considerations which are explored later in the book.

While the above is helpful in gaining a better understanding of the boundaries of the error-correction function of judicial review of economic evidence, it does not directly address the elephant in the room, that is, the perceived epistemic asymmetry that exists between the expert regulatory agency and the generalist judge when called upon to review economic evidence. If we are interested in minimising the likelihood of error stemming from this unequal epistemic position, should our conception of 'error correction' entail the judge becoming an expert economist himself, capable of falsifying the outputs of the discipline of economics? The answer is 'no', because as we shall be able to appreciate in the next few pages with the help of systems theory, minimising the likelihood of erroneous decisions does not require the judge to assess whether the regulatory decision under review conforms to the economists' true/false convictions, but rather, whether it conforms to the requirements of both 'thin' and 'thick' legality. Let us explain this point further.

According to systems theory, law is a normatively closed, but cognitively open system.[30] Economics, as a discipline, works with the categories of true/false. The law, by contrast, insists on the normative reference to legal/illegal, which unlike economics, is not linked to probabilistic inferences. Hence economic concepts and reasoning needs to be integrated into the normative legal framework. What the externalist-economist brings to the internalist-judge's world, via the recourse to economic evidence in regulatory decision-making, will be independently assessed by the internalist. We cannot expect courts to run their own regression analyses or undertake empirical studies themselves, let alone falsify the findings of another discipline. Rather, judges assess what the externalist delivers in the context of their internalist methodology.[31] Even

[27] *BT v OFCOM* (MCT) [2012] CAT 11.

[28] *TalkTalk v OFCOM* [2020] CAT 8.

[29] See *Hutchison 3G UK Ltd v OFCOM* [2008] CAT 11 [132].

[30] Gunther Teubner (ed), *Autopoietic Law: A New Approach to Law and Society* (de Gruyter 1988); Niklas Luhman, *Law as a Social System* (OUP 2004).

[31] For an analysis, see Katja Langenbucher, *Economic Transplants: On Lawmaking for Corporations and Capital Markets* (CUP 2017).

when procedural rules allow for calling in an economic expert, they require judges to independently evaluate expert witnesses' testimony.

Consider for example the judicial assessment of an econometric study. The judge may ask questions about the data coverage, the products, or market participants. She may also ask questions about the suitability of the econometric approach: is it appropriate for the market concerned and considering the available data? If she instructs the expert to assess how such an analysis would impact the determination of market power, she will ask a normative, internalist question. The expert's answer will not require the judge to retrain as an expert in economics. Instead, she will compare the expert's answer to how she interprets the applicable legal rules and principles. She may find that they fit in very well with the externalist's suggestions. Or the judge may realise that what at first glance seems a pure description of facts, for example consumers' revealed preferences, does raise several normative issues that avert deference to economic expertise.

Precisely because law is normatively closed, but cognitively open, when the judge is called upon to evaluate and assesses economic evidence in regulatory disputes, this does not necessarily entail that she needs to become an expert economist herself to minimize the likelihood of error. This is because the error-correction function of judicial review is not solely concerned with the economists' true/false convictions, but rather, with whether the agencies' discretionary economic assessments conform to the requirements of both 'thin' and 'thick' legality. 'Thin legality' entails an assessment of whether the regulatory decisions conform to the requirements of the applicable law. 'Thick legality' can be said to encompass substantive (eg rationality) and procedural (eg due process requirements) values which naturally derive from the public aspect of regulation and reflect constitutional, human rights, and administrative law principles drawn from a largely formal conception of the rule of law. We shall see in Chapter 4 the interplay of these values in the decision-making process of regulators and their role in constraining the perceived flexibility of the economic approach in advancing regulatory objectives. Some of these values, such as rationality, inform well-established grounds of review. We shall elaborate on these in Chapter 3.

The law's reference to legal/illegal does not of course render the epistemic asymmetry an unimportant factor. Rather, it will be shown that epistemic asymmetry is a matter of degree and the court's scrutiny of economic evidence depends on several institutional variables. These include, but are not limited to, the nature of the proceedings (administrative or court proceedings); the degree of specialisation of the regulatory agencies and courts; the distribution of the powers of investigation, prosecution, and adjudication within the agency; and the adversarial or inquisitorial character of the proceedings. The thorough examination of these factors yields a more nuanced account of the error-correction function of judicial review, one which is devoid of single-factor considerations, such as that economic evidence is too complicated for generalist judges, in favour of a richer set of variables that do and should inform both the jurisprudential (standard of review) and the institutional (generalist versus specialist courts) dilemma. The comparative institutional analysis of the regulatory and adjudicative process in the US and the UK, explained in section 1.3 below, serves to illuminate such factors.

## 1.3 Methods

The book ranges over legal doctrine and judicial decisions, economics, and socio-legal studies. It is a profoundly comparative and interdisciplinary endeavour. This is not out of methodological ambition. It is rather that the issue of adjudicating economic evidence in regulatory disputes is a complex one. It depends in part on normative arguments about which institutions in the regulatory state should have primary interpretive authority over defining economically informed concepts (eg cost-orientation) upon which our enjoyment of essential services depends. It also requires an understanding about how judicial and other institutions respond to the demands of judicial review of economic evidence, how they perceive their role, and how their role evolves over time. It is essentially about regulatory and judicial discretion, and its constraints and limits at the intersection of two distinct 'rationalities': legal and economic.

In a bid to uncover the wider set of institutional factors that determine the reception of economic evidence in different regulatory and adjudicative settings, the book advances an institutional analysis of the study of judicial review of economic evidence. Such analysis is very much influenced by the 'socio-political' strand[32] of institutionalist approaches in the study of law and courts. Unlike the 'rationalist' strand, which views judges as pure rational choice maximisers and courts as the mere aggregation of judges' preferences, the socio-political strand[33] allows us to easily reject single-factor explanations, such as that judges do not understand economics in favour of a richer set of macro-level (eg cultural and environmental factors) and micro-level (eg court's rules of procedure) institutional factors.

The institutional approach draws significantly on Neil Komesar's analytical framework of comparative institutional analysis.[34] Komesar approaches institutions, such as the adjudicative and regulatory process, as imperfect alternative mechanisms by which societies carry out their goals. Because one institution may be better able to implement those goals than another institution, comparative institutional analysis stresses the primary role of institutional choice: 'the decision of who decides'.[35] Komesar approaches these choices in 'participatory terms' (the direct or indirect participation of the affected stakeholders in the decision-making process). Which institution brings out the diversity of affected interests on a given issue, while avoiding situations of both 'minoritarian bias' (the over-representation of minority interests seeking rents) and 'majoritarian bias' (the over-representation of majority interests, such as consumers).[36] If the regulatory and adjudicative institutional process are

[32] Tom Ginsburg and Robert A Kagan, 'Institutionalist Approaches to Courts as Political Actors' in Tom Ginsburg and Robert A Kagan (eds), *Institutions and Public Law: Comparative Approaches* (Peter Lang 2005) 1–3. See Michael A Bailey and Forrest Maltzman, *The Constrained Court: Law, Politics and the Decisions Judges Make* (Princeton Univ Press 2011).

[33] Under this approach, the judiciary is thought to have its own 'utility maximising function'. See Richard Posner, 'What do Judges Maximize? The Same Thing as Everyone Else' (1993) 3 S Ct Econ Rev 1, 3; Lawrence Baum, 'What Judges Want: Judges' Goals and Judicial Behavior' (1994) 47 Pol Res Q 749; Barry Friedman, 'The Politics of Judicial Review' (2005) 85 Texas L Rev 257, 258.

[34] Neil K Komesar, *Imperfect Alternatives: Choosing Institutions in Law, Economics and Public Policy* (Univ Chi Press 1997) 26.

[35] ibid 3.

[36] ibid 27.

imperfect alternatives, as this book contends, it follows that the challenges posed by economic evidence in regulatory disputes should be addressed by a comparative institutional analysis of these imperfect alternative choices to select the least imperfect one. However, this is not as simple as it may sound. As will be discussed in Chapter 3, the examination of the main actors involved in the regulatory process in the US and the UK and the different avenues that exist for challenging regulatory decisions, will reveal a plethora of imperfect decision-makers that are involved in the regulatory and adjudicative process. Those imperfect decision-makers vary significantly with respect to their expertise in regulatory matters and the ways in which they apply and/or scrutinise economic evidence.

Before we move on to the next and final section of this introductory chapter, we owe the reader a bit more explanation on the reasons informing the selection of the two comparator jurisdictions. At first glance, it is fairly evident that the US is a far more mature system with regard to the role of economic evidence in regulation compared to the UK, where the boundaries between the role of economists and lawyers are more pronounced in view of the little impact economic analysis of law has had in legal academia and consequently the bar and the bench. Beyond that, historical and institutional considerations also have a role to play in the selection. Historically, the US is the antecedent of the modern regulatory state, where regulation through independent regulatory commissions was first documented. At the same time, it is the jurisdiction that first experienced the rise of professional expertise in utility regulation. Those features allow the observation of an evolutionary response to the challenges posed by the presentation of economic evidence in regulatory disputes. By contrast, the British regulatory state is a more recent phenomenon, as it emerged after the late 1980s' vast privatisation programmes. There were no precedents for the regulators to work with at the time, hence the reactions to the challenges posed by economic evidence developed in an incremental fashion.

On the institutional level, three significant differences exist in the way the US and the UK have sought to deal with the increased recourse to expert economic evidence and analysis. Firstly, as will be discussed in greater detail in Chapter 3, the two jurisdictions have adopted different models for the review of economic evidence. Briefly, the US has adopted an internal, administrative litigation model: when a decision involving economic evidence made by a US federal agency is challenged or disputed a common pattern is for the decision to be first reviewed by an adjudicatory institution embedded in the regulatory agency, that of the Administrative Law Judge (ALJ). By contrast, the UK has adopted an external model of review: economic evidence is (most of the time) reviewed in the first instance by a body external to the regulators, the Competition and Markets Authority (CMA). Secondly, differences exist with regard to the standard of review of regulatory decisions. Contrary to the US, in the UK both the options of merits review and judicial review are (in principle) open for challenging regulatory agencies' decisions. Thirdly, while the US has resisted the idea of establishing specialist courts for the resolution of regulatory disputes, in the UK one can witness an institutional response to the challenges posed by economic evidence, exemplified with the establishment of the specialist CAT.

Those three differences together permit the observation of how economic evidence is received in different institutional settings (ie generalist courts and specialist tribunals, internal review and external review) and of the role of the different standards of review in the judicial scrutiny of such evidence. Moreover, the institutional analysis facilitates the comparative nature of this study, as the differences in the degree of scrutiny of economic evidence across the two jurisdictions can be interpreted not solely as differences between institutions and procedure, but also as stemming from the different incentives presented to judges by the broader socio-political and constitutional landscape in which they are embedded.

The judgments examined in this study are petitions for review of the FERC and FCC decisions in the US and appeals from the sector-specific regulators OFCOM, OFWAT, and OFGEM in the UK. They cover the period from the liberalisation of the network industries in the US and the UK up to November 2021. Only those judgments that involve the judicial assessment of the economic evidence informing the decision under review are included in the analysis. In the US context, a review was conducted of forty-four judgments involving petitions for review of FCC orders covering the period 1996–2021[37] and 121 judgments involving petitions for review of FERC's orders covering the period 1984–2021.[38] In the UK context, a review was conducted of twenty final judgments of the CAT involving appeals from OFCOM covering the period 1998–2021,[39] one judgment involving an appeal from OFGEM in the same period, and five judgments involving appeals from OFWAT. A review was conducted of eleven judgments of the Court of Appeal concerning appeals from the CAT. Finally, a review was undertaken of seventeen High Court judgments involving appeals from regulatory authorities covering the period 1984–2013.[40]

The purpose of the review was not to describe in detail the use of economics in any specific case, but rather to gain a broad view of the input of economic evidence across all decisions and all adjudicatory settings. The decisions were reviewed with the following considerations in mind: (i) the nature of the decision appealed (eg *ex ante* regulation, ratemaking decision); (ii) the status of the court or tribunal (eg generalist or specialist); (iii) the elements of decisions being appealed; (iv) the type of review (eg merits review or judicial review); (v) the grounds of review under which decisions were appealed; (vi) the type of economic evidence enshrined in each case (eg econometric evidence, qualitative evidence); and, (vii) the outcome and/or remedy imposed.

## 1.4 The Argument in a Nutshell

The central argument advanced in the book is embedded in the case law of the US and UK courts and has both descriptive and prescriptive components. The book shows that courts not only should, but for the most part do adopt a modest and deferential posture towards the agencies' discretionary economic assessments. In fact, recourse to

[37] The US Telecommunications Act was enacted in 1996 and introduced competition into the local exchange market.

[38] FERC's Order No 380 (1984) was the first stage in the deregulation of natural gas markets.

[39] The CAT was established in 1998.

[40] BT was privatised in 1984, whereas the electricity and water and sewerage industries were privatised in 1989.

economic evidence and analysis has by and large transformed the scope, process, and intensity of review of regulatory decisions in both jurisdictions. In the US there has been an evolutionary transformation of the scope and nature of judicial review: from an intrusive 'hard look' review epitomised in the 1980s by the Supreme Court's *State Farm*[41] decision to what is really an undemanding version of rationality, referred to as 'thin rationality' review[42] (Chapter 5). The UK has seen an institutional response to the challenges posed by economic evidence epitomised by the establishment of the specialist CAT (Chapter 6). At the same time, the introduction of statutory appeals has marginalised judicial review as a primary means to challenge the regulatory agencies' decisions. The by-product of this transformation is the gradual rise of a complementary relationship between the judge and the regulatory agency. Rather than a state of institutional conflict between the two actors in the realms of law and policy, or a state of blanket deference, one can observe a measure of judicial restraint predicated upon considerations of relative institutional competence (Chapter 7).[43]

But how should we understand the notion of 'relative institutional competence' and how does it inform the scope of review and the institutional design of regulatory appeals? At their most basic, relative institutional competence considerations are built on the assumption that one branch of government (eg regulatory agency) is better at performing a specified function than the other (eg court). The integration of Neil Komesar's insights into the discussions on the appropriate scope of review of economic evidence invites the assessment of the relative attributes of both the regulatory agencies and the courts (or in some cases of other actors such the CMA) as well as the assessment of which of these institutions allows the broadest representation of interests, before deciding on the appropriate degree of dereference or the optimal adjudicative forum.[44] Seen this way, deference emerges as the institutional choice between imperfect alternative decision-makers. It reflects a judgment about which of the candidate institutions (eg the court, the regulatory agency, the specialist tribunal) is best suited, when compared to the other candidates, to carrying out the assessment of economic evidence enshrined into the regulatory decisions. The weight given to comparative institutional competence considerations depends on several macro-level (eg constitutional factors) and micro-level (eg court's rules of procedure and its access to epistemic competence) factors; Chapter 7 provides a synthesis thereof. The book shows that in reviewing the regulators' economic assessments, courts do embrace and should embrace comparative institutional competencies considerations alongside constitutional, institutional, and historical considerations that have traditionally informed the scope and intensity of substantive review of the regulatory agency's discretion.

The comparative imbalance in epistemic competency provides a basis for judicial deference to the regulatory agency's economic assessments grounded on the latter's 'epistemic authority'.[45] In such a case, the judge acknowledges her 'epistemic deficit'[46]

[41] *Motor Vehicle Manufacturers Association of the United States v State Farm Mutual Automobile Insurance Co*, 463 US 29 (1983).

[42] Adrian Vermeule, *Law's Abnegation* (Harvard Univ Press 2016) ch 4.

[43] Komesar (n 34) above.

[44] ibid 3–13.

[45] See Paul Horwitz, 'Three Faces of Deference' (2008) 83 Notre Dame L Rev 1061, 1079–1090.

[46] Scott Brewer, 'Scientific Expert Testimony and Intellectual Due Process' (1998) 107 Yale L J 1535, 1586.

in evaluating the economic evidence enshrined in regulatory decisions and accords greater weight to the judgement of the agency, which is closer to the facts on the ground. Aileen Kavanagh refers to this kind of deference as 'substantial'[47] deference, in the course of which the judge recognises her 'institutional shortcomings'[48] in respect of an issue. It follows that failure on the part of the court to afford substantial deference to the regulator will lead to the court giving a wrong pronouncement on the issue at stake. We shall be able to observe in Chapter 5 that substantial deference is reflected in 'thin rationality' review that has been adopted by the US courts. Crucially, it differs from the 'minimal' deference that is owed to the agency because of constitutional reasons.[49]

But comparative institutional analysis does not only throw light on the allocation of decision-making power across institutions when it comes to the assessment of economic evidence, but it also informs the institutional dilemma. An examination of the institutional alternatives to the incorporation of economic expertise in the courtroom (eg specialist court, expert witnesses, assessors, court-appointed experts), undertaken in Chapter 7, will reveal that a specialist court, enjoying both subject-matter specialisation and a combination of non-legal/economic and legal expertise, could present the optimal solution for addressing the epistemic asymmetry that exists between the judge and the expert agency in regulatory disputes and could minimise the likelihood of error. Taken together, the normative prescriptions advanced on institutional choice and institutional design are not mutually exclusive, but complementary in nature. The 'recipe' for adjudicating economic evidence requires a balance to be struck, in which deference is accorded to regulatory agencies on institutional competencies grounds and a degree of epistemic diversity is introduced in courts.

[47] Aileen Kavanagh, 'Deference or Defiance' in Grant Huscroft (ed), *Expounding the Constitution: Essays in Constitutional Theory* (CUP 2008) 191.

[48] ibid 139, 192.

[49] ibid.

# 2
# Unpacking Economic Evidence

## 2.1 Introduction

The book on the whole advances a positive and normative argument about the appropriate scope of judicial review in the era of regulatory economics and the optimal institutional response to the pervasiveness of economic evidence in regulation. But before we engage in this debate, we should first address a valid question: what is so special about economic evidence in the regulatory state that merits a book length discussion? Surely, the sceptic would argue, whether the last generalists are institutionally capable of dealing with the complexity of a specialised world and to what extent they may legitimately do so are concerns that have been voiced against all types of evidence reaching the courtroom.[1] Why then single out economic evidence as our main concern? How does it relate to the decision-making process of regulators and courts? And what specific challenges does it raise for rulemaking, adjudication, and the error-correction function of judicial review? The present chapter aims to address these questions.

## 2.2 Economics versus Natural Sciences

A natural starting point in explaining the peculiarity of economic evidence would be to compare economics, which is generally classified as a social science, to natural sciences. As we shall see, like physical sciences, economics uses a methodology that produces refutable implications and tests these implications holding solid statistical techniques. In fact, the beginnings of a distinct methodology for economics can been traced as early as the end of the sixteenth century and is often associated with the work of Francis Bacon. The quest for scientific objectivity that stems, in the Popperian view of 'science',[2] from the use of a certain scientific methodology, led economists to focus on measuring, quantifying, and delivering evidence in ways in which were perceived to resemble the standards of mathematics and physics.[3] Popper claimed that the scientific method consists of drawing up hypotheses and testing these, which is reflected in describing economics as producing refutable implications and testing these with statistical techniques. The rise of econometrics and empirical research offer an apt

[1] See, eg, Sheila Jasanoff, *Science at the Bar: Law, Science, and the Technology in America* (Harvard Univ Press 1995).

[2] Karl Popper, *The Logic of Scientific Discovery* (Routledge 1959).

[3] Philip Mirowsky, *More Heat Than Light: Economic as Social Physics, Physics as Nature's Economics* (CUP 1989).

*Courts, Regulators, and the Scrutiny of Economic Evidence.* Despoina Mantzari, Oxford University Press.
 DOI: 10.1093/oso/9780198851608.003.0002

illustration of how theoretical hypotheses are put to test in the ways the Popperian scientific method would suggest.

Yet, as much as economics tried to emulate natural sciences in their methods two main differences still exist between the two realms. The first one relates to the dual—positive and normative—dimension of economics, which is not found in the natural sciences. The second one refers to the distinctive methodology of economics. But let's examine these in turn. First, unlike natural sciences, in economics there are two modes of discourse: positive (what is) and normative (what ought to be). Economists study the workings of social institutions that constitute the economic system (eg firms, markets) in the same way researchers in a number of natural sciences study the workings of living organisms. That is, to simplify greatly, the positive dimension of economics, which is concerned with describing economic life through value-free, testable predictions that can be verified by empirical evidence. For example, economists tell us that the quantity demanded will decrease as prices increase, other things remaining the same. This positive statement can be proven to be true or false, meaning it can be supported or refuted by evidence. Positive economics, so we read in one famous Milton Friedman essay, 'is in principle independent of any particular ethical position or normative judgments ... in short, positive economics is, or can be, an "objective science", in precisely the same sense as any of the physical sciences'.[4]

Nevertheless, economists do not merely explain or predict economic phenomena. They also prescribe, with more or less self-consciousness, whether some economic outcomes are better than others in their ability to raise social welfare. In doing so, they select relevant concerns and identify the appropriate underlying assumptions. For example, supply side economists would argue that statutory minimum wages are a bad policy that will overburden small business. Demand side economists would argue that they are effective in achieving equity goals, such as that fair wages are paid to workers. These propositions represent the normative dimension of economics, which is concerned with value judgements, and which is mostly felt in the policy arena. Normative statements are statements that cannot be supported or refuted. Ultimately, they are opinions about how economies and markets should work. It is the dual—normative and positive—dimension of economics that distinguishes the latter from natural sciences and causes much controversy. The Nobel Laureate economist George Stigler could not have put in a better way this dual nature of his profession:

> A curious tension emerges from the simultaneous workings of two influences upon us. We wish to be scientists, with sound logic in our theories, reliable procedures in our empirical applications of those theories, and objective and fair-minded statements of the limitations of our knowledge. We wish also to be important – or in the language of this day we wish to do good – much good, and generally recognised as such.[5]

The tension between the roles of the 'economist-scientist' on the one hand, and the 'economist-advisor' on public economic policies on the other, is entangled with the well-known 'fact-value' distinction of philosophical positivists. David Hume in his *Treatise on*

[4] Milton Friedman, 'The Methodology of Positive Economics', in Milton Friedman (ed), *Essays in Positive Economics* (Univ Chicago Press 1953) 2.

[5] George J Stigler, 'Do Economists Matter?' (1976) 42 Southern Econ J 347, 353.

*Human Nature*[6] emphatically cautioned against inferring an 'ought' out of an 'is'; or in other words, he emphasised that moral judgements are logically independent from empirical beliefs. The proposition that naturally follows is that a person who aspires to be a good scientist ought to keep his subjective value judgements out of the factual analysis. Positive economics are thought to be fact-driven, while normative economics are value-laden.[7]

Second, unlike natural sciences, economics faces insurmountable difficulties in empirically testing the predictive power of theories using data from the complex real world. Because of the immense complexity of the economic system, the dominant aesthetic in economics sacrifices realism for tractability. Economics, therefore, traditionally relies on models, which are key to the 'scientific' nature of economics, to elucidate the workings of the complicated system that is the economy. Models are built up from a set of hypotheses and assumptions about the economic agents and their interactions that are simplified reflections of the system in question. For example, the model of perfect competition and its underlying assumptions can hardly be found when one looks at firms in the real world, let alone falsified.[8] Given these difficulties, the dominant, positivist methodology for economics, as developed by Milton Friedman, is *instrumentalistic* in nature rather than descriptive.[9] Economic models may not include all 'variables' of the world, but this is not considered necessarily bad. For what counts is the theory's predictive power and simplicity.[10] Positive economics is therefore designed:

> to provide a system of generalisations that can be used to make correct predictions about the consequences of any change in circumstances. Its performance is to be judged by the precision, scope, and conformity with experience of the predictions it yields.[11]

Friedman argued in favour of a positivist method built upon the formulation and subsequent falsification of hypotheses through empirical observation. The hypothesis that cannot be falsified is said to be predictive. Such a method would eliminate what were thought of as 'normative' controversies[12] and free economics from 'subjective' components, which may distort what other social scientists may produce. In this sense, policy advice, if given, would not rest on some pre-existing ethical positions, but would deductively follow from scientific, 'objective' research:

> Any policy conclusion necessarily rests on prediction about the consequences of doing one thing rather than another, a prediction that must be based ... on positive economics.[13]

Consider the following example. The concept of Pareto efficiency is defined in value-neutral terms: a distribution is Pareto-efficient if there is no other distribution that

[6] David Hume, *A Treatise of Human Nature* (Dover Philosophical Classics 2003), first published in 1740.
[7] Mark Blaug, *The Methodology of Economics. Or How Can Economists Explain* (2nd edn, CUP 1992).
[8] George J Stigler, 'Perfect Competition, Historically Contemplated' (1957) 65 J Pol Econ 1.
[9] Friedman (n 4) 3–43.
[10] ibid 40.
[11] ibid 4.
[12] ibid 5–6.
[13] ibid 5.

benefits some individuals without harming at least one individual. Whether or not a distribution is Pareto-efficient can be determined without making any ethical or value-based judgements. The concept of distributive justice is not value-neutral: it invokes the idea that some distributions are better because they are fairer or more just than others. The positive economist holds that such distinctions are legitimate to make, in principle. But within economics considerations of justice and equity have no place. The economist, according to this view, can work out the technical characteristics of various economic arrangements, but it is up to the political process or the policy decision-maker to arrive at a governing set of normative standards (the 'separability thesis').[14]

Notwithstanding the zeal for insisting on 'positive analysis' to render economics 'objective', 'scientific', and 'value-free', critics have argued that this is far from the truth. Research topics chosen, the assumptions made, the methodology used, the variables picked, and the data selected will inescapably reflect the economists' personal values and views.[15] Philosophers such as Hilary Putnam and Amartya Sen dispute the 'separability thesis' as wholly untenable and argue that the discipline is free to have a rational and reasoned discussion of the pros and cons of various principles of distributive justice.[16]

In the realm of utility regulation, which concerns us here, we shall see that questions of economic efficiency and issues of distribution are intertwined and inseparable: economists working in regulatory agencies are required to grapple with both in order to claim legitimacy for their normative prescriptions. For instance, economists try to achieve economic efficiency but within the constraints deriving from the essential nature of the services they regulate. Regulated firms in the realm of energy, telecoms, and water carry out activities which are essential for the functioning of the society and on which many other activities depend. These activities are also important for social cohesion, as being cut off from electricity can amount to social exclusion. Hence, issues of distributive justice and social solidarity considerations in the form of social and territorial cohesion underpin much of the economic models informing regulatory decisions such as access pricing. This raises the question of how courts should approach regulatory decisions where economic and non-economic values are intertwined. Should they defer to agency expertise in making economic but also value-laden assessments? We shall closely examine how courts in our two comparator jurisdictions approach and ought to approach such decisions in Chapters 5 to 7. In the meantime, the remainder of this chapter will unpack the different faces of economic evidence and demonstrate their relevance in the regulatory and adjudicative decision-making process (section 2.3). It will also delve deeper into the challenges that economic evidence and analysis raises for adjudication (section 2.4), before drawing some general conclusions (section 2.5).

[14] See John R Hicks, 'The Foundations of Welfare Economics' (1939) 49(196) Econ J 696; Nicholas Kaldor, 'Welfare Propositions in Economics and Interpersonal Comparisons of Utility' (1939) 49(145) Econ J 549.

[15] Amartya Sen, *Collective Choice and Social Welfare* (Harvard Univ Press 1970) 56; Hilary Putman and Vivian Walsh (eds), *The End of Value-Free Economics* (Routledge 2011).

[16] Hilary Putnam, *The Collapse of the Fact/Value Dichotomy and Other Essays* (Harvard Univ Press 2002); Amartya Sen, 'The Nature and Classes of Prescriptive Judgements' (1967) 17(66) Philos Q 46.

## 2.3 Economic Evidence and its Relevance in the Regulatory and Adjudicative Decision-making Process

### 2.3.1 Economic Evidence: Scope

Economic evidence, as used in this book, refers to the theories, methods, and tools used by the discipline of regulatory economics with the aim to advance normative claims on matters of regulatory policy. For example, economic evidence informed by the branch of neoclassical economics, known as industrial organisation economics, is crucial in determining the price that a supplier of gas should pay to access the network and serve consumers. Access pricing regulation represents one of the core tasks of economic regulation with wide ranging implications for the affordability of energy supply. To take a different example, economic evidence informed by behavioural economics has been increasingly employed in overcoming consumers' systematic irrational behaviour and thus reinforcing their engagement with the market.

Regulatory economics draws from different strands of economics. The most dominant strand is microeconomics and, more specifically, industrial organisation economics; the latter described as a branch of neoclassical economics concerned with how markets work and how rivals react strategically to each other's actions under various circumstances. The models of microeconomic theory describe or predict causal relationships involving a limited number of variables. Central to the analysis are the concepts of profit maximising, equilibrium, and efficiency. Profit-maximising actors are usually modelled on a market, some supplying a product, others demanding it. Assuming perfect competition, equilibrium is reached where supply and demand are equal. In such circumstances price will be set at marginal cost, all other things remaining equal. Supply and demand also provide the tools for restoring equilibrium where it is lacking. Finally, the concept of efficiency allows the economist to better understand whether an equilibrium reached makes economic sense. Industrial organisation economics is considered mainstream and accepted within these strands. The main disagreements among economists (and lawyers) in regulatory disputes are mostly about how a particular theory has been applied to the particular facts of the case and how case-specific facts have been analysed.

Another important, but less mainstream, theoretical strand of economics is behavioural economics. Rather than assuming that consumers act as if they are (close to being) rational, psychologists and behavioural economists armed with a broad array of research tools (ranging from controlled and field experiments to interviews and neuro-imaging studies) have identified a number of biases that consumers face across markets.[17] Such biases provide evidence that actual consumer behaviour 'differs in systematic ways from that predicted by the standard economic model of unbounded

[17] See generally Richard Thaler and Cass Sunstein, *Nudge-Improving Decisions about Health, Wealth and Happiness* (Yale Univ Press 2008); Amos Tversky and Daniel Kahneman, 'Judgment Under Uncertainty: Heuristics and Biases' (1974) 185 Science 1124; Dan Ariely, 'Controlling the Information Flow: Effects on Consumers' Decision Making and Preferences' (2000) 27 J of Consum Res 233.

rationality'.[18] Behavioural economics have been very influential during the last decade, not surprisingly in a period of financial crisis and turmoil in which the rationality of markets has been questioned. For example, in the UK energy regulation context mounting evidence suggests that consumers rarely conform to the model of self-interested utility maximisation inherent in the Austrian economics paradigm that informed the original regulatory framework of privatised UK industries because of several biases that impede rational choice.[19] For instance, empirical research suggests that consumers fail to investigate alternative energy contracts that may be more beneficial to them. This is because they tend to prefer the status quo[20] ('loss aversion' or 'status quo bias'). As we shall see in Chapter 4, a behavioural approach to utility regulation has been employed to permit the better design of regulatory policy and provide a clear understanding of when regulatory intervention in the market is necessary or desirable. Hence, regulatory focus in the UK has gradually shifted from an effort to control market power and the prices offered to consumers to controlling the ways in which 'behavioural' consumers respond to these offers. Notwithstanding, however, their influence on the workings of sectoral regulators behavioural economics have not yet been influential on the bench.

Turning to the 'outputs' of economic evidence, these may include the following: (a) economic theory that may derive from the field of industrial organisation or behavioural economics; (b) economic reasoning, which refers to the economists' methodological approach regarding which questions to ask and which indicators and evidence to examine; (c) economic techniques and tools, which refer to quantitative and qualitative techniques, such as econometrics and regression analysis; and, (d) economic data, which may refer to prices, sales, economic reports, and studies. The presentation of economic evidence before the courts may encompass all or some of the above. For example, the regulatory dispute may involve predictions of economic theory, for instance whether lower termination charges will result in higher prices for mobile subscribers—a phenomenon known as the 'waterbed' effect—or economic reasoning employed to support the conclusions drawn from the facts. Additionally, it may involve the presentation of econometric evidence or economic data, in the form of external economic studies and reports.

Quantitative economic techniques merit particular attention, as they are highly influential in utility regulation. Quantitative techniques are those designed to test a hypothesis formulated based on economic theory. These techniques can range from simple statistical tests to complex structural econometric estimation models of demand and supply. As the real-world data on consumer and business behaviour availability has improved over the last years, so too has the use of econometric

[18] Cass Sunstein, Christine Jolls, and Richard Thaler, 'A Behavioral Approach to Law and Economics' 50(5) Stanford L Rev (1998).

[19] See OFT 1324, 'Consumer Behavioural Biases in Competition: A Survey' (Final Report) (May 2011); Behavioural Insights Team, 'Applying Behavioural Insights to Regulated Markets' (26 May 2016). See Daniel McFadden, 'Free Markets and Fettered Consumers' (2006) 96(1) Am Econ Rev 3; Catherine Waddams Price and Minyan Zhu, 'Empirical Evidence of Consumer Response in Regulated Markets' (2016) 12(1) J Compet L Econ 113–49.

[20] Michael Pollitt and Irina Shaorshadze, 'The Role of Behavioral Economics in Energy and Climate Policy', ESRC Electricity Policy Research Group (Cambridge 2011).

analysis testing for statistical patterns and relationships in the available data expanded. However, rarely will quantitative techniques alone decide matters on a particular case. Quantitative analysis interacts with qualitative analysis. For example, in defining relevant markets under the Framework Directive[21] of electronic communications, two quantitative tools are typically used, that is, regression analysis and price-cost correlation tests. These are combined with qualitative tools such as survey analysis. Regression analysis allows one to estimate demand elasticities, that is, how customers respond to price charges, by observing actual prices and quantities for the product. How much of the product customers have actually purchased at different price levels tells you something about their 'revealed preferences', as opposed to 'stated preferences' that will be inferred by surveys. A sufficient number of observations allows one to identify the demand curve and price elasticities.

### 2.3.2 The Relevance of Economic Evidence in the Rulemaking Process

Broadly speaking there are three ways in which economics and economists relate to and influence the field of utility regulation. First, economics influences the content of 'hard law', such as the EU regulations and directives that are transposed in the UK regulatory statutes. Indeed, rulemaking emerges as a natural institutional point of entry for economic evidence into the legal world. For example, EC Regulation 2887/2000 requires notified operators (ie those operators of fixed public telephone networks designated by the NRAs as having Significant Market Power (SMP)) to 'charge prices for unbundled access to the local loop and related facilities set on the basis of cost-orientation'.[22] In the same vein, both the US Telecommunications Act 1996[23] and the Natural Gas Act 1984[24] instruct federal regulators to disallow prices that are not 'just and reasonable'. Moreover, with the rise in the number of economists employed in the regulatory agencies in the EU, the UK and the US, economic theory and analysis is also incorporated into the plethora of 'soft law' instruments, such as guidelines and recommendations issued by the regulatory agencies. For example, since the early 1990s, with the publication of guidelines on the application of competition law to the telecommunications sector[25] and the Access

[21] See Directive 2009/140/EC of the European Parliament and of the Council of 25 November 2009 amending Directives 2002/21/EC on a common regulatory framework for electronic communications networks and services, 2002/19/EC on access to, and interconnection of, electronic communications networks and associated facilities, and 2002/20/EC on the authorisation of electronic communications networks and services, [2009] L337/37.

[22] Regulation (EC) 2887/2000 of the European Parliament and of the Council of 18 December 2000 on unbundled access to the local loop [2000] OJ L336/4, Art 3(3).

[23] The Telecommunications Act constitutes one of the numerous amendments to the Communications Act 1934, the governing statute for the regulation of all sectors of the telecommunications industry in the US. For an extensive analysis of the main provisions of the US Telecommunications Act 1996, see Stuart M Benjamin, Douglas G Lichtman, and Howard Shelanski, *Telecommunications Law and Policy* (2nd edn, Carolina Academic Press 2006) 771–902. The mandatory unbundling provisions are enshrined in § 251(d) of the US Telecommunications Act of 1996, Pub L No 104-104, 110 Stat 56, codified at 47 USC §§ 151 et seq.

[24] See, eg, Natural Gas Act, § 4(a) 15 USC § 717(a) (1976).

[25] Commission Guidelines on the application of EEC competition rules in the telecommunications sector [1991] OJ C233/02.

Notice,[26] the European Commission has made extensive use of 'soft law' instruments while building up the electronic communications market.

As will be shown in Chapter 4, economic evidence plays a significant role in operationalising the open-ended statutory terms. In fact, economic evidence informs both questions of law (eg whether the price set by the regulator is a 'reasonable' one) and questions of fact, if one adheres to such a distinction.[27] There are good reasons for the legal process to distinguish questions of law from questions of fact. If a question before a court is one of fact, it is to be answered by inferences from the body of evidence, whereas a question of law is to be answered by recourse to statutory interpretation and precedent. But the correct interpretation itself depends to a large extent, as we shall see, on what the body of specialised economic knowledge indicates. Furthermore, it is not always possible to entirely separate the two: questions of law and questions of fact are often intertwined. For instance, a question of fact will be governed by the rules on admissibility of evidence, by the requisite standard of proof and inference, which are all matters of law. By way of illustration, the definition of the relevant market for the purposes of *ex ante* regulation in telecommunications is a fact-intensive exercise, and the assessment of the facts must be made according to an economic method of analysis (eg the hypothetical monopolist test). The EU General Court, as well as various national jurisdictions, such as the UK, consider the definition of the relevant market to be a question of law. It can be argued that the selection of the analytical framework for market definition is a question of law, while the application of that framework to the facts of the case may qualify as a question of fact. Finally, economic evidence also informs questions of policy. For example, the regulatory decision to move away from access-based regulation in telecoms to instead promoting competition and investment through network-based competition, raises a question of policy, and the court's role is confined to checking whether such policy is consistent with the regulator's duties.

The second way in which economics influence the realm of utility regulation is by providing a set of principles and standards, such as the market-type model, against which to judge the open-ended statutory objectives. Policy objectives such as 'the promotion of innovation', 'efficient investment', 'maximum benefit in terms of choice, price, quality', 'reasonable profits for firms' are close to the benefits obtained by a competitive market. In fact, regulation boils down to ensuring that output and prices are as close as possible to the competitive outcome without jeopardising the financial viability of the operators. As we shall be able to appreciate in Chapter 4, economics have helped to develop practical tests and criteria that make the application of the law more workable and provide a range of statistical and econometric techniques to produce empirical evidence to back up theories and arguments made. Going back to the EU statutory requirement of 'cost-orientation', this has led to the application of specific price-cost tests to assess whether the prices for certain telecommunications services

[26] Commission Notice on the application of competition rules to access agreements in the telecommunications sector [1998] OJ C265/2 (Access Notice).

[27] See Bernard Schwartz, 'Mixed Questions of Law and Fact and the Administrative Procedure Act' (1950) 19 Fordham L Rev 73; Ronald J Allen and Michael S Pardo, 'The Myth of the Law – Fact Distinction' (2003) 97 Northwestern Univ L Rev 1769.

are cost-oriented. The application, however, of such tests is not a straightforward exercise and several criticisms have been made about how such tests are being applied. We shall study closely in the following chapters to what extent institutional factors, such as the degree of specialisation of the court (generalist versus specialist), the model of review of economic evidence (internal or external), and the adversarial or inquisitorial character of the procedure determine whether and how courts review the contested nature of economic tests when assessing the legality of regulatory decisions.

Finally, economic evidence may contribute to a greater understanding of the welfare effects of regulatory interventions. Take for example the mobile termination rates (MTRs) in the context of electronic communications. There has been much debate on the merits of different approaches to regulating MTRs. Should they be limited to the incremental costs of providing call termination to other communication providers (a method called, pure long-run incremental cost (LRIC) or should they include additionally a mark-up for joint and common costs, such as the cost of the spectrum used by the network (an approach called LRIC+). In deciding which method to use to set charges, economic evidence and analysis offers a logic framework of analysis in considering how each one of these approaches will affect the different consumer groups the regulator has a primary duty to protect. This framework is reflected in the so-called 'welfare analysis' that regulatory agencies frequently undertake. But there is a very close nexus between the regulator's policy preference and the welfare analysis that is appropriate in light of that policy preference, in the sense that it is the latter which shall determine whose economic interests ought to be taken into account (eg callers or call recipients). This in turn entails value judgements informed by the regulator's statutory duties. For this reason, as we shall see, courts afford a margin of appreciation to questions of policy.[28]

### 2.3.3 The Relevance of Economic Evidence in Adjudication

When it comes to adjudication, there are at least two ways in which economic evidence influences the adjudication of regulatory disputes. The first one is *direct* and refers to the presentation of economic evidence in the courtroom. Economists are routinely called upon to testify as economic expert witnesses and prove specific economic facts. Depending on the court's rules of procedure, they may be invited by the parties or appointed by the courts. Economists may also act as factual witnesses and assist the judge in grasping the economic concepts that permeate the body of law governing the regulation of utilities. They may also sit as lay members in specialist courts or tribunals, such as the CAT in the UK. The second one is *indirect* and refers to the increased recourse to economic evidence and analysis when interpreting the economic concepts (eg 'cost orientation' or 'significant market power') enshrined in the substantive law governing utility regulation.

The direct and indirect influence of economic evidence in regulatory disputes discussed above has two crucial implications for adjudication. First, economic evidence

[28] See the relevant discussion in Chapter 6.

presents cognitive challenges for the judge, in the sense that she may be called upon to rely on economic authority[29] as opposed to legal authority as a conceptual basis of her reasoning—for example when considering whether the factual nature of the ratemaking process comes within the legal definition of a 'just and reasonable' price. In such cases, the judge may seek interpretive guidance in 'soft law' instruments, such as guidelines and recommendations which often incorporate economic authority. These documents reflect a hybrid discourse, as they are informed by communications characterising the domains of both law and economics. In fact, 'soft law' can be viewed as the institutional embodiment of the 'conversations' between lawyers and economists working together in the regulatory agency.[30]

The judge may also rely on the assistance of an economic expert, who will provide her with a passport to the world of economic facts. The judge may reframe what appears to be a difficult question of law—for example whether the mobile termination rates were 'fair and reasonable'—as being one of fact, open to an assessment by expert witnesses. Consider once again the example of how to interpret the legal term 'fair and reasonable' according to the Access Directive.[31] The judge may either address the question of how the European legislator meant this concept to be understood and applied in the Member States, or she might interpret it as a question of fact. She might argue that there are economic data to consider and formal methods to be consulted. She may also hear an economic expert on that question. The economic expert will describe the relevant facts often combined with an economic theory. In relying on the assistance of an economic expert, the judge may be said to admit limitations to her authority to proclaim 'what the law is', precisely because the economic dimension of the law invites the assistance of an economic expert. Scot Brewer summarises this phenomenon in the term 'epistemic deference'.[32]

The second crucial implication for adjudication deriving from the influence of economic evidence is that the latter frequently informs regulatory decisions which involve technical aspects (eg the design of the appropriate pricing methodology) and value judgements. For example, the implementation of the unbundling provisions of deregulatory acts in the telecommunications sector—those provisions which require the incumbent to share the components of its network (eg switches, trunks, loops) with a rival party—involves a huge trade-off between the objectives of static[33] and dynamic efficiency.[34] Mandating access to all components of the network can potentially diminish the incentives of the new entrants to build their own network infrastructure and those of the incumbents to keep up and improve their property.[35] Denying access, on the other hand, may increase the incumbents' market power, thus impeding competition from new entrants. In such cases, courts are confronted with a policy choice

[29] Ioannis Lianos, 'Lost in Translation? Towards a Theory of Economic Transplants' (2009) 62 Curr Leg Probl 364, 404.

[30] Julia Black, 'Talking about Regulation' [1998] PL 77; Lianos (n 29).

[31] Access Notice (n 26).

[32] Scott Brewer, 'Scientific Expert Testimony and Intellectual Due Process' (1998) 107 Yale LJ 1535, 1586.

[33] Static efficiency occurs when marginal production costs are minimised (productive efficiency) or when the goods and services are allocated to the uses in which they have the highest value (allocative efficiency).

[34] Dynamic efficiency relates to demand in investment and innovation.

[35] The mandatory unbundling provisions are enshrined in §251(d) of the US Telecommunications Act of 1996.

and judges are required to assess whether the economic methodologies employed by the regulatory agency are fit for purpose and whether the inferences drawn from economic analysis are sufficiently robust to support the regulator's policy decision.

### 2.3.4 The Case of Polycentric Regulatory Disputes

The challenges posed by economic evidence merit special attention in the case of regulatory disputes that present 'polycentric' elements.[36] In the Fullerian sense, a polycentric task is one that encompasses a large and complicated web of interdependent relationships.[37] In such cases, a decision taken may affect many actors, thus leading to a fluid state of affairs if all affected interests are taken into account. However, polycentricity may as well refer to situations where a decision affecting one actor could have a different set of repercussions for other parties, leading to a redefinition of the parties affected.

A perfect example of a polycentric task is how to set the appropriate regulatory access price; that is, the price under which competing firms will have access to essential inputs (eg, the electricity transmission network) provided by the incumbent. In access pricing the regulator must strike a balance between the divergent interests of the new entrants, the incumbent, and ultimately the consumers. The best outcome of this balancing exercise demands comprehension of a highly complex range of cause-and-effect relationships. And each of the separate consequential effects of the price determination, in turn, affects other networks of relationships. First, there is a distributional concern. Pricing at marginal cost maximises efficiency but does not compensate the incumbent for his fixed costs related to investments in the network. Secondly and relatedly, there is a dynamic efficiency concern. In other words, the regulator must ensure that the method employed will also contribute to the long-term interest of the consumer, the encouragement of technological innovation, and the growth and viability of the sector at issue. However, little guidance is provided in the agencies' governing statutes in such cases, hence allowing the regulators a large measure of discretion to balance the competing interests at stake.[38]

Consider for a moment OFCOM's review of the retail leased lines markets[39] and the cost-orientation obligation (the Distributed Standalone Cost (DSAC)) imposed on the incumbent, British Telecoms (BT), in the wholesale low alternative interface symmetric broadband origination (AISBO) bandwidth market in which it was found to have SMP. Imposing the obligation involved the balancing of different forms of economic efficiency (allocative, dynamic, and productive efficiency) and determining the appropriate trade-off between the benefits of increased access-based competition in downstream markets and the potential for more competition in the wholesale AISBO

[36] Lon L Fuller, 'The Forms and Limits of Adjudication' (1978) 92 Harvard L Rev 353.

[37] ibid 394.

[38] See, eg, Telecommunications Act of 1996, Preamble.

[39] OFCOM, 'LLMR 2008 Business Connectivity Market Review: Review of the retail leased lines, symmetric broadband origination and wholesale trunk segments markets – Statement and Consultation' ('the 2008 BCMR') available at: <https://www.ofcom.org.uk/__data/assets/pdf_file/0019/33823/bcmr08.pdf> accessed 6 June 2022.

market; all matters of policy.[40] Short-run allocative efficiency required that prices were set in a way that maximised the total level of demand in order to produce the greatest possible benefits to end users. Dynamic efficiency required that prices were set in a way that provided the appropriate incentives for the incumbent BT to undertake efficient investments in the provision of the cost-oriented services in question and to introduce new and innovative services. The prices set should also encourage downstream competition and efficient downstream investment by rivals who purchase the cost-oriented services as well as efficient new entry in the provision of such services. Finally, productive efficiency in relation to the provision of services that are subject to cost-orientation by BT required the latter to produce the cost-oriented services at as low a cost as possible. These questions are linked with how markets, consumers, and new entrants will react and all of this must be balanced against similar calculations in respect of alternative policy options. This is a polycentric problem because the soundness of some proposals is dependent on the comparative merits of others, the complete comprehension of which is extremely difficult and involves considerable guesswork. The court is also asked to make a finding about the substantial and heterogenous interests of many non-represented persons. Crucially, polycentric disputes increase the likelihood of judicial error as the judge may make a false assumption about certain interests.

Fuller argued that polycentric disputes are inherently unsuited for adjudication and thus best resolved through managerial discretion or through negotiation and contract,[41] or left to the forces of the market.[42] Nonetheless, Fuller conceded that polycentric elements are present in all problems resolved by adjudication. What becomes important is knowing when 'the polycentric elements have become so significant and predominant that the proper limits of adjudication have been reached'.[43] It follows that the polycentric dimension of certain regulatory disputes does not imply the removal of the court's supervision altogether (non-justiciability) but may warrant a special weight to be accorded to the economic assessments of the regulatory agency. This, however, as we shall see in Chapter 7, presupposes a case-by-case assessment of the factors that may attenuate the polycentric dimension of the dispute in question, thus making it amenable to the adjudicative process.

## 2.4 The Distinct 'Institutional Logics' of the Scientific-Economic and the Legal Processes

So far, we have been able to appreciate the different points of entry of economics and economic evidence in rulemaking and adjudication. This section will argue that despite the pervasiveness of economic evidence in rulemaking and adjudication, there are limits to the import of economic evidence in courts. Such limits derive and reflect the distinct 'institutional logics' (or 'rationalities') of the scientific-economic and the legal processes. Institutional logic should be understood as the different practices and beliefs that shape

[40] *BT v OFCOM* (Ethernet Determinations) [2014] CAT 14 [183]
[41] Fuller (n 36) 400.
[42] ibid 398.
[43] ibid 397.

institutions. In that sense, the regulatory and adjudicative processes are above all administrative processes and as such they are distinguished from the 'logic' of the broader scientific process. Justice Breyer has summarised vividly the differences between the two:

> [T]he economist, as a type of scientist, is bound by his discipline to seek truth. He may change his findings from one day to the next as he learns new facts. Although simplicity is a virtue in his theory, he needs not to reject complexity, for it may simply reflect the state of the world he investigates ... The lawyer, however, is immediately concerned with the workability of the principles for which he argues. Indeed, the professed aim of the legal system is not truth, but justice. Those involved in a controversy are given an opportunity to build a record and to present proofs and arguments to a legal, fair-minded person for decision on the basis of that record. The record may or may not reflect the true state of the world, but the process is working well if it provides a fair method for resolving the dispute between the parties, and the rules used to decide the controversy must satisfy minimal criteria of admissibility.[44]

In other words, law is a conservative institution and judges often display a conservative bias, pricing legal certainty and the rule of precedent above reformist ideas. Thus, law's desire for finality and certainty may clash with the contested nature of economics and the instability of empirical results. If, therefore, the externalist's findings are vague or inconclusive the judge may refuse to incorporate them in its reasoning, for example if the methods by which these have been produced are incompatible with more general principles represented by 'thick legality'. For example, the judge may question the underlying assumptions of an economic model that does not consider the specific interests the sectoral regulator has a duty to promote.

The distinct rationalities of the legal and scientific-economic processes further entail that the economic concepts that are enshrined in the agencies' governing statute will be understood differently from an internalist (judge) as opposed to externalist (economic expert) standpoint. We shall return to this point in Chapter 4, where we shall see how legal rationality, governed by the rule of precedent and the provisions of the agency's legislative framework may constrain an, otherwise, 'economically right' approach. Take, for example, the concept of a 'reasonable price' for an essential service such as retail energy supply. Though the EU (and the UK) energy *acquis* repeatedly refers to the objective of ensuring *reasonable* prices for electricity and gas, the concept is not defined anywhere in the text of the energy liberalisation directives. Should one adopt an economic understanding whereby a price shall be deemed reasonable solely in relation to the underlying wholesale costs or should one also take into account the consumer's *willingness* and/or *ability* to pay? And, which type of consumer, given the different images of energy consumers enshrined in the energy directives (ie household customers, industrial customers, vulnerable consumers)?[45] Andrew Lang's

[44] Stephen Breyer, 'Economics for Lawyers and Judges' (1983) 33 J Legal Educ 294, 296–97.

[45] See Saskia Lavrijssen, 'The Different Faces of Energy Consumers: Toward a Behavioral Economics Approach' (2014) 10(2) J Compet L Econ 257. For an analysis see Despoina Mantzari, 'The Quest for Reasonable Retail Energy Prices in Europe: Positive and Normative Dimensions' (2017) 36 Yearb Eur Law 599.

'as if' modes of reasoning,[46] offers some helpful insights in this respect. He argues that the incorporation of economic concepts into substantive law may be said to give rise to two modes of legal reasoning: the 'functionalist' mode, whereby the jurist draws heavily on economic knowledge on the interpretation of such concepts and gives the tools of economic expertise the primary role in the determination of such facts, and the 'as if' mode of reasoning, according to which the incorporation of economic concepts into law transforms their very nature; they become legal concepts. Applied to the concept of a 'reasonable price', the 'functionalist' mode of reasoning, reflecting the internalist's viewpoint, would give rise to an economic understanding of reasonableness, whereby a reasonable price would be linked directly with the benefits of competition. In this context, it would be almost synonymous with the economic concept of an *efficient* price. In contrast, the 'as if' mode of reasoning would point to a broader understanding of reasonableness, informed by the principle of social solidarity, that would encompass non-economic and non-competition law considerations. Unlike the first shade of reasonableness, it would also necessitate state intervention to further a broader range of regulatory objectives that lie beyond the realm of competition policy and are not in principle achieved by competitive markets. In this context reasonableness would hinge on the notion of an *affordable* price.

A logical consequence that follows when we reflect on the distinct rationalities or logics of the scientific-economic and legal processes is that even when 'epistemic deference' is in order, there are limits to the import of economics in the adjudicatory process. Because the legal system is 'cognitively open' but 'normatively closed' epistemic deference does not always come naturally to the judge. Possibly, the judge will only be willing to partially defer to what has been settled in the economist's world and according to that discipline's methodology for reasons which reflect epistemic, but also institutional logic considerations. In this sense, the judge, adopting the 'as if' mode of reasoning, accepts that economic expertise may be helpful, but by no means determinative. 'Reasoning as if' entails the courts focusing on the process of agency decision-making and economic analysis playing a prominent role only if carefully and fully explained. The explanation should indicate what methods or models of economics have been employed and how these work, why those models or methods are suited to the specific task of, say, understanding the relevant market or the actual or likely effect of the access pricing rule, and how those methods or models support conclusions based on the facts of the case. It should also indicate why the suggested model is more appropriate than the competing model, why it is more consistent with the facts of the case or economic literature, and so on. It is then a question of institutional design whether a specialist court or a generalist court or other possible institutional combination of legal and non-legal expertise is best suited to perform this assessment to minimise the likelihood of erroneous decisions. We shall return to this point in Chapters 7 and 8.

[46] Andrew Lang, 'Governing 'As If': Global Subsidies Regulation and the Benchmark Problem' (2014) 67(1)Curr Leg Probl 135.

## 2.5 Conclusion

The chapter sought to explain how economic evidence relates to and is incorporated in the decision-making processes of regulators and courts. Having made clear the distinction between economics and natural sciences, it then discussed the specific challenges economics and economic evidence raise for rulemaking and adjudication foreshadowing to a large extent several key themes that emerge as the book unfolds. One such theme is the inseparability between questions of economic efficiency and issues of distribution in utility regulation, explored in detail in Chapter 4. This raises the question how courts should approach such regulatory decisions where economic and non-economic values are intertwined. The chapter also introduced the concept of polycentric regulatory disputes. It deconstructed the main tenets of Lon Fuller's theory and explained its relevance to utility regulation. One of the key objectives was to demonstrate that polycentricity may warrant a special weight to be accorded to the economic assessments of the regulatory agency. This however presupposes a case-by-case assessment of the factors that may attenuate the polycentric dimension of the dispute in question, thus making it amenable to the adjudicatory process, a theme explored in Chapter 7. Finally, the chapter alluded to the contested nature of economics and the additional challenges this raises for the error-correction function of judicial review. But as systems theory would suggest, instead of becoming the arbiter of conflicting economic models, the judge needs to assess what the externalist economist delivers in the context of her internalist methodology. Thus, reviewing the legality of such decisions will entail an 'as if' mode of reasoning: the judge testing the adequacy of justification in reasoning, the plausibility of the premises of an economic theory or model, the validity of any inferences drawn from that model, and in polycentric disputes, as we shall see later in the book, the degree of participation of affected interests against the specific statutory objectives at play and any other relevant piece of legislation.

# 3
# Imperfect Alternatives
## Actors and Processes for the Review of Economic Evidence in the US and the UK

### 3.1 Introduction

Drawing on Neil Komesar's framework of comparative institutional analysis, the introductory chapter contended that the regulatory and adjudicative processes are imperfect alternatives. This entails that the challenges posed by economic evidence in regulatory disputes should be addressed by a comparative institutional analysis of these imperfect alternative choices to select the least imperfect one. However, this is not as simple as it may sound. The examination of the main actors involved in the regulatory process in the US and the UK will reveal a plethora of imperfect decision-makers that are involved in the regulatory and adjudicative processes as well as a variety of appeal processes against regulatory decisions.

Against this background, this chapter aims to first, briefly introduce the main actors involved in the regulatory process in the US and the UK and, secondly, examine in a systematic and comparative manner the various procedures available for the review of economic evidence included in regulatory agencies' decisions and the types of scrutiny applied to agency's action. This exercise, descriptive as it may sound, nonetheless offers a useful institutional map of regulatory appeals in the two comparator jurisdictions that will facilitate the systematic examination of the rationales and determinants of the reception of economic evidence in the US and the UK courts, undertaken in Chapters 5 and 6 respectively.

To simplify greatly, the main overarching difference between the two jurisdictions concerns the model of review of economic evidence: in the US it is 'internal', whereas in the UK it is 'external'. To explain this further, in the US, review of economic evidence takes place within the institution in which the original decision-maker was located at the time the decision was made. In other words, the US has adopted an administrative litigation model for the review of economic evidence, which reflects its long tradition of administrative adjudication in the regulation of natural monopolies. So when a decision involving economic evidence made by the Federal Energy Regulatory Commission (FERC) or the Federal Communications Commission (FCC) is challenged or disputed, a common pattern is for the decision to be reviewed first by an adjudicative institution embedded in the regulatory agency, that of the Administrative Law Judge (ALJ). Crucially, the ALJ is functionally separated from the investigatory and prosecution arm of the agency and has no legislative rulemaking functions. If the agency affirms the original decision or varies it in a way that does not satisfy the affected party, that party may seek external review of the decision in the federal courts.

*Courts, Regulators, and the Scrutiny of Economic Evidence.* Despoina Mantzari, Oxford University Press.
 DOI: 10.1093/oso/9780198851608.003.0003

In contrast, in the UK review of economic evidence is usually 'external' to the regulatory agency, as it takes place in a different institution, the Competition and Markets Authority (CMA).[1] Contrasting, however, appeal arrangements exist for the review of price controls and licence modifications decisions of each of the regulatory authorities for energy, telecommunications, and water.

Two further differences stand out, one substantive and one institutional. In the case of the US, federal regulatory agencies' decisions are reviewed by means of judicial review only. In contrast, in the UK, the routes of both judicial review and merits review are offered to challenge sector-specific regulators' decisions. Finally, while the US has resisted the idea of establishing specialist courts for the resolution of regulatory disputes, in the UK a specialist tribunal, the Competition Appeal Tribunal (CAT) has been established, charged with the review of economic evidence implicated in competition law and regulatory disputes.

The chapter is structured as follows. Section 3.2 will discuss the actors and processes for the review of economic evidence in the US, section 3.3 will discuss the actors and the review of economic evidence in the UK, and section 3.4 will conclude.

## 3.2 Actors and Processes for the Review of Economic Evidence in the US

We can now move on to introduce the main actors involved in the regulatory process in the US and explore the process and scope of review of economic evidence enshrined in the federal regulatory agencies' decisions. Substantial information for this purpose can be extracted from the text of the Administrative Procedure Act (APA),[2] which provides a default procedural framework governing federal regulatory policymaking. A brief discussion of its origins and of its main procedural provisions will facilitate our understanding of the procedure provided for the review of economic evidence and of the varying types of scrutiny applied to federal regulatory agencies' actions.

### 3.2.1 The Administrative Procedure Act

Enacted in 1946, amid a political controversy between the defenders and the critics of the New Deal, the APA does not solely represent the product of a political compromise between two opposing forces.[3] It can also be interpreted as a compromise between the respective functions of the judicial and administrative processes in the regulatory state. To compensate for the combination of rulemaking, adjudicatory and executive functions, the regulatory agencies were required to closely align their behaviour to that of the courts. This was made possible through the imposition of various

[1] Enterprise and Regulatory Reform Act (ERRA) 2013, ss 25–28.

[2] See APA Pub L No 79-404, Ch 324, 60 Stat 237 (1946) (codified as amended in scattered sections of 5 USC).

[3] See Martin Shapiro, *Who Guards the Guardians? Judicial Control of Administration* (Univ of Georgia Press 1988) 36–54; Mathew D McCubbins, Roger G Noll, and Barry R Weingast, 'The Political Origins of the Administrative Procedure Act' (1999) 15 J L Econ Org 180.

trial-type procedures on agencies, such as formal adversary proceedings, cross-examination, and rules of evidence aimed at standardising their adjudicative and legislative functions.

The APA established a distinction between rulemaking and adjudication. Rulemaking resembles legislative action, whereas adjudication is similar to court proceedings. Two kinds of rulemaking are envisioned by the APA: formal and informal rulemaking. Formal rulemaking refers to 'rules required by the statute to be made on the record after an opportunity for an agency hearing'.[4] Informal rulemaking, otherwise known as 'notice-and-comment rulemaking', is triggered by a notice to the public of the 'subjects and issues involved'[5] followed by an opportunity for outsiders to provide comments or objections to the proposed rule. The FERC, for example, frequently solicits comments from regulated industries, competitors, interested citizens, and organisations, collectively referred to as interest groups. Generally, informal rulemaking generates rules made pursuant to congressionally delegated authority. The legislative rules, if valid, operate like a statute. Although 'notice-and-comment rulemaking' represents the most followed process for issuing legislative rules, agencies may resort to the use of other rulemaking options, including formal, hybrid, direct final, and negotiated rulemaking. In the 1960s and 1970s the regulatory process opened up to allow greater participation by interest groups, 'reforming' American administrative law.[6] As will be explored in Chapter 5, courts also played an important role in this process through promoting the 'interest representation' model of rulemaking. Consequently, agencies were required to expand opportunities for meaningful participation of those interest groups. The side effect of the reformation was the transformation of the 'notice and comment' rulemaking process from a swift and flexible procedure to a burdensome one. Such 'ossification' of the rulemaking process hindered the effective promulgation of policy.[7]

Adjudication is defined broadly in the APA as a 'process for the formulation of an order'.[8] An order binds only the party to the proceeding, but some orders, such as those issued at the conclusion of the FERC's adjudication operate as precedent.[9] Both formal rulemaking and formal adjudication require prescribed hearing procedures with the aim of creating a factual empirical basis upon which the agency will form its decision. Formal adjudication, however, affords a more limited class of persons, often the parties only, to present evidence and to have the opportunity for cross-examination.[10]

[4] 5 USC § 553(c).

[5] 5 USC § 553(b)(3).

[6] For a seminal account see Richard B Stewart, 'The Reformation of American Administrative Law' (1975) 88 Harvard L Rev 1669, 1775.

[7] For an empirical support of the 'ossification' thesis, see Jason W Yackee and Susan W Yackee, 'Administrative Procedures and Bureaucratic Performance: Is Federal Rulemaking "Ossified"?' (2010) 20 J Pub Admin & Theory 261.

[8] 5 USC §551(7). 'Order' is defined as 'the whole or part of a final disposition … in a matter other than rule but including licencing' see 5 USC § 551(6). See generally, Ronald A Cass, 'Models of Administrative Action' (1986) 72 Virginia L Rev 363.

[9] See Jim Rossi, 'Redeeming Judicial Review: The Hard Look Doctrine and Federal Regulatory Efforts to Restructure the Electric Utility Industry' (1994) (4) Wisconsin L Rev 763, 833.

[10] 5 USC §§ 556–557.

There are also proceedings that are referred to as 'informal adjudications', which may be governed by special statutory requirements or by the agency's organic statute.

In the decades following the passage of the APA, case-by-case adjudication was the primary means for policymaking.[11] This can be explained historically. The archetype of the American federal regulatory agency, the Interstate Commerce Commission (ICC), established under the Interstate Commerce Act in 1887 to determine 'reasonable and just' rates for railroad services, developed policy in an incremental fashion. Ratemaking was developed through case-by-case adjudication of rate disputes between shippers and carriers. Those administrative proceedings were closely modelled on common law trials. This began to change in the 1960s when agencies such as the Federal Trade Commission (FTC) and the Federal Power Commission (FPC)[12] increasingly pursued their mandate through informal rulemaking. The reasons for this shift to rulemaking are well documented: in part it was a response to allegations of arbitrariness stemming from the lack of predictable rules and in part it was a reaction to the increase of agency caseloads following the extension of the regulatory state into the new areas of environmental and consumer protection.[13] At the same time, critics portrayed agencies as inefficient and captured by the very interests they were supposed to regulate.[14] The promulgation of rules with prospective effect which would bind the agency itself was regarded as a more efficient and fair policymaking tool.

Although the APA envisions two kinds of routes that the agency may follow to effectuate its statutory mandate, that is, the adoption of a legislative rule or the administrative enforcement action, in reality the latter is free to select from a wider set of policymaking tools.[15] The FERC, for example, is authorised to promulgate legislative rules, conduct administrative adjudication, and/or initiate judicial enforcement. It may also choose instead to provide guidance in the form of speeches or releases. It can be argued that as a general pattern the FCC relies heavily on rulemaking, whereas the FERC relies on both adjudication and legislative rules.[16] Crucially, ratemaking for electric and gas utilities is classified as rulemaking, but is conducted very much like formal adjudication before an ALJ.[17] As we shall see, the choice of action may have significant consequences for both the procedures the agency is required to undertake and the availability and scope of external review of the agency's action by the courts.

[11] See Martin Shapiro, 'Administrative Discretion: The Next Stage' (1983) 92 Yale LJ 1487.

[12] Congress established the FPC in 1920, restructured it as an independent agency in 1930, and tasked it with regulating electricity, natural gas, and oil pipelines and hydroelectric projects.

[13] Reuel E Schiller, 'Rulemaking's Promise: Administrative Law and Legal Culture in the 1960s and the 1970s' (2001) 53 Admin L Rev 1139, 1145–47; Skelly Wright, 'The Courts and the Rulemaking Process: The Limits of Judicial Review' (1974) 59 Cornell L Rev 375, 376. See further, Cass R Sunstein, *After the Rights Revolution-Reconceiving the Regulatory State* (Harvard Univ Press 1990).

[14] See George J Stigler and Claire Friedland, 'What Can Regulators Regulate? The Case of Electricity' (1962) 5 J L Econ 1.

[15] For a discussion see Elizabeth M Magill, 'Agency Choice of Policymaking Form' (2004) 71 Univ Chicago L Rev 1383. See also cases *Securities and Exchange Commission v Chenery Corp.*, 318 US 80 (1943) (Chenery I); 332 US 194 (1947) (Chenery II) which established the principle that an agency is free to choose between rulemaking and adjudication.

[16] Rossi (n 9).

[17] See *Shell Oil Co v FPC*, 520 F2d 1061 (5th Cir 1975). See further Richard J Pierce, Jr., 'The Choice between Rulemaking and Adjudication for Formulating and Implementing Energy Policy' (1979) 30 Hastings LJ 1.

### 3.2.2 Overview of the Main Actors in the Regulatory Process

Having analysed the procedural provisions of the APA, the main actors in the regulatory process in the US can now be brought into sharper focus. On the federal level, jurisdiction for the review of economic evidence is split between specialised regulatory agencies and generalist courts. The regulatory agencies, the ALJ, and the federal courts thus emerge as the chief actors in the regulatory process.

#### 3.2.2.1 Federal Regulatory Agencies: The FERC and the FCC

As with all administrative agencies, the FERC and the FCC combine rulemaking, adjudicative, and executive functions and often seem to operate in conjunction with and independently of the Congress, the President, and the courts.[18] Unlike many independent agencies, the FERC is an agency officially organised within the Department of Energy[19] and has assumed many of the responsibilities previously held by the FPC. It regulates, *inter alia*, rates and services for the interstate transmission of electricity, natural gas, and oil. The agency is charged with implementing and enforcing the Federal Power Act,[20] the Natural Gas Act,[21] the Natural Gas Policy Act,[22] and various other pieces of federal energy legislation. Administrative procedures are governed by both the organic legislation creating the agency and the APA.

The FERC is headed by a collegial body of five commissioners appointed by the President and confirmed by the Senate, of whom only three may be from one political party. The commissioners serve staggered five-year terms. The FERC staff, comprising of specialists in various aspects of energy development, are organised into several offices, including an Office for Energy Projects,[23] an Office of Energy Market Regulation,[24] and an Office of Energy Policy and Innovation.[25] The agency employs economists who collaborate with experts from different fields to provide direction on economic matters that affect FERC and the industry. Additionally, economists monitor and evaluate competition in emerging markets and analyse market access and rate proposals filed by major interstate companies.

Turning to the FCC, the agency was established by the Communications Act of 1934[26] and is responsible for regulating interstate and international communications

[18] For an analysis, see Peter Strauss, 'The Place of Agencies in Government: Separation of Powers and the Fourth Branch' (1984) 84 Colum L Rev 573.

[19] See The Department of Energy Organisation Act, 42 USC §7134, 7101(a) establishing the Department of Energy in 1977 for the purpose of coordinating action in response to the energy crisis of the 1970s. Before the creation of the DOE, the federal regulation of energy resources was scattered throughout the government.

[20] See the Federal Water Power Act of 1929, known as Part I of the Federal Power Act (FPA), 16 USC § 791a through 823c and Parts II and Parts III of the FPA, 16 USC §§ 824–825r.

[21] Natural Gas Act 1938, 15 USC §§ 717 through 717w.

[22] Natural Gas Policy Act 1978, §§ 42 USC 7101 through 7256.

[23] Which has oversight over hydroelectric facilities and natural gas and oil pipeline facilities and services.

[24] Which analyses findings submitted by public utilities and natural gas/oil companies to ensure that rates, terms, and conditions of service are just and reasonable and not unduly discriminatory or preferential.

[25] Which advises on policies to ensure the efficient development and use of transmission, generation, demand-side resources, storage, emerging technologies, as well as wholesale and interstate markets more generally.

[26] Communications Act of 1934, § 401, 47 USC 151 et seq.

by radio, television, wire, satellite, and cable across the US. It is directed by five commissioners, who are appointed by the President of the United States and confirmed by the US Senate. All commissioners have a fixed five-year-term. The FCC is organisationally separated into bureaus, such as the Consumer and Government Affairs Bureau, and into offices, such as the Office of the ALJs. The agency benefits from a chief economist, whose role is critical to directing policy in the areas under the FCC's purview.

#### 3.2.2.2 The Administrative Law Judge

Within the regulatory agency, the institution of the ALJ deserves special attention, as it is the body charged in the first instance with reviewing the agency's decision. Reflecting a long tradition of review of administrative litigation in the realm of regulation of the natural monopolies industries,[27] the institutional roots of the ALJ can be traced back to the 'hearing examiners' of the ICC. 'Hearing examiners' were charged with the adjudication of highly technical rate cases by conducting trials, producing a record of the case, and issuing recommended decisions to the agency heads. In fact, the US administrative litigation model is very similar to court adjudication, in the sense that 'it involves the participation of the affected interests in the decision-making through proofs and reasoned arguments'[28] whereas the role of ALJs is comparable to that of a trial judge presiding over non-jury trial proceedings. ALJs' main duty is to preside over the taking of evidence and to act as fact-finders in the course of formal adjudicatory and rulemaking administrative proceedings. They make decisions in these proceedings and their determinations must be based on the record of trial-type hearings. But ALJs may also serve multiple other roles. For example, under the FERC's Rule 602, they may act as settlement judges, mediators, facilitators, or arbitrators.[29]

Because the resolution of contested matters first takes place in an adjudicatory body internal to the agency, and not in a separate agency or in an administrative court of some kind, the APA provides for the ALJs' *de jure* and *de facto* independence. ALJs are appointed under the provisions of the APA[30] following competitive examinations, and may not be removed, suspended, or suffer a reduction of grade or salary except when there is a 'good cause established and determined by' the Independent Merits System Board following a hearing on the record.[31] Their compensation is established independently of agency recommendations. Finally, to insulate them from agency influence, the APA expressly provides for the functional separation of the ALJ from the investigatory and prosecution arm of the agency.[32] But when the case is appealed to the top level of the agency—the level of the Commissioners themselves—there is no separation of functions at all. This institutional design reflects, in the words of the Supreme Court, an 'equilibrium compromise'[33] that seeks to balance competing

[27] See Jerry L Mashaw, 'Recovering American Administrative Law: Federalist Foundations, 1787-1801' (2006) 115 Yale LJ 1256.

[28] Lon Fuller, 'The Forms and Limits of Adjudication' (1978) 92 Harvard L Rev 353.

[29] 18 CFR § 385.602. For an analysis, see James H McGrew, *FERC: Federal Energy Regulatory Commission* (2nd edn, ABA 2010).

[30] 5 USC § 551–559.

[31] 5 CFR § 930.211; 5 USC § 7521.

[32] 5 USC § 554(d).

[33] *Wong Yang Sung v McGrath*, 339 US 33, 40–41 (1950).

considerations such as the need to ensure unbiased decision-making on the one hand and expertise on the other.

3.2.2.3 Federal Courts

Although in principle all the US Circuit courts can hear petitions for review of federal regulatory agencies, the DC Circuit merits particular attention. Technically speaking, the DC Circuit is a regional court staffed by judges from all over the US. Its location, however, right in the heart of the federal's government capital and its exclusive jurisdiction over a variety of legal challenges to administrative law action has rendered it a 'semi-specialised'[34] court. With over half of the court's docket being comprised of administrative law appeals, it has rightly been called a 'de facto administrative law court'.[35] Over 90 per cent of the FCC's and the FERC's order challenges are heard in the DC Circuit rendering it a watchdog of the agencies' fidelity and consistency with the statute. In the telecommunications realm, as we shall see in Chapter 5, the court played a pivotal role in the break up of the AT&T[36] as well as in the implementation of the local competition provisions of the US Telecommunications Act 1996.[37]

Consequently, although the US has long resisted the idea of establishing specialist courts staffed by specialist judges for the resolution of administrative law disputes, nonetheless, it can be argued that the DC Circuit's members achieve a certain degree of specialisation through their repeated exposure to regulatory cases. This kind of specialisation, resulting from venue rules and geographical patterns in litigation, is better captured in the notion of 'subject-matter' specialisation. Additionally, the so-called Washington's 'uptown bar',[38] which represents the court's repeat players, also contributes to specialising the Justices, as well as shaping their attitude towards the regulatory matters they confront.

But subject-matter specialisation is not the only factor that might affect the reception of economic evidence in courts. The courts' internal procedural rules may also enable judges to develop subject-matter expertise. Two mechanisms merit special attention: case assignment and opinion specialisation. Studies of the Supreme Court[39] and of the federal courts of appeals have found some evidence of opinion specialisation. Prominent among these is Edward Cheng's study on the 'Myth of the Generalist Judge', which sheds empirical light on the *de facto* specialisation of the judge through the process of opinion assignment in the federal courts of appeals.[40]

Although the DC Circuit is the court of final resort for most cases, there is always the possibility of further appeal to the Supreme Court. There is a special relationship

[34] See John M Golden, 'The Federal Circuit and the D.C. Circuit: Comparative Trials of Two Semi-Specialised Courts' (2010) 78 George Wash L Rev 553. See further Richard L Revesz, 'Specialised Courts in Administrative Law-Making System' (1990) 138 Univ Pennsylvania L Rev 1111.

[35] See Patricia Wald, 'The Contribution of the D.C. Circuit to Administrative Law' (1988) 40 Admin L Rev 507, 509.

[36] *US v American Tel&Tel Co*, 552 F Supp 131 (DC Cir 1982).

[37] Telecommunications Act of 1996 (1996 Act), Pub L 104-104, 110 Stat 56. See, eg, *AT&T Corp v Iowa Utilities Board*, 525 US 366, 372–73 (1999).

[38] Lawrence Baum, *Specialising the Courts* (Univ Chicago Press 2010) 73.

[39] See, eg, Saul Brenner and Harold J Spaeth, 'Issue Specialisation in Majority Opinion Assignment on the Burger Court' (1986) 39 West Pol Q 520.

[40] Edward K Cheng, 'The Myth of the Generalist Judge' (2008) 61 Stanford L Rev 519.

between these two courts, as the DC Circuit acts as a 'table-setter',[41] identifying important administrative law issues for resolution by the highest court.

### 3.2.3 Overview of the Process for the Review of Economic Evidence

This section will first discuss the process for the internal review of economic evidence undertaken by the adjudicatory institution of the ALJ and will then explore the grounds and scope of the external review of economic evidence by the federal courts. In doing so, we shall consider both the standards of review of agencies' action found in the relevant provisions of the APA and the judge-made standards. Judge-made standards of review are of particular significance, as they embody assumptions about what courts are or are not doing in judicial review of administrative discretion. For example, in the US the promulgation of the 'hard look' review may signal that the judge has assumed a corrective role for the failures of the legislative and regulatory processes caused by interest group activity. Contrary to the US, the *Wednesbury*[42] test for unreasonableness review employed by English judges conveys the impression of an 'ill suited' judge to second-guess the policy choices made by the regulatory agencies. But by no means are we attempting to offer here an exhaustive, administrative law textbook account of judicial review of regulatory decisions in the US. The ambition is much narrower and is critical: to provide an institutional map of the different avenues that exist for challenging economic evidence in regulatory disputes in the US to better equip the reader for the substantive discussion in Chapter 5.

#### 3.2.3.1 Internal Review of Economic Evidence by the Administrative Law Judge

Internal review of economic evidence takes place before the ALJ in the course of what is labelled 'administrative litigation'. Most of the time, however, the ALJ will attempt a negotiated settlement before conducting a formal hearing. Only when such a settlement cannot be reached will contested matters be referred for administrative litigation. For example, rate cases are set for hearing if the proposed rates and conditions have not been shown to be just and reasonable. The Chief ALJ assigns a presiding judge and sets a hearing schedule. The administrative hearing is trial-like, with testimony and evidence presented by trial staff, such as attorneys and technical staff, who assist the ALJ and participate in the hearings as impartial representatives of the public interest. They may also serve as expert witnesses, without excluding the possibility of testimony given by outside expert witnesses.[43] The trial staff possesses a wide array of tools, from data requests and depositions to inspections and interrogatories. Their role is, *inter alia*, to prepare and present oral arguments, to conduct oral and cross-examination in the proceedings, to prepare and file legal briefs, and to ensure that the evidentiary record developed in each case is adequate for decision-making by the ALJ

[41] To this effect, see Richard J Pierce, Jr, 'The Special Contributions of the D.C. Circuit to Administrative Law' (2002) 90 Georgetown LJ 779, 779–80.

[42] *Associated Provincial Picture Houses Ltd v Wednesbury Corporation* [1948] 1 KB 223.

[43] See 18 CFR 385.102(b).

and the Commission. The opportunity for oral testimony by witnesses and the opportunity for cross-examination enable the agency to test its factual record.

The process is governed by the provisions of the APA. The APA has endorsed liberal standards for the admissibility of evidence in formal proceedings, providing that 'any oral or documentary evidence may be received'[44] except for 'irrelevant, immaterial or unduly repetitious evidence'.[45] In fact, the provisions codified the existing case law. Well before the enactment of the APA, the US Supreme Court recognised the necessity of accepting hearsay and non-admissible forms of evidence in a series of decisions involving rate-setting proceedings before the ICC.[46] Initially, the Court's main concern was to strike a balance between allowing broad admissibility of evidence and respecting due process. Later, the Supreme Court crafted the requirements of agencies' conduct in administrative proceedings, namely fair hearing and the evidential judicial review standard, and examined whether the agency hearing was supported by 'substantial evidence'.[47] However, because the APA's role is residual, agencies are free to complement the standards of the APA with those found in the Federal Rules on Civil Procedure or the Federal Rules of Evidence.

The ALJ's initial or recommended decision is final subject to a *de novo* review or appeal by the agency itself—either by commissioners or by members of the agency's governing body. Agency heads thus perform a 'second pair of eyes' review of the decisions and are free to substitute their judgement for that of the ALJ on questions of law, fact, and discretion.[48] The Federal Power Act, the Natural Gas Act, and the Natural Gas Policy Act provide that orders issued by the FERC will be subject to requests for rehearing at the FERC before they can be subject to review by the appellate courts. If the regulatory agency affirms the original decision-maker or varies it in a way that does not satisfy the affected party, that party may seek external review of the decision in the federal courts.

#### 3.2.3.2 External Review of Economic Evidence by the Federal Courts

External review of economic evidence is governed both by the standards of review enshrined in the APA and those which are judge-made. Following exhaustion of the administrative remedies, any person adversely affected or aggrieved by a 'final'[49] agency action may lodge a petition for judicial review on the various grounds of review listed in the APA. In principle, the courts review the agency head's decision, not that of the ALJ.[50] Federal courts are limited to the record produced by the agency itself—be that the product of a formal or an informal decision-making process[51]—and refrain from

[44] 5 USC § 556(d).

[45] ibid.

[46] See *Interstate Commerce Commission v Baird*, 194 US 25 (1904); *Interstate Commerce Commission v Louisville and Nashville RR Co*, 227 US 88 (1913); *Spiller v Atchison, Topeka and Santa Fe Ry Co*, 253 US 117 (1920) (permitting the Commission to receive and act upon hearsay); *Consolidated Edison Co v NLRB*, 305 US 197 (1938) (Consolidated Edison).

[47] *Consolidated Edison* (n 46) [229].

[48] 5 USC § 557(b).

[49] 5 USC § 704. The ripeness doctrine also affects the availability of judicial review as it requires that the issue in question have progressed to a point where it might be resolved by a court.

[50] *Universal Camera Corp v NLRB*, 340 US 474 (1951).

[51] See *Citizens to Preserve Overton Park v Volpe*, 401 US 402, 420 (1971) (Overton Park).

a *de novo* examination of the facts. It is not for the courts to substitute their views for that of the agency[52] nor to provide the reasonable basis for the agency's action.[53] The US Supreme Court enjoys *certiori* jurisdiction in reviewing lower courts' judgments *de novo*. The *certiori* jurisdiction enables the court to control its caseload and, where necessary, make a 'policy statement' through its power of granting or denying judgment.[54]

*3.2.3.2.1 Judicial Review under the Administrative Procedure Act*

The availability and scope of review of administrative decisions are mainly prescribed by the APA. For example, the APA provides that policies adopted in the course of adjudication can only be challenged following the promulgation of the agency's order.[55] The various grounds under which the courts may set aside administrative action are listed in § 706(2) of the APA.

Reviewable agencies' decisions[56] are subject, at the minimum, to the arbitrary and capricious test of the APA,[57] essentially a rationality standard of review. As the DC Circuit puts it, '[t]he "arbitrary and capricious" standard deems the agency action presumptively valid provided the action meets a minimum rationality standard'.[58] Hence, courts applying the arbitrary and capricious test essentially review the rationality of agency decisions. That test, however, is enormously wide. It varies in intensity depending on the nature of the agency's action.[59] In engaging in this type of review, courts also review the component parts of the discretionary decisions that agencies make and can strike them down if they are 'unsupported by substantial evidence in cases subject to sections 556 and 557 of this title or otherwise reviewed on the record of an agency hearing required by statute . . . '.[60] For instance, the record of the FCC and the FERC cases illustrates that courts increasingly review agencies' action under the arbitrary and capricious test of the APA deferring to agency findings of fact, provided they are supported by substantial evidence on the record.[61]

Under the APA's bi-polar approach to agency action, which differentiates between rules and orders, rules made on the 'record' are subject to the 'substantial evidence

[52] *Universal Camera* (n 50) (stating that the court may not 'displace' the agency's 'choice between two fairly conflicting views, even though the Court would justifiably have made a different choice had the matter been before it *de novo*); *Overton Park* (n 51), 401 US at 416.

[53] *SEC v Chenery Corp*, 332 US 194, 196 (1947).

[54] See H W Perry, *Deciding to Decide: Agenda Setting at the United States Supreme Court* (Harvard Univ Press 1991); Supreme Court Rule 10.

[55] 5 USC § 704.

[56] Congress can statutory preclude review of agency action, subject of course to constitutional constraints, see 5 USC § 701(a)(1).

[57] 5 USC § 701, 706(2)(A) (a 'court shall . . . hold unlawful and set aside agency action, findings, and conclusions found to be . . . arbitrary, capricious, an abuse of discretion, or otherwise not in accordance with law').

[58] *White Stallion Energy Ctr LLC v EPA*, 748 F3d 1222, 1233 (DC Cir 2014) quoting *Natural Resources Defense Council v EPA*, 194 F3d 130, 136 (DC Cir 1999).

[59] Magill (n 15).

[60] 5 USC § 706(2) (A), (E) (2006).

[61] *American Gas Association v FERC*, 593 F3d 14, 19 (DC Cir 2010); *Achernar Broad v FCC*, 62 F3d 1441, 1445 (DC Cir 1995); *Covad Communications Committee v FCC*, 450 F3d 528, 531, 533–34 (DC Cir 2006).

standard'.[62] The same standard applies to an agency's factual finding in the course of adjudication, which will be assessed to see whether it is based on the 'whole record'.[63]

Although the provisions of the APA indicate that the type of judicial review may differ depending on whether the court is reviewing formal or informal rulemaking, Congress has sometimes required informal rulemaking to be reviewed under the substantial evidence test. In fact, US commentators have drawn attention to the increased convergence of the two standards in the context of judicial review of informal rulemaking.[64] Finally, an agency's decision may be reversed when the Constitution has been violated[65] or when the agency has violated its statutory mandate.[66]

*3.2.3.2.2 The Evolution of Judge-made Standards of Review*

Although the APA attempts to 'pigeon-hole' the varying forms of agency action to specific standards of review, in reality the formality of an agency's action plays little role in selecting the standard of review. Courts, rather than the APA, are the primary architects of the scope of review of administrative action. Hence, additional standards of review may apply to an agency's action. Courts can craft these standards in two distinct ways. First, they are free to engage in their own interpretation of the open-ended standards of review. Secondly, they are free to select from the several provisions of the APA. What will be attempted here is a very brief exposition of the judge-made standards of review, before delving deeper into their application in the context of utility regulation in Chapter 5.

Consider, first, the 'arbitrary, capricious, [or] abuse of discretion' standard of review under s 706(2)(A) of the APA. Neither the text nor the legislative history of the APA clarifies the intensity of this form of review. Over time it has given rise to both light-touch review and intrusive review of administrative action, the latter commonly referred to as 'hard look' review. Developed by the DC Circuit in the late 1960s and early 1970s in response to agencies' turn to informal rulemaking as a means of policy-making and to the beliefs in 'agency capture',[67] 'hard look' review required the latter to develop 'rule-making' records and imposed procedural requirements that an agency must follow to survive a challenge to its action in court. For instance, the agency should satisfy the court that it had considered all the dimensions of the matter before it and that it had engaged in reasoned decision-making.[68] Rather than engaging in an intense substantive review of the agency's action, the DC Circuit demanded that agencies use procedures (ie 'reasoned decision-making' requirements) that were above and beyond anything mandated in the APA. The Supreme Court significantly tempered

[62] 5 USC § 706(2)(E).

[63] 5 USC § 706.

[64] See, eg, Matthew J McGrath, 'Convergence of the Substantial Evidence and Arbitrary and Capricious Standards of Review During Informal Rulemaking' (1986) 54 George Wash L Rev 541.

[65] § 706(2)(B).

[66] § 706(2)(C).

[67] See Thomas W Merrill, 'Capture Theory and the Courts: 1967-1983' (1997) 72 Chicago-Kent Law Rev 1039, 1043.

[68] See *Overton Park* (n 51). The arbitrary and capricious standard requires that agencies have made a decision 'based on a consideration of the relevant factors' without 'clear error of judgment'. The *Overton Park* principle that review should be applied on 'administrative record' has been extended to informal rulemaking cases.

the DC Circuit's activist stance in the *Vermont Yankee* case.[69] It substantially limited the lower courts' power to control agency discretion by imposing procedural requirements not found in either the APA or in the agencies' governing statutes or required by due process. The Court was concerned that if 'hybrid' processes could be imposed on agencies, the latter would use highly adversarial procedures in each case. Most worryingly, the proceduralisation of the agency's rulemaking process that the DC Circuit had mandated would eliminate the speed and efficiency of rulemaking leading to its 'ossification'.[70] Judicial review, the Supreme Court said, was to be substantive.[71]

A few years later in the *State Farm* case,[72] the Supreme Court approved the requirement of 'reasoned decision-making', declaring the rejection of the 'post hoc rationalisations of agency action'.[73] Agencies' explanations, the Court said, must be based on the record of the rulemaking itself. *State Farm* involved a decision by President Reagan's National Highway Traffic Safety Administration (NHTSA) to rescind a rule issued under the Carter Administration that would have required manufacturers to install either airbags or automatic seatbelts ('passive restraints') in vehicles produced after a certain date. The agency was of the view that manufacturers would choose to include seatbelts rather than airbags, and that the regulation would not increase seatbelt use. The Supreme Court criticised the NHTSA for failing to consider an alternative proposal that would encourage the use of airbags and unanimously held that the agency's decision to rescind the rule was arbitrary and capricious. The rescission of the regulation requiring 'passive restraints' in new automobiles was invalidated on the ground that the NHTSA had 'failed to present an adequate basis and explanation'[74] for its action. In doing so the Court held:

> [A]n agency rule would be arbitrary and capricious if the agency has relied on factors which Congress has not intended it to consider, entirely failed to consider an important aspect of the problem, offered an explanation for its decision that runs contrary to the evidence before the agency, or is so implausible that it could not be ascribed to a difference in view or the product of agency expertise.[75]

Hence, the Court embraced not only the procedural but also the substantive dimensions of the 'hard look' review. Though, following the *Overton Park* decision, courts may not require agencies to adopt procedures outside of those prescribed by the APA or other sources of law, with the *State Farm* decision, agencies are required to furnish detailed explanations of the courses of action, consider viable alternatives, justify departure from prior policy, and make policy choices that are reasonable. Until today, in ratemaking cases, the federal courts employ a rationality type of review to examine whether the agency considered 'the relevant data and articulate[d] a satisfactory

[69] *Vermont Yankee Nuclear Power Corporation v Natural Resources Defence Council, Inc.*, 435 US 519 (1978). See further A Scalia, 'Vermont Yankee: The APA, the D.C. Circuit, and the Supreme Court' (1978) 1978 Sup Ct Rev 345.

[70] *Vermont Yankee* (n 69) at 547.

[71] ibid 549.

[72] *Motor Vehicle Mfrs Ass'n v State Farm Mot Auto Ins Co* 463 US 29 (1983).

[73] ibid 50.

[74] *State Farm* (n 72) at 34.

[75] ibid 43.

explanation for its action including a rational connection between the facts found and the choices made'.[76] However, as Chapter 5 will demonstrate, this has evolved over time to become an undemanding version of rationality—what we shall refer to as 'thin rationality' review—a standard of review that is primarily informed by institutional competencies considerations relating, *inter alia*, to the regulatory agencies' superior expertise in regulatory matters.

The application of the so-called *Chevron* doctrine in the context of judicial evaluation of agency interpretations of law is another illustration of a judicially crafted standard of review. In the *Chevron* case,[77] the Supreme Court established a two-part test for judicial deference to agencies' reasonable interpretation of their empowering statutes. Under what came to be known as the *Chevron* test of review, a court that reviews an agency's interpretation of the statute has to proceed as follows: in step one, using the tools of statutory interpretation, the court has to verify whether 'Congress has directly spoken to the precise question at issue'.[78] If so, the statute is 'unambiguous'.[79] '[T]hat is the end of the matter for the court as well as the agency must give effect to the unambiguously expressed intent of Congress.'[80] If, however, the court decides that the statute is ambiguous, the court proceeds to step two and examines whether the agency's construction of the statute it administers is 'permissible' or 'reasonable'.[81] According to the reasoning set forth by the Supreme Court, if a statute is ambiguous, Congress has implicitly delegated that question to the agency. In that case, a court 'may not substitute its own construction of a statutory provision for a reasonable interpretation made by the administrator of an agency'.[82] The end result is that an agency's interpretation of the law should be upheld if it does not run contrary to the instructions of Congress. Prior to *Chevron*, there were two main lines of precedent, one requiring courts to engage in full *de novo* review of agency decisions, and the other according agencies deference under certain circumstances, such as the degree of agencies' expertise or the technical complexity of the issue.[83] Scholars, however, have discerned two additional steps in the current judicial approach to applying *Chevron*: a 'step zero', which uses various analytical tools to determine whether the *Chevron* framework is in principle applicable for evaluating the agency's statutory interpretation and a 'step-one-and-a-half' approach, whereby if a court determines that the agency failed to recognise that it was interpreting an ambiguous statutory provision, the court may remand the decision back to the agency to interpret the ambiguous provision.[84] Yet, other scholars have advocated jettisoning *Chevron*'s two-step

[76] *Midwest ISO Transmission Owners v FERC*, 373 F3d 1361, 1368 (DC Cir 2004) (quoting *State Farm*).

[77] *Chevron USA Inc v Natural Resources Defence Council, Inc*, 467 US 837 (1984).

[78] ibid [842].

[79] ibid.

[80] ibid.

[81] ibid [843]–[845]. Interestingly, Peter Strauss perceives judges as wearing a 'Deciders' hat under step one inquiry and an 'Overseers' hat under step two, in Peter Strauss, '"Overseers" or "Deciders" – The Courts in Administrative Law' (2008) 75 Univ Chicago L Rev 815.

[82] *Chevron* (n 77) [844].

[83] See Antonin Scalia, 'Judicial Deference to Administrative Interpretations of Law' (1989) Duke LJ 511, 513, See, eg, *Skidmore v Swift & Co*, 323 US 134, 140 (1944).

[84] See Daniel J Hemel and Aaron L Nielson, 'Chevron Step-One-and-a-Half' (2017) 84 Univ Chicago L Rev 757.

framework arguing that *Chevron* calls for a single inquiry into the reasonableness of agencies' interpretation.[85]

The *Chevron* doctrine merits particular attention for two main reasons. First, it still represents the leading authority in the course of judicial review of the FCC's and the FERC's interpretations of the statutes they administer.[86] Because these statutes often contain ambiguous and vague terms—such as 'unduly discriminatory[] or preferential' in s 5 of the Natural Gas Act—courts are prepared to afford substantial deference to agencies' interpretation of these terms. Second, it constitutes the finest example of a judicial creativity, for it seems to conflict with the wording of the APA, which requires courts to decide all relevant questions of law.[87]

The judge-made standard of *Chevron* has been further refined by the Supreme Court's case law. In its decision in *Mead*,[88] the Court limited the types of agency interpretations that bind courts, such as when it appears that 'Congress delegated authority to the agency to make rules carrying the force of law'.[89] If an agency's interpretation of the statute is given when the agency is not acting with the 'force of law'[90] (ie when it does not act with the necessary degree of formality in arriving at the interpretation), then a less deferential standard of review to the agency's views applies.[91]

Finally, the conflict that may arise between an agency interpretation that is eligible for *Chevron* deference and an earlier judicial precedent established before the agency construed the relevant ambiguous statutory provision, was resolved by the Supreme Court in the *Brand X* case.[92] *Brand X* concerned the debate on net neutrality, that is, the principle that internet service providers should treat all data on the internet equally, allowing non-discriminatory access to all contents and applications, regardless of source and without blocking or favouring particular products or websites. The issue before the Court was whether the FCC had appropriately classified broadband cable Internet service under the Federal Communications Act. In other words, was the FCC's determination that cable companies selling broadband Internet service do not provide 'telecommunications service' a lawful construction of the Act under *Chevron* and the APA?[93] The Act defines two categories of regulated entities: telecommunications carriers and information service providers, the former regulated as common carriers. This entails that telecommunications carriers

[85] Matthew Stephenson and Adrian Vermeule, 'Chevron Has Only One Step' (2009) 95 Virginia L Rev 597, 599.

[86] *Iowa Utilities Board* (n 37); *USTA v FCC*, 359 F3d 554 (2004); *Public Service Corporation v FERC*, 832 F2d 1201 (10th Cir 1987); *Northern Natural Gas Co v FERC*, 827 F2d 779 (DC Cir 1987); *Philips Petroleum Co v FERC*, 792 F2d 1165 (DC Cir 1986).

[87] See APA, 5 USC § 706.

[88] *United States v Mead*, 533 US 218 (2001).

[89] ibid [227]. See also *Christensen v Harris*, 529 US 576 (2000) holding that 'the applicability of Chevron would largely depend on the formality of the process in the course of which the agency adopted its interpretation, excluding from its reach policy statements, agency manuals, interpretive letters' at 587.

[90] *Mead* (n 88) [227].

[91] Those interpretations which failed to qualify for Chevron deference (ie those reached with less formal procedures) could still receive the Skidmore deference, *Skidmore v Swift & Co*, 323 US 134 (1944) to the extent that the interpretation is a persuasive on. See *INS v Cardoza-Fonseca* 480 US 421, 466–48 (1987) holding that Chevron will apply only in cases involving mixed questions of law and fact rather than in cases involving pure questions of law.

[92] *National Cable and Telecomms. Ass'n v Brand X Internet Servs*, 545 US 967, 982–83 (2005).

[93] ibid [974].

must charge just and reasonable and non-discriminatory rates to their customers, facilitate interconnection, and contribute to the universal service fund. In contrast, information-service providers are subject to more light-handed regulation and are not regulated as common carriers under the Act, although the FCC has authority to impose additional regulatory obligations. Finding, therefore, that cable modem providers were telecommunications service providers would impose common carrier obligations on them provided under Title II of the Communications Act and would facilitate net neutrality. The Court of Appeals for the Ninth Circuit overturned the FCC's finding that cable modem operators were not deemed telecommunications service providers,[94] ruling that the Ninth Circuit's prior precedent was binding upon the FCC.[95] However, the majority of the Supreme Court overturned the Ninth Circuit decision. In doing so it made two key rulings. First, under *Chevron* a court's precedent trumps an authorised agency interpretation only when that court finds that the statute 'unambiguously forecloses the agency's interpretation'.[96] Thus, the FCC ruling was entitled to deference. Second, a court must afford deference even if the agency ruling is not the best interpretation, provided the ruling is at least reasonable.

The application of the *Chevron* doctrine has given rise to two contentious issues. The first concerns whether the case is to be decided at step one or step two of *Chevron.* This is owing to the absence of a set of statutory interpretation rules that all interpreters would adhere to when deciding whether a statute is 'ambiguous'. The second one concerns the doctrinal relationship between *Chevron* step two (the 'reasonableness' requirement) and the arbitrary and capricious test of the APA. Does the *Chevron* step 2 'reasonableness' analysis incorporate the *State Farm* reasonableness test? When courts reach step two, they sometimes examine the reasoning process followed by the agency in constructing the statutory provision. Arbitrary and capricious review requires the court to determine whether the agency exercised its discretion in a reasoned way. For this reason, commentators argue that the step two 'reasonableness' standard should be treated as equivalent to the arbitrary and capricious standard of the APA.[97] However, this does not necessarily entail that any determinations as to whether interpretive decisions are reasonable and therefore entitled to *Chevron* deference should depend on the factors articulated by the Supreme Court in the *State Farm* case.[98] In other words, the arbitrary and capricious standard applied under *Chevron* step two does not always invite the application of the 'hard look' review.[99] As will be shown in Chapter 5, courts rarely invalidate an agency construction of the statute

[94] *FCC Cable Modem Ruling*, 17 FCCR 4798, 4819 (2002).

[95] *Brand X Internet Servs v FCC*, 345 F3d 1120, 1130-32 (9th Cir 2003). The precedent relied upon by the Ninth Circuit was *AT&T Corp v City of Portland*, 216 F3d 871 (9th Cir 2000).

[96] *Brand X* (n 92) [2700].

[97] See, eg, Strauss (n 81) 826; Ronald M Levin, 'The Anatomy of Chevron: Step Two Reconsidered' (1997) 72 Chicago-Kent L Rev 1253; Elizabeth M Magill, 'Step Two of *Chevron v Natural Resources Defense Council*' in John E Duffy and Michael Hertz (eds), *A Guide to Judicial and Political Review of Federal Agencies* (ABA 2005) 85, 99; Stephenson and Vermeule (n 85) 604. See further *Verizon v FCC*, 740 F3d 623, 635 (DC Cir 2014).

[98] Stephenson and Vermeule (n 85) 602–3.

[99] See, eg, *Brand X* (n 92) [1001] n 4, which differentiated between Chevron step two and arbitrary and capricious analysis.

under *Chevron* step two. On the rare occasions they have done so, such as in the *AT&T Corp v Iowa Utilities Board*[100] case, they did not apply the 'hard look' review but invalidated the FCC's order on a variety of statutory grounds. 'Hard look' review is mostly applied in the review of an agency's exercise of policymaking expertise in light of a technical, economic, or scientific record, such as that which exists in rate-setting cases. Furthermore, as Kenneth Bamberger and Peter Strauss rightly point out the *State Farm* factors do not 'always identify the totality of factors involved in a reasonableness process of statutory construction'.[101]

Finally, the courts have also significantly elaborated on the 'substantial evidence' standard of review often accompanied by the 'whole record' requirement, which applies to matters required to be decided in 'on the record' proceedings. Prior to adoption of the APA, the Supreme Court had defined the 'substantial evidence' test as fairly deferential: 'it is more than a mere scintilla, but it is less than a preponderance of evidence . . . such relevant evidence as a reasonable mind might accept as adequate to support a conclusion'.[102] Later on, the test required only that the reviewing court determine whether the agency had gathered substantial evidence on its side.[103] Eventually the test became 'substantial evidence on the record as a whole' and the substantiality of the evidence was established only after the reviewing court had discounted the agency's evidence by considering rebuttal evidence.[104] Thus, the Court had to make some independence assessment of both sides of the evidence.

In sum, as shown in Figure 3.1, which depicts the process for the review of economic evidence, the US has adopted an administrative litigation model for the review of economic evidence, which reflects its long tradition of administrative adjudication first undertaken by the hearing examiners and later by the ALJs. The existence of the APA should not be underestimated: a federal piece of legislation codifying procedural requirements for the exercise of rulemaking and adjudication acts as a motivation force within agencies for the collection of evidence and for the enhancement of the case record. The opportunity for oral testimony by witnesses and the opportunity for cross-examination enable the regulatory agency to test its factual record whereas the further review undertaken by the agency's head enables the latter to concentrate on issues of policy. Consequently, the nature of the US internal review of economic evidence model facilitates and even constrains as we shall see, the external review by the federal courts, in the sense that the DC Circuit rarely gets into the facts of the case before it. Although the wording of the APA has largely remained unchanged over the years, institutional forces have given rise to both light touch and 'hard look' review of agencies' actions. We shall trace in Chapter 5 the evolutionary transformation of the scope and nature of judicial review of economic evidence from an excessively intrusive 'hard look' review to a 'thin rationality' review which is far more attentive to the interplay of the various

[100] 525 US 366, 387–92 (1999).
[101] Kenneth A Bamberger and Peter L Strauss, 'Chevron's Two Steps' (2009) 95 Virginia L Rev 611, 622.
[102] *Consolidated Edison* (n 46) above.
[103] *NLRB v Universal Camera Corp*, 179 F2d 749 (2nd Cir 1950).
[104] See *Universal Camera* (n 50) above.

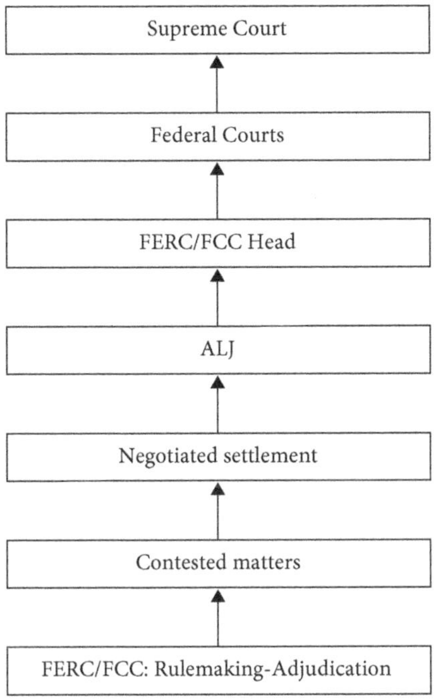


**Figure 3.1** The Process for the Review of Economic Evidence in the US

values and institutional competencies considerations that inform regulatory agencies' actions.

## 3.3 Actors and Processes for the Review of Economic Evidence in the UK

Compared to the US, four major differences exist in the way the UK has sought to deal with the review of economic evidence. First, such review is (most of the times) undertaken in the first instance by a body external to the regulators, the CMA. This can be explained historically: the CMA's predecessors, that is, the Competition Commission (CC) and the Monopolies and Mergers Commission (MMC), have had a long history in the resolution of financially significant issues, such as price controls and licence modification references. In fact, the bulk of review of regulators' decisions are done by the CMA, under a hybrid referral/review procedure inherited from the CC which is inquisitorial in nature and involves a mixture of review and reconsideration.

Secondly, the appeal routes against sector-specific regulatory agencies' decisions vary depending on the nature of the case and further, differ significantly for each of the regulated sectors. This is an issue that has been the focus of many government reviews seeking to streamline the appeals process, most notably the 2013 Regulatory Appeals

Consultation[105] and the most recent proposals of Lord Tyrie, requiring the CMA to relinquish or share some of its existing powers and functions in regulatory appeals.[106] To these one should add the independent study of John Penrose MP, recommending, *inter alia*, to send all regulatory appeals to the CAT to streamline the process.[107] The UK has, indeed, a very complex institutional architecture for appeals, that can be explained historically: there were no precedents for the regulators to work with when the first industries were privatised back in the 1980s and the early 1990s thus the whole policy process developed in an incremental fashion. Evolution has played a much more significant role in the British regulatory process than revolution. This feature coupled with the absence of any tradition of administrative litigation in the UK or any kind of legislative document close to the US APA impeded the development of a uniform procedural framework governing the appeals processes across the regulated sectors.

Thirdly, reflecting a long tradition of assigning the adjudication of disputes involving non-legal expertise to specialist tribunals, the UK has established a specialist tribunal, the CAT, to review the economic evidence implicated in competition law and regulatory disputes.

Finally, both the options of merits review and judicial review are (in principle) open for challenging regulatory agencies decisions. This is a significant shift from the original legislation establishing the utility regulators which made little provision for appeals. Until the introduction of statutory rights of appeal with the Telecommunications (Appeals) Regulations 1999, their decisions could only be challenged by way of judicial review.[108] Figure 3.2 illustrates the process for the review of economic evidence in the UK. The chapter is accompanied by a number of tables. Table 3.1 depicts the various UK appeal bodies involved in regulatory appeals. Table 3.2 provides a summary of CMA Determinations in the telecoms sector. Table 3.3 provides a summary of CMA Energy Licence Appeals. Table 3.4 provides a summary of CMA Energy Codes Appeals, and Table 3.5 provides a summary of OFWAT Redeterminations.

[105] See Department for Business, Innovation and Skills (DBIS), 'Streamlining Streamlining Regulatory and Competition Appeals: Consultation on Options for Reform' 19 June 2013, available at: <https://assets.publishing.service.gov.uk/government/uploads/system/uploads/attachment_data/file/229758/bis-13-876-regulatory-and-competition-appeals-revised.pdf> accessed 6 June 2022.

[106] See letter from Andrew Tyrie, CMA Chair, to the Secretary of State for Business, Energy and Industrial Strategy available at: <https://assets.publishing.service.gov.uk/government/uploads/system/uploads/attachment_data/file/781151/Letter_from_Andrew_Tyrie_to_the_Secretary_of_State_BEIS.pdf> accessed 6 June 2022 outlining proposals for reform, including that of requiring the CMA to relinquish or share some of its existing powers and functions in regulatory appeals.

[107] In September 2020, John Penrose MP was commissioned by the UK Chancellor of the Exchequer and the Secretary of State for Business, Energy, and Industrial Strategy to write an independent report on how the UK's approach to competition and consumer issues could be improved. The report was published in February 2021, see 'Power to the People: Independent Report on Competition Policy' available at: <https://www.gov.uk/government/publications/power-to-the-people-independent-report-on-competition-policy> accessed 6 June 2022.

[108] See Telecommunications (Appeals) Regulations 1999, SI 1999/3180l; Damien Géradin and Michel Kerf (eds), *Controlling Market Power in Telecommunications: Antitrust vs Sector-Specific Regulation* (OUP 2003) 182.

### 3.3.1 Overview of the Main Actors in the Regulatory Process

#### 3.3.1.1 Sector-specific Regulatory Agencies

Sector-specific regulatory agencies were first established following the privatisation and subsequent liberalisation of essential services in the late 1980s.[109] These agencies are institutionally and organisationally separated from the ordinary bureaucracy but are accountable to Parliament. They are governed by corporate boards, which provide strategic direction to the organisations, each of which is supported by an office. The Board usually comprises a Chair, and executive and non-executive members. Non-executive members bring experience and expertise from a range of backgrounds including industry, social policy, environmental work, and finance. The organisational structure differs radically from that conceived under the original privatisation legislation, which vested individuals (eg the DG for Telecommunications) rather than Boards with the task of overseeing, directing, and controlling the newly privatised industries.[110] The regulatory agencies are characterised by a high degree of membership expertise. Such expertise depends on many factors: from formal recognition of competence sealed by a PhD to extensive experience in regulatory matters.

OFGEM was set up by the Utilities Act[111] in 2000, as a non-ministerial department following the merger of the OFFER and OFGAS. It operates under the direction and governance of the Gas and Electricity Markets Authority (GEMA), which makes all major decisions and sets the policy priorities of the economic regulation of the electricity and gas industries in Great Britain. The members of the Authority are appointed and reappointed by the Secretary of State for Business, Energy, and Industrial Strategy in consultation with the administrations. OFGEM is headed by a Chief Executive and who is further supported by a senior management team. OFGEM is charged with implementing the Gas Act 1986, the Electricity Act 1989, the Utilities Act 2000, the Competition Act 1998, the Enterprise Act 2002, and the Energy Acts of 2004, 2008, 2010, 2011, 2013, and 2016. Its role, however, has widened in recent years to include administration of several environmental programmes on behalf of the government. Such programmes include, *inter alia*, the administration of the renewable's obligation, that is, a statutory requirement on electricity suppliers to buy an annually increasing percentage of their electricity from renewable sources, and the Feed-in-Tariffs, that is, a scheme that aims to encourage smaller scale energy generation.

Economists at OFGEM work on issues related to market design, monitor structural reform in wholesale and retail energy markets, produce market analysis, and meet with industry representatives. Crucially, an Office for Research and Economics has been recently established headed by a chief economist. The office was established following the lengthy, in-depth energy market investigation undertaken by the UK

[109] See Christopher D Foster, *Privatisation, Public Ownership and the Regulation of Natural Monopoly* (Blackwell 1992).

[110] For a comprehensive account, see Tony Prosser, *Law and the Regulators* (Clarendon Press 1997); Telecommunications Act 1984, s 1.

[111] Utilities Act 2000, s 1.

CMA,[112] where it was felt that OFGEM had not used economic evidence as robustly as it should have done, and that economics did not have sufficient prominence in the organisation. We shall return to this point in Chapter 4.

OFCOM is responsible for regulating the TV and radio sectors, fixed line telecoms, mobiles, postal services, and the airwaves over which wireless devices operate.[113] It was established under the Office of Communications Act 2002 and operates under a number of Acts of Parliament and other statutes. These include the Communications Act 2003, the Wireless Telegraphy Act 2006, the Broadcasting Act 1990, the Digital Economy Acts 2010 and 2017, and the Postal Services Act 2011. OFCOM's main decision-making body is the Board, which provides strategic direction for the organisation. Most crucially for our purposes here, the competition group has a prominent role over all sectors OFCOM regulates. It provides expert competition and regulatory economic analysis in relation to a diverse range of OFCOM projects that span all the industry areas for which the authority has responsibility (eg regulatory policy development, market reviews, market investigations under the Enterprise Act, competition investigations, resolution of disputes between communications providers, spectrum policy, and impact assessments). The competition group consists of competition economists, a team focusing on competition policy and *ex ante* regulation, a quantitative financial economics team, and the enforcement group. The competition group also collaborates closely with the chief economist's team.

OFWAT, created by the Water Act 1989, is responsible for the regulation of the water and sewerage industries in England and Wales. Its main overarching duties are to protect the interests of consumers, wherever appropriate by promoting competition, to ensure that the functions of water and sewerage companies are properly carried out, and to ensure that the companies are able to finance their functions by securing reasonable returns on their capital. Since 2005, OFWAT has had a duty to contribute to the achievement of sustainable development. The Water Act 2014 placed a new 'resilience' duty on the water regulator to highlight the importance of the long-term resilience of water and wastewater systems in light of environmental pressures and population growth. Furthermore, it created new powers under which the Secretary of State (ie the Department for Environment, Food and Rural Affairs (DEFRA)) may publish a statement setting out strategic priorities and objectives for OFWAT to guide how it regulates water services in England. Prior to 2006, its functions rested with the Director General of Water Services. The framework for the changeover was outlined in the Water Act 2003.[114] The market now includes eighteen large regional independently run private companies. Because water companies are monopoly suppliers to most consumers, OFWAT limits the prices they can charge by setting price limits for fixed five-year periods. OFWAT has carried out seven price reviews since privatisation. The Water Act 2014 extended retail competition to all non-household customers of English water companies from 2017 and provides for possible future competition in

[112] See CMA (2016), 'Energy Market Investigation: Final Report', available at: <https://assets.publishing.service.gov.uk/media/5773de34e5274a0da3000113/final-report-energy-market-investigation.pdf> last accessed 6 June 2022.

[113] See Communications Act 2003 and Office of Communications Act 2002, s 1.

[114] Water Act 2003, s 34.

wholesale markets.[115] Currently, the UK government is considering the evidence base to understand the case for extending competition to household customers in England in the future.

As will be explored in more detail in Chapter 4, all three regulatory agencies operate under certain statutory objectives and have a general duty to promote the interests of consumers. Furthermore, they are accountable to Parliament for all their statutory functions. Finally, a unique feature of the UK regulatory process is the concurrent jurisdiction shared by the sector-specific regulatory agencies and the CMA, the central institution responsible for the enforcement of competition law in the UK, with regard to the application of national competition law by sector-specific regulators in their areas of competence.[116] In order to address the small number of cases brought by the sector-specific regulators under the concurrency regime, the government strengthened the primacy of general competition law over sector regulation by imposing an obligation on sector regulators to use their competition powers in preference to their sectoral powers whenever legally permissible and appropriate. The CMA has published several guidelines on the concurrency regime and has issued more specific guidance on the application of competition law provisions to the regulated industries.[117]

#### 3.3.1.2 The CMA's Role in Economic Regulation

The CMA was created following the amalgamation of the OFT and the CC; the latter being in part a successor to the MMC.[118] With regard to regulatory matters the CMA has six distinct functions.

First, as explained above, the CMA has an enhanced role in supporting sectoral bodies to initiate competition inquiries and most controversially it has the power to take cases away from the regulators in certain circumstances. Second, the CMA can perform market investigations in regulated sectors following a market investigation referral of the relevant regulator.[119] For example, in June 2014, the UK energy regulator OFGEM referred the UK energy market for a full competition investigation by the CMA following a joint OFT/OFGEM assessment of the state of competition

[115] Martin Cave, 'Independent Review of Competition and Innovation in Water Markets – Final Report', April 2009, available at: <https://assets.publishing.service.gov.uk/government/uploads/system/uploads/attachment_data/file/69462/cave-review-final-report.pdf> accessed 6 June 2022.

[116] See ERRA 2013, ss 51–53. For an analysis, see Niamh Dunne, 'Recasting Competition Concurrency under the Enterprise and Regulatory Reform Act 2013' (2014) 77(2) Modern L Rev 254.

[117] CMA (2014), 'Regulated Industries: Guidance on Concurrent Application of Competition law to Regulated Industries' available at: <https://www.gov.uk/government/publications/guidance-on-concurrent-application-of-competition-law-to-regulated-industries> accessed 6 June 2022.

[118] Section 45(3) of the Competition Act 1998 dissolved the MMC, which had been in existence under various names since the Monopolies and Restrictive Trade Practices Act of 1948. For a general account of the work of the MMC from 1948 to 1998, see Stephen Wilks, *In the Public Interest: Competition Policy and the Monopolies and Mergers Commission* (Manchester Univ Press 1999).

[119] The Market Investigation Reference process was instituted by Part 4 of the Enterprise Act 2002 and substantially reformed by the ERRA Act 2013. See CMA (2017), 'Markets Studies and Market Investigations: Supplemental Guidance on the CMA's Approach' available at: <https://assets.publishing.service.gov.uk/government/uploads/system/uploads/attachment_data/file/624706/cma3-markets-supplemental-guidance-updated-june-2017.pdf> accessed 6 June 2022.

in the energy market in Great Britain.[120] This notoriously broad tool granted by the Enterprise Act 2002 enables the CMA to consider whether there are features of a market, structural (e.g. concentration, entry barriers and regulation) or conduct-related (supplier or customer conduct) that have an adverse effect on competition (AEC).[121] If one or more AECs are found, then the CMA must determine whether it should take action itself to remedy the AEC, and/or whether it should recommend actions to be taken by others (such as the government or the regulator).[122] A broad range of remedies can be imposed, ranging from structural remedies (ie divesture) to licence modifications, price controls, informational remedies, and recommended actions.[123] These may then be subject to judicial review by the specialist CAT. Third, the CMA can hear energy licence modification appeals. Fourth, the CMA has an appeal function in relation to price control decisions by OFCOM following a reference by the CAT under the Communications Act 2003. In an appeal under s 193 of the Communications Act 2003 against an OFCOM decision the CAT must refer that part of the appeal that relates to price control matters to the CMA for a decision.[124] The CAT must decide the appeal on those matters in accordance with the CMA's determination, unless it decides that the determination would be set aside on an application for judicial review.[125] Fifth, the CMA has an appeal function following decisions by the GEMA to modify certain energy codes under the Energy Act 2004[126] and following decisions by OFWAT to modify water codes.[127] Finally, the CMA can hear appeals against OFWAT's price determinations.[128]

In each case referred to the CMA a group will be appointed to conduct the investigation. Economists work closely with the group to provide economic analysis and advice. The exact work carried out by CMA economists depends on the type of inquiry and on the industry involved. As well as conducting their own evidence, economists appraise evidence submitted by the parties. When conducting an investigation concerned with the regulation of the water, electricity, or gas sectors or an energy code modification appeal, the Chairman must appoint at least one member from the utility panel, while when the group is involved in communications matters, at least one specialist communications panel member should be appointed.[129]

[120] OFT/Ofgem (2014), 'State of the Market Assessment' available at: <https://www.ofgem.gov.uk/sites/default/files/docs/2014/03/assessment_document_published_1.pdf> accessed 6 June 2022.

[121] EA 2002, s 134(2).

[122] EA 2002, s. 134(4).

[123] EA 2002, s 161 and Schedule 8. See further, *BAA Ltd v CC* [2009] CAT 35 [117].

[124] Pursuant to s 193(10), a 'price control matter' is defined as an imposition of any form of price control authorised by ss 87(9), 91, or 93(3) of the Communications Act 2003.

[125] Communications Act 2003, s 193 and rule 117 of the Competition Appeal Tribunal Rules 2015, SI 2015/1648; see case *BT Plc v OFCOM* [2010] CAT 15 [9]–[53].

[126] Section 173.

[127] Under Regulation 4 of the Water Industry Designated Codes (Appeals to the Competition and Markets Authority) Regulations 2017 (SI 2017/447); such codes that have been designated for the purposes of s 207A(2) of the Water Industry Act 1991. See further CMA (2017), Water Codes Appeals: Competition and Markets Authority Rules, available at: <https://assets.publishing.service.gov.uk/government/uploads/system/uploads/attachment_data/file/1019391/water-codes-appeals-rules-cma67.pdf> accessed 6 June 2022.

[128] Water Industry Act 1991, Part I.

[129] ERRA Act 2013, Explanatory Notes, Part 3.

### 3.3.1.3 The Competition Appeal Tribunal

The CAT was established by the Enterprise Act 2002 to hear appeals on the merits and applications for review of the decisions of the CMA and the sector-specific regulators. In essence, the CAT is primarily a competition tribunal, with the regulator functions added because of its expertise and specialised knowledge. It is an independent judicial body funded and supported in its administration through a body called the Competition Service. It consists of a President,[130] a panel of Chairmen, and a panel of ordinary members. The current President of the CAT is a High Court judge appointed to the Chancery Division, and a number of other Chancery Division judges sit regularly as Chairmen in the CAT. The Tribunal exemplifies the continuation of a long tradition in the UK of the use of lay members in the assessment of competition law issues. The Restrictive Trade Practices Act 1956 provided for the establishment of a Supreme Court of Record to be known as the Restrictive Trade Practices Court consisting of five judges and ten members appointed from persons having knowledge of or experience in industry, commercial, and public affairs.

The CAT has four distinct functions in relation to regulatory matters. First, it is responsible for hearing appeals against certain decisions taken by OFCOM or the Secretary of State under the provisions of the Communications Act 2003. Those decisions principally concern the exercise by OFCOM of its powers to regulate electronic communications networks and services under Part 2 of the Communications Act, the use of the radio spectrum under the Wireless Telegraphy Act 2006, and the exercise of Broadcasting Act 1990 powers for a competition purpose.[131] As mentioned in the introduction to this chapter, although there have been various government reviews of regulatory appeals aimed at streamlining the overall process, the only change thus far implemented concerns the standard of review in telecommunications appeals. Considerations relating to the length of an appeal and the high costs of continuing litigation in the fast-moving markets of electronic communications led to a relegation of OFCOM's decisions under ss 192–196 of the Act to a judicial review standard.[132] In other words, there no longer exists a rehearing on the merits of the decision, as the CAT must decide these appeals by applying the same principles as would be applied by a court on an application for judicial review.[133] However, the combined reading of Article 4(1) of the retained Framework Directive,[134] which requires an effective appeal mechanism taking due account of the merits that exist at a national level for any user or undertaking affected by the decision of an NRA, and Article 194(A) of the Communications Act 2003 stipulates that the Tribunal has to ensure that the merits of the case are also duly taken into account. We shall return to this point in Chapter 6,

[130] EA 2002, s 12(2)(a).

[131] Communications Act, ss 192 and 317(6). The competition aspects of certain decisions concerning the Channel 3 networking arrangements may also be appealed to the Tribunal.

[132] Digital Economy Act 2017, s 87 (Commencement No 1) Regulations 2017 (SI 2017/765).

[133] Communications Act 2003, § 194A(2).

[134] See Directive 2009/140/EC of the European Parliament and of the Council of 25 November 2009 amending Directives 2002/21/EC on a common regulatory framework for electronic communications networks and services, 2002/19/EC on access to, and interconnection of, electronic communications networks and associated facilities, and 2002/20/EC on the authorisation of electronic communications networks and services, [2009] L337/37.

where we shall examine in detail how the CAT has understood and applied this change in the standard of review in the telecommunications cases before it. Regarding remedies, the CAT may dismiss the appeal or quash the whole or part of that decision, remit the matter back to OFCOM with a direction to reconsider, and make a new decision in accordance with its ruling. Second, it has been given certain functions under the Mobile Roaming (European Communities) Regulations 2007,[135] Schedule 2A of the Electricity Act 1989, and Schedule 18 of the Energy Act 2004 in relation to determinations by OFGEM in respect of property schemes. Third, an appeal to the CAT may be made under the Energy Act 2010 against either the imposition of a final order or the imposition or amount of a penalty (or the date by which such penalty may be made) in relation to the breach of the transmission constraint licence condition.[136] Fourth, the CAT hears appeals on the merits in respect of decisions made under the Competition Act 1998 by the CMA and the sectoral regulators.

The Tribunal epitomises the essence of a hyper-specialised judicial body. There are several reasons for this. The first relates to the Tribunal's membership and composition. Contrary to the ordinary courts, the CAT's bench combines legal and non-legal expertise. The membership consists of two panels: a panel of chairmen and a panel of ordinary members. The majority on the panel of chairmen are judges of the Chancery Division of the High Court. Some chairmen and all the other members come from academia, private practice, the civil service, business, and industry. Typically, a three-member tribunal (a chairman and two ordinary members) will be constituted by the President to hear a particular case. Although the Tribunal's lay members may not claim a deep level of specialisation in a specific sector, such as that characterising the CMA members, they do possess cross-disciplinary expertise in economics, business, and accountancy or have experience in the public sector.[137] The second reason relates to the CAT's limited jurisdiction over regulatory and competition law disputes, which in turn strengthens its capacity to deal with complex economic evidence. The third reason relates to the judge's perception of their role. To put it another way, the institutional identity of the 'expert Tribunal' has a direct impact on judicial behaviour: in seven out of eighteen appeals from OFCOM the CAT has not hesitated to engage in a forensic review of complex regulatory issues, to delve into the detail of the regulator's reasoning, and eventually overturn its decision.[138] Overall, the CAT's combination of special or exclusive jurisdiction over fields of legal policy with the recruitment of specialist-expert judges create incentives for its self-proclaimed 'profound and rigorous scrutiny'[139] of the agencies' findings and economic analysis.

[135] SI 2007/1933.

[136] Energy Act 2010, ss 20–21. The licence conditions prohibit generators from obtaining an excessive benefit from electricity generation in relation to a period of transmission constraint.

[137] See *British Sky Broadcasting Group Plc v CC* [2008] CAT 25 [60]: 'the Tribunal's composition is required by statute to contain competition expertise, and its members are selected for their relevant knowledge and experience'.

[138] See, eg, *Vodafone Ltd v OFCOM* [2008] CAT 22, where the Tribunal conducted a detailed analysis of OFCOM's cost-benefit analysis of proposed changes to the telephone number portability regime.

[139] See *Hutchison 3G UK Ltd v OFCOM* [2008] CAT 11 [164]; *Vodafone Ltd v OFCOM* [2008] CAT 22 [46]; and *TalkTalk v OFCOM* [2012] CAT 1 [71].

#### 3.3.1.4 Ordinary Courts

Amongst the ordinary courts, the Administrative Court of the Queen's Bench Division (part of the High Court) in England and Wales (hereinafter 'High Court') constitutes the main venue for bringing actions for judicial review against sector-specific regulators' decisions. In fact, prior to the Enterprise Act 2002, the High Court enjoyed a near total monopoly in reviewing regulatory decisions.

The High Court and the CAT enjoy similar status in the judicial hierarchy and share some judges. High Court cases are, however, heard by a single judge although the court can choose to sit with assessors. In both cases, appeals against their decisions on points of law or in penalty cases as to the amount of any penalty are heard with the permission of the Court of Appeal in England and Wales.[140] From the Court of Appeal a further appeal may be taken with permission to the Supreme Court, formerly the House of Lords.

Although the CAT's jurisdiction is governed by statute, the High Court enjoys inherent jurisdiction governed by the rules of precedent.[141] There remains the possibility that a claim for judicial review may be brought before the Administrative Court, for example where there are infringements of Articles 101 and 102 TFEU or of the Chapter I and II prohibitions of the Competition Act 1998. Such actions are usually brought in the Chancery Division, but sometimes may be dealt with by the Commercial Court. The CMA's decisions are also subject to judicial review by the High Court. Nonetheless, permission to apply for judicial review would be refused if the court were to consider that a particular case could be addressed within the statutory appeal procedure.

### 3.3.2 Overview of the Process for the Review of Economic Evidence

Having provided a broad overview of the various actors the chapter moves on to consider the process and scope of external review of economic evidence. Depending on the nature of the case this is undertaken by the CMA, the CAT, or the ordinary courts.

#### 3.3.2.1 External Review of Economic Evidence by the CMA

This section will review the process of external review of economic evidence referring to each of the CMA's functions detailed above. It is important to note at the outset that the CMA's decision-making autonomy is significantly greater when considering appeals against OFGEM's decisions. This is mainly attributed to the implementation of the EU Third Energy package,[142] which strengthened affected parties' rights to appeal

[140] In relation to Tribunal proceedings in Scotland, the appeal lies to the Court of Session; and in relation to Tribunal proceedings in Northern Ireland to the Court of Appeal for Northern Ireland.

[141] Supreme Court Act 1981, s 31 and Civil Procedure Rules, Part 54.

[142] The Third Package comprises two Directives and three Regulations: Directive 2009/72/EC of the European Parliament and of the Council of 13 July 2009 concerning common rules for the internal market in electricity and repealing Directive 2003/54/EC [2009] OJ L211/55 (Electricity Directive 2009); Directive 2009/73/EC of the European Parliament and of the Council of 13 July 2009 concerning common rules for the internal market in natural gas and repealing Directive 2003/55/EC [2009] OJ L211/94 (Gas Directive

against the NRAs' decisions[143] and transformed the CMA to a fully fledged appeal body charged with merits-based review of OFGEM's decisions.

*3.3.2.1.1 Energy Licence Modification Appeals and Water Redeterminations*

Under the Gas Act[144] and the Electricity Act,[145] each company involved in the generation, distribution, transmission, supply, transportation shipping, or provision through interconnectors of electricity or gas requires a licence, unless specifically excluded from needing one by the Secretary of State (eg small operators). Licences are, therefore, the principal mechanism of *ex ante* regulatory control. OFGEM decides the content of such licences (which generally impose obligations upon the licence holders to prevent, *inter alia*, anticompetitive, discriminatory, or exploitative conduct) and is responsible for monitoring and enforcing compliance with them. In broad outline, the relevant legislation sets out a statutory procedure for the regulator to modify an energy licence and for appeals to be brought to the CMA against a decision of the regulator to proceed with such a modification, including price control decisions. Price control is a key element of regulation. Licensees may appeal price controls[146] and interested third parties may also make representations or observations to the CMA about the grounds on which the appeal has been brought.[147]

Several changes have been introduced to the energy licence modification process following the implementation in the UK of the EU Third Energy Package. First, the CMA is not to consider afresh the licence modifications imposed by the Authority, as was the case in the original privatisation regime. The appeal regime is now more adversarial in nature and the CMA is required to decide whether or not to consider the appeal on defined criteria and not by recourse to the abstract notion of 'public interest', as in the first privatisation statutes.[148] In other words, the CMA will only allow an appeal where it is satisfied that the appellant has shown on the balance of probabilities that the Authority's decision was wrong on one or more of the grounds set out in the Acts: that is, that GEMA failed properly to have regard, or to give appropriate weight to the matters to which GEMA must have regard in the carrying out of its principal

2009); Regulation (EC) No 714/2009 on conditions for access to network for cross-border exchanges in electricity and repealing Regulation (EC) No 1228/2003 [2009] OJ L211/15 (Electricity Regulation 2009); Regulation (EC) 715/2009 of the European Parliament and of the Council of 13 July 2009 on conditions for access to the network for cross-border exchanges in electricity and repealing Regulation (EC) 1775/2005 (Gas Regulation 2009) and Regulation (EC) 713/2009 establishing an Agency for the Cooperation of Energy Regulators [2009] OJ L211/1.

143 Electricity Directive 2009, Art 37(5) and Arts 16 and 41(1–17) Gas Directive 2009. The specific procedures enshrined in paras 11 and 12 of Art 37 Electricity and Art 41 Gas are 'without prejudice to the exercise of rights or appeal under EU or National Law' para 15 of both Articles. On the specific issue concerning tariffs/ methodologies, see Art 37(2) Elec and Art 41(12) Gas.

144 Gas Act 1986, s 5(1) (as amended).

145 Electricity Act 1989, s 6(1)(c) (as amended).

146 Electricity Act 1989, s 11C.

147 CMA (2017), 'Energy Licence Modification Appeals: Competition and Markets Authority Rules' (October 2017), Rule 10, available at: <https://assets.publishing.service.gov.uk/government/uploads/system/uploads/attachment_data/file/1019199/energy-licence-modification-appeals-rules.pdf> accessed 6 June 2022.

148 See, eg, Telecommunications Act 1984, ss 13 and 15.

objectives and certain duties; that the decision was based, wholly or partly, on an error of fact; that the modifications fail to achieve, in whole or in part, the effect stated by GEMA in its decision that the decision was wrong in law. To the extent that the CMA does not allow the appeal, it must confirm the decision appealed against. The 'public interest test' contained a variety of objectives, from the maintenance of 'effective competition' to the promotion of the 'balanced distribution of industry and employment' and the 'promotion of the interest of consumers'.[149] It has now been declared incompatible with the Third Energy Package and has been replaced by the requirement that the CMA applies the same criteria as the regulator. The CMA therefore assumes a 'gatekeeper role' in deciding whether to allow the appeal or not.

Secondly, in response to the EU Third Energy Package requirement to strengthen the NRAs autonomous decision-making, the veto rights of companies over changes to their own licenses have been abolished and the CMA can directly enforce its decisions, by issuing binding directions. This is a significant change as it transforms the CMA to a fully fledged quasi-judicial appeal body.

Thirdly, standing requirements have been widened and all licensees (eg network companies, generators, or retailers) and consumer representative bodies have a right of appeal in relation to license decisions that materially affect them.[150] These generous standing rules encourage more rigorous analysis of the potential impacts of license modification decisions on all parties.

The CMA considers the evidence submitted by the parties and has the power to require the submission of additional information and clarification of the evidence. It may also commission expert advice to help it interrogate evidence submitted by the appellant and by OFGEM. Parties are permitted to introduce new evidence in so far as the appeal body considers it is relevant to the issue before it. The CMA enjoys quite wide remedial powers: in relation to a price control decision,[151] it can quash GEMA's decision, remit the matter back to GEMA for reconsideration and determination in accordance with any directions given by the CMA, or it can substitute its own decision for that of GEMA's decision (to the extent that the appeal is allowed) and give any directions to GEMA or any other party to the appeal. In relation to any other decision, it can quash GEMA's decision and remit the matter back to GEMA for reconsideration and determination in accordance with any directions given by the CMA.

The standard of review was tested and clarified in the first set of appeals under s 11C of the Electricity Act 1989 against OFGEM's price control decisions brought by British Gas and Northern Powergrid.[152] British Gas, a supplier, appealed on the basis that OFGEM's price control decision was too generous to distributors. It advanced several grounds of appeal, but won only one, with the CMA finding that OFGEM's recalibration of one of its incentive mechanisms had been on the facts excessive, but the regulator was right in principle. Northern Powergrid, a distributor, conversely

[149] See Fair Trading Act 1973, s 84.

[150] See CMA (2017) (n 147) above.

[151] See Electricity Act 1989, s 11(F) and Gas Act 1986, s 23 E(7).

[152] CMA, *British Gas Trading Ltd v the Gas and Electricity Markets Authority – Final Determination* (29 September 2015) and *Northern Powergrid (Northeast) Ltd and Northern Powergrid (Yorkshire) plc v the Gas and Electricity Markets Authority – Final Determination* (29 September 2015).

appealed on the basis that the allowances were not generous enough. The CMA found for Northern Powergrid on only one of the three grounds it advanced, holding that the savings that OFGEM anticipated distributors would make through the advent of smart technology were probably not too important and they were also premised on an unsound methodology.

Crucially, the CMA, seeing itself as an expert appellate body, stated that the standard of review to be applied to OFGEM's decision is more intense than the judicial review standard. The CMA was required to look at the merits of the decision under appeal and determine whether it was wrong on one of the grounds laid down in the legislation.[153] At the same time, the CMA placed clear limits on the extent to which it would interfere with OFGEM's decisions, stressing that it would not substitute its views for OFGEM's simply because it would have taken a different approach; rather, OFGEM's decision had to be wrong. Nor did it accept the submissions of intervening parties that it was required to conduct a rehearing and, if necessary, decide matters afresh; rather, the CMA confines its inquiry to the grounds advanced.

The situation is however different in the context of water redeterminations. Here, the CMA is tasked with a new determination (a 'redetermination') rather than with simply deciding whether it considers OFWAT's determination to have been reasonable. The process is inquisitorial in nature and there is no limitation on the scope of CMA's review. In carrying out the redetermination of the price controls, the CMA is required to determine the reference in accordance with OFWAT's primary and secondary statutory duties and is subject to the same principles of best regulatory practice as applied to OFWAT when it made the disputed determinations. The CMA exercises its own regulatory discretion as to how to appropriately balance these statutory duties.

*3.3.2.1.2 Energy and Water Code Modifications Appeals*

The CMA is also responsible for hearing appeals on the merits from market participants in respect of modifications to codes covering the energy industry, subject to that decision being eligible for a right to appeal.[154] In fact, some licences require the licensee to accede to and comply with industry codes and agreements. These multilateral industry codes establish detailed rules for the gas and electricity industries that govern market operation, the terms for connection and access to energy networks, supply point administration, and security of supply. For example, in the electricity industry, the National Grid Company is required by its transmission license to have in force at all times a Balancing Settlements Code, a Connection and Use of System Code, and a Grid Code. In the gas industry, all gas transporters are required to produce a network code, which governs the commercial arrangements between it and gas shippers.

Each code has a panel or committee that oversees the assessment of proposed changes to the codes, proposed by code signatories or by consumer representative

[153] Electricity Act 1989, s 11E.

[154] See Energy Act 2004, ss 173–175, as amended by the Electricity and Gas Appeals (Designation and Exclusion) Order 2005 SI 2005/1646 (2005 Order) and the Electricity and Gas Appeals (Designation and Exclusion) Order 2009 SI 2009/648 (2009 Order); see further CC10, 'Energy Code Modification Rules' (July 2005), adopted by the CMA Board.

bodies. Some codes, however, may only be altered with the consent of, or at the direction of, OFGEM. Appeals will be allowed where OFGEM disagrees with the decision of the industry panels that govern the codes. OFGEM's views are informed by its statutory duties and functions and by its mission to protect consumers. Until the introduction of the Unified Network Code for gas in 2005 there was no panel recommendation in the gas code modification process. Furthermore, there has never been a judicial review on the gas network code although a successful judicial review has been carried out against OFGEM's electricity code decision.[155] The right of appeal is available to anyone 'materially affected' by the regulatory decision or a body or organisation representing such persons, for example an industry or consumers' association.[156] The procedure is closely modelled on that available for licence modification references; active case management by the Commission and the parties to an appeal may be permitted to rely on expert evidence. Regarding the nature of the appeal, it falls somewhere between a full appeal on the merits and review. The Commission may only allow an appeal on specified grounds, but these are wide enough to include an error of fact or failing to give appropriate weight to the regulator's statutory objectives.[157]

The nature and intensity of the CMA's review function was developed in detail in the *E.ON UK plc v GEMA* decision.[158] The appeal concerned the decision made by OFGEM to reform the regime of the off-take of gas from Great Britain's high pressure National Transmission System. The CMA at the time considered challenges to each of GEMA's proposals for modifications to the Uniform Network Code and to the aspects of 116V relating to user commitment, flexibility, and interruptibility as well as to the cost-benefit analysis in GEMA's decision. The CMA took the view that the grounds for appeal enabled it to go beyond the narrow judicial review approach and consider the merits of the case. In considering code modification appeals OFGEM is required to perform a broad assessment of whether a particular proposal better facilitates the achievement of the relevant objectives. And such a task undoubtedly falls within the agency's broad discretionary power. The CMA while highlighting that it will not consider afresh the modification proposed with a view to deciding whether it would have reached the same decision as GEMA, had the Commission rather than GEMA had to decide whether to allow the modification,[159] still identified several errors in GEMA's cost-benefit analysis, as the decision did not contain sufficient evidence to support OFGEM's conclusions. In addition, the Commission found that GEMA had erred in its approach to upfront transporters' costs. The CMA can apply a wide range of remedies: it has the power to quash OFGEM's decisions, to approve modification decisions, to direct that recommended modifications 'vetoed' by OFGEM have a direct effect, or to remit decisions to OFGEM for reconsideration and redetermination in line with its directions.

[155] See *R (on the application of Teeside Power Ltd and others) v Gas and Electricity Markets Authority* [2008] EWCH 1415 (Admin).

[156] See Energy Act, ss 173(3) and 174(4).

[157] See Energy Act, s 175(4).

[158] See CC02/07, *E.ON UK plc and GEMA and British Gas Trading Ltd*: Decision and Order of the Competition Commission (10 July 2007).

[159] CC11, 'Guide to Appeals in Energy Code Modification Cases' (July 2005) adopted by the CMA.

In the water sector, the introduction of codes, which were put forward by the Water Act 2014 governing agreements between incumbent undertakers and water supply and sewerage licensees wishing to compete to provide water and sewerage services in the new market, also include regulations governing appeals to the CMA against a decision by OFWAT to make or not to make a revision to the code. DEFRA suggested an appeals approach similar to the adversarial, quasi-judicial procedure that exists for the energy sector, although the government limited the right to appeal only to an undertaker or licensee in possession of a water supply and sewerage license.[160]

*3.3.2.1.3 Appeals against Price Control Decisions by OFCOM*

Appeals against price control decisions by OFCOM are made to the CAT, but there is an obligation for the CAT to refer price control matters to the CMA, while retaining for itself non-price control appeals.

More specifically, the Communications Act gives OFCOM the power to impose various conditions on communications providers, including conditions on operators that OFCOM has determined to have significant market power (SMP conditions).[161] Such conditions may include price controls.[162] Appellants have a right to appeal to the CAT against such decisions and the Tribunal must decide these appeals by reference to the grounds of appeal set out in the Notice of Appeal and, following the changes introduced by the Digital Economy Act 2017, by applying the same principles as would be applied by a court on an application for judicial review.[163] Regarding remedies, the CAT may dismiss the appeal or quash the whole or part of the decision to which it relates and where it quashes the whole or part of that decision, remit the matter back to the regulator with a direction to reconsider and make a new decision in accordance with its ruling.[164]

But where the Tribunal determines that a particular appeal raises a specified price control matter,[165] this is referred to the CMA for determination. In broad terms, a specified price control matter is a matter which relates to the design of a price control, as opposed to the question as to whether or not to impose a price control at all. The CMA makes its determination by reference to the grounds of appeal and, in light of the changes introduced by the Digital Economy Act 2017, having regard to the same principles as would be applied by a court on an application for judicial review.[166] Unlike the CMA procedures against OFGEM's

[160] DEFRA (2015), 'Water Supply and Sewerage Licencing Regime: Standard Licence Conditions and the Approach to Secondary Legislation,' available at: <https://consult.defra.gov.uk/water/water-supply-and-sewerage-licensing-regime/> accessed 6 June 2022.

[161] Communications Act 2003, s 42(2)(b). The SMP provisions implement Articles 14–16 of the Framework Directive and Articles 9–13 of the Access Directive. See Directive 2009/140/EC of the European Parliament and of the Council of 25 November 2009 amending Directives 2002/21/EC on a common regulatory framework for electronic communications networks and services, 2002/19/EC on access to, and interconnection of, electronic communications networks and associated facilities, and 2002/20/EC on the authorisation of electronic communications networks and services, [2009] L337/37.

[162] See Communications Act 2003, ss 87(9), 91 and 93(3).

[163] Communications Act 2003, s 194A(2).

[164] Communications Act 2003, s 194A(3)(a) and (b).

[165] See Communications Act 2003, s 193(10).

[166] Communications Act 2003, ss 193(2) and 194A(2). See further, CMA (2017), 'Price control appeals under section 193 of the Communications Act 2003: Competition and Markets Authority guidance',

decisions, participation in the CMA proceedings is limited to the parties to the case, the appellant, the regulator, and any interveners who are admitted by the CAT. Concurrently with this process, the CAT must determine the non-price control matters and review of the CMA's determinations applying the principles applicable on an application for judicial review. The Tribunal is not concerned with the correctness, but with the 'lawfulness' of the CMA's review.[167] The CAT has held that the disposal of the appeal should result in as high degree of finality as possible, having regard to the grounds of the appeal and the nature of the CMA's findings.[168] Only an error of 'sufficient importance'[169] can vitiate the regulator's determinations.

#### 3.3.2.2 External Review of Economic Evidence by the UK Courts

External review of economic evidence is undertaken by both the CAT and the High Court. Although, as already stated, the two courts have similar status in the judiciary hierarchy, their jurisdiction and rules of procedure differ greatly. The real distinction arises between cases that require a full assessment of the merits of the factual and legal arguments and cases in which the judicial review standard applies.

As already mentioned in the introduction, in the UK there is a categorical distinction between judicial review (inherent jurisdiction) and merits review (which requires express statutory authorisation). The most popular classification of the grounds of review is found in Lord Diplock's *CCSU* case division into illegality (unlawfulness), irrationality (unreasonableness), and procedural impropriety (unfairness).[170] Crucially, in cases where there is real unfairness the courts are now willing to intervene where the public body has made a serious factual error in reaching its decision.[171]

Under the illegality ground of review, the courts will intervene where a public body has acted in a manner which is incompatible with a higher legal authority, such as domestic primary or subordinate legislation; in other words, where a body has acted *ultra vires*. For instance, in the *Teeside Power* case[172] the Court determined that OFGEM had no general power to approve proposed modifications to an industry code, which are not in accordance with a timetable for implementation previously set. In approving proposed modifications to the code outside of the set timetable OFGEM had acted unlawfully.

Under the irrationality ground of review, or what has come to be known as 'Wednesbury unreasonableness'[173] the courts can set aside the decision of a public authority entrusted by Parliament with discretion on a matter if this decision is wholly absurd; that is, if it is

available at: <https://assets.publishing.service.gov.uk/government/uploads/system/uploads/attachment_data/file/652741/telecoms-price-control-appeals-cma-guidance.pdf> accessed 6 June 2022.

[167] *British Telecommunications and Others v CC* [2012] CAT 11 [118, 3].
[168] *Hutchison 3G UK Ltd v OFCOM* [2008] CAT 5 [15].
[169] ibid [132].
[170] *Council of Civil Service Unions v Minister for the Civil Service* [1985] AC 374 (*CCSU*).
[171] *E v Secretary of State for the Home Department* [2004] EWCA Civ 49; [2004] QB 1044. For an analysis of the case, see Paul Craig, 'Case Comment – Judicial Review, Appeal and Factual Error' (2004) Pub L 788.
[172] *Teeside Power* (n 155).
[173] *Wednesbury* (n 42) [234].

one which 'no reasonable body would have come to', a very heavy evidential burden to satisfy.[174] Hence, the *Wednesbury* test demarcates the respective provinces of executive and judicial power within the constitutional order. In the *CCSU* case Lord Diplock observed that *Wednesbury* unreasonableness '... applies to a decision which is so outrageous in its defiance of logic or of accepted moral standards that no sensible person who had his mind to the question to be decided could have arrived at it'.[175] To the knowledge of the author no challenge has so far succeeded on the ground of irrationality in the Administrative Court in appeals from utility regulators. The courts are willing to grant to the regulator 'a wide measure of discretion and width of decision'[176] in such cases.

Finally, challenges can also be made with respect to the procedure by which the decision was made. Procedural impropriety refers to broader considerations of procedural fairness[177] founded upon the principle of natural justice. For example, an alleged bias in taking a decision,[178] the failure to give each party to the dispute an opportunity to be heard,[179] or the failure to give adequate reasons,[180] and the breach of legitimate expectations[181] may also lead to the annulment of the decision. Until the case of *Interbrew*,[182] however, all attempts to invoke procedural failings in judicial review applications against the MMC's decisions had been unsuccessful.

Nevertheless, the above list is neither exhaustive nor mutually exclusive. It is open to the courts to consider new grounds of review. Indeed, following the incorporation of the European Convention on Human Rights (ECHR) into domestic law via the Human Rights Act 1998 (HRA), potentially new grounds of review, such as that of proportionality,[183] have blurred the distinction that is firmly embedded in the English courts between 'merits' review and 'judicial' review.[184] Subsequently the courts' review of the decisions of agencies is moving from a position of traditional reluctance to intervene in areas of policy to a position of greater intensity of scrutiny.[185] At the

[174] ibid [230].

[175] *CCSU* (n 170).

[176] *Wildman v OFCOM* [2005] EWCA (Admin) 1573. See further *R (London and Continental Stations and Property Ltd) v The Rail Regulator* [2003] EWCA Civ 2607.

[177] See, eg, *R (on the application of Tate & Lyle Industries Ltd) v Secretary of State for Energy and Climate Change and the Gas and Electricity Markets Authority* [2011] EWCA Civ 664 (where broader considerations of fairness, such as the need to take account of material data to avoid over-subsidising renewable obligations certificates took precedence over adopting a consistent approach to all affected parties).

[178] See *Magill v Porter* [2001] UKHL 67; *BAA v CC* [2009] CAT 35. See further, *R (Walker) v Secretary of State for Energy and Climate Change* [2011] EWHC 2048 (Admin).

[179] *R v Deputy Industrial Injuries Commissioner, ex p Moore* [1965] 1 QB 456.

[180] *Secretary of State for Education and Science v Tameside Metropolitan Borough Council* [1977] AC 1014; [1976] 2 WLR 641 HL; *R v Ministry of Defence, ex parte Murray* [1998] COD 134; *R v Civil Service Appeal Board, ex p Cunningham* [1991] 4 All ER 310; *R v Home Secretary, ex p Fayed* [1997] 1 All ER 228.

[181] *R v North and East Devon Health Authority, ex p Coughlan* [2002] 2 WLR 622.

[182] *Interbrew v Competition Commission and DTI* [2001] EWHC (Admin) 367 [2001] UKCLR 954.

[183] See, eg, *Tesco plc v Competition Commission* [2009] CAT 6, at para 137.

[184] See *CCSU* (n 170), where Lord Diplock foresaw that 'further development on a case-by-case basis may ... in course of time add further grounds. I have in mind particularly the possible adaption in the future of the principle of proportionality which is recognised in the administrative law of several of our fellow members of the European Community'. *R (Daly) v Secretary of State for the Home Department* [2001] UKHL 26, [2001] 2 AC 532; *R v Secretary of State for the Home Department ex p Leech* [1994] QB 198. See further Michael Fordham, 'Common Law Proportionality' (2002) 7 Jud Rev 10.

[185] *Daly* (n 184) 5: 'the doctrine of proportionality may require the reviewing court to assess the balance which the decision-maker has struck, not merely whether it is within the range of rational and reasonable decisions'. See further Jaime Arancibia, *Judicial Review of Commercial Regulation* (OUP 2011).

same time, the intensity with which the courts review agency choices varies: heightened scrutiny applies in rights based claims[186] while the generality of cases are subject to the ordinary *Wednesbury* test.[187]

Article 1 of the First Protocol (A1P1) of the ECHR enshrining the right to property[188] has also proven to be of particular relevance to businesses, in view of the significant assets upon which their profitability depends. The *Infinis*[189] case is a case in point. The two claimants (who were respectively the owner and the operator of two generating stations fuelled with landfill gas) disagreed with OFGEM's interpretation of the statutory regime for subsidising renewable energy that resulted in them being refused the Renewable Obligation Certificates (ROCs) and sought judicial review arguing that the authority had acted unlawfully. Interestingly, the claimants presented their case as one rooted not solely in legal entitlement under the statutory scheme to which they had been denied due to OFGEM's error of law, but also involving a violation of their rights under A1P1; and they argued that an award of damages under s 8(3) of the Human Rights Act was necessary to afford just satisfaction.[190] The High Court found that the Authority's decision was unlawful and its consequence was 'to deny the claimants a pecuniary benefit to which they were statutorily entitled'.[191] Given that the ROCs were past their sell by date, the judge proceeded to decide that the claimants would not derive just satisfaction from quashing and mandatory orders alone. No claim in private law was available to them. The only means by which Infinis could recover what they were entitled to under the statutory scheme was indeed through the award of damages.[192] Part of the judge's rationale was that losses 'were clearly calculable'.[193] The sums of money involved were considerable: the claimants were awarded £93,454.38 with a further £2,656,743.84 subject to mitigation. The Court of Appeal upheld the award

[186] *R v Secretary of State for the Home Department, ex p Brind* [1991] 1 AC 606. In cases involving fundamental rights, the courts have established that the relevant decision will be 'rigorously examined and subjected to the most anxious scrutiny' in *R v Secretary of State for the Home Department ex p Turgut* [2001] 1 All ER 719; *R (Thangarasa) v Secretary of State for the Home Department* [2002] UKHL 36. See further Lord Steyn, 'Deference: A Tangled Story' [2005] Pub L 346. See further *R (Wilkinson) v Broadmoor Special Hospital* [2001] EWCA Civ 1545, [2002] 1 WLR 419 where the Court of Appeal endorsed a merits review approach and reached its own view of the need for medical treatment on the basis of oral evidence from medical witnesses including cross-examination.

[187] For an early account, see Paul Craig, 'Regulation and Judicial Review: Perspectives from UK and EC Law' in Christopher McCrudden (ed), *Regulation and Deregulation. Policy and Practice in the Utilities and Financial Services Industries* (OUP 1999).

[188] See *Stretch v United Kingdom* (2004) 38 EHRR 12, 32.

[189] *R (on the application of Infinis Plc) v GEMA* [2011] EWHC 1873 (Admin).

[190] Under HRA, § 8(3) the victim of the violation will only be awarded damages where the court, taking into account (i) any other remedy, relief, or order granted in relation to the act in question, and (ii) the consequences of the decision in respect of that act, is satisfied that the award is necessary to afford just satisfaction. HRA, § 8(4) requires domestic courts to consider the principles set out by the ECtHR in determining whether to award damages and the amount to award.

[191] See *Infinis* (n 189) [103].

[192] ibid [106].

[193] See the distinction in *Anufrijeva v Southwark London Borough Council* [2003] EWCA Civ 1406; [2004] QB 1124 between two types of infringements, namely those giving rise to readily computable type of losses (special damages) and those leading to distress (general damages) upheld by the House of Lords in *R (Greenfield) v Secretary of State for the Home Department* [2005] UKHL 14; [2005] 1 WLR 673.

of damages.[194] The case is significant as it introduces an important protection for companies in the form of a novel action for damages for unlawful state actions in violation of Convention rights. Most crucially, given the considerable amount of money awarded, *Infinis* will most probably encourage strategic litigation, as companies may be willing to use human rights claims to seek more favourable forms of redress in judicial review proceedings. What remains to be seen, however, is what approach the court will take in circumstances where the regulator has a degree of discretion in making its decisions, as well as in cases where the loss is not readily quantifiable.

Another important recent judgment engaging the right to property comes from the High Court in *Npower Direct Ltd v OFGEM*.[195] The High Court dismissed Npower's claim for judicial review of a direction by OFGEM that Npower was required to circulate information to its customers designed to make them consider Npower's terms of supply and potential alternative sources of supply in the context of regulatory measures to stimulate retail competition and consumer engagement. Npower argued, *inter alia*, that there had been an unlawful interference with its rights under Article 1 Protocol 1 of the ECHR because OFGEM had failed to undertake a 'lawful structured proportionality analysis' when deciding the selection criteria for the collective switching trials, including that it had failed to assess the costs and benefits of the trial and failed to strike a fair balance between the collective good and Npower's rights. The Court afforded a wide margin of appreciation to OFGEM's analysis that also extended to the methodology used to apply its proportionality analysis and stressed the Court's reluctance to interfere with the regulator's assessment.

Finally, appeals against decisions of the sector-specific regulators as to the infringement of Article 101 or 102 TFEU, or the equivalent provisions of the Chapter I and Chapter II prohibitions of the Competition Act 1998 are on the merits. In the latter case the CAT's powers go beyond confirming, setting aside, revoking, or quashing the decisions of the sector-specific regulator's decision or penalty, but also extend to substituting the decision for that of the agency.[196] Procedural shortcomings in the decision being appealed can, in principle, be cured.[197] The CAT may also set aside any finding of fact on which the decision is based. The CAT has interpreted the reference to an appeal 'on the merits' to mean that it has 'full jurisdiction to find facts, make its own appraisals of economic issues, apply the law to those facts and appraisals, and determine the amount of any penalty'.[198] Nonetheless, as we shall see in Chapter 6, the Court of Appeal has placed certain limits on the Tribunal's far-reaching powers in scrutinising the agencies' decisions.

[194] *GEMA v Infinis* [2013] EWCA Civ 70.

[195] [2018] EWHC 3576 (Admin).

[196] Competition Act 1998, Sch 8, para 3(1) subject to the limitations articulated in *Imperial Tobacco Ltd v OFT* [2011] CAT 41; Communications Act, s 195(3).

[197] See *TalkTalk v OFCOM* (n 139) [123]–[127].

[198] *Freeserve v DGT* [2003] CAT 5 [107].

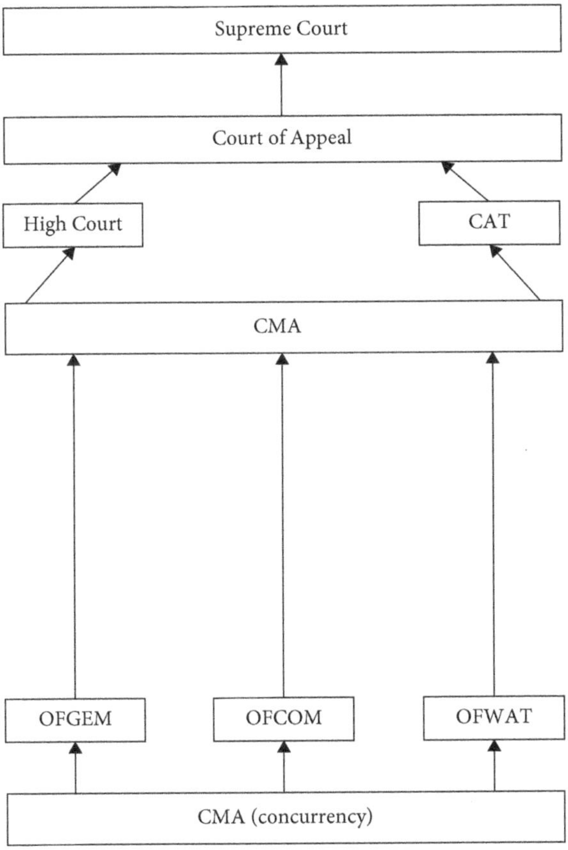


**Figure 3.2** The Process for the Review of Economic Evidence in the UK

## 3.4 Conclusion

The chapter offered a broad overview of the main actors involved in the regulatory process in the US and the UK and discussed the internal (ie 'administrative litigation') and external processes for the review of economic evidence in these two jurisdictions. The imperfect alternatives of the regulatory and adjudicative process in the two comparator jurisdictions discussed in detail here allowed us to appreciate the different mechanisms that exist for the review of economic evidence and the varying types of scrutiny applied to agencies' actions. At the same time, the chapter hinted at an array of institutional and larger environmental factors that affect the scope of the judicial review of economic evidence in the US and the UK.

For example, it is not hard to see how the US institutional framework for the review of economic evidence significantly insulates the courts from the assessment of such evidence. As discussed, much of the complex fact-finding process takes place in an adjudicative body internal to the agency and not before a court of some kind. The procedure, which is governed by the provisions of the APA and/

or by those of the Federal Rules on Civil Procedure and/or by the Federal Rules of Evidence, is designed to motivate the agencies' evidence-collection process and to encourage the broad admissibility of evidence. Consequently, the federal courts are limited to the record produced by the agency itself—be that the product of a formal or informal decision-making process—and refrain from a *de novo* examination of the facts.

The distinctiveness of the UK model of external review of economic evidence by the CMA reflects the piecemeal and evolutionary transformation of the British regulatory state. Despite the reform of the competition regime in 2003, the CMA remains the primary review body charged with the resolution of price control matters and licence modification reference decisions involving complex economic assessments. At the same time, the introduction of statutory rights of appeal led to the marginalisation of judicial review as the primary means to challenge the regulatory agencies' decisions and the establishment of the CAT largely replaced the High Court as the primary venue for hearing such challenges.

## Appendix to Chapter 3
## CMA Regulatory References and Appeals

### 1. CMA Determinations—OFCOM

*CityFibre and TalkTalk v OFCOM* (Case 1259/3/3/16), 6 April 2017
Leased lines price control appeals: CityFibre and TalkTalk 2 telecoms appeals concerning the amount BT can charge other providers for purchasing leased line services, available at:<https://www.gov.uk/cma-cases/leased-lines-price-control-appeals-cityfibre-and-talktalk> accessed 6 June 2022

*BT and TalkTalk v OFCOM* (Case 1238/3/3/15), 25 July 2016, available at:
<https://www.gov.uk/cma-cases/superfast-broadband-price-control-appeals-bt-and-talktalk> accessed 6 June 2022

*Verizon and Vodafone v OFCOM* (Case 1210/3/3/13), 20 May 2014, available at:
<https://www.gov.uk/cma-cases/verizon-vodafone-appeal> accessed 6 June 2022

*British Telecommunications Plc v OFCOM* (Case 1193/3/3/12) and *British Sky Broadcasting Ltd and TalkTalk Telecom Group Plc v OFCOM* (Case 1192/3/3/12), 27 March 2013, available at:
<https://www.gov.uk/cma-cases/llu-wlr-charge-control-review-2012-appeals> accessed 6 June 2022

*Everything Everywhere Ltd v OFCOM* (Case 1181/3/3/11); *Hutchison 3G UK Ltd v OFCOM* (Case 1182/3/3/11); *Vodafone Ltd v OFCOM* (Case 1183/3/3/11) and *Telefónica UK Ltd*, Determination, 9 February 2012, available at:
<https://www.gov.uk/cma-cases/bt-everything-everywhere-hutchison-3g-and-vodafone-v-ofcom-wholesale-mobile-voice-call-termination-price-control-appeals> accessed 6 June 2022

*Cable & Wireless UK v OFCOM* (Case 1112/3/3/09), 30 June 2010, available at:
<https://www.gov.uk/cma-cases/cable-wireless-uk-v-ofcom-leased-lines-charge-control-price-control-appeal> accessed 6 June 2022

*The Carphone Warehouse Group plc v OFCOM* (Case 1149/3/3/09), Determination, 30 September 2010, available at: <https://www.gov.uk/cma-cases/carphone-warehouse-v-ofcom-local-loop-unbundling-price-control-appeal> accessed 6 June 2022

*Hutchison 3G UK Ltd v OFCOM* (Case 1083/3/3/07) and *British Telecommunications v OFCOM* Case 1085/3/3/07), 16 January 2009, available at: <https://www.gov.uk/cma-cases/hutchison-3g-and-bt-v-ofcom-mobile-call-termination-price-control-appeals> accessed 6 June 2022

## 2. Appeals from OFGEM

### (a) Energy Licence Modifications Appeals

RRIO-2 Energy Licence Modification Appeals, 28 September 2021 <https://www.gov.uk/cma-cases/energy-licence-modification-appeals-2021> accessed 6 June 2022

Energy licence modification appeal: SONI, 11 May 2017 <https://www.gov.uk/cma-cases/energy-licence-modification-appeal-soni> accessed 6 June 2022

Energy licence modification appeal: Firmus Energy, 28 September 2016 <https://www.gov.uk/cma-cases/energy-licence-modification-appeal-firmus-energy> accessed 6 June 2022

### (b) Energy Price Control Appeal

Energy price control appeal: British Gas Trading, 23 March 2015 <https://www.gov.uk/cma-cases/energy-price-control-appeal-british-gas-trading> accessed 6 June 2022

Energy price control appeal: Northern Powergrid, 23 March 2015 <https://www.gov.uk/cma-cases/energy-price-control-appeal-northern-powergrid> accessed 6 June 2022

### (c) Energy Code Modification Appeals

SSE code modifications appeal, 14 January 2021 <https://www.gov.uk/cma-cases/sse-code-modifications-appeal> accessed 6 June 2022

EDF/SSE code modification appeal, 3 May 2018

<https://www.gov.uk/cma-cases/edf-sse-code-modification-appeal> accessed 6 June 2022

E.ON UK plc v GEMA: energy code modification appeal (CC), 1 August 2007

<https://www.gov.uk/cma-cases/e-on-uk-plc-v-gema-energy-code-modification-appeal> accessed 6 June 2022

Utilita Electricity Ltd v GEMA: energy code modification appeal (CC), 9 May 2006 <https://www.gov.uk/cma-cases/utilita-electricity-ltd-v-gema-energy-code-modification-appeal> accessed 6 June 2022

## 3. OFWAT Redeterminations

Anglian Water Services Ltd, Bristol Water plc, Northumbrian Water Ltd, and Yorkshire Water Services Ltd price determinations, 17 March 2021 <https://assets.publishing.service.gov.uk/media/60702370e90e076f5589bb8f/Final_Report_---_web_version_-_CMA.pdf> accessed 6 June 2022

Bristol Water plc price determination, 4 March 2015 <https://www.gov.uk/cma-cases/bristol-water-plc-price-determination> accessed 6 June 2022

Bristol Water plc price determination (CC), 14 September 2010 <https://www.gov.uk/cma-cases/bristol-water-plc-price-determination-cc> accessed 6 June 2022

Sutton and East Surrey Water plc price determination (CC), 17 August 2009 <https://www.gov.uk/cma-cases/sutton-and-east-surrey-water-plc-price-determination> accessed 6 June 2022

**Table 3.1** UK Appeals Bodies

| Type of Decision | Legislation | Appeal Body | Standard of Review |
|---|---|---|---|
| Energy licence modifications (*ex ante*) | Electricity Act 1989, the Gas Act 1986 | CMA | Merits review |
| Water licence modifications (*ex ante*) | Water Industry Act 1991, s 13 | CMA | Merits review |
| Water price determinations | Water Industry Act 1991, s 12 | CMA | Merits review |
| Communications dispute resolution (*ex post*) | Communications Act 2003, s 195 | CAT | Merits review |
| Telecommunications market power determinations (*ex ante*) | Communications Act 2003, s 193 | CMA | Judicial review |
| Telecommunications price controls (*ex ante*) | Communications Act 2003, s 193 | CMA | Judicial review |
| Energy code modification appeals (*ex ante*) | Energy Act 2004, s 173 | CMA | Merits review |
| Competition decisions (*ex post*) | Competition Act 1998 | CAT | Merits review |
| Water codes appeals | Water Industry Act 1991, s 16 | CMA | Merits review |

**Table 3.2** CMA Determinations—OFCOM

| Case Name | Year | Appeal Body | Outcome/Remedy |
|---|---|---|---|
| *CityFibre and TalkTalk v OFCOM* (Case 1259/3/3/16) | 2017 | CMA | Remitted to OFCOM |
| *BT and TalkTalk v OFCOM* (Case 1238/3/3/15) | 2016 | CMA | Upheld OFCOM's decision |
| *Verizon and Vodafone v OFCOM* (Case 1210/3/3/13) | 2014 | CC | Upheld OFCOM's decision |
| *BT v OFCOM* (Case1193/3/3/12) and *BSB and TalkTalk T v OFCOM* (Case 1192/3/3/12) | 2013 | CC | Upheld OFCOM's decision in part |
| *EE v OFCOM* (Case 1181/3/3/11); *Hutchison 3G UK Ltd v OFCOM* (Case 1182/3/3/11); *Vodafone v OFCOM* (Case 1183/3/3/11) | 2012 | CC | Remitted to OFCOM |
| *Cable & Wireless UK v OFCOM* (Case 1112/3/3/09) | 2010 | CC | Remitted to OFCOM |
| *The Carphone Warehouse Group plc v OFCOM* (Case 1149/3/3/09) | 2010 | CC | Upheld OFCOM's decision |
| *Hutchison 3G UK Ltd v OFCOM* (Case 1083/3/3/07) and *British Telecommunications v OFCOM* (Case 1085/3/3/07) | 2009 | CC | Upheld OFCOM's decision in part |

**Table 3.3** CMA Energy Licence Appeals

| Case Name | Year | Appeal Body | Outcome/Remedy |
|---|---|---|---|
| *Energy price control appeal: British Gas Trading* | 2015 | CMA | Upheld OFGEM's decision in part |
| *Energy price control appeal: Northern Powergrid* | 2015 | CMA | Upheld OFGEM's decision in part |

**Table 3.4** CMA Energy Codes Appeals

| Case Name | Year | Appeal Body | Outcome/Remedy |
|---|---|---|---|
| *SSE code modifications appeal* | 2021 | CMA | Dismissed appeal |
| *EDF/SSE code modification appeal* | 2018 | CMA | Dismissed appeal |
| *E.ON UK plc v GEMA: code modification appeal (CC)* | 2007 | CC | Decision quashed and remitted to the Authority |
| *Utilita Electricity Ltd v GEMA: energy code modification appeal (CC)* | 2006 | CC | Utilita Electricity Ltd decided not to proceed |

**Table 3.5** OFWAT Redeterminations

| Case Name | Year | Appeal Body | Outcome/Remedy |
|---|---|---|---|
| *Anglian Water Services Ltd, Bristol Water plc, Northumbrian Water Ltd and Yorkshire Water Services Ltd* | 2021 | CMA | Upheld in part |
| *Bristol Water plc price determination* | 2015 | CMA | Upheld in part |
| *Bristol Water plc price determination (CC)* | 2010 | CC | Upheld in part |
| *Sutton and East Surrey Water plc price determination (CC)* | 2009 | CC | Rejected the appeal |

# 4
# Transforming Discretion

## 4.1 Introduction

By now the reader should have been, hopefully, convinced that economists and economic evidence play a crucial, yet underexplored, role within the regulatory and adjudicative decision-making processes. Given the pervasive role of economic evidence and analysis in the workings of regulatory authorities, she might also have assumed that economic regulation is largely a technocratic enterprise: the 'Economists' Kingdom', where the 'universalistic' language of economics is employed. Indeed, the complexity surrounding the use of economics in the exercise of discretion coupled with the arcane body of economically informed discretionary assessments has contributed to the latter being perceived as too 'technical' assessments, thus often concealing the important value judgements that they embody. Regrettably, competition law and public law scholarship have rarely engaged with the essence of the work of regulatory agencies and have by and large ignored the important role of economists therein.

Against this background, the chapter casts light on these neglected actors by exploring the root source of their power and influence, that is delegated discretionary power. Delving into their arena of discretion will also serve to identify the various goals that infuse their statutory objectives and the trade-off between economic efficiency and equity that economists are routinely called upon to perform. Over the next few pages, we shall zoom into the workings of the UK regulatory agencies and explore how economic evidence enters the realm of regulatory discretion and transforms the way regulators (and courts) understand and conceptualise the very idea of discretion and what constraints they face when making discretionary economic assessments. This is crucial for our purposes, as both the jurisprudential dilemma (scope of review) and the institutional one (generalist versus specialist courts) cannot be meaningfully addressed without a deeper, context-specific understanding of how regulators perceive and exercise their discretionary powers. In doing so, the chapter draws on both the competition law and regulation scholarship, which informs the substantive rules governing utility regulation, and the administrative law scholarship, which informs the procedural rules governing this area in the hope of blending these two rich fertile sources of scholarship.

This endeavour is novel and significant not only because it sheds light on the underexplored interrelationship between economic evidence and discretion in the regulatory state, but also methodologically: while existing legal scholarship attempts to locate the sphere of regulatory discretion within the confines of judicial review, the focus here is on the perspective of those internal to the regulatory agencies. The court-centric approach is rife with categorical, artificial, most of the time, distinctions

*Courts, Regulators, and the Scrutiny of Economic Evidence.* Despoina Mantzari, Oxford University Press.
 DOI: 10.1093/oso/9780198851608.003.0004

between economic assessments that are often couched as questions of fact and value judgements often deemed as matters of regulatory policy, which courts draw in an attempt to tame discretion and its exercise. When delving, however, on the perspective of those exercising discretion within the regulatory agencies it will become apparent that the relationship between economic evidence and discretion is much broader than the judicial paradigm allows us to envisage. Sure, as we shall see in subsequent chapters, there is plenty of indirect evidence from court judgments and regulatory decisions on the way economic facts and considerations feed into the decision-making process; to the process, for example, that led to the adoption of a given economic model rather than another when making discretionary trade-offs. But, still, we never really learn directly how those undertaking regulatory tasks perceive their scope of decisional freedom relative to their overall statutory mandate and the influence that economic evidence may or may not have on the reach and breadth of their discretion. This chapter aims to address this gap in the literature by blending theoretical with empirical insights deriving from fourteen semi-structured elite interviews with regulatory economists working in OFGEM, OFCOM, and OFWAT. While the jurisdictional focus of the empirical exercise is on the UK, we shall see towards the end of this chapter and in (Chapter 5) how some findings are also relevant to the US context, given the similar trade-offs between equity and efficiency that federal agencies routinely address.

The chapter puts forward a theoretical framework inspired by Craig Parsons' typology of political action[1] to uncover the possible constraints to the influence of economic evidence in regulatory decision-making. It thus seeks to explore the relative influence of 'structural',[2] that is, exogenous constraints (eg the political or economic climate), 'institutional',[3] that is, forces that affect regulators' actions with respect to their position 'within man-made organizations and rules',[4] and 'ideational'[5] constraints, such as the influence of epistemic communities, in the context of three rich case studies which represent diverse areas of regulatory action where economists are called upon to exercise discretionary assessments.

The argument advanced unfolds in two parts. The first part is conceptual in nature and seeks to explore how economic evidence enters the realm of discretionary decision-making. In doing so, it offers a taxonomy of administrative discretion that is primarily informed by the economists' perception of their role and unpacks its interrelationship with economic evidence. The second part is operational in nature and examines the use and influence of economic evidence, particularly in the context of specific regulatory episodes that emerged during the case study design as having significant importance. The findings render a stark disparity between these two levels of analysis. While on a conceptual level virtually all regulators perceived economic evidence as the main 'tool' for translating their broad statutory mandate to operational policies and procedures, hence allowing them to trade off between efficiency

[1] Craig Parsons, *How to Map Arguments in Political Science* (OUP 2007).
[2] ibid 12.
[3] ibid 12, 49–65.
[4] ibid 12, 66–93.
[5] ibid 12, 94–132.

and equity goals, this perception is extremely variable between the three regulatory agencies at the operational level of analysis. The chapter seeks to explain this variation by drawing on Craig Parsons' rich framework of analysis. It shows that economists do take advantage of the use of economics to increase their discretionary space and make complex trade-offs between the diverse goals of the regulatory enterprise. This is especially the case when they exercise interpretive and operational discretion. But, contrary to the prevailing assumptions they are not always Kings, as the discrepancy between the conceptual and operational level of the analysis reveals. The chapter identifies, examines, and critiques the nature and scope of constraints that inform and shape the influence of economics in the exercise of regulatory discretion.

Section 2 discusses the methodological approach taken, section 3 explores, using examples, the interrelationship between economic evidence and the exercise of discretionary power and offers a taxonomy thereof, section 4 explores the various constraints to the exercise of discretion, and section 5 concludes.

## 4.2 Methodology

A mixed-methods approach was adopted that combined doctrinal, theoretical, and empirical analysis. To prepare for the interview stage, a review was performed of all regulatory decisions issued by OFGEM, OFCOM, and OFWAT so as to gain a broad view of the input and manifestation of economic evidence employed to support a range of discretionary assessments. When such decisions had been appealed the analysis included the relevant court judgments. The regulatory decisions covered the period between the enactment of the relevant regulator's governing statute and December 2018; that is, since the Communications Act 2003 in the case of OFCOM, the Utilities Act 2000 in the case of OFGEM, and the Water Act 2003 in the case of OFWAT. The analysis conducted led to the methodological choice of focusing on three case studies, one from each regulatory agency. During the interviews, the interviewees were asked, *inter alia*, to reflect on the influence economic evidence exerted over regulatory judgments and the reasons why it might not have been as effective in the context of these specific case studies related to their organisation. To allow for a reliable testing of the hypothesis, the selection of case studies was subjected to two main constraints. First, 'closed episodes' were selected to be able to examine the use and influence of economic evidence throughout the decision-making process under examination. Second, such episodes represented relatively recent cases in order to increase the chances of locating the relevant interviewees and ensure a relatively accurate recollection of facts.

In the case of OFGEM, the case study was related to the use of neoclassical/Austrian economics in introducing competition in the retail energy market and the reregulation thereof as well as the use of behavioural economics in enhancing consumer participation in the market.[6] In the case of OFCOM, the case study was related to the use of

[6] See, eg, OFGEM, 'Ofgem launches probe into energy supply markets', 21 February 2008, available at: <https://www.ofgem.gov.uk/publications/ofgem-launches-probe-energy-supply-markets> accessed 6 June 2022; CMA, 'Energy Market Investigation: Final Report', 24 June 2016, available at: <https://assets.publishing.service.gov.uk/media/5773de34e5274a0da3000113/final-report-energy-market-investigation.pdf> accessed 6 June 2022.

neoclassical economics in the termination rates disputes.[7] In the case of OFWAT, the case study was related to the use of neoclassical economics in introducing competition to the non-residential retail market.[8] Delving into these regulatory episodes allowed generating original insights on the respective positions and beliefs of economists in each episode, reinforced by their own account of the story. Because the institutional organisation of economic expertise varies greatly across the three regulatory agencies involved, the range of interviewees was balanced to involve economists in various positions within the agencies. Interviews were conducted between June 2017 and December 2017 'on the record', face-to-face, and were audio recorded and transcribed. Interviewees received the interview protocol before the interviews and expressed both their written and oral consent to the interview being recorded and used to inform this research. Due consideration was given to interviewees' requests to keep certain pieces of information off the interview record. When specifically requested, interviews were conducted under the promise of anonymity. The transcripts were manually coded. The coding aimed at identifying the regulators' perceptions of constraints and their response to such constraints in terms of their decision-making process. Interviewees were given ample scope to self-direct their contributions within the context of a framework of prepared questions and issues for discussion deriving from the case studies. The qualitative analysis performed allowed to better contextualise the insights generated from the interviews and the breadth of the analysis allowed offsetting any possible tendency for interviewees to exert bias in their recollections. Evidence gathered via interviews was then triangulated with analysis of regulatory judgments and relevant policy reports, shedding light on the regulatory process and the various constraints on agency decision-making.

Craig Parsons' typology of political action directly informs the theoretical framework adopted and serves as an analytical tool for identifying the various constraints to the influence of economic evidence in discretionary assessments. Of course, Parsons' framework is not the only, or even the best way of making sense of the interrelationship between economic evidence and discretion. But its inclusion of various macro- and micro-level factors at play in decision-making renders it well suited to the task at hand. Parsons identifies structural, institutional, ideational, and psychological constraints.[9] For methodological reasons explained below the chapter focuses only on the first three sources of constraints.

'Structural' claims explain people's actions 'as a function of their position vis-à-vis exogenously given "material" structures like geography, a distribution of wealth, or a distribution of physical power'.[10] Applied in the context at hand, they refer to exogenous constraints, such as the political or economic climate in which regulators

[7] See, eg, OFCOM, 'Determination to resolve a dispute between BT and each of Vodafone, T-Mobile, H3G, O2, Orange and Everything Everywhere about BT's termination charges for 0845 and 0870 calls', 10 August 2010, available at: <https://www.ofcom.org.uk/__data/assets/pdf_file/0026/82961/final_determination.pdf>accessed 6 June 2022.

[8] See, eg, OFWAT, 'Residential Retail Market', 19 September 2016, available at: <https://www.ofwat.gov.uk/regulated-companies/markets/future-markets/extending-retail-competition-to-households/rrr/>accessed 6 June 2022.

[9] Parsons (n 1) 12.

[10] ibid.

operate as well as broader societal pressures and the way these constrain or otherwise the way they employ economics when exercising discretion.

Institutional claims also explain people's actions with respect to their position but 'within man-made organizations and rules (and within the "path-dependent" process implied by man-made constraints)'.[11] For our purposes here, the more pluralistic understanding of institutions is adopted, whereby the latter are not merely organisations that set the 'rules of the game';[12] rather, they provide operating procedures, behavioural norms, and identities to those who function within them. Hence, this allows us to explore how legal factors, such as the threat of judicial review or the standard of review, and quasi-legal factors, such as organisational factors, values, and the attitudes of officials affect the way economic evidence is used in discretionary assessments.

'Ideational' claims also explain regulatory action based on cognitive and/or affective elements but see those as 'created by certain historical groups of people'.[13] For example, epistemic communities or elite beliefs may affect the type of economic evidence used, as we shall see in section 4 below.

'Psychological' claims explain people's actions by relying on 'cognitive, affective, or instinctual elements that organize their thinking, but see these elements as general across humankind, as hard-wired features of "how humans think"'.[14] Examining such constraints would require a different methodological approach than the one adopted here and are thus outside the scope of this study. Such an approach would be based on lab experiments to reveal the existence or otherwise of biases, such as confirmation bias, and how these affect the use of economic evidence when exercising discretion.[15]

## 4.3 Conceptualising the Interrelationship between Economic Evidence and Discretion

A natural starting point would be to explore how economic evidence enters the realm of discretionary decision-making. In other words, how regulatory discretion is 'filled out' with economic context. This will allow us to better appreciate the input of economic evidence in diverse areas in which regulators are called to exercise discretion, explored in greater detail in subsection B below, as well as the various constraints to the use of economic evidence, discussed in section 4.

In examining the interrelationship between economic evidence and discretion, we follow a largely inductive approach that is informed by the interviewees' own understanding of the *purpose* ('why') for which discretion was awarded in the first place and the *way* it will be exercised ('how'), that is, how the regulatory agency will achieve its substantive goals and what trade-offs should it make when multiple substantive goals interact. It will be shown that economics have added a layer to discretionary power composed of their own methodology and tools. This is not solely confined to

[11] ibid.

[12] Douglass C North, 'Institutions' (1991) 5(1) J Econ Perspect 97.

[13] Parsons (n 1) 12.

[14] Parsons (n 1) 12.

[15] See, eg, James Cooper and William Kovacic, 'Behavioral Economics: Implications for Regulatory Behavior' (2012) 41 J Reg Econ 41.

the operationalisation of the traditional core objectives of economic regulation, such as the promotion of competition, but also applies to the broader set of non-economic objectives, such as social and environmental statutory objectives and the concomitant efficiency/equity trade-offs that regulators have increasingly been called upon to perform.[16] In doing so, we shall see that economics provides a logic framework of analysis in making these trade-offs; for example equity objectives can be pursued as long as they are not too costly or have too strong negative effects of competition thus structuring the arena of discretionary power. We shall be able to appreciate that discretion in relation to efficiency decisions is significantly more limited relative to the discretion in relation to the weight agencies need to assign to efficiency and equity, respectively.

Specifically, the interviewees understood economic evidence and analysis to inform three relatively distinct dimensions of regulatory discretion: (a) the interpretation of their statutory mandate (what may be referred to as 'interpretive discretion'); (b) the way they formulate policy when 'Parliament has expressly or impliedly left a specific policy domain undetermined'[17] (what may be referred to as 'operational discretion');[18] and (c) the procedures and enforcement tools they choose and employ to this end (what may be referred to as 'enforcement discretion'). This widespread input of economic evidence and analysis has allowed economists to expand their own understanding of the range of decision-making freedom open to them. As we shall see, in the case of interpretive discretion this expanded freedom is externally recognised from other actors in the regulatory space, notably the courts, but the section will also allude that it is significantly constrained in the case of operational and enforcement discretion. Section 4 will explore this claim in greater detail.

Before elaborating further on the three dimensions of discretion, it is first necessary to appreciate how discretion manifests itself in the statutory objectives of utility regulators to which the next subsection turns to. We will then offer a taxonomy of the use of economic evidence in regulatory decision-making processes by exploring the various ways in which economic evidence and analysis informs interpretive, operational, and enforcement discretion.

### 4.3.1 How Discretion Manifests Itself: Scope and Implications

Utility regulation, like all forms of regulation, is purposive in orientation in the sense that it seeks to implement collective goals, that is, goals, which are considered by the society to be socially valuable and worthy of pursuit, but which would not otherwise be achieved in the absence of regulation. Such goals are reflected in the regulatory agencies' governing statute—the source of regulatory discretion—which is infused by statutory objectives of both an economic nature, such as the promotion of competition, and a social nature, such as the protection of vulnerable consumers. Regulators are required to interpret, consider, and trade-off such objectives when exercising

[16] See Tony Prosser, *The Regulatory Enterprise: Government, Regulation and Legitimacy* (OUP 2010) ch. 1.
[17] Eric C Ip, 'Taking a "Hard Look" at 'Irrationality': Substantive Review of Administrative Discretion in the US and UK Supreme Courts' (2014) 34(3) Oxf J Leg Stud 481, 485.
[18] ibid.

discretionary powers. In doing so, they largely employ economic evidence and analysis. In a sense, economic evidence and analysis translates regulatory objectives, such as the promotion of competition, to operational policies and procedures that guide their day-to-day activities.

A careful reading through the statutory frameworks of the UK regulatory agencies will immediately reveal that discretion manifests itself through standards, rather than narrowly construed rules, if one adheres to such distinction. Although the term 'rules' may be used to refer to all 'general norm(s) mandating or guiding conduct or action in a given type of situation',[19] it is the narrower sense of 'rules', which in turn distinguishes the latter from the more flexible norms of standards and principles, that is used here.

As we shall see, the very fact that discretion manifests itself in the form of open-ended standards has 'important effects on the allocation of decision-making authority'.[20] In sharp contrast to rules, that 'vest authority in the rule formulators rather than in those who apply the rule in particular cases at a later time',[21] 'standards delegate decision-making authority to the decision-maker at the point of application'.[22] Hence, standards contribute to the *ex post* formulation of the content of the law, as they allow the decision-maker to gather, process, and finally incorporate into his reasoning information obtained after the promulgation of the standard.[23] For Vermeule, rules 'require more information and decisional competence ex ante, at the time the rule formulators decide what the content of the rule should be', whereas '[s]tandards require more information and decisional competence ex post, at the time of application'.[24]

Furthermore, unlike narrowly construed rules which may be overinclusive or underinclusive in their application, standards guide the exercise of discretion by encompassing an open-ended framework comprising, in our case, various substantive regulatory objectives (economic and non-economic) which the regulator should interpret, consider, and trade-off when exercising discretionary power. These objectives reflect both efficiency and equity considerations. For example, OFCOM's principal statutory objective is 'to further the interests of consumers in relevant markets, where appropriate by promoting competition',[25] but also 'to further the interests of citizens in relation to communications matters'.[26] The efficiency maximisation objective is mostly apparent in the market mechanisms governing spectrum auctioning and management, or in the need to ensure 'the availability throughout the United Kingdom of a wide range of electronic communications services',[27] whereas equity considerations are mostly reflected in the non-economic objectives that the regulator 'must secure' or 'have regard to' in performing its duties that relate to the interests of 'citizens'.[28] Those

19 William Twining and David Miers, *How to Do Things with Rules* (4th edn, Butterworths 1999) 123.

20 Adrian Vermeule, 'Interpretive Choice' (2000) 75 NY Univ L Rev 74, 95.

21 ibid 93.

22 ibid 92.

23 To this effect, see Louis Kaplow, 'Rules versus Standards: An Economic Analysis' (1992) 42 Duke LJ 557.

24 Vermeule (n 20) 92.

25 Communications Act 2003, s 3(1)(b).

26 Communications Act 2003, s 3(1)(a).

27 Communications Act 2003, s 3(2)(b).

28 See Sonia Livingstone, Peter Lunt, and Laura Miller, 'Citizens, Consumers and the Citizen-Consumer: Articulating the Citizen Interest in Media and Communications Regulation' (2007) 1 Discourse Commun 85.

include 'plurality considerations'[29] and 'the needs of persons with disabilities, of the elderly and of those on low incomes'.[30]

In the same vein, OFGEM's principal statutory objective is not limited to the protection of 'existing' consumers, but, echoing sustainability considerations, further encompasses the protection of 'future consumers'.[31] Additionally, OFGEM 'must have regard' to the financeability of license holders and the achievement of sustainable development.[32] Similarly, OFWAT duties consist, *inter alia*, of promoting the interests of consumers, whenever appropriate by promoting effective competition in the provision of water and sewerage services[33] and the financeability of license holders.

All three regulators, alongside their general duty to protect the interests of all consumers, have particular responsibilities towards certain groups in society, such as the disabled or chronically sick, pensioners, individuals with low incomes, and those living in rural areas.[34] Promoting the interests of these groups involves a departure from the purely economic rationale for public intervention in markets summarised in the concept of 'market failure', in order to achieve a socially, rather than economically desirable outcome. Finally, all regulators have a duty to promote effective competition 'where relevant/appropriate'. Naturally, this leaves considerable discretion to the regulator as to the interpretation and application of the standard to the case at issue.

There is, however, one recent exception to the legal primacy of competition. The Energy Act 2010 requires OFGEM to consider in the regulation of both electricity and gas 'whether there is any other manner (whether or not it would promote competition ...) in which the Secretary of State or the Authority [OFGEM and GEMA] ... could carry out those functions which would better protect those interests [the interests of current and future consumers]'.[35] The role of competition in the electricity and gas industries has, indeed, come under considerable criticism and scepticism, rendering, as we shall see below, the energy regulator more vulnerable to structural constraints.

The following subsection will focus on how economic evidence informs the *ex post* formulation of the content of the law granted by standards. It will thus attempt to open the 'black box' of discretionary decision-making and appreciate using illustrative examples the diverse ways in which economic evidence influences the breadth of regulatory discretion vis-à-vis the statutory wording or otherwise.

### 4.3.2 The Use of Economic Evidence in Discretionary Assessments: A Taxonomy

> In terms of our overarching statutory objectives of protecting the interests of existing and future consumers we have fairly wide discretion (emphasis added) in terms of

[29] Communications Act 2003, s 58(2B).
[30] ibid, s 3(4) (i).
[31] Gas Act 1986, s 4AA(1); Electricity Act 1989, s 3A.
[32] Gas Act 1986, s 4AA(2); Electricity Act 1989, s 3A2.
[33] Section 39(3) adding a new s 2(2B) to the Water Industry Act 1991 as amended.
[34] Water Industry Act as amended by the Water Act 2014, § 39(2C).
[35] Energy Act 2010, ss 16 (for natural gas) and 17 (for electricity).

> how we achieve them. I do think in practice that has gone down fairly well established and well-worn routes really. We set principles that we expect companies to follow, we set price controls, clearly, we will take enforcement action, if need be, there's a set of well-understood set of tools we have to influence the market, the sector as a whole. There can be questions of balance between them, take the balance between enforcement action and compliance work . . . I think there are questions about how you get the right balance there. Equally, there are questions . . . we have a certain toolkit, but does that need to change if we see big changes in the sector? (OFGEM, chief economist)

The above quote is quite illustrative of the regulators' own understanding of the significant leeway they enjoy in operationalising their statutory objectives, but also of the role economic logic, evidence, and analysis play in structuring their discretion. It also serves to highlight the three relatively distinct dimensions of discretion that interviewees understood economic evidence to directly inform: interpretive, operational, and enforcement discretion.

Of course, while these are presented here as conceptually distinct, pragmatically speaking they are very much interdependent on the larger institutional analysis of agency decision-making. For example, economic evidence and analysis employed to inform interpretive discretion as to what a 'fair and reasonable' price entails are impossible to separate from enforcement discretion, as the regulatory agency's procedural framework and rules will determine, at least in part, whether and how the agency will achieve such a goal, what trade-offs it will be required to make, and which affected interests it will consult. Similarly, the process of interpreting the statutory mandate unavoidably involves consideration of how the statutory objectives will be implemented. Despite these shortcomings, the distinction adopted reflects the interviewees' perception of the different faces of their discretionary powers and serves well our analytical purposes. The remainder of this section will explore, using examples, the ways in which economic evidence informs these three dimensions of discretion.

#### 4.3.2.1 Economic Evidence and Interpretive Discretion

Interpretive discretion can be said to broadly refer to the leeway in determining the meaning of the agency's statute in pursuance of its policy ends. Of course, this is closely related to agency implementation of its statutory mandate, but the process of interpretation is an unavoidable first step. We tend to think of legal interpretation as the domain of the judiciary, but much statutory interpretation is done, at least in first instance, by regulatory agencies. This is so in part because the legislature and the courts allow such an expansive role for regulators by drafting vague statutory language and by deferring to agencies' interpretation of their governing statutes. A prime example of the influence of economic evidence on interpretive discretion relates to the interpretation of Article 13 of the Access Directive,[36] as implemented by the Communications

[36] Directive 2002/19/EC on access to, and interconnection of, electronic communications networks and associated facilities [2002] OJ L108/51 (Access Directive). For a discussion, see Alexandre de Streel, 'Remedies in the Electronic Communications Sector' in Damien Geradin (ed), *Remedies in Network Industries: EC Competition Law vs. Sector-Specific Regulation* (Intersentia 2004) 67.

Act 2003 (otherwise referred to as 'Significant Market Power conditions'). Section 88(1)(b) provides that 'the cost recovery mechanism or pricing methodology must be designed to confer the greatest possible benefits on end-users and to achieve the other specified purposes, namely that of promoting efficiency and sustainable competition'.[37] The interpretation of this provision is a necessary step towards the implementation of regulatory remedies. But before elaborating on the exercise of interpretive discretion, let's pause for a second to place this provision within the larger context of the so-called market review process in electronic communications to which it forms an integral part.

In meeting its principal objective to promote the interests of consumers, OFCOM has a specific statutory duty to periodically review the operation of the relevant markets in the telecoms sector so as to determine whether each of those markets is 'effectively competitive' and to impose regulatory remedies (price controls or quality standards) to undertakings found to enjoy a Significant Market Power (SMP), in accordance with the EU framework governing electronic communications.[38] The determination of SMP is a forward-looking exercise, equivalent to the test of dominance that is used in European competition law and enables the *ex ante* regulation of the sector. Such *ex ante* regulation is *asymmetric* in nature as it is imposed only on operators found to enjoy SMP and aims to prevent or remedy the abuse of dominance and create a level playing field.[39] The determination of SMP expressly relies on economic assessments that OFCOM must perform on a case-by-case basis. Those include, first, a market definition exercise often through the application of the hypothetical monopolist test, which is one way of assessing the existence of demand-side substitutability. The hypothetical monopolist test asks what products (or geographic areas) a hypothetical monopolist would need to dominate in order to be able to profitably raise prices by 5 to 10 per cent above the competitive level—otherwise known as the SSNIP test (ie small but significant and non-transitory increase in price test). The likely responses by consumers to such a price increase help in determining whether substitutable products exist and, if so, where the boundaries of the relevant product market should be delineated. The second step involves the determination of dominance. This is based on a case-by-case assessment that is not limited to market shares of the undertaking concerned, but also involves other criteria, such as the overall size of the undertaking, vertical integration, the existence of barriers to enter the market, and the absence of potential competition, in accordance with the European Commission Guidelines on the issue.[40] In identifying markets subject to *ex ante* regulation, OFCOM is required to

[37] Communications Act 2003, s 88(1)(b).

[38] See Directive 2009/140/EC of the European Parliament and of the Council of 25 November 2009 amending Directives 2002/21/EC on a common regulatory framework for electronic communications networks and services, 2002/19/EC on access to, and interconnection of, electronic communications networks and associated facilities, and 2002/20/EC on the authorisation of electronic communications networks and services, [2009] L337/37.

[39] For an analysis of the evolution of *ex ante* regulation in telecoms, see Martin Cave, Christos Genakos, and Tommaso Valletti, 'The European Framework for Regulating Telecommunications: A 25-year Appraisal' (2019) 55 Rev Ind Organ 47.

[40] See, eg, EC, 'Guidelines on market analysis and the assessment of significant market power under the EU regulatory framework for electronic communications networks and services' [2018] C159/1.

take the utmost account of such recommendations and guidelines as to what product and service markets should be analysed.

> I think if you are on the telecoms side, particularly anything to do with the market review process, where there's a very clear market definition, analysis of competition remedies, I think the economics is very heavily embedded into that and the way in which the competition group is set up. That's what they do. If we need a market, fine we go to the economists; SMP analysis we go to the economists; a network charge control, we need to get the economists to do that and even within the economists' function now, we have recognized that sort of more specialized modelling role and sort of carved out specific financial economics team, which combines accounting function and people with modelling expertise (OFCOM 3).

While the determination of SMP is a strictly regulated exercise, the second stage in the process that involves the selection of the appropriate regulatory remedy to be imposed—typically price controls at the wholesale level—leaves considerable leeway to the regulator regarding which pricing principle and pricing methodology will be adopted.[41] Article 13 of the Access Directive,[42] as implemented by the Communications Act 2003, plays a central role in this process. As noted above, it provides that the cost recovery mechanism or pricing methodology must be designed to confer the greatest possible benefits on end-users and achieve the other specified purposes, namely that of promoting efficiency and sustainable competition.[43] Of course, these are broad objectives that require interpretation before being translated to regulatory action. There are choices to be made and thus discretion must be exercised in choosing the appropriate pricing methodology. Hence, pricing methodologies embody value judgements as to which of the various objectives is to be promoted. This was echoed by an interviewee when asked to comment on the disputed 'welfare standard' that was adopted in the context of the termination rates appeals dispute:[44]

> Many economists would view that as being neutral, but I don't think it is neutral; that is making a particular set of value judgments … some economists may disagree with me, but I don't think it is judgment free. That involves judgement and you have to be clear what those are because they are not always appropriate (OFCOM 4).

As will be shown, economists enjoy a wide margin of discretion in choosing the most appropriate pricing methodology considering their statutory objectives, but that also economic evidence and analysis is itself *the tool* for mediating between these objectives. But the final decision is of course, made by the Board, precisely because they are value judgments to be made. This institutional feature provides an important constraint to the discretion economists perceive to enjoy and allow the latter to be better

[41] Janice Hauge and David Sappington, 'Pricing in Network Industries' in R Baldwin, M Cave, and M Lodge (eds) *Oxford Handbook of Regulation* (OUP 2010) 462–99.
[42] See n 36.
[43] Communications Act 2003, s 88(1)(b).
[44] See n 7.

exercised. Nonetheless, economists are crucial in offering a framework for analysis based on facts and empirical observation which allows the ultimate decision-maker to make a reasoned choice.

A useful example of the discretion economists enjoy in determining the most appropriate pricing methodology, but also the constraints they face comes from the 2011 market review of the wholesale mobile voice call termination.[45] That is, the service provided by the intended recipient's mobile communications provider to the originating communications provider, which is necessary for mobile and fixed communications providers to connect their customers with recipients on different mobile networks. For this service, operators impose a wholesale charge known as 'mobile termination rates' (MTR). These have been subject to regulatory control on the basis that absent control the significant market power exercised by operators would be detrimental to competition and to consumers. OFCOM was of the view that this price control should be based on either the so-called Long Run Incremental Cost (LRIC) or LRIC+. The fundamental difference between the LRIC and the LRIC+ is that the former is intended to cover the terminating operator's direct costs of terminating a call, whereas LRIC+ is intended to make a contribution to the terminating operators' fixed and common costs, such as the costs that are involved with running a network. Economic theory suggests that ideally access prices should reflect the marginal costs of an efficient network operator and thus LRIC was regarded by the regulator as a better approximation of marginal costs that would result in lowering mobile termination rates. It also had the merit of following a Recommendation of the European Commission.[46]

But efficiency considerations alone could not form the basis of OFCOM's judgment. OFCOM was, therefore, required to consider and ultimately balance the benefits and the detriments of each of these two pricing methodologies against the broad policy objectives, which further involved making several hypothetical assessments on the effects of the pricing methodologies on economic efficiency (allocative and dynamic) and on competition, also bearing in mind their distributional implications: an essentially polycentric judgement. For example, the interests of dynamic efficiency or the protection of vulnerable consumers, the latter being a specific group that OFCOM has a statutory duty to protect,[47] favoured the adoption of LRIC+, while the interests of competition pointed towards pure LRIC. OFCOM eventually reasoned that a pure LRIC approach would confer the greatest possible benefits on consumers.

Crucially, in interpreting the statutory mandate and determining the appropriate price control standard and its proper application to the facts, OFCOM enjoyed a large degree of interpretive freedom that is not only observed internally but was also externally recognised by the courts. The Court of Appeal afforded a large measure of

[45] OFCOM, 'Wholesale Mobile Voice Call Termination', 15 March 2011, available at: <https://www.ofcom.org.uk/__data/assets/pdf_file/0025/38581/mct_statement.pdf > accessed 6 June 2022. See further, OFCOM, 'Disputes between each of Sky, TalkTalk, Virgin Media, Cable & Wireless and Verizon and BT regarding BT's charges for Ethernet Services—Determinations and Explanatory Statement', 13 March 2013, <https://www.ofcom.org.uk/about-ofcom/latest/bulletins/competition-bulletins/all-closed-cases/cw_01052> accessed 6 June 2022.

[46] See further, Commission Recommendation of 7 May 2009 on the Regulatory Treatment of Fixed and Mobile Termination Rates in the EU [2009] OJ L124/67, Recital 13.

[47] Article 8(4) of Access Directive (n 36); Article 8 of the Framework Directive (n 38).

discretion to OFCOM's determinations highlighting the complexity of the economic judgement the regulator was called upon to perform that involved 'questions of policy in a highly technical field':[48]

> The subject matter of the appeal is a complex question of economic judgment. It involves questions of policy in a highly technical field. The regulator, Ofcom and the Competition Commission are required to make educated predictions for the future as to the effect of any price control measure to be imposed. Although decisions relating to the control of charges are of great importance to communication providers and to the general public, the exercise of seeking an appropriate solution is necessarily imprecise; when looking to the future there is unlikely to be any one right answer.[49]

In the same vein, the Court of Justice of the European Union (CJEU) has also highlighted the interpretive freedom national regulatory authorities (NRAs) should enjoy when operationalising pricing principles enshrined in EU legislation, such as the one prescribing 'cost-oriented' wholesale access prices.[50] Indeed, in the *Arcor*[51] and *Mobistar*[52] preliminary rulings, the CJEU confirmed the NRAs' broad discretion in interpreting and applying the principle of cost-orientation.[53] It further conceded that in the absence of Community legislation, it is the task of the NRAs to define detailed rules for calculating the actual costs that have to be taken into account. Perhaps, most crucially, the CJEU affirmed that the boundaries of their discretion are not limited to the methodology employed, but further extend to the choice of analytical cost models for establishing the costs incurred by the notified operator,[54] as well as for other aspects of those costs and tariffs. Seen another way, the CJEU may be said to defer to the regulatory agency's economic interpretation of the principle of cost-orientation. Those rulings epitomise what Denis Galligan referred to as the 'central sense' of discretion,[55] in the sense that there exists both 'significant freedom'[56] for the regulator in exercising his power and 'the courts recognise this freedom'.[57]

We need to pause here for a second to note that, as we shall see in Chapter 6, the specialist CAT has on many occasions constrained OFCOM's interpretive discretion and overturned its expert assessments by laying down its own understanding of the economic test that should be employed. This propensity towards a heightened review

[48] In *Everything Everywhere Ltd v OFCOM (Mobile Call Termination)* [2013] EWCA Civ 154 [35], Moses] LJ.

[49] Ibid. See further *Everything Everywhere Ltd v OFCOM* [2016] EWCA 2134 (Admin), Cranston J; *British Telecommunications Plc v OFCOM* [2016] CAT 3.

[50] See, eg, Regulation (EC) No 2887/2000 of the European Parliament and of the Council of 18 December 2000 on unbundled access to the local loop [2000] OJ L336.

[51] See C-55/06, *Arcor AG & Co KG v Bundesrepublik Deutschland* [2008] ECR I-2931 [94].

[52] C-438/04, *Mobistar SA v Institut belge des services postaux et des télécommunications* [2006] ECR I-6675. This case concerned whether one-off set-up costs associated with the porting of mobile numbers also fell within Article 30(2) USD, which at that time referred to 'interconnection related to the provision of number portability'.

[53] See (n 51) [150].

[54] See (n 51) [132] and [134].

[55] Denis Galligan, *Discretionary Powers: A Legal Study of Official Discretion* (Clarendon Press 1990) 23.

[56] Ibid.

[57] Ibid.

of OFCOM's multifactorial decisions comes at a cost in the sense that it has rendered the regulator legalistic in its approach which may in turn undermine sound economic analysis. We shall discuss in Chapter 6 how the Court of Appeal ultimately constrained the CAT by invoking relative institutional competence considerations. Those primarily refer to the regulatory agency's superior institutional legitimacy in deciding cases involving multifaceted policy considerations.

#### 4.3.2.2 Economic Evidence and Operational Discretion

In contrast to interpretive discretion, operational discretion 'is exercised independently of statutory provisions if Parliament has expressly or impliedly left a policy subdomain undetermined'.[58] Eric C Ip nicely captures the difference between the two senses of discretion: 'while interpretive discretion might be constrained, at least in theory, by better legislative drafting technique and judicial legality review (of the procedural correctness with which legislation is construed), however, the same cannot be said of operational discretion'.[59] Operational discretion is far more open-ended as it encompasses the range of choices regulators have to make as to *when* to intervene in the markets (what can be understood as a first-order judgment) and *how* to intervene in the markets (what can be understood as a second-order judgment). It includes the process of choosing the policies, strategies, standards, and procedures that may suit a particular situation. Having said that, in some cases the second-order judgment may precede that of the first, as it is more useful to understand what remedies are feasible before deciding to intervene if no appropriate remedies are available.

Regarding the first-order judgment, all regulators conceded that it is economic logic deriving from the concept of market failure that informs their operational discretion on *when* to intervene. But, when regulators arrive at the second-order judgment as to *how* to intervene and what remedies to impose, the use of neoclassical economics has been enriched by the advent of behavioural economics, which focuses on imperfections in the demand side that allow firms to exploit market power on the supply side.

The interrelationship between behavioural economics and operational discretion is better understood in the context of the ongoing *metamorphosis* of the regulatory state from a model of economic regulation largely concerned with the promotion of competition, to a broader framework of market organisation, where objectives such as security of supply, sustainability, and affordability have all risen in salience.[60] As Frank Vibert observes 'regulators have moved from creating conditions "sufficient" for consumers to be able to make choices (a "satisficing" role) to a trustee role, or, to acting in the "best interest" of the consumer (a role that tries to "optimize" conditions for consumers)'.[61] Because competition alone does not necessarily ensure that consumers will access and act upon the information needed to make sensible choices for themselves, regulators have become increasingly activist in the demand side of the

[58] See Ip (n 17) 485.

[59] Ibid.

[60] For an excellent analysis, see Frank Vibert, *The New Regulatory Space: Reframing Democratic Governance* (Edward Elgar 2014).

[61] Ibid 55–60.

market. Rather than assuming consumer rationality, they turn to the insights of behavioural economics to explore when and under what conditions consumers systematically depart from rationality. For instance, status quo bias explains why consumers fail to investigate alternative contracts that may be beneficial to them. This was in turn incorporated in OFGEM's and OFCOM's ban on automatic renewal of contracts;[62] an exercise of operational discretion. Perhaps the most representative example relates to OFGEM's Retail Market Review.[63] OFGEM introduced measures aiming at the simplification of tariffs ('simpler choices' component).[64] These measures included a ban on complex tariffs, a maximum limit on the tariffs offered, and a simplification of cash discounts. Tariff simplification was premised on the findings of behavioural economics regarding consumers' cognitive limits and aimed at facilitating consumer switching.[65]

It is important not to underestimate the breadth and scope of operational discretion. Unlike the price control remedies imposed by OFCOM in the market review process, which are prescribed in detail in the Communications Act 2003, OFGEM's remedies in the retail energy market represent the translation of the deliberately broad statutory mandate regarding the protection of consumers into operational policies and procedures. This gives rise to a wide arena of administrative discretion, which has been given form and purpose by recourse to economic evidence and analysis. This is not a negative development: freedom in decision-making is what allows regulators to tailor their response to different conditions and avoid making errors. However, as we shall see in the next section this expanded arena of operational discretion has been constrained by structural and ideational factors which, in significant cases, undermine the role of economic evidence in the final decisions adopted.

#### 4.3.2.3 Economic Evidence and Enforcement Discretion

All regulators employ a spectrum of enforcement ranging from increased monitoring to a full-blown investigation. In carrying out their enforcement actions, regulatory authorities wield vast discretionary powers, yet their statutory mandate provides little guidance as to how this discretionary power should be exercised. Accordingly, regulators are confronted with a number of very significant decisions in enforcing regulatory standards. Such decisions may not only have a serious impact on those against whom enforcement action is targeted but may also profoundly influence the overall

[62] See OFCOM, 'Removing Barriers to Switching: OFCOM Bans Rollover Contracts', 13 September 2011, available at: <https://www.ofcom.org.uk/about-ofcom/latest/media/media-releases/2011/removing-barriers-to-switching-ofcom-bans-rollover-contracts> accessed 6 June 2022.

[63] OFGEM (2010), 'Retail Market Review', available at: <https://www.ofgem.gov.uk/energy-policy-and-regulation/policy-and-regulatory-programmes/retail-market-review> accessed 6 June 2022.

[64] OFGEM, 'Simpler, Clearer, Fairer', 19 October 2012, available at: <https://www.ofgem.gov.uk/publications/ofgem-publishes-plans-deliver-simpler-clearer-and-fairer-energy-market-consumers> accessed 6 June 2022.

[65] In particular, framing bias can be exacerbated in an environment where consumers are presented with a lot of information. This information can be purposefully presented in a confusing manner creating the problem of *confusopoly*. On framing biases, see Amos Tversky and Daniel Kahneman, 'The Framing of Decisions and the Psychology of Choice' (1981) Science 211. Confusopoly was first coined in Scott Adams, *The Dilbert Future* (Harper Collins 1997).

implementation of regulatory objectives. Enforcement discretion may involve some questions of general enforcement policy, for example whether to investigate a particular segment of the market, such as standalone landline telephone services. Others are more operational in nature and may relate to specific complaints. Unlike interpretive and operational discretion, the exercise of enforcement discretion is predominantly influenced by legal and bureaucratic considerations.

A central part of enforcement powers resides, in the case of energy and water regulation only, in the licence which is granted from the regulator to companies, and which allows them to operate in their respective industry. Each licence contains the terms and conditions under which a company is entitled to operate. Regulators are responsible for policing the licences and they can amend the provisions of the licence. They can also act when industry behaviour fails to meet obligations for consumers, especially those in vulnerable circumstances, and when companies do not observe the Standards of Conduct. Enforcement action may also include imposing financial penalties and making consumer redress orders for breaches of relevant conditions and requirements under the governing statute or consumer protection legislation.[66] Finally, regulators also enjoy competition law powers in the sectors for which they are responsible under the concurrency regime.[67] Whether to take enforcement action or not is not a straightforward matter for regulators, but a culmination of deliberations among lawyers and non-lawyers, including economists, regarding the desirability of triggering formal legal procedures. This is not to argue that economic evidence does not have a role to play. On the contrary, legal considerations and economic evidence are in a constant dialectic process:

> We work very closely with lawyers; they are kind of involved throughout, and a lot of the time. I mean the way we tend to operate it's not siloed; you don't say 'you go away and do the economics, we go away and do the policy, you go away and do the legal analysis.' Yes, there are elements of that but it's an integrated whole, they interplay with each other. What are we trying to achieve in policy terms? How does that fit with the economic analysis? How is that consistent with our objectives and the legal analysis? How does it apply to what we should be doing and also limits on what we might want to do? Or the test, and actually one of the key areas in the interaction between economics and law that is very important is understanding what legal condition we are doing. Is it market review with SMP conditions? What does that imply for the legal test that would need to be satisfied for us to impose? (OFCOM 4)

Economic evidence influences the regulatory authority's decision to take enforcement action in the first place. In deciding whether to open an investigation, regulators must

[66] See, eg, *Virgin Media Ltd v OFCOM* [2020] CAT 5 (OFCOM decided that Virgin Media had breached GC 9.3 and GC 9.2(j), principally by charging customers who terminated contracts inside the minimum commitment period more than it had promised it would in its terms and conditions; a fine of £7 million was imposed).

[67] Enterprise and Regulatory Reform Act 2013, ss 51–53.

assess the seriousness of the case according to the potential harm to consumers and to competition:

> I think it comes down to whether you can demonstrate an effect and by that I mean can you convey to somebody that the action that one party or several parties have taken has adversely impacted generally consumers we are worried about, or some of the intermediate markets? But we need to demonstrate this as a first step (OFWAT 3).

Because regulatory resources are scarce, economic evidence allows regulatory agencies to prioritise investigations where the alleged harm to the consumer or to competition is most serious. Economists are crucial in quantifying this harm:

> We have been involved in enforcement cases. That's two roles: one is in terms of calculating gain; say a company failed to provide good service for consumers, how much detriment resulted, my team has a role of quality assurance in the assessment of the level of detriment resulted. The second is in competition enforcement cases where my team have contributed to enforcement cases and the analysis therein (OFGEM, chief economist).

But this quantification of harm is then subject to scrutiny by the 'legal frame'.[68] It is the latter that will determine whether the evidence of harm marshalled in support of opening a case can meet the evidentiary requirements set by the law, that is, the legal standard of proof. In cases relating to competition law infringements, the impact of the law is not merely procedural, but substantive: 'what is an abuse of dominance, or refusal to supply? '[E]conomists may disagree about legal conditions' (OFWAT 2), but economics need to be marshalled to support these legal conditions, that is, the appropriate and relevant legal test for proving a competition law infringement, as this is set by the case law.[69] It is the influence of legal considerations in the regulators' exercise of enforcement discretion that constrains their discretion, rendering them vulnerable to institutional constraints, as the following section will demonstrate.

This conceptual part of the analysis provided an overview of the input of economics in the regulatory decision-making process by exploring the various ways in which economic evidence and analysis informs interpretive, operational, and enforcement discretion. It was shown that recourse to economic evidence is pervasive across all three regulatory agencies and that regulators enjoy significant leeway in employing economic evidence and analysis when furthering regulatory objectives. This is particularly the case with interpretive discretion. However, the section alluded that economists are significantly constrained in the case of operational and enforcement discretion. The following section will explore the nature of these constraints by drawing on Parsons' rich framework of analysis.

[68] See Keith Hawkins, *Law as Last-Resort: Prosecution Decision-making in a Regulatory Agency* (OUP 2002) 54–57.

[69] *BT v OFCOM* [2016] CAT 3.

## 4.4 From the Conceptual to the Operational: What Constraints to the Influence of Economic Evidence in Discretionary Assessments?

> I don't feel that we have broad latitude, when you are inside a body you feel quite hemmed in by all kinds of factors (OFGEM 1).

Economists do not operate in a vacuum. As the previous discussion demonstrated, their decisions are made in a particular institutional setting, which reflects among others the interplay of various values, such as economic values, human rights values and norms, as well as constraints. The analysis, therefore, of the influence of economic evidence in discretionary assessments could not be complete without an understanding of how these values and constraints affect or otherwise the way economists perceive the limits of their discretion. In line with Parsons' typology the remainder of this chapter explores the relative influence of structural, institutional, and ideational constraints on the use and influence of economic evidence in discretionary assessments in the context of the three case studies. The findings are extremely variable between the three regulatory agencies examined. In fact, the following pattern emerges from the interviews: The greater the influence of institutional constraints, such as the threat of the decision being appealed in courts, the weaker the weight of economic evidence in the final decision reached and the more legalistic the regulator becomes in its approach, as the case of OFCOM reveals. Economic authority and wisdom while relevant, are not always dispositive, and economists are not Kings. In contrast, when competitive markets are nascent, such as that of water, and the degree of exposure to courts and litigation has remained low, such as in the case of OFWAT, the more unconstrained economists perceive themselves in the exercise of discretion: economists emerge as Kings. However, this regulatory reality can at any time be shattered when regulators become vulnerable to structural and ideational constraints, as the case of OFGEM paradigmatically reveals. Sound economic analysis was sidelined and the role of economic expertise within the organisation was undermined.

### 4.4.1 Structural Constraints

According to Parsons, structural constraints are 'exogenous' in nature, occupying what Keith Hawkins refers to as 'the surround', that is 'the broad setting in which regulatory (or other) decision-making activity takes place'.[70] This may involve the political or economic climate in which regulators operate and/or broader societal pressures. The 'surround', however, is not static or unchanging. As Hawkins underlines, 'political and economic forces may shift, and in these circumstances the social surround of the organisation changes'.[71] While all regulatory agencies are exposed to structural constraints, these have been more pronounced, as we shall see, in the case of OFGEM.

[70] Hawkins (n 68) 48–49.
[71] Ibid 49.

Before we elaborate further on this point, it is important to appreciate the influence of such constraints on the use of economic evidence. As will be shown throughout this section, these constraints do not necessarily limit the recourse to economic evidence and analysis in the workings of regulators, but rather limit the influence of economic values. In particular, structural constraints downplay the pursuit of economic efficiency in favour of non-economic and non-competition law values that have infused the regulatory objectives such as that of affordability, especially when regulators exercise operational discretion. This is exacerbated by the broadening of regulatory objectives to include social and environmental objectives, which has brought regulators closer to the concerns of government, including those of redistribution. Hence, in sharp contrast to the firmly embedded in neoclassical economics 'separability thesis' that enables questions of economic efficiency to be separated from issues of distribution,[72] economists working in regulatory agencies are required to grapple with both so as to claim legitimacy for their normative prescriptions. A senior manager at OFGEM emphasised the need to take more firmly into account considerations other than economic efficiency, given the nature of the regulated service:

> I am of the view that for an essential public service, like energy, which has major environmental impacts and consequences, then it is inevitable you will make complex trade-offs. I think it would be damaging to us to say we are responsible for economic efficiency and everything else is a political issue because it would mean that our roles would be very much more limited than they are at the moment. I prefer the approach where we have a degree of discretion, which enables us to take a broader role and get involved in things that do have environmental and social impacts. Actually, there's a very few things that we do that are purely technocratic. Most things we do have distributional impacts, social, environmental, security of supply impacts (OFGEM 2).

The need to engage more closely with distributional questions, because of the broadening of regulatory objectives, has expanded the regulator's arena of discretion, in the sense that their implementation requires making trade-offs between efficiency and equity. To the above one should also add the gradual decline of the 'Littlechild model' of economic regulation. Conveniently overlapping with the New Public Management's (NPM) oversimplified distinction between 'policy' and 'administration' (or 'steering' and 'rowing'), the 'Littlechild model' reserved a tight remit to regulators to promote competition free from central government interference.[73] The influential Littlechild Report from 1983, which provided the intellectual backbone for the privatisation of British Telecommunications perceived that economic regulation would be a temporary phenomenon, to be phased out as competition increased; simply a means of 'holding the fort' until effective competition developed.[74] But the reality showed that

[72] Following the Kaldor-Hicks criterion of efficiency, economic policy recommendations should be determined by efficiency, distribution remaining a problem for the political realm (the separability thesis). See John R Hicks, 'The Foundations of Welfare Economics' (1939) 49 Econ J 696; Nicholas Kaldor, 'Welfare Propositions in Economics and Interpersonal Comparisons of Utility' (1939) 49 Econ J 549.

[73] Christopher Hood and Michael Jackson, *Administrative Argument* (Dartmouth 1991); Stephen Littlechild, *Regulation of British Telecommunications' Profitability* (London: Department of Industry 1983).

[74] Littlechild (n 73), para. 4.11.

first, the underlying assumptions of the privatisation model were ambitious about the ability of markets with natural monopoly elements to be subjected to competition forces only, and secondly, that there is a much greater degree of cooperation between the realm of independent regulation and the realm of central government than that envisaged under NPM.[75] But as an OFCOM economist explained:

> Sectoral regulation has always been more deeply involved in those kinds of distributional questions, and justice questions and fairness questions than historically competition authorities, and as an economist it's a fascinating area, because economics has little to contribute. A lot of the formal neoclassical economics is kind of trying to avoid getting into questions of fairness. What does an economist think about fairness? Most economists have nothing to say about fairness! And it is really important to understand one of these areas where understanding your limits of your specialism has to contribute, but also what it does not have to contribute. Economics and economists can really contribute to identify a framework that encompasses different perspectives and identify key trade-offs and the key issues and economics is just generally very good at that (OFCOM 2).

Hence, economic evidence and analysis allows a more structured exercise of discretion vis-à-vis the ever-expanding statutory objectives. For example, equity objectives can be pursued as long as they are not too costly or have too strong negative effects on competition. But this broadening of statutory objectives comes at a cost, in that it renders regulators more exposed to the prevailing political and economic imperatives, undermining the role of sound economic analysis.

While OFWAT interviewees also mentioned the political environment and public acceptability, especially in relation to opening the domestic water market to competition, the analysis deriving from the interviews suggests that these structural constraints have been particularly pronounced in the workings of the energy regulator OFGEM:

> There are important and difficult constraints in terms of changing how we regulate; the way economics is involved in how we make decisions. We have high levels of formal discretion but in practice we are quite constrained (emphasis added). Some of the external constraints include the political environment and the public acceptability (OFGEM 1).

Two plausible explanations of OFGEM's vulnerability to their surrounding environment are offered here. First, a correlation seems to emerge between the degree of political influence observed in the workings of OFGEM and the institutional organisation of professional economic expertise within the agency. Recent evidence suggests that there was a 'reduced involvement of economists in senior roles at OFGEM'[76] that led,

[75] David Coen and Mark Thatcher, 'The New Governance of Markets and Non-Majoritarian Institutions' (2005) 18(3)Governance 329.

[76] Stephen Littlechild, 'Promoting Competition and Protecting Customers? Regulation of the GB Retail Energy Market 2008–2016' (2019) 55 J Reg Econ 107, 126.

inter alia, to economically uninformed retail energy market policies against the experts' consensus and advice.[77] This was again picked up in the in-depth energy market investigation undertaken by the UK CMA,[78] which was, amongst others, a catalyst for institutional changes in the organisation of economic expertise within the regulatory authority including the appointment, for the first time, of a chief economist:

> I did join recently but the role was set relatively recently. The role followed the CMA investigation into the energy market, where it was felt that Ofgem had not used economic evidence as robust as it might do, economics did not have sufficient prominence in the organization and a formal office of the chief economist should be set up accordingly. There were people who had chief economist role before, but they tended to be senior people with economic background rather than people who did economics as a big part of their job (OFGEM, chief economist).

The second reason has to do with the fact that energy prices and their affordability became a hotly debated political issue, and together with the prevailing economic climate presented important constraints to the monolithic pursuit of economic efficiency:

> You are trying to achieve economic efficiency within constraints and those constraints are set by society, by politicians, by and large security of supply, environmental constraints and limits on the degree of differential outcomes you might have, treatment of vulnerable customers, USOs, all these things. If everything was left to the market you would find that 15% of the households would not have electricity at all because they are uneconomic to supply... Once something has gained this public utility status, issues of universal access justice become quite important, fairness becomes important, I think we need to recognize that we operate within that context. A while ago I think there was a belief that energy could be made to be just like any public service, but it was a period of low energy prices, before climate change became such a high-profile issue, and a period of significant surplus generation capacity, and now we've got tighter margins, climate change is really important, and oil and energy prices are so much higher (OFGEM 2).

Finally, notwithstanding the crucial role of economic evidence and analysis in offering a logic framework for analysis when making trade-offs between efficiency and equity, evidence suggests that structural constraints relating to the political climate expose the limits of economists and economic evidence in areas of substantial redistribution:

> There are areas of very substantial redistribution that are matters best left to government rather than the regulator because the government has the political support, the public accountability and mandate to make these decisions (OFGEM 1).

[77] ibid 115.
[78] See CMA, 'Energy Market Investigation: Final Report' (n 6) above.

This is perhaps nowhere more apparent than in the heated political and regulatory debate surrounding the return to price cap regulation for all household energy consumers on poor value tariffs; a debate that culminated in the enactment of the UK Domestic Gas and Electricity (Tariff Cap) Act.[79] In particular, the Act puts in place a requirement on OFGEM to set an absolute price cap on standard variable (SVTs) and default tariffs;[80] that is, a rate above which no energy supplier can charge. It is estimated that this price cap will protect around 11 million households in England, Wales, and Scotland, who are currently on poor value tariffs. Unlike the existing price cap that protects consumers on prepayment meters, the cap on SVTs necessitated legislative action because of its wide remit and distributional implications. The initial price cap was designed and delivered by OFGEM and applied until the end of 2020.[81] A new cap rate was announced in August 2021. In such a major intervention in the market, economists rightly perceive their role as presenting evidence that allows political decision-makers to take decisions on distributional issues versus making the decisions themselves:

> I think it would be uncomfortable if technocrats were making substantial redistribution decisions, but I do think it can be useful for us to lay out evidence based on that and provide the information to make that decision' (OFGEM, chief economist).

This section explored the structural, that is exogenous, constraints to the influence of economic evidence in discretionary assessments. Such constraints do not render the use of economic evidence redundant, but rather downplay the pursuit of economic efficiency in favour of non-economic considerations such as those of affordability. This is exacerbated by the broadening of regulatory objectives, which has brought regulators closer to the concerns of government, and the concomitant decline of the 'Littlechild model' of economic regulation. This has led in the case of OFGEM to economic expertise, at least up to the CMA enquiry into the energy market, being ignored and sound economic analysis being sidelined. The section hypothesised on why OFGEM, amongst the other two regulatory agencies examined here, has been more vulnerable to such constraints and highlighted the outer limits of the use of economic evidence in discretionary assessments that are triggered in matters of substantial redistribution.

### 4.4.2 Institutional Constraints

According to Parsons, institutional constraints differ from structural ones in the sense that they do not exist independently of the institution but are rather forces that affect regulators' actions with respect to their position 'within man-made organisations

[79] Domestic Gas and Electricity (Tariff Cap) Act 2018 (c 21).

[80] SVTs are the suppliers' default tariffs charged when consumers do not choose a specific price plan. They are normally higher than fixed tariffs, which offer guaranteed prices for the duration of the supply contract. For an analysis, see Maria Ioannidou and Despoina Mantzari, 'The UK Domestic Gas Electricity (Tariff Cap) Act: Re-regulating the Retail Energy Market' (2019) 82(3) Modern L Rev 488.

[81] Ibid.

and rules'.[82] Institutional explanations serve as a broader organising framework from which several constraints flow, legal and quasi-legal.

Legal constraints stem first and foremost from the provisions of legislation establishing the agency's powers and from which its interpretive, operational, and enforcement discretion is derived. While, as we have seen above, economics have been crucial in operationalising discretion, the 'legal frame' is prominent throughout much of the economists' work as senior economists and their teams work closely with lawyers. Economic evidence is not only integrated into legal norms and legal analysis but is also regulated by the 'legal frame'. For example, administrative law, which requires regulatory authorities to exercise their powers lawfully, in accordance with the requirements of procedural fairness and on rational grounds, as well as its component that deals with judicial review of discretionary powers all regulate and constrain the exercise of economists' discretion.[83] As one interviewee conceded:

> The economic analysis is not the totality of it. We have to show evidence, to be rational, to be proportional, we cannot do more than can be justified by the evidence, which I think is all part of the framework that properly constrains us (OFGEM 2).

The above quote hints to considerations of both 'thin' and 'thick' legality that preoccupy economists when exercising discretion. In other words, regulators are not merely concerned with whether their discretionary assessments are authorised by the relevant law ('thin' legality), but also whether their overall approach to the use of economic evidence in their exercise of interpretive, operational, and enforcement discretion respects and reflects broader constitutional and human rights values inherent in the rule of law ('thick' legality). This should not come as a surprise. The conferral of broad discretionary powers makes it, at times, difficult to determine whether the regulatory action is legally authorised in the narrow sense of 'thin legality'. Therefore, a plurality of considerations and values deriving from the rule of law are likely to bear upon the requirement of legality and these considerations may well vary from case to case.

Quasi-legal constraints can be said to derive from the behaviour of other actors within the regulatory agency, most prominently the Board, and outside the regulatory agency, such as the relevant Ministry, as well as from the 'deeper values and principles reflecting the principles and "ethos" or "shared culture" of the community that may not be expressly reflected in legal rules'.[84] We shall examine each in turn.

#### 4.4.2.1 Legal Constraints

The 'legal frame' carries with it its distinct 'logic' of what a reasonable regulatory decision entails that it imposes on economists' discretionary assessments; something that economists find at times 'frustrating': 'You think action X is economically the right thing to do, but we cannot do it essentially' (OFGEM, chief economist). Hence, legal rationality may be in direct conflict with economic rationality. It is typically legal

[82] Parsons (n 1) 12.
[83] *Council of Civil Service Unions v Minister for the Civil Service* [1985] AC 374.
[84] Karen Yeung, *Securing Compliance: A Principled Approach* (Hart 2004) 10.

precedent and the provisions of the legislative framework that constrain an otherwise 'economically right' approach. But this is not always a one-way process: Legal interpretation is influenced by economic theories, and both can change over time. Legal interpretations do also evolve in light of economic theories and can be challenged when deemed incorrect. The two distinct rationalities—legal and economic—are thus in a dialectic relationship.

Take, for example, the imposition of regulatory obligations on telecommunications operators found to enjoy SMP. Economists may strongly favour a price control condition whereby the regulator uses information about the historic costs of a service provider with SMP to impose maximum prices which it may charge for its services in the future, than the less intrusive cost orientation condition, which simply requires a reasonable relationship to be maintained between the costs of a service provider with SMP and the prices it charges for its services.[85] But the legislative requirement of regulatory remedies being a proportionate response to the finding of SMP may instruct otherwise.[86] The same applies to the pricing methodology. For example, in OFCOM's determination regarding ethernet services,[87] the regulator considered that a different methodology for cost-orientation should be employed, that of Distributed Stand Alone Cost (DSAC), than the one used by the incumbent, British Telecom. In exercising interpretive discretion, OFCOM relied on previous regulatory decisions and case law in the so-called *PPC* case[88] and emphasised the identical wording of the cost orientation condition that applied in the latter case that rendered it consistent with its approach, taking into account the relevant regulatory concerns in the particular circumstances of the market and the policy objective of developing competition in the wholesale AISBO market.[89]

Considerations relating to 'thick' legality become prominent in the workings of economists precisely because of the contested nature of economics as a source of wisdom. Recourse to economic evidence and analysis rarely lends itself to a single 'right' answer. Economics, as one interviewee conceded, 'does not say oh well, the right answer is this, there cannot be another right answer. In almost any real-world circumstance there's a range of possible decisions, or views.' (OFCOM 4). Therefore, considerations relating to procedural fairness and the meaningful participation of affected interests become important in driving the overall discretionary judgement and determining the weight of economic analysis in the final decision reached, especially in the context of polycentric disputes. There might be 'other considerations than the economic analysis, but we have to be clear that you have to have those other justifications or rationales if we are doing it on that basis' (OFGEM 1). For example, adequate

[85] See Condition HH3.1 put in place by OFCOM. On 24 June 2004, OFCOM issued its final form Leased Lines Market Review ('the 2004 LLMR'), available at: https://www.ofcom.org.uk/consultations-and-statements/category-2/llmr accessed 6 June 2022. This was a substantial document, which included analyses of various markets and the extent of market power within them. OFCOM identified BT as having SMP in the AISBO market. It imposed Condition HH3, entitled 'Basis of Charges', as an SMP condition on BT as the Dominant Provider in that market.

[86] See Access Directive (n 36), Recital 6.

[87] OFCOM (2012), 'Disputes between each of Sky, TalkTalk, Virgin Media, Cable & Wireless and Verizon and BT regarding BT's charges for Ethernet services' (n 45) above.

[88] *BT v OFCOM* (PPC) [2012] EWCA Civ 1051.

[89] See *BT and others v OFCOM and others* [2017] EWCA Civ 330 [120].

procedures that satisfy the requirements of democratic legitimacy structure and constrain economic analysis.[90]

Human rights values, as these find their expression in the European Convention on Human Rights (ECHR), also constrain the use of economic evidence, particularly when the latter engage Article 1, Protocol 1 of the ECHR, which enshrines the right to property. For example, in setting the level of the energy price cap, an exercise of operational discretion that unavoidably interferes with the companies' licences, OFGEM must strike a fair balance between the public interest, namely the protection of certain household consumers from unjustifiably high energy prices, and the rights of individual firms.[91] Furthermore, Article 6 of the ECHR on the right to a fair trial and the related underlying values of procedural fairness influence the use of economic evidence in the exercise of enforcement discretion. Regulators do strive to ensure that their decisions are substantively fair; that is, that they reflect some 'substantive notion of fairness in rationally pursuing regulatory goals':[92]

> The economic model is a support to our decision-making, it does not drive it entirely itself. There needs to be a good rational logic as to why we are doing things. That's really important as good regulatory practice but also in making sure our decisions are robust legally because the last place you want to be is arguing the toss over bits of modelling code in court, which is ... once you got to that stage you probably lost (OFGEM 2).

Appeals on the merits are a significant constraint to bad economic analysis and can curtail the freedom economists perceive to enjoy in choosing, say, appropriate pricing methodologies: 'Legal review comes into essentially everything we do and there is a fairly substantial internal legal review' (OFGEM, chief economist). Most notably, among all utility regulatory agencies, OFCOM is the regulator most frequently challenged in courts. On the one hand, this is due to the shorter regulatory period set for price controls in the sector (three years versus five years for the other two regulators). On the other hand, the multiplicity of market players active in the sector renders almost every regulatory decision susceptible to creating winners and losers. This in turn presents a strong incentive for companies to challenge OFCOM's decisions. A crucial point to be made is that the majority of the decisions have been challenged on the merits before the specialist CAT. This should not be underestimated. The composition of the Tribunal, which combines legal and non-legal expertise, allows the latter to exercise its self-proclaimed 'profound and rigorous scrutiny'[93] over all aspects of OFCOM's decisions. Hence, when the regulator produces the body of economic analysis supporting its decisions, statutory appeals emerge as an important factor guiding the type and quality of economic evidence produced. As one interviewee conceded:

[90] See, eg, OFCOM's approach to enforcement available at: <https://www.ofcom.org.uk/consultations-and-statements/category-2/ofcoms-approach-to-enforcement> accessed 6 June 2022.

[91] See further *R (on the application of Infinis Plc) v OFGEM* [2011] EWHC 1873 (Admin) discussed in Chapter 3.

[92] See Yeung (n 84) 42–43.

[93] See *Hutchison 3G UK Ltd v OFCOM* [2008] CAT 11 [164]; *Vodafone Ltd v OFCOM* [2008] CAT 22 [46]; and *TalkTalk Telecom Group Plc v OFCOM* [2012] CAT 1 [71].

> ... we have the appeals process, merit appeals, which can be really very onerous and have actually driven a huge amount of complexity in the policy formulation and actually in terms of the staffing, we have a lot of people because the actual policy projects now have to be so thorough, because they are forensically challenged by stakeholders, both pre-court, but as soon as we move to statement they are invariably challenged in court ... There's all the work associated with the proceedings themselves, but actually because we have to be so thorough so that we are more secure in the legal process, we have to probe ... my assessment is we do even more work at the policy stage as well to buttress our position, because we have to be sure that what we are doing is correct and right and that we have looked through all the evidence very thoroughly (OFCOM 1).

Another interviewee stressed the 'reputational' aspect of losing in court:

> I don't think regulators like to be seen to try something that does not work and then they have to withdraw it. I am not entirely sure where that comes from, you'd have thought if we put in place a remedy that is not working then we should take it off but there is a reputational aspect to that (OFCOM 3).

On the positive side, appeal on the merits can be seen as a means to clarify OFCOM's wide statutory remit and instil greater rigour in the regulatory decision-making process. But OFCOM interviewees suggested that statutory appeals are being strategically deployed by market-players with deep pockets—an argument that the regulator used to eventually get rid of the statutory appeal and relegate its decisions to a judicial review standard.[94] As mentioned in Chapter 3, following the coming into force of Digital Economy Act, the CMA and the CAT will both be required to review telecommunications appeals 'having regard to judicial review principles', rather than, as in the previous regime 'on the merits'. This may decrease in the future the quality of economic analysis within the organisation and increase the regulator's arena of discretion. In other words, economic analysis can be downplayed in the face of legal considerations and the need to avoid litigation. We will return to this point in Chapter 6.

We shall not attempt to summarise here the intensity of review of regulatory decisions in the UK; a theme explored in detail in Chapter 6. But what is crucial for our purposes is that the intensity of review not only affects what regulatory agencies may do, but *who* within regulatory agencies might do it. As Adrian Vermeule argues, weak oversight of agency's rationality empowers non-lawyers within agencies, whereas strong rationality empowers lawyers.[95] This seems to be confirmed when comparing OFCOM, a repeat player before the specialist CAT, to OFWAT, which has so far limited, albeit of significance, exposure to appeal bodies, such as the CMA and the CAT. Against this background, an interesting pattern emerges: the greater the threat of institutional constraints, such as that of an appeal against the regulator's decision, as in the case of OFCOM, the more legalistic the regulator becomes, which may in turn undermine sound economic analysis. Economic authority and wisdom while

[94] Digital Economy Act 2017 (Commencement No 1) Regulations 2017 (SI 2017/765), § 87. See Chapters 3 and 6.

[95] Adrian Vermeule, *Law's Abnegation* (Harvard Univ Press 2016) ch 6.

relevant are not dispositive and economists are not Kings. Indeed, strong oversight of OFCOM's decision-making by the specialist CAT has empowered lawyers at the expense of economists. Moreover, it has also embedded a high degree of 'legal consciousness'[96] within the group of competition economics:

> I think (the threat of appeal) does run through quite a lot of the work we do, because I know the lawyers are very alive to that threat of litigation ... We are cautious about recognising the threat of litigation, that we do need to have a robust case for us to proceed, particularly if we are proceeding in the face of industry opposition (OFCOM 3).

All interviewees stressed the power lawyers enjoy at OFCOM during internal agency deliberations to veto policy decisions that are otherwise desirable and indeed legally supportable on the ground that they are legally incorrect. Perhaps the most interesting account of the law's hegemony in the workings of OFCOM is offered from a senior economist at OFWAT who had also spent significant time at OFCOM:

> Based on early impression here (at OFWAT), I think probably economics or decisions based purely on economics are more important, are given more relevance here at OFWAT than OFCOM ... It seems to me that OFWAT is willing to take more risks, the message from the Chairman recently has been we may want to try new things, make mistakes, if you make mistakes, we accept that it is a potential outcome. OFCOM is much more conservative, it tends to rely more on precedent, simply because I think it is a big organisation and it has been more subject to appeal than others. OFCOM is a bit more conservative (OFWAT 1).

The interviewee, however, conceded that if OFWAT 'gets challenged, it may change its mind about that [ie relying strongly on economic analysis]' (OFWAT1). In fact, OFWAT has recently come to appreciate the threat of appeal on the way economic analysis is deployed. A case in point is the *Bristol Water* case,[97] an appeal to the CMA against OFWAT's price control determination. Bristol Water was concerned about the difference between its business plan and OFWAT's final determination in relation to the appropriate level of wholesale costs required to deliver the agreed outcomes. Reducing bills to the degree proposed by OFWAT would have meant that the company would not have enough funds to invest and run its business. Bristol Water argued that the resilience duty required long-term planning to address supply challenges and, in any event, it needed to invest in a reservoir that would be invaluable in the case of a drought. At the heart of the dispute lay OFWAT's econometric modelling. Bristol Water claimed that OFWAT had relied too much on the latter and did not consider whether the reduction suggested was achievable in practice. The CMA scrutinised in detail the econometric evidence and modelling supporting OFWAT's decision and ultimately substituted these with its own model. It argued that Bristol Water should have been able to demonstrate that additional supplies would be needed and when they would be needed if resilience

[96] Patricia Ewick and Susan Silbey, *The Common Place of Law: Stories from Everyday Life* (Univ Chicago Press 1998).

[97] CMA (2015), 'Bristol Water plc price determination'.

concerns were pressing. Although not frequently appealed in courts, OFWAT appears to become aware of the threat of litigation. In the words of one interviewee:

> There are lots of checks and balances in terms of when we make decisions; we can be held to account. Either companies can refer our decisions in the context of cases, to the CAT for judicial review or in cases of price determination to the CMA, so we are very alert to the fact that we are not making these decisions alone, without prospect of a review. What would a reasonable person interpret our duties, or whatever particular party, there's plenty of cases that tell you how what's reasonable would be interpreted. We have pushed the boundaries on some of those things, certainly when we have looked at certain cost measures or how to apply cost of capital in particular cases, we have said we think that the case law is not necessarily the right starting place, given what happens in our sector is different (OFWAT 3).

#### 4.4.2.2 Quasi-legal Constraints

Quasi-legal constraints allow us to observe the influence of actors who are both internal to the regulatory agency, such as the Board, and external, such as the relevant Ministry, on the use of economic evidence in regulatory decision-making. The role of the Board as an important source of quasi-legal constraints to the use of economic analysis is prominent in the work of all regulatory agencies. This is because the Board is separated from the departments conducting economic analysis thus leaving greater room for a broader set of considerations, besides the merely economic ones, to influence the final regulatory judgment. As one interviewee explained:

> There's a lot of good economics work at OFCOM, but I think the decision-makers (i.e., the Board) are a bit removed from the economics. Often what happens is that a direction is set at the very high level and then the work of the economists is more to justify the policy direction, the decision; it's not that economics shapes the decision so much (emphasis added), it may do indirectly if the original suggestion does not prove correct, but it's not the main driver, essentially (OFWAT 1).

A somewhat similar view was offered on OFGEM:

> I think the role of the Authority, the Gas and Electricity Markets Authority, which is the ultimate decision-maker here, that body's role is to exercise judgement. There will be evidence that we present, with suitable caveats about the quality of it, but as far as we can we will give evidence on the costs and benefits of different options. Then there is an important role for GEMA in using its judgement based on the experience of its members that goes beyond the evidence that is presented (OFGEM, chief economist).

The government, through its role in making appointments to the Board, emerges as an important external actor. Most crucially, the relevant Ministry can exercise influence over the exercise of regulatory discretion through issuing guidance, which signals the government's priorities and views on how legislation should be interpreted. For instance, OFGEM operates under the Social and Environmental Guidance, which reflects, among others, the government's social and environmental energy goals with respect to fuel poverty and energy consumption, and intergenerational equity concerns relating to sustainability. The CMA investigation in the energy market brought into greater focus the influence of the Ministry on the regulatory decisions adopted and the deployment of economic expertise. The report stated that OFGEM's interventions in the retail energy market were based less on thorough economic analysis and more on concerns that the relevant Ministry (at the time the Department of Energy and Climate Change (DECC)) will intervene and take powers away from the regulator:

> Two of OFGEM's most important decisions in recent years (neither of which we consider to have benefited customers)[98] were taken against a backdrop of DECC taking powers – or stating its readiness to take powers – to implement changes in primary legislation in the event that OFGEM did not act. We do not know how material this context was in influencing OFGEM, but the coincidence of DECC's and OFGEM's actions risked creating the perception of a lack of independence on the part of OFGEM.[99]

Similarly, the Water Act 2014 created new powers under which the Secretary of State (ie the Department for Environment, Food and Rural Affairs-DEFRA) may publish a statement setting out strategic priorities and objectives for OFWAT to reflect in the way it regulates water services in England.[100] Together with the strategic policy statement, OFWAT is required to have regard to DEFRA's Social and Environmental Guidance, which seeks to provide the regulator with a steer on key environmental and social policies to which the government expects it to contribute in carrying out its role when discharging its statutory functions.[101] Crucially, compared to other regulators, Ofwat operates under more direct guidance from the government. As one interviewee observed: 'there is this sort of influence of the Ministry which you have to get buying into it; they have to issue a commencement order, guidelines; that is different from the other regulators' (OFWAT 1). Commencement orders are a form of Statutory Instrument designed to bring into force the whole or part of an Act of Parliament, which for some reason it is not desired to put into effect immediately upon Royal Assent. The gradual opening of the market to competition, deriving from the Water Act 2014, in fact depends on such commencement orders. For example, in OFWAT's recently published 2019 price review of the sector, the regulator envisages a bilateral market in water resources in which retailers will contract directly with upstream providers of water resources, with an access charge paid to the network business (competition in the market).[102] However, such a market depends on government activation of the relevant provisions of the Water Act.[103]

[98] These were the introduction of the simpler choices component of the Retail Market Review reforms in 2013 and the Standard Licence Condition 25A in 2009 prohibiting regional price discrimination.

[99] CMA (2016), 'Energy Market Investigation. Final report' (n 6) at para 304.

[100] DEFRA (2017), 'The Government's Strategic Priorities and Objectives for OFWAT—Presented to Parliament pursuant to section 2A of the Water Industry Act 1991'.

[101] DEFRA (2013), 'Defra's Social and Environmental Guidance to Ofwat'.

[102] OFWAT (2019), '2019 Price Review', available at:<https://www.ofwat.gov.uk/regulated-companies/price-review/2019-price-review/> accessed 6 June 2022.

[103] OFWAT, 'Delivering Water 2020. Consulting on our Methodology for the 2019 Price Review', 30 August 2017, available at: <https://www.ofwat.gov.uk/consultation/delivering-water2020-consulting-on-our-methodology-for-the-2019-price-review/> accessed 6 June 2022.

> OFWAT is slightly different from other regulators in the sense that in some areas it needs approval by the Ministry in order to do things. It got approval to open up competition at the retail level for non-households, it has not got yet approval to do that for households. There have been attempts, some cost-benefit analysis done, the government is not too convinced, it has postponed the decision. It's basically driven by government. I think if it was for us we would extend it because that would work better in the bilateral market, retailers would have a bigger share of customers with stronger incentive to go and look for resources. (OFWAT 1).

This section highlighted the role of institutional constraints to the use of economic evidence. It first discussed the relative influence of legal constraints, such as considerations of 'thin' and 'thick' legality and the way these affect the translation of economic inputs to legal outputs. It then moved on to consider quasi-legal constraints relating to the organisational constraints. Perhaps the most striking finding relates to the impact that the threat and intensity of review has had on the use of economic evidence in OFCOM: despite the mature state of competition in the retail telecommunications market and the dedicated competition economics teams that exist at OFCOM, lawyers, and the distinct logic of the 'legal frame' seem to prevail over purely economic considerations so as to minimise the threat of appeal. While the existence of the CAT provides a valuable check on the quality of economic decisions, evidence from the interviews suggests that the approach undertaken is overtly legalistic with the concomitant risk that inadvertently the goal becomes either avoiding or winning an appeal, instead of promoting the consumer's interests. The return to a judicial review standard may render the regulator less legalistic in its approach, but it may come at the expense of sound economic analysis, which will eventually increase OFCOM's discretionary power.

#### 4.4.2.3 Ideational Constraints

Ideational constraints refer to the influence of ideas and 'epistemic communities' on the workings of economists and their normative prescriptions. 'Epistemic communities' are 'network[s] of professionals with recognised expertise and competence in a particular domain and an authoritative claim to policy-relevant knowledge within the domain or issue'.[104] They are typically providers of external expertise, as opposed to the expertise that resides with the regulatory agency and may include academics and expert consultants. Their advice and support can, at times, be requested by the regulator, when for example they provide additional evidence or cooperate in modelling exercises during the decision-making process:

> We've obviously got economic expertise within the organisation but then there is quite an important role for economics outside, particularly in academia but also in other organizations, of providing a challenge function. My role is partly that, challenging things the rest of OFGEM is doing. Inevitably you can only get so far internal challenge, and you need that external challenge. It's always going to be quite

[104] Peter Haas, 'Introduction: Epistemic Communities and International Policy Coordination' (1992) 46 Int Organ 1, 3.

uncomfortable, and some of the people who provide that external challenge are quite robust ... but broadly it's a good thing. Compared to other jurisdictions I've seen there is a greater level of external challenge, which probably gets us to better decisions more quickly than it's the case in more consensual or internally focused regimes (OFGEM, chief economist).

An example comes from OFGEM, whose interventions in the retail energy market adopted following the Energy Supply Probe[105] in 2009 attracted wide criticism from the academic community of economists at the time of their introduction[106] and led to their subsequent withdrawal. Ideational constraints may also derive from the diffusion of ideas originating in the academy to the policy arena, as the rise of behavioural economics in regulatory policymaking amply illustrates. This set of ideas has justified an increased role for OFGEM when exercising operational discretion as we saw in the previous section.

However, economists and economic ideas may sometimes have conflicting impact on various policies. A notorious example concerns the access and interconnection pricing policies in telecoms. The Baumol-Willig efficient component pricing rule (ECPR), which was initially embraced and then expressly banned in the New Zealand regulatory context for its long-term damage in the telecommunications sector[107] has been has been one of the most hotly debated access pricing rules in the academic literature.[108] The ECPR deducts from the retail price of a product the cost that an undertaking would avoid (ie opportunity cost) if it did not provide an upstream service. In the UK context, as we shall see in Chapter 6, it was extensively discussed in the *Albion* saga,[109] where the specialist UK CAT decided that the ECPR adopted by OFWAT was not a safe methodology to use in the case before it.[110]

It is, arguably, the job of sociologists and political scientists to explain how economic ideas travel from epistemic communities and the academy and find their way to policymaking and why some economic theories become more prominent than others.[111] But, what this section demonstrates is that the influence of ideational constraints on

[105] OFGEM (2008), 'Ofgem launches probe into energy supply markets' (n 6).

[106] Stephen Littlechild, 'The Competition Assessment Framework for the Retail Energy Sector: Some Concerns about the Proposed Interpretation' (2014) Eur Compet J 181, 191; Stephen Littlechild, 'Ofgem's Retail Choice: A Response to Ofgem's Consultation on SLC 25A', 28 May 2012, available at: <https://www.ofgem.gov.uk/sites/default/files/docs/2012/07/25a_stephen-littlechild-response_0.pdf> accessed 6 June 2022. ; Morten Hviid and Catherine Waddams Price, 'Non-discrimination Clauses in the Retail Energy Sector' (2012) 122 Econ J 236; Catherine Waddams Price and Minyan Zhu, 'Prices and Consumer Switching in the British Retail Electricity Market', Working Paper 13-12 (Centre for Competition Policy 2013).

[107] This legislation followed litigation in the telecommunications sector culminating in the decision of the Privy Council in *Telecom Corporation of New Zealand Ltd v Clear Communications Ltd* [1994] UKPC 36, [1995] 1 NZLR 385.

[108] The ECPR is widely attributed to William Baumol and Robert Willig. For a discussion, see William Baumol and Gregory Sidak, *Toward Competition in Local Telephony* (MIT Press 2013); Nicholas Economides and Lawrence J White, 'Access and Interconnection Pricing: How Efficient is the Efficient Component Pricing Rule?' (1995) XL Antitrust Bull 557; 'The Inefficiency of the ECPR Yet Again: A Reply to Larson' (1998) XLIII Antitrust Bull 429.

[109] The Albion saga is long and complicated. Emphasis is placed upon the following judgment [2006] CAT 23.

[110] ibid [31] and [853].

[111] For an example, see Marion Fourcade, *Economists and Societies* (Princeton Univ Press 2010).

the use of economic evidence in regulatory decision-making is not always a straightforward exercise and that legal constraints mostly prevail.

## 4.5 Conclusion

This chapter demonstrated that economic evidence informs a wide array of discretionary assessments and the trade-off between efficiency and equity which has been more pronounced in the last two decades due to the broadening of regulatory objectives. The conceptual part of the argument (section 3) showed that recourse to economic evidence and analysis is pervasive in all three dimensions of discretion: interpretive, operational, and enforcement discretion. Furthermore, the role of economic evidence and analysis has increased as it is used to inform both economic efficiency considerations and the weight agencies need to assign to efficiency and equity respectively. However, this enhanced role of economic evidence and analysis has not had the effect of increasing the discretion agencies enjoy. Discretion does not run wild. On the contrary. First, against the backdrop of an ever-increasing statutory remit, economics offers a logic framework for decision-making and a strong focus on empirical and factual evidence, which structures the expanded statutory remit thus allowing discretion to be better exercised. Secondly, while economists enjoy formal discretionary powers, they are quite constrained, as the discrepancy between the conceptual and operational level of the analysis reveals. Economists are constrained by structural factors, such as the political and economic climate, and broader societal concerns. Such constraints emanate from the need to cater for social and environmental objectives, arguably more fitted to the role of the government. The upshot, however, of this development is that sound economic evidence and analysis may be sidelined, as the case of OFGEM revealed. Economists are also constrained by institutional factors, including the desire to produce substantively fair decisions, which may increase the quality of economic evidence. Hence, although the effective achievement of policy outcomes is appropriately given prominence considering the instrumentalist nature of the regulatory enterprise, the chapter demonstrated that there are other values that have an important role in limiting the pursuit of regulatory goals. And these values derive from both *thin* and *thick* legality. In a way, judicial review of economic evidence acts as a compass steering the agencies away from the monolithic pursuit of economic rationality towards the requirements of legal rationality reflected in both *thin* and *thick* conceptions of legality. Finally, economists are constrained by ideational factors, such as scrutiny by the academic community, as the case of OFGEM and OFWAT revealed. However, when specialist courts, such as the CAT, exercise too much zeal in second-guessing the regulators' expert assessments, the latter become more legalistic in their approach, as the case of OFCOM reveals, which may in turn undermine sound economic analysis.

A similar zeal on the part of the DC Circuit can be observed in the US context. A telling example comes from the early days of telecommunications regulation. As we shall see in the following chapter, the early stages of telecommunications deregulation were characterised by a highly intrusive, substantive review of the FCC's interpretive discretion when implementing the mandatory sharing provisions of the Telecommunications Act. Though the legal issues confronting the courts were akin to the policy considerations of the expert FCC, federal and Supreme Court judges assumed a quasi-regulatory role. During a decade-long 'serial litigation' generated by the FCC's primary unbundling rule, judges increasingly framed and directed the agencies' choices about which elements of the local exchange network would be shared with new entrants[112] by pointing to some specific alternative approaches or relevant factors that the agency should have considered, or at least explained. This can impact the agency's recourse to economic evidence and analysis.

There are many benefits to understanding whether and to what extent such constraints shape the decisions of economic regulators. First, we can better explain the on-going evolution of the British regulatory state from a project largely fuelled by a strong market ideology and the concomitant New Public Management (economic) values of efficiency and effectiveness to one concerned with the promotion of non-economic objectives and the pursuit of 'thick' legality. Secondly, understanding the constraints faced by economists helps us assess and possibly reform the regulatory and/or adjudicatory process. If economists operate largely unconstrained when exercising interpretive discretion, as the chapter posits, then perhaps a more adversarial and less inquisitorial decision-making process might be necessitated. Such a reform would subject economic facts and arguments to more detailed scrutiny and allow for a greater representation of affected interests. And if legal constraints, such as the threat of appeal, render the regulator legalistic and undermine the significance of economic evidence in the regulatory decision-making process, then this may invite a reconsideration of the scope and intensity of review. Indeed, we shall see in the following chapter how the DC Circuit moved away from 'hard look' review and adopted a 'thin rationality' review of economic evidence.

## Acknowledgements

Reproduced with permission from Oxford University Press. Mantzari, D, 'Are Economists Kings? Economic Evidence and Discretionary Assessments at the UK Utility Regulatory Agencies' (2020) 8 J Antitrust Enforce 535–71. (doi: <https://doi.org/10.1093/jaenfo/jnaa007>) © 2020, Oxford University Press.

[112] The Commission's first effort to identify the network elements that would be unbundled was invalidated by the Supreme Court in *AT&T Corp v Iowa Utilities Board*, 525 US 366, 387–92 (1999). The Commission's second effort was invalidated in *United States Telecom Association v FCC*, 290 F3d 415 (DC Cir 2002) ('USTA I'). The third effort was assessed in *United States Telecom Association v FCC*, 359 F3d 554 (DC Cir 2004) ('USTA II'). Finally, the Commission's fourth attempt was upheld in *Covad Communications Committee v FCC*, 450 F3d 528, 531, 533–34 (DC Cir 2006).

# 5
# From 'Hard Look' Review to 'Thin Rationality' Review
## The US Courts' Response to Economic Evidence

### 5.1 Introduction

This chapter will offer a nuanced account of the US federal courts' reaction to the regulatory agencies' increased recourse to expert economic evidence and analysis. It will show that an evolutionary transformation of the scope and nature of judicial review has taken place: from an intrusive 'hard look' review epitomised in the 1980s by the Supreme Court's *State Farm*[1] decision, to what is really an undemanding version of rationality, referred to as 'thin rationality' review.[2] Under the latter, agencies are not required to consider all relevant variables that strike judges as reasonable, but they must make decisions by making a rational connection between the facts found and the choices made. 'Thin rationality' review emphasises institutional competence and historical considerations and is more attentive to the interplay of the various values that inform agencies' actions. As we shall see, institutional competence and historical considerations are mostly pronounced in polycentric disputes, such as those involving rate-setting, whereas in cases concerning access to bottleneck facilities and universal service obligations judicial scrutiny is determined by the emphasis given to the underlying values of efficiency and equity. Taken together, they yield a picture of deference to agencies' economic expertise in regulatory matters.

A closer look at the record of petitions for review of the FCC's and FERC's orders under the 'arbitrary and capricious' standard of review shows that in matters where judges have been declared to be at their most deferential, such as in rate-setting cases, they consistently employ a 'thin rationality' type of review to examine whether the agency took into account 'the relevant data and articulate[d] a satisfactory explanation for its action including a rational connection between the facts found and the choice made'.[3] With regard to factual matters, judges typically defer to agency findings of fact, provided that they are supported by substantial evidence on the record.[4] Of course, there are outliers; cases where judges have mandated the kind of decision-making record the agency must produce to survive judicial review.[5] One such case concerns,

[1] *Motor Vehicle Mfrs Ass'n v State Farm Mot Auto Ins Co*, 463 US 29 (1983).

[2] Adrian Vermeule, *Law's Abnegation* (Harvard Univ Press 2016) ch 4.

[3] See, eg, *Midwest ISO Transmission Owners v FERC*, 373 F3d 1361, 1368 (DC Cir 2004) (quoting *State Farm* (n 1).

[4] *American Gas Ass'n v FERC*, 593 F3d 14, 19 (DC Cir 2010); *Achernar Broad v FCC*, 62 F3d 1441, 1445 (DC Cir 1995); *Covad Communications Committee v FCC*, 450 F3d 528, 531, 533–34 (DC Cir 2006).

[5] See, eg, *City of Idaho Falls, Idaho v FERC*, 629 F3d 222, 231 (DC Cir 2011).

*Courts, Regulators, and the Scrutiny of Economic Evidence.* Despoina Mantzari, Oxford University Press.
 DOI: 10.1093/oso/9780198851608.003.0005

as we shall see below, the DC Circuit's aggressive application of 'hard look' review which distorted FERC's policy initiatives and ultimately caused harm to the natural gas industry. But this should not be allowed to blur the overall picture of 'thin rationality' review. The judgments reviewed for the purposes of this chapter are included in Tables 5.1 and 5.2. Table 5.1 includes a review of all appeals from FCC between 1996 and November 2021 and Table 5.2 includes a review of all appeals from FERC between 1984 and November 2021.

Section 2 takes a closer look at the roots and evolution of 'hard look' review of economic evidence. Section 3 examines the determinants of judicial scrutiny in rate-setting cases. Section 4 explores the determinants of judicial scrutiny in cases involving access conditions to bottleneck facilities by new entrants and in cases involving the scope and funding mechanisms of universal service. Section 5 concludes.

## 5.2 The Roots and Evolution of 'Hard Look' Review of Economic Evidence

Placing 'hard look' review of economic evidence in its broader historical and institutional context will allow us to better appreciate its evolutionary transformation towards 'thin rationality' review. And this is what this section aims to achieve.

### 5.2.1 Agency Expertise and the Early 'Institutional Choice' Dilemma

The transformation of the scope and nature of judicial review towards an intrusive review was first triggered by the rise of agencies' expertise in the fields that they regulated. The arrival of the first regulatory agencies, namely the Interstate Commerce Commission (ICC) and the Federal Trade Commission (FTC), and the establishment of state Public Utilities Commissions (PUCs) during the first decades of the twentieth century, gradually challenged the courts' authority in the realm of economic regulation.[6] Emanating from the Progressives' ideal to separate politics from administration, regulatory agencies embodied the commitment to expertise-based administration and the 'rational public interest perspective'.[7] The Progressives and their New Deal-era descendants criticised the courts' involvement in industry regulation and urged that the courts should stay out of the regulatory process.[8]

Under the contours of substantive due process, judges had for a long time reserved for themselves an almost monopoly position in regulating several aspects of economic life. The Supreme Court generally presumed constitutionality of regulatory statutes. If, however, a statute interfered substantially with a right guaranteed by the Fourteenth

[6] For a historical analysis, see Robert L Rabin, 'Federal Regulation in Historical Perspective' (1985) 38 Stanford L Rev 1189, 1216.

[7] José Gómez-Ibáñez, *Regulating Infrastructure: Monopoly, Contracts and Discretion* (Harvard Univ Press 2003) 10.

[8] Reuer E Schiller, 'The Era of Deference: Courts, Expertise, and the Emergence of New Deal Administrative Law' (2007) 106(3) Michigan L Rev 399, 402.

Amendment, such as the exclusive right to use one's property as one see fit, then it would be upheld only if there existed strong public interest. The substantive due process doctrine rendered the inexpert judge the final arbiter of the constitutionality of state regulations aiming to curb market imperfections.

Faced with the complexity of commercial life, the Supreme Court upheld rate regulation for a variety of businesses, avoiding, however, any commitment on the level of price: 'We know that [rate regulation] is a power which may be abused; but that is not the argument against its existence.'[9] [F]or protection against abuses by legislators, the people must resort to the polls, not to the courts.'[10] Nevertheless, the judiciary defined the constitutional limits of the legislative power to set rates by stating that regulated industries had the right to a 'fair return',[11] refraining, however, from any explanation of what constitutes a fair return.

New Dealers argued that judges did not have the necessary expertise to understand the issues that agencies had to address in an increasingly industrialised world, such as the design of a sound rate methodology, nor the special knowledge to second-guess administrators.[12] New Deal opponents on the other hand, were sceptical about the rapid growth of the administrative state and the combination of policymaking, prosecution, and adjudication in a single agency. The Committee on Administrative Management, established by President Roosevelt in 1939 largely echoed the courts and lawyers' views on agencies, which were described as a headless fourth branch of government. The expansion of the regulatory state gradually gave rise to an 'institutional choice' dilemma. Simply and crudely, whether to establish a federal administrative court to oversee the agencies or to impose court-like procedures on agencies and strengthen judicial review. The American Bar Association Special Committee on Administrative Law largely abandoned the institutional response of a specialised court because it was inconsistent with the strong American Diceyan tradition of general courts enshrined in the Constitution.[13] Efforts were therefore directed towards a plan to reform administrative proceedings and strengthen judicial review of agency decisions. The choice to impose court-like procedures and the subsequent judicialisation of the agency's decision-making process led to the adoption of 'hard look' review that is mostly applied to FCC's and FERC's actions examined here.

### 5.2.2 The Advent of Aggressive 'Hard Look' Review: A View From FERC

You may recall from Chapter 3 the court-like procedures imposed on the regulatory agencies in the wake of the enactment of the APA. These included trial-type

[9] *Munn v Illinois*, 94 US 113, 114 (1877).
[10] ibid [134].
[11] *Smyth v Ames*, 171 US 361 (1898). See further John Bickey, 'A Fair Return for Public Utilities' (1927) 3 J Land Public Util Econ 61.
[12] Schiller (n 8) 402–03.
[13] See Kenneth C Davis and Richard Pierce, Administrative Law Treatise (3rd edn, Aspen Publishers 1994) 1.4, at 19 quoting 59 ABAR 539, 549 (1934) and HR Rep No 79-1980, at 7–16 (1946) (providing a detailed history of legislative developments).

procedures, such as formal adversary proceedings, cross-examinations, and rules of evidence with the aim of creating a factual empirical basis upon which the agency will form its decision. Because the APA's role is residual, agencies are free to complement the standards of the APA with those found in the Federal Rules of Evidence or in the Federal Rules on Civil Procedure. Formal proceedings are conducted by the ALJ whose determinations must be based on the record of trial-type hearings. The APA prescribes such procedures only regarding formal rulemaking or formal adjudication.

However, in the 1960s, agencies increasingly pursued their mandates through informal rulemaking and adjudication. The courts reacted to agencies' turn to informal rulemaking by imposing procedural requirements that the latter should follow to survive a challenge to their action in court. Under the 'hard look' review, regulatory agencies were required to develop 'rule-making' records to satisfy the court that they had considered all matters before them and explained their resolution in a reasoned way. In the *State Farm*[14] case the Supreme Court summarised its position towards agencies' rules stating that the latter:

> would be arbitrary and capricious if the agency has relied on factors which Congress had not intended it to consider, entirely failed to consider an important aspect of the problem, offered an explanation for its decision that runs counter to the evidence before the agency, or is so implausible that it could not be ascribed to a difference in view or the product of agency expertise.[15]

Consequently, if in adopting a final policy choice, the agency failed to consider alternatives or based its decisions on factors that Congress had not intended it to consider, the court would reverse the decision and remand to the agency for further explanation. Those procedural requirements were above and beyond anything mandated in the APA.

While the Supreme Court has been careful about policing the boundaries of *State Farm*, the DC Circuit has, at times, over-read the requirements of agency rationality. Perhaps the most aggressive application of 'hard look' review concerns the era of federal energy restructuring. As we shall explain below, the DC Circuit's 'adequate consideration' doctrine enshrined in the *Associated Gas Distributors v FERC* (AGD)[16] and *American Gas Association* (AGA) cases[17] distorted FERC's policy initiatives and ultimately caused harm to the natural gas industry. At the same time, the case demonstrates the radically different prism through which the agency and courts evaluate economic facts, such as the evaluation of 'stranded costs', which were central to the case.

FERC's Order No 436[18] radically changed the wholesale natural gas market as well as the incentives of participants in the market by applying antitrust principles in gas regulation. It reduced the regulatory barriers to entry, exit, and competition by making interstate pipelines open-access transporters of natural gas. Prior to Order

[14] See n 1.
[15] ibid [43].
[16] *Associated Gas Distributors v FERC*, 824 F2d 981 (DC Cir 1987).
[17] *American Gas Association v FERC*, 888 F2d 136 (DC Cir 1989).
[18] See FERC, Order No 436 (50 Fed Reg 42408, Ferc Stats & Regs § 30, 6665).

No 436 pipelines were buying gas from independent producers and reselling it to distributors and end-users. As a result, pipelines could exclude potential competitors from the sales market by denying them access to pipeline transportation. Order No 436, however, substantially increased the transportation of third-party gas by, *inter alia*, permitting pipelines to apply for 'blanket transportation facilities' in return for the open, non-discriminatory transmission of gas.[19]

In the *AGD* case[20] the DC Circuit affirmed most of the FERC's order, except for the 'take-or-pay' provisions, which were remanded on the ground that the agency had not 'adequately considered' the adoption of a regulatory mechanism to allocate a greater proportion of transition/stranded costs to gas producers, who benefit from the equal access regime. Stranded costs, otherwise known as transition costs, are the inevitable consequence of the arrival of competition in the supply of utility services. These costs represent 'expenditures incurred by the utility in the past in meeting its obligation to serve all customers within the area in which it held an exclusive franchise'.[21] They might be historical investments in generation plants, or take-or-pay costs,[22] such as those deriving from long-term contracts with gas producers and incurred by the natural gas pipelines in the wake of the open access transportation rules enshrined in FERC's Order No 436. Stranded costs sat comfortably in the rate base during the years of pervasive state regulation, and it was anticipated that they would gradually be recovered through charges to consumers. The imposition, however, of market-based prices rendered them costs for which no-one in the competitive environment wanted to pay.[23] The question of whether the former monopolists should be allowed to recover their stranded assets has been the subject of much academic and policy analysis. From a purely economic perspective the costs generated from a change in an agency's policy are sunk costs. They cannot be eliminated or retrieved.[24] Policy analysts, however, have approached the issue by employing a cost-benefit analysis. If the costs of transition are high and the probability of significant long-term gains from the change in policy are low, then the proposed policy change should be rejected. If, on the other hand, there is proof that the societal benefits will increase from the policy change, then the transition costs should be endured.[25]

[19] For an analysis, see Richard J Pierce, Jr, 'Reconstituting the Natural Gas Industry from Wellhead to Burner Tip' (1988) 9 Energy LJ 12, 24.

[20] See n 16. See also *Consolidated Edison Co v FERC*, 823 F2d 630 (DC Cir 1987).

[21] Gregory Sidak and William Baumol, 'Stranded Costs' (1995) 18 Harv J L Public Policy 835.

[22] Take-or-pay costs or liabilities are attributed to pipeline's long-term contractual commitments to purchase gas above the market price.

[23] Jeffrey Harrison, Thomas Morgan, and Paul Verkuil, *Regulation and Deregulation: Cases and Materials* (2nd edn, Thompson/West 2004) 4. See also *Cajun Electric Power Cooperative, Inc v FERC*, 924 F2d 1132 (DC Cir 1991).

[24] To this effect, see Louis Kaplow, 'An Economic Analysis of Legal Transitions' (1986) 99 Harvard L Rev 509.

[25] To this effect, see Richard J Pierce, Jr, 'The Unintended Effects of Judicial Review of the Agency Rules: How Federal Courts Have Contributed to the Federal Crisis of the 1990s' (1991) 43 Admin L Rev 7, 21; Paul Joskow and Richard Schmalensee, *Markets for Power* (MIT Press 1983) 199–209. See also, however, Gregory Sidak and Daniel F Spulber, 'Deregulatory Takings and Breach of the Regulatory Contract' (1996) 71 NY Univ L Rev 851 (arguing that the 'implicit regulatory contract' between regulated utilities and government entitles the utility to stranded cost recovery. Failure to do so is a violation of the Fifth Amendment

The Court suggested that FERC considered two possible mechanisms (cross-contract crediting or modification of the provisions of jurisdictional contacts between producers and pipelines). Yet, when FERC adopted the cross-contract crediting device,[26] the DC Circuit in the *AGA* case[27] reversed FERC's order on the basis that the agency did not engage in 'reasoned decision-making'. The Court found 'inadequate' FERC's explanation of its reasons for implementing cross-contract crediting than exercising its power to modify the provisions of jurisdictional contracts between producers and pipelines.[28] The DC Circuit seemed oblivious to the benefits to consumers of FERC's policies, by attaching increased significance to the transition cost problem. Not all costs, however, are transition costs, as others might be generated because of the imprudence of pipelines. Therefore, allocating transmission costs through a regulatory mechanism may distort the agency's efforts to create a competitive gas sales market. In fact, take-or-pay liabilities had already been resolved with lower transaction costs through negotiation settlements between pipelines and producers. As has been remarked, the DC Circuit's insistence on the 'adequate consideration doctrine', when reviewing regulatory action held 'hostage the entire reconstitutive strategy for the gas industry'.[29]

The case amply illustrates the aggressive reading of the *State Farm* requirements and the increased judicialisation of the regulatory agencies' decision-making process. Gradually, however, the meaning of the phrase 'hard look' review came to connote the idea that courts should scrutinise the agencies' decision-making processes. In the context of review of the FERC's orders issued under the FPA and the NGA, much of the appellate courts' task on appeal is to assure themselves that those orders satisfy the requirement of 'reasoned decision-making'. In *Columbia Gas Transmission Corporation v FERC*[30] the Court explained this requirement in greater detail:

> Judicial scrutiny under the Natural Gas Act is limited to assuring that the Commission's decision-making is reasoned, principled and based upon the record. For a reviewing court to perform this task it is imperative that the Commission articulate the critical facts upon which it relies when it decides to reallocate cost responsibility. Similarly, when the Commission finds it necessary to make predictions or extrapolations from the record, it must fully explain the assumptions it relied on to resolve unknowns and the public policies behind those assumptions. Where the Commission balances competing interests in arriving at its decision it must explain on the record the policies, which guided it. Only if the Commission

(Takings Clause) of the Constitution). Oliver Williamson criticises this approach by stating that the authors ignore that the previous regulatory regime might have been captured and opportunistically exploited by the incumbent monopolist; see Oliver Williamson 'Deregulatory Takings and Breach of the Regulatory Contract: Some Precautions' (1996) NY Univ L Rev 71, 1007–20.

[26] Interim Rule and Statement of Policy, Regulation of Pipelines After Partial Wellhead Decontrol, 52 Fed Reg 30,334 (to be codified at 18 CRF pts 2, 284) (FERC Order No 500, 7 August 1987).
[27] See n 17.
[28] ibid.
[29] Pierce (n 25) 42.
[30] 628 F2d 587 (DC Cir 1979).

> observes these minimum standards can we be confident that missing facts, gross flaws in agency reasoning, and statutory irrelevant or prohibited policy judgements will come to a reviewing court's attention. Moreover, by requiring that the Commission fully articulate the basis for its decision, we assure the Commission itself, the first opportunity to correct any defects, which may emerge from such disclosure.[31]

Thus, agencies' 'rationality' is not judged in the abstract but by reference to factors made relevant by the statute. An agency's consideration of statutorily irrelevant factors, or its failure to consider relevant ones, render its decision procedurally flawed.

Similarly, in the *Permian Basin Area Rate Cases:*[32]

> It follows that the responsibilities of a reviewing court are essentially three. First, it must determine whether the Commission's order viewed in light of the relevant facts and of the Commission's broad regulatory duties, abused or exceeded its authority. Second, the court must examine the manner in which the Commission has employed the methods of regulation, which it has itself selected, and must decide whether each of the order's essential elements is supported by substantial evidence. Third, the Court must determine whether the order may reasonably be expected to maintain financial integrity, attract necessary capital, and fairly compensate investors for the risks they have assumed, and yet provide appropriate protection to the relevant public interests, both existing and foreseeable. The court's responsibility is not to supplant the Commission's balance of these interests with one more nearly to its liking, but instead to assure itself that the Commission has given reasonable consideration to each of the pertinent factors.[33]

Following a broad overview of the application of the 'hard look' review in petitions for review of FERC's orders, the remainder of this chapter will examine the variable intensity of review of economic evidence in the following three distinct areas of regulatory action: (i) rate-setting cases (section 5.3); (ii) in cases involving access conditions to bottleneck facilities (section 5.4), and (iii) in cases involving the scope of universal service obligation (section 5.5).

## 5.3 The Determinants of Judicial Scrutiny of Economic Evidence in Rate-Setting Cases

The APA treats rate orders as legislative rules, hence FERC's rate determinations are subject to the arbitrary and capricious standard of review. As we shall see, federal

[31] ibid [593].

[32] *Permian Basin Area Rate Cases*, 390 US 747 (1968) (the Court rejected a challenge to the FPA's ability to set area-wide rates for natural gas, reasoning that there is no constitutional obligation to determine individual rates on a cost-of-service basis).

[33] ibid [791]–[792].

courts have adopted an approach to rationality review that is more aware and tolerant of the limits of rationality against the background of polycentric disputes, such as rate-setting which involves economic, technical, and policy assessments.[34] Federal courts consistently defer to agencies' expertise on 'fairly technical'[35] issues while judges routinely hold that the implementation of the legislative requirement of 'just, reasonable and non-discriminatory rates' involves 'policy judgements that lie at the core of the regulatory mission'.[36] Thus, federal courts have explicitly embraced institutional competence considerations to inform the scope and intensity of review. Over time, judicial review of ratemaking has shifted from substance to procedure, focusing on whether the Commission provided sufficient support and a proper rationale for its decisions.[37]

### 5.3.1 Judicial Scrutiny of FERC's Ratemaking Orders

Prior to exploring the judicial scrutiny of FERC's ratemaking orders, it is helpful to first understand the ways in which economic evidence informs rate-setting and the rate-setting process itself. In the US, it is the regulated firms that initiate the rate-setting process. For instance, in the natural gas sector, interstate pipelines apply for rates with the FERC, which ensures that the rates, terms, and conditions are 'just and reasonable' and not unduly discriminatory.[38] The FERC may pursue rate changes on its own initiative or after receiving a complaint from an interested party.[39] The Natural Gas Act (NGA) requires that rates charged for interstate pipeline services be 'just and reasonable', which entails a balancing of equities between the interests of pipeline and its ratepayers. The basic methodology to establish just and reasonable rates is cost-of-service ratemaking, whereby rates are designed based on a pipeline's cost of providing service including an opportunity for the pipeline to earn a reasonable return on its investment.

Similarly, in the electricity sector, the FPA requires integrated utilities to file with the FERC open access, non-discriminatory transmission tariffs showing the terms, conditions, and rates that they will charge for the transmission or sale of energy.[40] Those have to be just, reasonable, and not unduly discriminatory or preferential, and apply to both transmission services offered to third-party generators and to the utilities' own electricity transmissions. FERC generally approves transmission rates based on cost-of-service principles in which the regulator determines an entity's revenue requirement. Public utilities, investor-owned utilities, and

[34] *Pacific Gas and Electric Co v FERC*, 306 F3d 1112, 1115–16 (DC Cir 2002) ('Because of the highly technical and policy-based nature of rate design, the court's review of whether a particular rate design is just and reasonable is highly deferential').

[35] *Alcoa Inc v FERC*, 564 F3d 1342 (DC Cir 2009).

[36] *Entergy Services, Inc v FERC*, 319 F3d 536, 541 (DC Cir 2003).

[37] *Town of Norwood v FERC*, 962 F2d 20, 22 (DC Cir 1992) ('we require only that the agency have made a reasoned decision based upon substantial evidence in the record').

[38] Natural Gas Act, s 4 (15 USC § 717c) establishes the procedures and standards pursuant to which interstate pipelines apply for rates and pursuant to which FERC sets rates.

[39] Ibid, s 5. It empowers the Commission to lower rates not to raise rates.

[40] Federal Power Act, s 205 (16 USC § 824d).

independent transmission system operators may initiate rate increase filings and other filings related to the terms and conditions of their service without waiting for prior authorisation or permission from the regulator.[41] Following a hearing before the ALJ, the FERC accepts or modifies the rate filing.[42] The FERC may also reduce rates that are found to be 'unjust, unreasonable, unduly discriminatory or preferential'.[43] The burden of proof rests with the Commission to prove it.[44] The approved rates, otherwise referred to as 'tariffs', reflect the regulator's careful evaluation of the firm's costs and prices and signal the 'exclusive authority of the agency to accept or challenge such tariffs'.[45] In disputes involving tariff interpretation, courts typically apply the *Chevron* two-step analysis and give substantial deference to the agency's interpretation of filed tariffs informed by institutional competence considerations,[46] even where the issue simply involves the proper construction of language:[47] 'So long as FERC adequately explains why it interprets the contract as it does, we assume that its explanation is drawn from its statutory responsibility and experience.'[48] Crucially, courts have employed the so-called 'filed rate doctrine',[49] which bars alleged violations of antitrust or other private claims where a firm has an approved 'tariff' on file with a federal or state regulator.

Regulators use their discretion to set rates in a 'zone of reasonableness'. In the *Permian Basin Rate Cases*[50] the US Supreme Court summarised its position towards the Commission's pricing methodology in a statement applicable to both the provisions of the NGA and the FPA:

> Moreover this Court has often acknowledged that the Commission is not required by the Constitution or the Natural Gas Act to adopt as just and reasonable any particular rate level; rather courts are without authority to set aside any rate selected by the Commission which is within a 'zone of reasonableness ... No other rule would be consonant with the broad responsibilities given to the Commission by Congress; it must be free within the limitations imposed by pertinent constitutional and statutory commands to devise methods of regulation capable of equitably reconciling diverse and conflicting interests.[51]

[41] ibid § 824d(d). These changes go into effect immediately.

[42] Ibid § 824d(a).

[43] Ibid § 824e(a).

[44] See *Cities of Campbell v FERC*, 770 F2d 1180, 1185 (DC Cir 1985).

[45] *Town of Norwood v New England Power Co*, 202 F3d 408, 418 (1st Cir 2000).

[46] *Colorado Interstate Gas Co v FERC*, 599 F3d 698, 701 (DC Cir 2010); *Old Dominion Electric Cooperative v FERC*, 518 F3d 43, 48 (DC Cir 2008); *Consol Edison Co of NY v FERC*, 347 F3d 964, 972 (DC Cir 2003).

[47] See *Koch Gateway Pipeline Co v FERC*, 136 F3d 810, 814 (DC Cir 1998); *TAPSG v FERC*, 225 F3d 667, 687 (DC Cir 2000); *CAISO v FERC*, 372 F3d 395, 399–400 (DC Cir 2004); *South Carolina Pub Serv Auth v FERC*, 762, F3d 41, 54 (DC Cir 2014).

[48] *Cajun Electric Power Cooperative, Inc v FERC*, 66 F3d 364 (DC Cir 1995). See also *City of Kaukauna, Wisconsin v FERC*, 214 F3d 888 (7th Cir 2000).

[49] The doctrine was established in case *Keogh v Chicago and Northwestern Railway Co*, 260 US 156 (1922). See further Jim Rossi, 'Public Choice, Energy Regulation and Deregulation' in Daniel Farber and Anne Joseph O'Connell AJ (eds), *Research Handbook on Public Choice and Public Law* (EE 2010) 420.

[50] See n 32.

[51] Ibid [767].

In the same vein, in the *Morgan Stanley*[52] case the Supreme Court contended that 'the statutory requirement that rates be "just and reasonable" is obviously incapable of precise judicial definition, and we afford great deference to the Commission in its rate decisions'.[53]

Substantial leeway is also afforded to the methodology for setting rates. The Commission need not show that each element of the ratemaking method or calculation is fully persuasive so long as the end result appears to be reasonably articulated and supported by substantial evidence. For instance, in the electricity sector rates for transport services are typically established by recourse to one of the following methodologies: (a) the cost-of-service-method,[54] which allows the operator to recover its cost of providing the service and earn a reasonable return on the investment; (b) the negotiated rate method, which allows the operator to charge a rate that is agreed upon by the pipeline operator and the shipper on the basis of a 'recourse rate'; and, (c) the market-based rate method, which allows certain sellers of wholesale electricity to charge market-based rates provided that they demonstrate to the FERC that they lack both horizontal and vertical market power.[55] Additionally, sellers are required to file an updated market power analysis every three years.

With regards to the first method, the US Supreme Court has affirmed FERC's authority to consider non-cost factors in setting rates[56] as well as its discretion to choose from among several 'cost-recovering rates'.[57] The courts, however, have imposed limits upon FERC's discretion to set 'market-based' rates in an effort to address the difficulty of aligning market-based rates with FERC's statutory obligation to ensure that rates are 'just and reasonable' and not 'unduly discriminatory or preferential'. In the *Texaco*[58] case the Supreme Court, while emphasising that the FPC enjoys 'great discretion as to how to ensure just and reasonable rates',[59] nonetheless ruled that FERC may not determine in advance that the prevailing market rate is by definition just and reasonable. Nor may FERC substitute prevailing market prices for its own judgement. Only in cases where sellers do not have market power or the ability to manipulate the market can FERC presume that rates are just and reasonable.[60] Market power was in turn defined by FERC as the seller's ability to 'significantly influence price in the market by withholding service and excluding competitors for a significant period of time'.[61] Thus, FERC's ability to detect and mitigate market

[52] *Morgan Stanley Capital Group, Inc v Public Utility District No 1 of Snohomish County*, 544 US 527.

[53] ibid [532].

[54] See *Canadian Ass'n of Petroleum Producers v FERC*, 254 F3d 289, 293 (DC Cir 2001) (CAPP I). In the electricity sector, see *Sithe/Independence Power Partners v FERC*, 285 F3d 1, 5 (DC Cir 2002).

[55] In the 1990s FERC began moving to a regulatory policy that allowed sellers of wholesale electricity to file 'market-based' rates with FERC's Order No 697. Sellers who elect to participate in the market-based policy must show that they lack (or have adequately mitigated) both horizontal and vertical market power. See Order No 697, Market Based Rates for Wholesale Sales of Electric Energy, Capacity and Ancillary Services by Public Utilities, FERC Stats and Regs, para 31,252, 72 Fed Reg 39, 904 (2007).

[56] *Permian Basin Area Rate Cases* (n 32) at 791–92, 815 (1968); *Public Utilities Commission of California v FERC*, 367 F3d 925, 929 (DC Cir 2004).

[57] *FPC v Conway Corp*, 426 US 271, 278 (1976).

[58] *FPC v Texaco*, 417 US 380, 397 (1974).

[59] ibid [394]–[396].

[60] *Louisiana Energy & Power Auth v FERC*, 141 F3d 364, 365 (DC Cir 1998); *Elizabethtown Gas Co v FERC*, 10 F3d 866, 870–71 (DC Cir 1993); *Montana Consumer Counsel v FERC*, 659 F3d 910, 916–17 (9th Cir 2011).

[61] *Citizens Power & Light Corp*, 48 FERC paras 61, 210 at 61,777 (1989).

power became an essential aspect in determining whether market-based rates were just and reasonable.

Over time, review of ratemaking has shifted from substance to procedure, focusing on whether the Commission provided sufficient support and a proper rationale for its decisions. Thus federal courts have vacated, remanded, or reversed agencies' orders for failure to explain their underlying policy,[62] for departure from prior policy,[63] for departure from precedent,[64] and for the refusal to consider new evidence.[65] For example, in *Petal Gas Storage, LLC v FERC*,[66] which concerned an appeal by two interstate natural gas pipeline companies to ratemaking orders, the Court agreed with the petitioners that FERC erred in the composition of the proxy groups that were used by FERC in establishing the pipelines' allowed returns on equity. The Court concluded that there was a lack of 'adequate support for the contention that the Commission's proxy group arrangements were risk-appropriate'.[67] The FERC had not adequately explained why its chosen proxy companies were risk-comparable to the pipelines, the Court reasoned, particularly in view of the FERC's exclusion of gas distribution companies from the proxy group in previous decisions.[68] Similarly, in *Sithe/Independence Power partners v FERC*[69] the Court remanded the FERC orders dismissing a complaint that had challenged the method of computing losses under a contract for transmission service holding that the FERC had not clearly explained its rationale or revealed the data and assumptions underlying its findings.

### 5.3.2 Judicial Scrutiny of FCC's Rate-setting Orders

FCC's rate-setting orders under the US Telecommunications Act 1996[70] have equally benefited from a large degree of deference. But prior to considering the use of

[62] *Transcontinental Gas Pipe Line Corp v FERC*, 54 F3d 893 (DC Cir 1995) (the DC Circuit remanded FERC orders which granted Transcontinental Gas Pipeline Corporation (TRANSCO) certificate authority to provide additional gas transportation service to existing customers during peak and shoulder months. The Court found no basis for FERC's conclusions that the rates Transco suggested should become effective a year after the start of the service); *Michigan Public Power Agency v FERC* 405 F3d 8 (DC Cir 2005) (the DC Circuit remanded for further explanation FERC orders); *FPL Energy Marcus Hook, L.P. v FERC*, 430 F3d 441 (DC Cir 2005) (The DC Circuit vacated and remanded FERC orders that allocated to Marcus Hook the costs of interconnection that had become unnecessary holding that FERC had failed to explain its new rationale).

[63] *Louisiana Public Service Commission v FERC*, 184 F3d 892, 230–31 (DC Cir 1999) (the DC Circuit vacated and remanded the orders reasoning that FERC's action to require public utility holding companies to count interruptible loads when allocating capacity costs among its several operating companies was arbitrary and capricious. FERC had not adequately explained why it refused to follow its long-standing precedent that does not assign responsibility for capacity costs to interruptible loads); *Panhandle E Pipe Line Co v FERC*, 196 F3d 1273 (DC Cir 1999).

[64] *Williston Basin Interstate Pipeline Co v FERC*, 165 F3d 54 (DC Cir 1999).

[65] *Port of Seattle, Washington v FERC* 499, F3d 1016 (9th Cir 2007) (The federal court found that the FERC acted arbitrarily and capriciously in refusing to consider new evidence on market manipulation in California).

[66] 496 F3d 695 (DC Cir 2007).

[67] ibid [699].

[68] ibid [699]–[700].

[69] 165 F3d 944 (DC Cir 1999).

[70] US Telecommunications Act of 1996, Pub L No 104-104, 110 Stat 56, codified at 47 USC §§ 151 et seq.

economic assessments in implementing the local competition provisions (otherwise known as unbundling provisions) of the Act it is necessary to briefly refer to its main spirit and objectives.

The US Telecommunications Act 1996 sought to enable local telephone companies, long distance carriers, and cable television companies to compete, for the first time, in one another's markets. The Act stroke right in the heart of the long-standing belief that the local market constituted a natural monopoly and envisioned a telephone network of interconnected networks that are composed of complementary components and generally provide both competing and complementary services.[71] In order to accomplish this goal the Act facilitated entry into the local exchange market by lifting state-imposed barriers to competition and by subjecting the former monopolist local exchange carriers (ILECs)[72] to competition with new entrants (CLECs)[73] in the downstream market. The duty of interconnection was imposed on all telecommunications carriers.[74] In addition to interconnection, CLECs were barred from either prohibiting or imposing discriminatory conditions on the resale of telecommunication services.[75]

ILECs were subjected to additional obligations to those listed above. They were required to interconnect their own facilities with the CLECs' network at any feasible point,[76] either by allowing the latter to purchase telecommunication services[77] for resale to end-users or by providing non-discriminatory access to particular components of their network, that is, network elements,[78] on an unbundled basis and at regulated rates. Thus, the pertinent question was which of the network elements (eg incumbent's switches, transport lines, customer loops) would be considered 'bottlenecks' to be shared with the CLECs and at what price should they be offered to competitors. Section 251(d)(2) of the Act introduced the 'necessary' and 'impairment' standard. With regard to the price at which various network elements would be made available for mandatory sharing the Act solely stipulated that a 'just and reasonable rate' should be 'based on the cost' of the shared facility, should be 'non-discriminatory', and 'may include a reasonable profit'.[79] The cost, however, should be 'determined without reference to a rate-of-return or other rate-based proceedings'.[80] A possible explanation for the rejection of the traditional public-utility model of rate regulation derives from

[71] See Nicholas Economides, 'The Telecommunications Act of 1996 and its Impact' (1999) 11 Jpn World Econ 455, 457. Local telephone services were traditionally provided by private, franchised monopolies with the majority of local lines owned and serviced by AT&T. Long-distance services were opened to competition following AT&T's divestiture.

[72] Section 251(h) refers to the term 'incumbent local exchange carrier' to include any local exchange carrier that provided telephone exchange service with respect to an area as of the date of the enactment of the Act.

[73] CLECs are in their turn divided into those competitors who choose to build up their own network (facilities-based competitors) and those who choose to purchase infrastructure and services from the ILECs.

[74] Section 251(a)(1).

[75] Section 251(b)(1).

[76] Section 251(3)(2)(B). For a general account of the duty to interconnect imposed upon the ILECs, see s 251 of the US Telecommunications Act. The obligation for interconnection was aimed at guaranteeing that the new entrant's subscribers would be able to communicate with existing telephone users.

[77] See US Telecommunications Act 1996, ss 251(b)(1) and 251(c)(4).

[78] The term 'network elements' is defined in s 153(29).

[79] See s 252(d).

[80] ibid.

the 'Averch-Johnson' hypothesis, which demonstrated that rate-of-return regulation created an incentive for utilities to make excessive capital investments that resulted in a profit-maximising overcapitalisation.[81] But the Act failed to provide a precise definition of what constitutes 'cost-based' rates for unbundled elements; would this entail forward-looking economic costs or historical costs?

FCC's TELRIC (ie Total element long run incremental cost) pricing rule focused on marginal costs, but also accounted for some of the ILEC's fixed costs.[82] Prices for unbundled network elements (UNEs) were to be set on the basis of 'forward-looking economic costs' rather than on the basis of historical costs related to the particular element at issue.[83] More specifically, these forward-looking costs of a network element should reflect the sum of the TELRIC plus a 'reasonable allocation of forward-looking common costs' where common costs are 'costs incurred in providing a group of elements that cannot be attributed directly to individual elements'.[84] Therefore, the FCC's methodology was not based on the 'embedded costs' of ILECs' investments, but on the costs associated with a hypothetically efficient network; 'the most efficient telecommunications technology currently available and the lowest cost network configuration, giving the existing location' of the incumbent's wire centre locations'.[85]

Unsurprisingly, the incumbent carriers challenged FCC's pricing methodology as UNE's prices would inevitably be lower than the cost of maintaining the elements of the network and would not allow them to recover the cost of their past investments in the element. In the *Verizon v FCC*[86] case, the Supreme Court upheld the Commission's TELRIC methodology as a reasonable construction of the agency's statutory mandate to promulgate 'just and reasonable rates' for access to network elements. The reasoning was predicated upon the legal fiction embodied in *Chevron*,[87] that Congress intends to delegate law-interpreting powers to agencies. This in turn was supported by the agencies' expertise in the sector they regulated, an institutional competence consideration. It further illustrates that agencies' interpretation of their statute is not entirely separable from policymaking so that the power to interpret the rules is a necessary component of the agency's policymaking expertise with respect to the industry it oversees. The following excerpt from the Court's decision is illustrative of the wide degree of deference courts are willing to afford to the FCC's rate-setting decisions:

> Whether the FCC picked the best way to set these rates is the stuff of debate for economists and regulators versed in the technology of telecommunications and microeconomic pricing theory. The job of judges is to ask whether the Commission made

[81] See Harvey Averch and Leland Johnson, 'The Behaviour of the Firm Under Regulatory Constraint' (1962) 52 Am Econ Rev 1053, 1058. The phenomenon finds some empirical support in the context of electric power. For a review of evidence, see Paul Joskow and Roger G Noll, 'Regulation in Theory and in Practice: An Overview' in Garry Fromm (ed), *Studies in Public Regulation* (MIT Press 1981).

[82] FCC, Implementation of the Local Competition Provisions in the Telecommunications Act of 1996, First Report and Order, 11 FCCR 15499, 4 Comm Reg (P&F) 844–49 (1996).

[83] ibid.

[84] Telecommunications Act of 1996, 47 CFR§ 51.505(a) (2002).

[85] ibid § 51.505(b)(1) (2002).

[86] *Verizon Communications v FCC*, 535 US 467 (2002).

[87] *Chevron USA Inc v Natural Resources Defence Council, Inc*, 467 US 837 (1984).

> choices reasonably within the pale of statutory possibility in deciding what and how items must be leased and the way to set rates for leasing them.[88]

Quoting Justice Breyer in *Iowa Utilities Board*,[89] the Supreme Court held that 'words like "cost" give rate-setting commissions broad methodological leeway; they say little about the "method employed" to determine a particular rate'.[90] A similar degree of deference to agencies interpretive discretion is afforded in disputes involving interconnection obligations, that is, obligations that relate to the terms on which carriers connect their networks for the mutual exchange of traffic.[91] The ILECs file a tariff with the Commission, which has to ensure that rates for telecommunication service are 'just and reasonable'. The Commission fulfils this duty by reviewing the tariffs that communications providers file, both before and after the tariffs become effective. It then determines whether certain carriers are charging just and reasonable rates by prescribing a maximum rate of return and leaving it to the carrier 'to set its rates at a level designed to yield up to the prescribed rate of return'.[92]

But how have courts arrived at this deferential position? What rationales inform 'thin rationality' review? The following section will argue that historical considerations as well as institutional competence considerations mostly account for the deferential stance observed vis-à-vis rate-setting cases.

### 5.3.3 Rationales for Deference

#### 5.3.3.1 Historical Antecedents

To understand how the US federal courts have arrived at this deferential position towards the agencies' ratemaking methodology, it is important to examine their stance in the early ratemaking cases decided during the substantive due process era. In the infamous ratemaking case, *Smyth v Ames*,[93] the Supreme Court required agencies to set rates at a level that would allow public utilities to receive a reasonable return on their investment. Rates that did not ensure a reasonable return on the investment were rejected as confiscatory and as such were regarded as violating the due process clause of the Fourteenth Amendment. Therefore, in order to determine whether a particular rate was constitutional, a court had to determine whether it would allow a company to receive 'a just and reasonable return upon the fair valuation of its property'.[94] This ratemaking approach thrust the inexpert courts into the process of valuing utility

[88] Ibid [69].

[89] *AT&T Corp v Iowa Utilities Board, et al*, 525 US 366 (1999).

[90] Ibid [423]

[91] *Competitive Telecommunications Ass'n v FCC*, 87 F3d 522 (DC Cir 1996); *MCI Telecomm's Corp v FCC*, 59 F3d 1407, 1409 (DC Cir 1995).

[92] *Virgin Islands Telephone Corporation v FCC*, 444 F3d 666 (DC Cir 2006).

[93] See n 11. The Supreme Court voided a Nebraska statute for the regulation of railroads, declaring that it violated the Fourteenth Amendment to the United States Constitution in that it takes property without due process of law. See also *Ben Avon Borough v Ohio Valley Water Co*, 68 Pa Super 561 (Supreme Court 1917), rev'd, 103 A. 744 (Pa 1918), rev'd, 253 US 287 (1920). See further AG Priest, 'Major Public Utility Decisions in Perspective' (1960) 46 Virginia L Rev 1327.

[94] *Ben Avon* (n 93) [747].

rates. During this period of activist judicial review, federal courts closely scrutinised all aspects of the ratemaking process. Courts concerned themselves with the methodology that the agency used, with which assets were to be included in the rate base, and with whether the values attributed were the correct ones. Though the Court acknowledged that the findings required could more easily be made by 'a commission composed of persons whose special skill, observation and experience qualify them so to handle great problems of transportation as to do justice both to the public and to investors',[95] Justice Harlan declared that the judiciary could not abstain from its duty to decide the reasonableness of rates within the confines of substantive due process.

Decided in the aftermath of the Great Depression, the case, which dominated rate regulation for more than forty years, explains the balance that must be struck in establishing just and reasonable rates that would not violate the Takings Clause of the Fifth Amendment (which states that 'private property [shall not] be taken for public use, without just compensation') at a time when price levels had fallen sharply. The Court declared that 'the basis of all calculations as to the reasonableness of rates to be charged by a corporation ... must be the fair value of the property'.[96] Not only would courts need to determine if a sufficient rate of return was permitted, but they would also have to ascertain the fair value of the assets upon which that rate of return should be earned. The inquiry into the fair value required courts to consider on an *ad hoc* basis a range of facts 'to be given such weight as may be just and right in each case'[97] in determining whether fair value was provided:

> The original cost of construction, the amount expended in permanent improvements, the amount and market value of its bonds and stock, the present as compared with the original cost of production, the probable earning of capacity of the property under particular rates prescribed by the statute, and the sum required to meet operating expenses.[98]

State agencies at the time acted as mere fact-finders in a process where the policy-making function was largely reserved to the courts.

Over the next few decades, the Supreme Court wrestled with the issues raised by *Smyth v Ames* in the context of utility regulation. In *Willcox v Consolidated Gas Co*,[99] the Supreme Court recognised the importance of risk in determining the proper rate of return. *Missouri ex rel Southwestern Bell*[100] also supported the role of the Supreme Court as the final arbiter of ratemaking. But Justice Brandeis, joined by Justice Holmes, attacked the judicial inquiry into the 'fair value' stating that the rule in *Smyth v Ames* was 'legally and economically unsound' because it 'set the laborious and baffling task of finding the present value of the utility'.[101] The present value of the utility can't be determined,

[95] *Smyth v Ames* (n 11).
[96] ibid [566].
[97] ibid [546]–[547].
[98] ibid [468].
[99] 212 US 19 (1909).
[100] *State of Missouri ex Rel Southwestern Bell Telephone Co v Public Service Commission et al*, 262 US 276 (1923).
[101] Ibid [292].

however, without capitalising its net earnings, since the earnings are determined, in large measure, by the rate, which the company will be permitted to charge.[102] So under the *Smyth v Ames* rule, the present value of utility is determined by its replacement cost, which requires 'forming an opinion, or exercising judgment, as distinguished from merely ascertaining facts'.[103] Hence, the fair value standard left little room for meaningful judicial review, as it 'not only fail[ed] to furnish any applicable standard of judgment, but direct[ed] consideration of so many elements, that almost any result may be justified'.[104] Brandeis rejected the fair value rule and proposed to replace it with the capital prudently invested in the enterprise as a basis for determining a reasonable rate.[105]

Despite Brandeis measured dissent, *Smyth v Ames* would continue to dominate the Supreme Court's ratemaking case law for another decade. The *Smyth v Ames* fair value rule would be finally abandoned in the *Hope* case,[106] decided in the post-New Deal era, in favour of a more flexible approach to determining the justness and reasonableness of rates. The Court refused to 'substitute [their] opinions for the expert judgment of the administrators to whom Congress entrusted the decision'[107] and adopted instead the 'end results test'.[108] Justice Douglas, writing for the majority, declared that:

> Under the statutory standard of 'just and reasonable' it is the result reached not the method employed which is controlling ... Moreover, the Commission's order does not become suspect by reason of the fact that it is challenged. It is the product of expert judgment that carries a presumption of validity.[109]

The Commission therefore is not bound to use any single formula or combination of formulae in determining rates: 'It is not the theory, but the impact of the rate order which counts. If the total effect of the rate order cannot be said to be unjust and unreasonable, judicial inquiry under the Act is at an end.'[110] The statutory standard requires the Commission to balance the interests of consumers with those of the industry.[111] The Commission is charged with preventing the exploitation of consumers, while ensuring that utilities can earn a return that is: '(1) commensurate with returns on investments in other enterprises having corresponding risks' and (2) 'sufficient to assure confidence in the financial integrity of the enterprise, so as to maintain its credit and to attract capital.'[112] A foundational part of the analysis the Commission undertakes in cost-based rate-setting involves examining the public utility's costs[113] (which include the cost of capital, which is the cost of debt and the cost of attracting equity investment). *Hope*, therefore, adopted an interpretation of the NGA's just and reasonable

102 Ibid [293]–[294].
103 Ibid [293].
104 Ibid [290].
105 Ibid [290] and [306].
106 *FPC v Hope Natural Gas Co*, 320 US 591 (1944).
107 Ibid [615].
108 ibid [615].
109 ibid [602].
110 ibid [602].
111 Ibid [613].
112 Ibid [613].
113 *Bluefield*, 262 US 679 [694].

rates as a balance of investor and consumer interests, with the latter including a requirement for enough revenue not only for operating expenses but also for the capital costs of business.

But *Hope* isn't only significant because it upheld historical cost as a valid basis on which to calculate a fair return, but also because it was founded upon a theory of procedural due process and repudiated substantive economic due process that underlay *Smyth v Ames*. Rather than being a 'taking' of private property for public use, rate regulation was viewed as price control, which would be unconstitutional 'only if arbitrary, discriminatory, or demonstrably irrelevant to the policy the legislature is free to adopt, and hence an unnecessary and unwarranted interference with individual policy'.[114]

Subsequent case law elaborated further on the *Hope* criteria, which gradually led the way to the 'zone of reasonableness' within which rates would not be challenged by the courts.[115] The result of this vague standard has been increased deference by courts to the Commission's expertise,[116] but with consistency in the application of a said methodology being a key element in the 'just and reasonableness' analysis.[117] These historical antecedents of judicial scrutiny of the ratemaking process explain the large degree of deference which courts have afforded to the regulatory agencies' rate-setting process.

#### 5.3.3.2 Institutional Competence Considerations

Apart from historical reasons, the courts' reluctance to exercise a more intensive judicial supervision over the regulators in the course of the ratemaking process may also be explained by reference to the comparative institutional competence between these two actors with regard to an essentially polycentric matter. The federal courts' deferential stance reflects the recognition of the agency's superior technical knowledge in the ratemaking field. This expertise does not derive solely from the professional qualifications of its staff. It has also been gained through cumulative years of experience in the rate-setting process. The judiciary, on the other hand, lacks the cognitive and material resources which would enable it to deal with the multifaceted matter of rate-setting. Furthermore, judges are insulated from the information required to reach a well-informed judgment in this area. In contrast, the ratemaking procedure provides a forum for the wide participation of affected parties and allows the regulators to balance the interests of firms, consumers, investors, and the state. Finally, judicial intervention in what is largely a self-correcting process may impose high error costs and have a detrimental effect on the operation of the market.[118] The doctrine of the 'zone of reasonableness' emerges as a concession by the courts that FERC's ratemaking process requires flexibility in balancing the interest of 'just and reasonable rates' against a variety of goals, such as security of supply and non-discrimination; a balancing exercise that courts are ill-equipped and ill-suited to

[114] *Nebbia v New York*, 291 US 5022, 539 (1934).
[115] *Permian Basin Rate Cases* (n 32).
[116] See Rossi (n 49) citing, amongst others, *Market Street Railway v Railroad Commission*, 324 US 528, 557, 564–65 (1945).
[117] *Duquesne Light Co v Barasch*, 488 US 299, 315–16 (1989).
[118] Rossi (n 49) 424.

perform. At best, courts can apply a 'thin rationality' review to ensure that regulators have taken decisions on the basis of a transparent record and being loyal to the legislative mandate. The spheres of special competence are clearly delineated: questions of method or technique, such as the appropriate rate base or rate of return fall entirely within the special competence of the agency. Courts cannot and should not substitute their own judgement as to what is a proper rate base or rate of return.

## 5.4 Efficiency versus Equity Concerns: Judicial Scrutiny of Access Conditions to Bottlenecks and the Scope of Universal Service

A close examination of judicial scrutiny of disputes related to access to bottlenecks and universal service in the telecommunications and energy sectors reveals varying standards of review. While judges scrutinise the unbundling process closely under the 'hard look' review, they are prepared to afford substantial deference to agencies' actions related to the scope of universal service. This part will argue that the intensity of review is determined chiefly by the relevance of efficiency versus equity considerations. It will become apparent that efficiency considerations are more pronounced in disputes related to access to bottlenecks, whereas equity concerns become relevant in the context of disputes involving the scope and funding mechanisms of universal service. While conditions for access to bottleneck services for new entrants are driven by efficiency considerations pertaining to equality of opportunity, universal service seeks to create equality of outcome by supporting the service to a legislatively defined category of users. As will be discussed, the US Telecommunications Act is committed to the redistributive goal of providing universal service to as many members of society as possible (eg to rural areas, to the poor, the middle class, and the educational and health system) and requires the explicit funding of such policy.

### 5.4.1 Judicial Scrutiny of Disputes Related to Access Conditions to Bottleneck Facilities

When examining the judicial scrutiny of disputes dealing with access conditions to 'bottleneck facilities' the record illustrates that the FERC's decisions benefit from a lower degree of scrutiny than that observed in the context of judicial review of the FCC's decisions. This can be explained by the fact that the process of unbundling in the natural gas sector requires a less delicate economic exercise. In contrast to the telecommunications sector, the homogeneity of the final product, that of energy supply, and the enormous economies of scale involved in the construction of natural gas pipelines render the transmission of gas or electricity the main natural monopoly to be constrained by regulatory action.[119]

[119] The Natural Gas Act's fundamental purpose is to protect natural gas consumers from the monopoly power of natural gas companies; see 15 USC § 717 c(b)(1). See also *United Distribution Co v FERC*, 88 F3d

#### 5.4.1.1 Telecommunications Sector

As briefly touched upon in Chapter 4, the early stages of telecommunications deregulation are characterised by a highly intrusive, substantive review of the FCC's implementation of the mandatory sharing provisions of the Telecommunications Act. Though the legal issues confronting the courts were akin to the policy considerations of the expert FCC, federal and Supreme Court judges assumed a quasi-regulatory role. In the course of a decade-long 'serial litigation' generated by the FCC's primary unbundling rule, judges increasingly framed and directed the agencies' choices with regard to which elements of the local exchange network would be shared with new entrants[120] by pointing to some specific alternative approaches or relevant factors that the agency should have taken into account, or at least explained.

US regulators focused directly on the wholesale network elements with high fixed costs that render them unlikely to be replicable by potential entrants. Section 251(d)(2) of the Act stipulated that the set of network elements that would be made available to new entrants (the UNEs) had to be determined by recourse to the 'necessary' and 'impairment' standard. In other words, access should be afforded to 'such network elements as are proprietary in nature is necessary' and to which 'failure to provide access would impair the ability of the telecommunications carrier to provide the services it seeks to offer'.[121] The FCC was left to devise the mandatory sharing provisions of the Act in its First Report and Order.[122]

Mandatory sharing is promoted in the Telecommunications Act as a means to facilitate competition. Without it, a competitor can enter the market either by building and interconnecting its own network with the existing telephone network (facilities-based competitors)[123] and/or by making some type of arrangement with the ILEC to use its network (services-based competitors).[124] Mandatory sharing, however, presents the advantage of removing heavy regulation requirements and allows the new entrant to enter the market in stages, building part of its network and purchasing access to the rest of the network elements (eg switches, transport lines, and copper wire loops) at regulated rates from the existing firms.

1105, 1122 (DC Cir 1996). See further *FPC v Louisiana Power & Light Co*, 406 US 621, 631 (1972). Before performing any significant act, such as construction of a new facility or initiation of sales, pipelines were required to secure a 'certificate of public convenience and necessity' from the Commission. Section 7 (15 USC § 717f). The Commission regulated both the wellhead price and the price charged by pipelines to end-users and local distribution companies.

[120] The Commission's first effort to identify the network elements that would be unbundled was invalidated by the Supreme Court in *Iowa Utilities Board* (n 89); The Commission's second effort was invalidated in *United States Telecom Association v FCC*, 290 F3d 415 (DC Cir 2002) (*USTA I*); The third effort was assessed in *United States Telecom Association v FCC*, 359 F3d 554 (DC Cir 2004) (*USTA II*). Finally, the Commission's fourth attempt was upheld in *Covad Communications Committee v FCC*, 450 F3d 528, 531, 533–34 (DC Cir 2006).

[121] See s 251(d).

[122] See FCC, Implementation of the Local Competition Provisions in the Telecommunications Act of 1996, 11 FCC Rcd. 15499 (1996). In Rule 319, the primary unbundling rule, the FCC applied the definition of 'network elements' to include items such as operator services, the local loop, and directory assistance.

[123] See s 253(a), which preempts state and local laws that create barriers to entry into the local exchange markets and ss 251(a) and 251(c) which require rival local carriers to exchange traffic with entrants.

[124] Under ss 251(b)(1) and 251(c)(4) (the resale provisions), a CLEC has the right to purchase at regulated telecommunications services from a rival and then resell those services directly to consumers.

The mandatory sharing provisions of the Act, commonly referred to as the 'unbundled network element' provisions, were amongst its most controversial pro-competitive provisions. The Act gave little guidance to the FCC with regard to which elements of the local competition network should be shared with new entrants (eg switches, trunks, or loops) stating only that the Commission should: 'consider, at a minimum, whether (A) access to such network elements as are proprietary in nature is necessary; and (B) the failure to provide access to such network elements would impair the ability of the telecommunications carrier seeking access to provide the services that it seeks to offer.'[125]

The Commission concluded that a CLEC was entitled to access a given UNE 'if the quality of the service the entrant can offer, absent access to the requested element, declines and/or the cost of providing the service rises'.[126] The Supreme Court in the *Iowa Utilities Board*[127] vacated the rule as unreasonable under *Chevron*'s second step of analysis. According to the Court, the Commission interpreted the first of the unbundling criteria 'as having been met regardless of whether requesting carriers can obtain the requested proprietary element from a source other than the incumbent'[128] and considered competition to be impaired if 'the failure of an incumbent to provide access to [some specific network element] would decrease the quality, or increase the financial or administrative cost of the service a requesting carrier seeks to offer, compared with providing that service over other unbundled elements'.[129] The Court concluded that the Commission had failed to apply 'some limiting standard rationally related to the goals of the Act'.[130]

In addressing the Supreme Court's concerns, the Commission promulgated a revised rule stating that a would-be entrant is 'impaired' if 'taking into consideration the availability of alternative elements outside the incumbent's network, including self-provisioning by a requesting carrier or acquiring an alternative from a third party supplier, lack of access to that element materially diminishes a requesting carrier's ability to provide the services it seeks to offer'.[131] The DC Circuit in the *USTA I* case found the Commission's impairment standard unlawful because it did not differentiate between these cost disparities that a new entrant in any market would be likely to face and those that arise from market characteristics 'linked (in some degree) to natural monopoly . . . that would make genuinely competitive provision of an element's function wasteful'.[132]

Though the DC Circuit had in the past interpreted the 'shall consider' phrase as requiring the FCC to 'reach an express and considered conclusion about the bearing of [each] factor' without having to 'give any specific weight'[133] to those factors, in the

[125] Section 251(d)(2). See also s 251I(3). In contrast to the resale provisions, the unbundling provisions apply only to ILECs.

[126] See n 122, Rule 285 (1996).

[127] See n 89 [389]–[90].

[128] ibid [389].

[129] ibid [389].

[130] ibid [388].

[131] UNE Remand Order, 15 FCCR (1999) [375].

[132] *USTA I* (n 120) [427].

[133] *Time Warner Entertainment Co v FCC*, 56 F3d 151, 175 (DC Cir 1995) (dispute over cable television rates).

*USTA I* case[134] it directed the FCC to build on the Court's recommendations about the scope of unbundling requirements in its final rules. The DC Circuit vacated and remanded the Commission's interpretation of the 'impairment standard' and the list of UNEs. The Court criticised the FCC's impairment analysis for not taking into account differences in particular markets. It also found that the Commission's analysis had failed to adequately weight the costs of unbundling,[135] such as the discouragement of investment in innovation, and had not distinguished between impairment caused by the natural monopolistic characteristics of the market and cost disadvantages faced by new entrants. Finally, it vacated and remanded the FCC's line sharing requirements, as the Commission had failed to consider competition from cable, which was the market leader.

In the *USTA II*[136] case, the DC Circuit while agreeing with the formulation of the Commission's revised impairment determinations nevertheless objected to the application of that test to specific network elements. More specifically, the Court rejected the FCC's attempt to extend ILEC's unbundling obligations to providers of wireless service (commercial mobile radio services) and directed the Commission to 'consider the availability of tariffed ILEC special access services when determining whether would-be entrants are impaired'.[137]

The DC Circuit's quasi-regulatory role in promoting its own vision of competition in the local exchange market can be explained by reference to two distinct factors. The first factor relates to the substantial power gained by the Court in telecommunications regulation ever since its involvement in the historical consent decree breaking up the AT&T.[138] While the terms of the consent decree were negotiated between the Antitrust Division of the Department of Justice and the AT&T (Bell at the time) its entry and final acceptance was a judicial act. The Court's role in reviewing the consent decree was not to address the merits of the case, but solely to determine whether the acceptance of the consent decree would be 'in the public interest'.[139] The Court, however, interpreted the phrase as authorising an expansive review. According to the Court, its duty was to 'harmonise competing values with other legitimate public interest factors';[140] essentially a policy-making exercise. The DC Circuit promulgated a revised two-part public interest standard: 'If the decree meets the requirements for an antitrust remedy—that is, if it effectively opens the relevant markets to competition and prevents the recurrence of anti-competitive activity, all without imposing undue and unnecessary burdens upon other aspects of the public interest—it will be approved.'[141] The second element of the test sharply narrowed the authority of the Attorney General and vested in the Court primary responsibility and discretion to accommodate the myriad competing interests.

The second factor relates to federalism concerns. The Court's aggressive posture towards the FCC's implementation of the broad statutory provisions of the

[134] *USTA I* (n 120).
[135] ibid [428].
[136] *USTA II* (n 120).
[137] ibid.
[138] *United States v AT&T Co*, 552 F Supp. 131 (DC Cir 1982).
[139] ibid.
[140] ibid [153].
[141] ibid.

Telecommunications Act can be interpreted as a revival of the non-delegation doctrine. According to the doctrine, the legislature cannot delegate its inherent law-making powers to agencies without laying down an 'intelligible principle' to guide an agency's exercise of delegated law-making. Though the doctrine was last invoked to repeal a statute in 1935,[142] 'courts have relied on statutory interpretation to address their persistent worries about broad delegations'.[143] It can therefore be argued that the DC Circuit and the Supreme Court refused to take the ambiguity of the Telecommunications Act as authorising an expansive agency interpretation.[144] In the same vein, two years before the enactment of the Act, in the *MCI Telecommunications Corp v American Telephone & Telegraph Co*[145] case, the Supreme Court, in an aggressive ruling, rejected the agency interpretation of the words 'modify any requirement'[146] under *Chevron*'s first step on the grounds that it went 'beyond the meaning the statute can bear'.[147] The dissenting views in the case had argued that, particularly in a 'technical and complex realm', the agency decision is entitled to deference when it is consistent with the purposes of the statute and reflects detailed and reasoned consideration.[148]

In contrast, however, with the intense scrutiny of the unbundling provisions of the Act, the federal courts substantially deferred to the Commission's application of the forbearance provisions of the Telecommunications Act on the grounds of institutional competence considerations. The federal courts have stressed the agencies' superior expertise in collecting and analysing data to assess the operation of markets on a permanent basis. The Telecommunications Act instructs the FCC to forbear from applying a given provision of the Communications Act to a telecommunications carrier 'in any or some of its ... geographic markets' if three conditions are met: (1) enforcement is not necessary to ensure that charges and practices are 'just, reasonable and non-discriminatory'; (2) enforcement 'is not necessary for the protection of consumers'; and, (3) forbearance 'is consistent with the public interest'.[149] In making the determination of the third element of the test, the FCC is required to undertake a forward-looking hypothetical assessment of the effects of forbearance on competition among providers of telecommunications services and on incentives to innovate.[150] This sort of assessment can prove to be a particularly intricate exercise, especially when undertaken against the backdrop of emerging and rapidly changing markets,

[142] *ALA Schechter Poultry Corp v United States*, 295 US 495 (1935).

[143] See Lisa Bressman, 'Chevron's Mistake' (2009) 58 Duke LJ 549, 610. See further Cass Sunstein, 'Nondelegation Canons' (2000) 67 U Chicago L Rev 315, 388.

[144] See also the Tenth Circuit's decision remanding a matter back to the FCC for failing to give effect to the Congress's directive on universal service policy, *Qwest Corp v FCC*, 258 F3d 1191, 1199–202 (10th Cir 2001).

[145] *MCI Telecomms Corp v AT&T Co*, 512 US 218 (1994) (MCI).

[146] ibid [224].

[147] ibid [231] ('it is highly unlikely that Congress would leave the determination of whether the industry will be entirely, or even substantially, rate-regulated to agency discretion and even more unlikely that it would achieve that through a subtle device as permission to "modify" rate-filling requirements.'); see further *Whitman v Am Trucking Ass'ns, Inc*, 531 US 457, 468 (2001).

[148] *MCI* (n 145) [231].

[149] 47 USC § 160(a).

[150] 47 USC § 160(b).

such as the broadband market.[151] In the *USTA II* case the DC Circuit upheld the FCC's decision to refrain from requiring unbundling of the fibre broadband elements[152] on the grounds that cable companies could provide loop alternatives and intermodal competition.[153] In assessing the level of retail competition and the role of the wholesale market, the Court held that the FCC is not tied to any particular mode of market analysis, nor is it required to make a 'painstaking analysis of market conditions'.[154]

Finally, in the *Brand X*,[155] case the Supreme Court was presented with yet another case raising questions regarding the degree of deference courts should afford administrative agencies when faced with the sort of technical and economic complexity caused by technological convergence. The Supreme Court was called upon to decide whether cable modem services should be considered 'telecommunications providers'[156] or 'information service providers'[157] within the meaning of the US Telecommunications Act 1996.[158] Classifying them as information service providers would have crucial implications, as they would be subject to mandatory regulation by the FCC as common carriers under Title II of the Act. The case thus rested on the ambiguity of the statutory terms 'telecommunications', 'telecommunications service', and 'information service'.

Under review was FCC's ruling ('Declaratory Ruling')[159] which classified broadband cable modem service as an 'information service', so that it is not subject to mandatory Title II common-carrier regulation. Hence, cable modem service providers were not required to carry competing Internet service providers (ISPs). The FCC reasoning was based on its own 1998 Universal Service Report[160] which held that third party ISPs do not offer telecommunications services (ie do not offer connectivity but merely use an embedded capacity). The upshot of this development was that DSL providers who owned their own facilities were required to lease access to their wires to competitors,[161] but cable modem service providers were not required to lease access to their cable connections to competitors.

Multiple parties petitioned for judicial review of the FCC's Declaratory Ruling in the Courts of Appeals for the Third, Ninth, and District of Columbia Circuits on the grounds

151 See *Earthlink, Inc v FCC*, 462 F3d 1 (DC Cir 2006).

152 *USTA II* (n 120) [578]–[587].

153 ibid [582].

154 *Verizon California, Inc v FCC*, 555 F3d 270 (DC Cir 2009).

155 *National Cable & Telecommunications Association v Brand X Internet Services*, 545 US 967 (2005).

156 Those 'offering ... telecommunications for a fee directly to the public ... regardless of the facility used' 47 USC § 153(46).

157 Those 'offering ... a capability for [processing] information via telecommunications' 47 USC § 153(20).

158 Such classifications were absent in the original Communications Act of 1934. They originated in the 1970s as the FCC attempted to develop rules to regulate data processing services offered over telephone wires. Amendment of s 64.702 of the FCC's Rules and Regulations (Second Computer Inquiry) 77 FCC 2d 384, 417–23 (1980) (Computer II Order). Those rules were codified later in the US Telecommunications Act 1996 which established the terms 'telecommunication services' (analogous to the former 'basic' service defined by the FCC as a 'pure transmission capability over a communications path that is virtually transparent in terms of its interaction with customer supplied information', in Computer II Order, at 417–23) and 'information services' (analogous to the former 'enhanced services' defined by the FCC as those in which 'computer processing applications (were) used to act on the content, code, protocol, and other aspects of the subscriber's information' in Computer II Order, at 420. Basic services were subjected to traditional common carrier regulation, but enhanced services were not.

159 Inquiry Concerning High Speed Access to the Internet Over Cable and Other Facilities, 17 FCCR 4798 (2002).

160 Federal-State Joint Board on Universal Service, 13 FCCR 11501, 11531 (1998).

161 DSL providers were subject to mandatory common carrier regulation under Title II of the Communications Act.

that the rulemaking was contrary to the intent of Congress and that it was arbitrary and capricious. These petitions for review were assigned to the Ninth Circuit by lottery. The substantive issue was whether the Court should accept FCC's classifications or whether its own *stare decisis* should govern instead. In the *City of Portland*[162] case, which was decided prior to the FCC's Declaratory Ruling, the Ninth Circuit had held that cable Internet broadband service was a 'telecommunications' service under the meaning of the statute.[163] Prior to the *City of Portland* ruling the issue of proper classification of cable broadband Internet service had not been the subject of the FCC's interpretation, hence the Court did not have to determine whether *Chevron* deference was warranted. Therefore, it proceeded with its own 'best reading'[164] of the ambiguous statutory terms and held that broadband cable service was a 'telecommunications service', primarily because of the integrated nature of cable Internet service.[165] This precedent was in sharp contrast to the FCC's Declaratory Ruling when the Ninth Circuit faced its decision in *Brand X*.[166] Hence, the Ninth Circuit had to consider whether deference to the agency decision was warranted. Though the federal court referred to the *Chevron* framework in its own *Brand X* opinion[167] it felt bound by its previous pronouncement in *Portland*[168] and vacated the FCC's ruling.

On appeal the Supreme Court rejected the Ninth Circuit's reasoning and ruled that the Ninth Circuit should have applied the *Chevron* deference test rather than adhering to its previous construction in *Portland*. The Court stated that a lower court's prior construction of a statute 'trumps an agency construction otherwise entitled to Chevron deference only if the prior court decision holds that its construction follows from the unambiguous terms of the statute and thus leaves no room for agency discretion';[169] without, however, offering any sort of test for what constitutes 'unambiguous'. The Supreme Court clarified this statement by further stating that judicial precedent can govern only if the precedent case explicitly holds that the judicial construction is the 'only permissible reading of the statute'.[170] Following the application of the *Chevron* two-step inquiry, the Supreme Court ruled that the FCC's construction of the definition of 'telecommunications service' was a permissible reading of the Telecommunications Act. By deferring to the FCC's ruling that cable modem providers are not required to provide access to the ISPs as they are not offering 'telecommunications services', the *Brand X* court afforded to the FCC a large degree of deference in the face of statutory ambiguity.

#### 5.4.1.2 Energy Sector

In stark contrast to the heightened scrutiny that was applied to the FCC's implementation of the unbundling provisions of the Telecommunications Act, the DC Circuit exercised a 'thin rationality' review towards the FERC's statutory constructions in the course of federal energy restructuring.

162 *AT&T Corp v City of Portland*, 216 F3d 871 (9th Cir 2000).
163 ibid [878].
164 *Brand X* (n 155) [2688].
165 ibid [877]–[878].
166 *Brand X Internet Services v FCC*, 345 F 3d 1120, 1130-31 (9th Cir 2003).
167 ibid.
168 ibid.
169 See *Brand X* (n 155).
170 ibid [982]–[983].

FERC's deregulatory efforts in the electricity sector introduced the functional unbundling of wholesale generation and transmission services and required public utilities to provide open access transmission.[171] Under this system, previously integrated utilities should maintain a wholesale marketing function separate from their transmission functions. The corollary of this obligation was the requirement to file separate rates for generation, transmission, and ancillary services. In *Transmission Access Policy Study Group (TAPS) v FERC*[172] the Court affirmed FERC's authority under the Federal Power Act (FPA)[173] to require public utilities to file open access transmission tariffs. The Court exercised a 'hard look' review and remanded the case on two respects only. First, the Court remanded Order No 888, which required that the FERC impose a 'reasonable cap' on the terms of competing offers that a firm transmission customer must match in order to exercise its right of first refusal. Second, the Court remanded the Order for the FERC to provide an adequate explained basis for its treatment of energy costs under the 'market option' in the stranded-cost rules.

### 5.4.2 Judicial Scrutiny of Disputes Related to Universal Service

This section will examine the judicial scrutiny of economic evidence in cases involving the scope and funding mechanisms of universal service in the telecommunications sector and will highlight the role of distributive justice considerations in determining the intensity of review.

The US courts have afforded a large degree of deference towards the FCC's implementation of the US Telecommunications Act provisions that relate to the funding mechanisms to preserve and advance universal service.[174] This deferential posture is informed by equity considerations that the FCC has to take into account in order to render the telephone service affordable. Universal service requires regulatory intervention in order to further a broader range of regulatory objectives that lie beyond the realm of competition policy and are not in principle achieved by competitive markets.

Historically, the universal service program focused on reducing the costs of the basic telephone service. This goal was easy to implement when the Bell monopoly ran

[171] See Parts II and III of the Federal Power Act (FPA) 16 USC §§ 824 through 825r; The Federal Power Act gives FERC jurisdiction over the transmission and sale of electric energy at wholesale in interstate commerce. See also Promoting Wholesale Competition Through Open Access Non-Discriminatory Transmission Services by Public Utilities, FERC Stats and Regs, para 31, 036, 61 Fed Reg 21,540 (1996) (Order No 888) 21,541 ('designed to remove impediments to competition in the wholesale bulk power marketplace and to bring more efficient, lower cost power to the Nation's electricity consumers'). See further *Public Util Dist No 1 of Snohomish Country v FERC*, 272 F3d 607, 610–11 (DC Cir 2001); *East Kentucky Power Coop, Inc v FERC*, 489 F3d 1299, 1301-02 (DC Cir 2007). Order No 888 encouraged the formation of Regional Transmission Organisations, that is, multi-utility entities that would manage all transmission services from a particular region so as to ensure competitive pricing of transmission services and reduce utilities' market power. See *Transmission Access Policy Study Group v FERC*, 225 F3d 667, 682–83 (DC Cir 2000) (Transmission Access Policy). By consolidating control but not ownership of the unbundled transmission services FERC sought to preserve the efficiencies of vertical integration. See also Regional Transmission Orgs, Order No 2000, FERC Stats & Regs § 31, 089 (1999), 65 Fed Reg 810 (2000) (Order No 2000) directing transmission-owning utilities either to participate in an RTO or to explain their refusal to do so.

[172] *Transmission Access Policy* (n 171).

[173] See Federal Power Act §§ 205–206, as amended, 16 USCA § 824d, 824e (1994).

[174] 47 USC §245(b)(5). See, eg, *National Association of State Utility Consumer Advocates v FCC*, 372 F3d 454 (DC Cir 2004); *Rural Cellular Association v FCC*, 588 F3d 1095, 1100 (DC Cir 2009); *Rural Cellular Association and Universal Service for America Coalition v FCC*, No 11-1094 (DC Cir 2012).

a unified national phone system, as prices charged for any service did not necessarily have to reflect the true costs of providing that service, provided that the company made a profit overall. Implicit cross-subsidies between rural and urban areas, resulting from the access fee the LECs charged interexchange carriers in order to recover LECs' expenses of building and operating local loops, were inherent in the Commission's rate structure. The creation, however, of the competitive telecommunications environment envisioned by the Telecommunications Act required the elimination of implicit cross-subsidies, if incumbent LECs were to compete against new entrants. Access charges reform and universal service therefore became intertwined.[175]

The Telecommunications Act authorises the FCC to define the scope of universal service on an ongoing basis[176] and includes in its distributive goals not only increased penetration of the basic telephone service, but also greater access to new telecommunication technologies and services. To this effect, the Act expands the range of universal service by adding subsidised access to advanced services for schools, hospitals, and libraries.[177] Furthermore, the Act sets the principle that prices must be 'just, reasonable and affordable',[178] and requires that rates and services in rural areas and high-cost areas be 'reasonably comparable'[179] to rates and services in urban areas. The latter legislative requirement has been characterised by the courts as 'a definitional matter left to the Commission's discretion'.[180] The Commission enjoys wide discretion in the selection of the appropriate 'range' benchmark, in this case the nationwide range of urban areas, as both urban and rural rates vary significantly from state to state.

## 5.5 Conclusions

This chapter addressed the US courts' response to the challenges posed by economic evidence in regulatory disputes. It examined closely the judicial scrutiny of economic evidence in petitions for review of the FERC's and the FCC's orders and showed that in fact courts apply a 'thin rationality' review informed by historical and comparative institutional competencies considerations. In cases involving access to bottleneck facilities and universal service obligations, the chapter argued that judicial scrutiny is determined by the emphasis given to efficiency or distributive justice considerations. In contrast to the scholarly portrayal of 'hard look' review, arbitrary and capricious review is in fact 'thin' and does not require agencies to pick the optimal policy or the most accurate policy. The standard of review is not one of correctness, because the courts are far more attentive to institutional competence considerations and the limits of correctness in polycentric decisions that agencies are required to make while constrained by limited resources, information, and time.

[175] See Federal–State Joint Board on Universal Service, Report and Order, 12 FCC Rcd 8776 (1997); Access Charge Reform, First Report and Order, 12 FCC Rcd 15982 (1997).

[176] 47 USC § 254(c)(1) and 254(h).

[177] 47 USC § 254(b)(1).

[178] 47 USC § 254(b)(1).

[179] 47 USC §254(g).

[180] See *Rural Cellular Ass'n v FCC*, 588 F3d 1095, 1101–02 (DC Cir 2009). See further *Vermont Public Service Board and Maine Public Utilities Commission v FCC*, No. 10-1184 (DC Cir 2011).

## Appendix to Chapter 5

**Table 5.1** Appeals from FCC

| Case Name | Nature of Decision Appealed | Grounds of Review | Outcome/Remedy |
|---|---|---|---|
| *City of Arlington v FCC*, 569 US 290, 133 S Ct 1863 (2013) | Regulation of wireless communication facilities | Statutory interpretation | Upheld FCC's interpretation |
| *Rural Cellular Ass'n v FCC*, 685 F3d 108 (DC Cir 2012) | USO | Arbitrary or capricious | Denied petition for review |
| *Gulf Power Co v FCC*, 669 F3d 320 (DC Cir 2012) | Cable: rents for pole attachment | Statutory interpretation | Denied petition for review |
| *Farmers and Merchants Mutual Telephone Co Wayland v FCC*, 668 F3d 714 (DC Cir 2011) | ILECs refund access fees | Arbitrary or capricious | Upheld FCC's decision |
| *Vermont Public Service Board and Maine PUC v FCC*, 661 F3d 54 (DC Cir 2011) | USO | Statutory interpretation | Denied petition for review |
| *MetroPCS California, LLC v FCC*, 644 F3d 410 (DC Cir 2011) | Termination rates for intrastate Traffic | Arbitrary or capricious | Denied petition for review |
| *Core Communications v FCC*, 592 F3d 139 (DC Cir 2010) | Termination charges | Arbitrary or capricious | Denied petition for review |
| *Rural Cellular Ass'n v FCC*, 588 F3d 1095 (DC Cir 2009) | USO | Arbitrary or capricious | Denied petition for review |
| *Ad Hoc Telecomms Users Comm v FCC*, 572 F3d 903 (DC Cir 2009) | Regulation: special access broadband lines | Arbitrary or capricious | Denied petition for review |
| *Covad Commc'ns Co v FCC*, 450 F3d 528 (DC Cir 2006) | Unbundling | Statutory interpretation | Denied petition for review |
| *Earthlink, Inc v FCC*, 462 F3d 1 (DC Cir 2006) | Forbearance provisions | Statutory interpretation | Denied petition for review |
| *BellSouth Telecom'tions v FCC*, 469 F3d 1052 (DC Cir 2006) | Special access services | Arbitrary or capricious | Vacated and remanded |
| *Virgin Islands Telephone Corporation v FCC* (DC Cir 2006) | Ratemaking | Arbitrary or capricious | Vacated in part/ remanded |

**Table 5.1** Continued

| Case Name | Nature of Decision Appealed | Grounds of Review | Outcome/Remedy |
|---|---|---|---|
| *Qwest Commc'ns Int'l, Inc v FCC*, 398 F3d 1222 (DC Cir 2005) (*Qwest II*) | USO | Statutory interpretation | Denied petition for review |
| *National Cable & Telecommunications Association v Brand X Internet Services*, 545 US 967 (2005) (*Brand X*) | Classification of cable broadband Internet service | Statutory interpretation | Reversed and remanded 9th Cir |
| *United States Telecom Ass'n v FCC* (*USTA II*), 359 F3d (DC Cir 2004) | Unbundling | Statutory interpretation | Vacated in part/ remanded in part |
| *National Association of State Utility Consumer Advocates v FCC*, 372 F3d 454 (DC Cir 2004) | LECs fixed costs recovery/ ratemaking | Arbitrary or capricious | Denied petition for review |
| *Verizon v FCC*, 374 F3d 1229 (DC Cir 2004) | Forbearance order | Arbitrary or capricious | Remanded in part |
| *Mountain Communications, Inc v FCC*, 355 F3d 644 (DC Cir 2004) | Terminating carrier compensation | Arbitrary or capricious | Vacated in part and remanded |
| *Brand X Internet Services v FCC*, 345 F3d 1120, 1130–31 (9th Cir 2003) | Classification of cable broadband Internet service | Statutory interpretation | affirmed in part, Vacated in part and remanded |
| *United States Telecom Association v FCC*, 290 F3d 415 (DC Cir 2002) (*USTA I*) | Unbundling: impairment standard | Statutory interpretation | Vacated |
| *United States Telecom Association v FCC*, 359 F3d 554 (DC Cir 2004) (*USTA II*) | Unbundling: network elements | Statutory interpretation | Vacated in part/ remanded in part |
| *Alabama Power Co v FCC*, 311 F3d 1357 (11th Cir 2002) | Access pricing: poles | Arbitrary or capricious | Denied petition for review |
| *Global NAPS, Inc v FCC*, 291 F3d 832 (DC Cir 2002) | Interconnection agreement | Statutory interpretation | Denied petition for review |
| *Southern Co v FCC*, 293 F3d 1338 (DC Cir 2002) | Poles attachment act: coverage | Statutory interpretation | Overturned FCC's guidelines |

(*continued*)

**Table 5.1** Continued

| Case Name | Nature of Decision Appealed | Grounds of Review | Outcome/Remedy |
|---|---|---|---|
| *Competitive Telecomms Ass'n v FCC*, 309 F3d 8 (DC Cir 2002) | CLEC's access to UNEs | Arbitrary or capricious | Denied petition for review |
| *ACS of Anchorage v FCC*, 290 F3d (DC Cir 2002) | Tariff terms interpretation | Arbitrary or capricious | Vacated in part/ remanded in part |
| *Verizon Communications v FCC*, 535 US 467 (2002) | TELRIC pricing methodology | Statutory interpretation | Upheld |
| *WorldCom v FCC*, 308 F3d 1 (DC Cir 2002) | Ratemaking | Arbitrary or capricious | Remanded in part |
| *Qwest Corp v FCC*, 258 F3d 1191 (10th Cir 2001) (*Qwest I*) | USO | statutory interpretation | Remanded in part/ affirmed in part |
| *MCI World Com Network Services v FCC*, 274 F3d 542 (DC Cir 2001) | Interconnection rates | Arbitrary or capricious | Denied petition for review |
| *Sprint Communications Co v FCC* (DC Cir 2001) | Ratemaking: TELRIC compliance | Arbitrary or capricious | Remanded |
| *WorldCom v FCC*, 246 F3d 690 (DC. Cir 2001) | Classification of DSL-based advanced services | Statutory interpretation | Vacated and remanded |
| *Global Crossing Telecommunications v FCC*, 259 F3d 740 (DC Cir 2001) | Payphones compensation | Arbitrary or capricious | Denied petition for review |
| *Bell Atlantic Telephone Companies v FCC* (DC Cir 2000) | ISPs categorisation | Statutory interpretation | Vacated and remanded |
| *Alenco Commc'ns, Inc v FCC*, 201 F3d 608 (5th Cir 2000) | USO | Statutory interpretation | Denied petition for review |
| *American Public Communications Council v FCC*, 251 F3d 51 (DC Cir 2000) | Payphone methodology | Arbitrary or capricious | Denied petition for review |
| *AT&T Corp v City of Portland*, 216 F3d 871 (9th Cir 2000) | Broadband internet service Classification | Statutory interpretation | Denied petition for review |
| *AT&T v FCC*, 220 F3d 607 (DC Cir 2000) | Switching rates | Statutory interpretation | Denied petition for review |
| *Cable & Wireless v FCC*, 166 F3d 1224 (DC Cir 1999) | Benchmark rates for foreign telecoms operators | Arbitrary or capricious | Denied petition for review |

**Table 5.1** Continued

| **Case Name** | **Nature of Decision Appealed** | **Grounds of Review** | **Outcome/Remedy** |
|---|---|---|---|
| *AT&T Corp v Iowa Utils Bd*, 525 US 366 (1999) | Unbundling | Statutory interpretation | Upheld FCC's rules |
| *Southwestern Bell Telephone v FCC* (DC Cir 1999) | Unbundling | Statutory interpretation | Vacated and remanded in part |
| *MCI Telecomms Corp v FCC*, 143 F3d 606 (DC Cir 1998) | Payphones compensation | arbitrary or Capricious | Remanded |
| *Competitive Telecomms Ass'n v FCC*, 87 F3d 522 (DC Cir 1996) | Interconnection charge | Arbitrary or capricious | Remanded |

**Table 5.2** Appeals from FERC

| Case Name | Nature of Decision Appealed | Ground of Review | Outcome/ Remedy |
|---|---|---|---|
| *International Transmission Co, et al v FERC*, No 19-1190 (DC Cir 2021) | Ratemaking | Arbitrary or capricious | Denied petition for review |
| *Public Service Electric and Gas Co v FERC*, No 19-1091 (DC Cir 2021) | Ratemaking | Arbitrary or capricious | Denied petition for review |
| *Louisiana Public Service Commission v FERC*, No 20-1024 (DC Cir 2021) | Tariff interpretation | Arbitrary or capricious | Denied petition for review |
| *Oklahoma Gas and Electric Co v FERC*, No 20-1062 (DC Cir 2021) | Tariff interpretation | Arbitrary or capricious | Denied petition for review |
| *SFPP, LP v FERC and United States of America*, No 19-1067 (DC Cir 2020) | Tariff filing | Arbitrary or capricious | Denied petition for review |
| *El Paso Natural Gas Co, LLC v FERC* (DC Cir 2020) | Ratemaking | Arbitrary or capricious | Denied petition for review |
| *National Association of Regulatory Utility Commissioners v FERC*, No 19-1142, (DC Cir 2020) | Ratemaking | Arbitrary or capricious | Denied petition for review |
| *Baltimore Gas and Electric Co v FERC*, No. 18-1298 (DC Cir 2020) | Tariff filing | Arbitrary or capricious | Denied petition for review |
| *Southwest Airlines Co and American Airlines, Inc v FERC*, No 18-1134, et al (DC Cir 2019) | Index-based rates | Arbitrary or capricious | Vacated and remanded |
| *Northwestern Corporation v FERC*, 16-1176 (DC Cir 2018) | Rate filling | Arbitrary or capricious | Denied petition for review |
| *Arkansas Public Service Commission v FERC, No 16-1305* (DC Cir 2018) | Settlement benefits | Arbitrary or capricious | Denied petition for review |
| *Old Dominion Electric Cooperative v FERC*, No 16-1111 (DC. Cir 2018) | Tariff filing | Arbitrary or capricious | Denied petition for review |
| *Ameren Services Co, et al v FERC*, (DC Cir 2018) | Ratemaking | Arbitrary or capricious | Denied petition for review |

**Table 5.2** Continued

| Case Name | Nature of Decision Appealed | Ground of Review | Outcome/ Remedy |
|---|---|---|---|
| *ESI Energy, LLC v FERC*, 892 F3d 321 (DC Cir 2018) | Ratemaking | Arbitrary or capricious | Denied petition for review |
| *ANR Storage v FERC*, 904 F3d 102 (DC Cir 2018) | Market power assessment | Arbitrary or capricious | Remanded |
| *Verso Corp v FERC*, 898 F3d 1 (DC Cir 2018) | Ratemaking/surcharges | Arbitrary or capricious | Denied petition for review |
| *NextEra Energy Resources v FERC*, 881 F3d 202 (DC Cir 2018) | Ratemaking | Arbitrary or capricious | Denied petition for review |
| *Emera Maine v FERC*, 854 F3d 9 (DC Cir 2017) | Ratemaking | Arbitrary or capricious | Vacated and remanded |
| *Association of Oil Pipelines v FERC* 876 F3d 336 (DC Cir 2017) | Ratemaking | Arbitrary or capricious | Denied petition for review |
| *Advanced Energy Management Alliance v FERC*, 860 F3d 656 (DC Cir 2017) | Capacity selling | Arbitrary or capricious | Denied petition for review |
| *NextEra Desert Center Blythe, LLC v FERC*, No 16-1003 (DC Cir 2017) | Rules for capacity markets | Arbitrary or capricious | Denied petition for review |
| *FERC v EPSA*, 136 S Ct 760 (2016) | Wholesale rates | Arbitrary or capricious | Reversed DC Cir |
| *United Airlines, Inc v FERC*, 827 F3d 122 (DC Cir 2016) | wholesale transmission rates | Arbitrary or capricious/ Chevron | Remanded |
| *Aera Energy LLC v FERC*, 789 F3d 184 (DC Cir 2015) | Ratemaking | Arbitrary or capricious | Denied petition for review |
| *Louisiana Pub Serv Comm'n v FERC*, 772 F3d 1297 (DC Cir 2014) | Ratemaking | Arbitrary or capricious | Denied petition for review |
| *BNP v FERC*, 373 F3d 1315 (DC Cir 2014) | Ratemaking | Arbitrary or capricious | Vacated and remanded |
| *Black Oak Energy, LLC v FERC*, 725 F3d 230 (DC Cir 2013) | Ratemaking/refunds | Arbitrary or capricious | Vacated and remanded |
| *Southern California Edison Co v FERC*, 17 F3d 177 (DC Cir 2013) | Ratemaking | Arbitrary or capricious | Vacated and remanded |

(*continued*)

**Table 5.2** Continued

| Case Name | Nature of Decision Appealed | Ground of Review | Outcome/ Remedy |
|---|---|---|---|
| *Indiana Utility Regulatory Comm'n v FERC* (IURC), 668 F3d 735 (DC Cir 2012) | Tariff/interconnection | Arbitrary or capricious | Denied petition for review |
| *City of Redding v FERC*, 693 F3d 828 (DC Cir 2012) | Ratemaking | Arbitrary or capricious | Denied petition for review |
| *Northern Natural Gas Co v FERC*, 700 F3d 11 (DC Cir 2012) | Market-based rates | Statutory interpretation/ Chevron | Denied petition for review |
| *Mobil Pipe Line Co v FERC*, 676 F3d 1098 (DC Cir 2012) | Market-based rates | Statutory interpretation | Vacated and remanded |
| *PSEG Energy Resources &Trade LLC v FERC*, 65 F3d 203, 210–11 (DC Cir 2011) | Market-based rates | Arbitrary or capricious | Remanded |
| *Alabama Municipal Electric Authority v FERC*, 662 F3d 571 (DC Cir 2011) | Tariff interpretation | Statutory interpretation | Denied petition for review |
| *Dynegy Midwest Generation, Inc v FERC*, 633 F3d 1122 (DC Cir 2011) | Ratemaking | Statutory interpretation | Denied petition for review |
| *Mark West Michigan Pipeline Co LLC v FERC*, 646 F3d 30 (DC Cir 2011) | Tariff interpretation | Statutory interpretation/ Chevron | Denied petition for review |
| *City of Idaho Falls, Idaho v FERC*, 629 F3d 222 (DC Cir 2011) | Transmission rates | Statutory interpretation/ Chevron | Denied petition for review |
| *NRG Power Mktg, LLC v Me Pub Utils Comm'n*, 130 S Ct 694 (2010) | Ratemaking/Mobile Sierra doctrine | Arbitrary or capricious | Reversed DC Cir |
| *Conn Dep't of Pub Util Control v FERC*, 593 F3d 30 (DC Cir 2010) | Mobile Sierra doctrine | Statutory interpretation | Reversed and remanded |
| *Montana Consumer Counsel v FERC*, 659 F3d 910 (9th Cir 2011) | Market-based rates | Arbitrary or capricious | Denied petition for review |
| *Transmission Agency of Northern California v FERC*, 628 F3d 538 (DC Cir 2010) | Tariff filing | Arbitrary or capricious | Denied petition for review |

Table 5.2 Continued

| Case Name | Nature of Decision Appealed | Ground of Review | Outcome/ Remedy |
|---|---|---|---|
| *Sacramento Municipal Utility District v FERC*, 616 F3d 520 (DC Cir 2010) | Electricity tariff amendment | Arbitrary or capricious | Denied petition for review |
| *Flint Hill Resources Alaska, LLC v FERC*, 627 F3d 881 (DC Cir 2010) | Electricity tariff design | Arbitrary or capricious | Affirmed |
| *Interstate Natural Gas Association of America v FERC*, 617 F3d 504 (DC Cir 2010) | Oil pipeline rate-setting methodology | Arbitrary or capricious | Denied petition for review |
| *Southern California Edison Co v FERC*, 603 F3d 996 (DC Cir 2010) | Retention of cost-based price ceilings on short-term capacity sales by pipelines | Arbitrary or capricious | Denied petition for review |
| *Sacramento Mun Util Dist v FERC*, 616 F3d 520 (DC Cir 2010) | Ratemaking/network transmission service | Arbitrary or capricious | Denied petition for review |
| *Missouri Public Service Commission v FERC*, 601 F3d 581 (DC Cir 2010) | Market design/ratemaking | Arbitrary or capricious | Denied petition for review |
| *Colorado Interstate Gas Co v FERC*, 599 F3d 698 (DC Cir 2010) | Ratemaking | Arbitrary or capricious | Vacated and remanded |
| *Florida Municipal Power Agency v FERC*, 602 F3d 454 (DC Cir 2009) | Ratemaking | Arbitrary or capricious | Denied petition for review |
| *Alcoa Inc v FERC*, 564 F3d 1342 (DC Cir 2009) | Ratemaking | Arbitrary or capricious | Denied petition for review |
| *Connecticut Department of Public Utility Control v FERC*, 569 F3d 477 (DC Cir 2009) | Ratemaking methodology/ jurisdiction | Statutory interpretation/ Chevron | Denied petition for review |
| *Illinois Commerce Commission v FERC*, 76 F3d 470 (7th Cir 2009) | Ratemaking | Arbitrary or capricious | Denied petition for review |
| *City of Anaheim v FERC*, 558 F3d 523 (DC Cir 2009) | Electricity transmission ratemaking | Statutory interpretation/ Chevron | Vacated and remanded |
| *Blumenthal v FERC*, 552 F3d 875 (DC Cir 2009) | Ratemaking | Arbitrary or capricious | Denied petition for review |
| *Westar Energy, Inc v FERC*, 568 F3d 985 (DC Cir 2009) | Ratemaking | Arbitrary or capricious | Denied petition for review |

(*continued*)

**Table 5.2** Continued

| Case Name | Nature of Decision Appealed | Ground of Review | Outcome/ Remedy |
|---|---|---|---|
| *Exxon Mobil Corp v FERC*, 571 F3d 1208 (DC Cir 2009) | Ratemaking methodology/ refunds | Arbitrary or capricious | Denied petition for review |
| *Morgan Stanley Capital Group v Pub Util Dist No 1 of Snohomish City*, Wash 554 US 527 (2008) | Mobile Sierra doctrine/ contract | Statutory interpretation | Remanded |
| *Western Area Power Administration v FERC*, 525 F3d 40 (DC Cir 2008) | Ratemaking | Arbitrary or capricious | Denied petition for review |
| *Louisiana Public Service Commission v FERC*, 522 F3d 378 (DC Cir 2008) | Ratemaking/cost recovery | Arbitrary or capricious | Denied petition for review in part/remanded in part |
| *Public Service Commission v Wisconsin*, 545 F3d 1058 (DC Cir 2008) | Ratemaking/cost allocation policy | Arbitrary or capricious | Denied petition for review |
| *Cogeneration Assoc of Cal v FERC*, 525 F3d 1279 (DC Cir 2008) | Ratemaking | Arbitrary or capricious | Denied petition for review |
| *Braintree Electric Light Department v FERC*, 550 F3d 6 (DC Cir 2008) | Ratemaking | Arbitrary or capricious | Denied petition for review |
| *Western Area Power Administration v FERC*, 525 F3d 40 (DC Cir 2008) | Ratemaking | Arbitrary or capricious | Denied petition for review |
| *Maine Public Utilities Commission v FERC*, 520 F3d 464 (DC Cir 2008) | Ratemaking/jurisdiction | Arbitrary or capricious | Denied petition for review |
| *Williston Basin Interstate Pipeline Co v FERC* 519 F3d 497 (DC Cir 2008) | Market design/ratemaking | Arbitrary or capricious | Remanded |
| *Old Dominion Electric Cooperative v FERC*, 518 F3d 43 (DC Cir 2008) | Ratemaking/cost recovery | Arbitrary or capricious | Denied petition for review |
| *Transcontinental Gas Pipe Line Corp v FERC*, 518 F3d 916 (DC Cir 2007) | Ratemaking | Arbitrary or capricious | Denied petition for review |
| *California Department of Water Res v FERC*, 489 F3d 1029 (9th Cir 2007) | Ratemaking | Arbitrary or capricious | Denied petition for review |
| *Petal Gas Storage, LLC v FERC*, 496 F3d 695 (DC Cir 2007) | Ratemaking | Arbitrary or capricious | Denied petition for review |

**Table 5.2** Continued

| Case Name | Nature of Decision Appealed | Ground of Review | Outcome/ Remedy |
|---|---|---|---|
| *North Baja Pipeline, LLC v FERC*, 483 F3d 819 (DC Cir 2007) | Rate filling | Arbitrary or capricious | Denied petition for review |
| *NSTAR Elec & Gas Corp v FERC*, 481 F3d 794 (DC Cir 2007) | Tariff filing | Arbitrary or capricious | Remanded |
| *Keyspan-Ravenswood, LLC v FERC*, 474 F3d 804 (DC Cir 2007) | Tariff filing | Arbitrary or capricious | Remanded |
| *Gas Transmission Nw Corp v FERC*, 504 F3d 1318 (DC Cir 2007) | Tariff filing | Arbitrary or capricious | Denied petition for review |
| *Colorado Office of Consumer Counsel v FERC*, 490 F3d 954 (DC Cir 2007) | Market-based rates | Arbitrary or capricious | Denied petition for review |
| *Public Service Electric and Gas Co v FERC*, 485 F3d 1164 (DC Cir 2007) | Tariff interpretation | Statutory interpretation/ Chevron | Denied petition for review |
| *National Fuel Gas Supply Corporation v FERC*, 468 F3d 831 (DC Cir 2006) | Pipelines regulation | Arbitrary or capricious | Vacated and remanded |
| *Pub Serv Comm'n of Ky v FERC*, 397 F3d 1004 (DC Cir 2005) | Ratemaking | Arbitrary or capricious | Reversed and remanded |
| *Edison Mission Energy, Inc v FERC*, 394 F3d 964 (DC Cir 2005) | Ratemaking | Arbitrary or capricious | Reversed and remanded |
| *FPL Energy Marcus Hook, L.P. v FERC*, 430 F3d 441, 448 (DC Cir 2005) | Ratemaking | Arbitrary or capricious | Vacated and remanded |
| *Southern California Edison Co v FERC*, 415 F3d 17 (DC Cir 2005) | Ratemaking | Arbitrary or capricious | Vacated and remanded |
| *Tenn Gas Pipeline Co v FERC*, 400 F3d 23 (DC Cir 2005) | Ratemaking/tariffs | Arbitrary or capricious | Denied petition for review |
| *The Industrials v FERC*, 426 F3d 405 (DC Cir 2005) | Ratemaking/tariffs | Arbitrary or capricious | Denied petition for review |
| *Am. Gas Ass'n v FERC*, 428 F3d 255 (DC Cir 2005) | Ratemaking/tariffs | Arbitrary or capricious | Denied petition for review |
| *ExxonMobil v FERC*, 430 F3d 1166 (DC Cir 2005) | Ratemaking/tariffs | Arbitrary or capricious | Denied petition for review |

*(continued)*

**Table 5.2** Continued

| Case Name | Nature of Decision Appealed | Ground of Review | Outcome/ Remedy |
|---|---|---|---|
| *Mich Pub Power Agency v FERC*, 405 F3d 8 (DC Cir 2005) | Ratemaking | Arbitrary or capricious | Remanded |
| *Midwest ISO Transmission Owners v FERC*, 373 F3d 1361 (DC Cir 2004) | Ratemaking | Arbitrary or capricious | Denied petition for review |
| *ChevronTexaco Exploration&Production Co v FERC* 87 F3d 892 (DC Cir 2004) | Ratemaking | Arbitrary or capricious | Denied petition for review |
| *Fla Mun Power Agency v FERC*, 315 F3d 362 (DC Cir 2003) | Ratemaking/pricing credits | Arbitrary or capricious | Denied petition for review |
| *Sithe New England Holdings, LLC v FERC*, 308 F3d 71 (1st Cir 2002) | Ratemaking | Arbitrary or capricious | Denied petition for review |
| *Pacific Gas & Elec Co v FERC*, 306 F3d 1112 (DC Cir 2002) | Ratemaking | Arbitrary or capricious | Remanded |
| *Sithe/Independence Power Partners v FERC*, 285 F3d 1 (DC Cir 2002) | Ratemaking | Arbitrary or capricious | Granted in part/remanded in part |
| *Association of Oil Pipelines v FERC*, 281 F3d 239 (DC Cir 2002) | Ratemaking | Arbitrary or capricious | Denied petition for review |
| *Canadian Ass'n of Petroleum Producers v FERC*, 308 F3d I 1 (DC Cir 2002) | Ratemaking | Arbitrary or capricious | Reversed and remanded in part |
| *Process Gas Consumers Group v FERC*, 292 F3d 831 (DC Cir 2002) | Ratemaking | Arbitrary or capricious | Denied petition for review |
| *Alliant Energy Corp v FERC*, 253 F3d 748 (DC Cir 2001) | Ratemaking | Arbitrary or capricious | Denied petition for review |
| *Central Maine Power Co v FERC*, 252 F3d 34 (1st Cir 2001) | Ratemaking | Arbitrary or capricious | Remanded |
| *Public Utils. Comm'n of Cal. v FERC*, 254 F3d 250 (DC Cir 2001) | Ratemaking | Arbitrary or capricious | Denied petition for review |
| *Canadian Ass'n of Petroleum Producers v FERC*, 254 F3d 289 (DC Cir 2001) | Ratemaking | Arbitrary or capricious | Remanded |

**Table 5.2** Continued

| Case Name | Nature of Decision Appealed | Ground of Review | Outcome/ Remedy |
|---|---|---|---|
| *Missouri Pub Serv Comm'n v FERC*, 215 F3d I (DC Cir 2000) | Ratemaking | Arbitrary or capricious | Vacated and remanded in part |
| *Missouri Pub Serv Comm'n v FERC*, 234 F3d 36 (DC Cir 2000) | Ratemaking | Arbitrary or capricious | Remanded |
| *Transmission Access Policy Group v FERC*, 225 F3d 667 (DC Cir 2000) | Market design/ratemaking | Arbitrary or capricious | Remanded in part |
| *Exxon Corp v FERC*, 206 F3d 47 (DC Cir 2000) | Ratemaking | Arbitrary or capricious | Reversed and remanded |
| *Western Mass Elec Co v FERC*, 165 F3d 922 (DC Cir 1999) | Ratemaking | Arbitrary or capricious | Denied petition for review |
| *Sithe/Independence Power Partners, LP v FERC*, 165 F3d 944 (DC Cir 1999) | Ratemaking | Arbitrary or capricious | Remanded |
| *Louisiana Pub Serv Comm'n v FERC*, 184 F3d 892 (DC Cir 1999) | Ratemaking | Arbitrary or capricious | Remanded |
| *Louisiana Energy & Power Auth v FERC*, 141 F3d 364 (DC Cir 1998) | Market-based rates | Arbitrary or capricious | Denied petition for review |
| *Northern Border Pipeline Co v FERC*, 129 F3d 1315 (DC Cir 1997) | Ratemaking | Arbitrary or capricious | Denied petition for review |
| *Association of Oil Pipe Lines v FERC*, 83 F3d 1424 (DC Cir 1996) | Ratemaking | Arbitrary or capricious | Denied petition for review |
| *Texas Eastern Transmission Corp v FERC*, 102 F3d 174 (5th Cir 1996) | Ratemaking | Arbitrary or capricious | Denied petition for review |
| *Transcontinental Gas Pipe Line Corp v FERC*, 54 F3d 893 (DC Cir 1995) | Ratemaking | Arbitrary or capricious | Reversed and remanded |
| *ANR Pipeline Co v FERC*, 71 F3d 897 (DC Cir 1995) | Ratemaking | Arbitrary or capricious | Reversed |
| *OXY USA, Inc v FERC*, 64 F3d 679 (DC Cir 1995) | Ratemaking | Arbitrary or capricious | Remanded in part |

(*continued*)

**Table 5.2** Continued

| Case Name | Nature of Decision Appealed | Ground of Review | Outcome/ Remedy |
|---|---|---|---|
| *City of New Orleans v FERC*, 67 F3d 947 (DC Cir 1995) | Ratemaking | Arbitrary or capricious | Denied petition for review |
| *Cajun Electric Power Coop, Inc v FERC*, 28 F3d 173 (DC Cir 1994) | Ratemaking | Arbitrary or capricious | Remanded |
| *Town of Norwood v FERC*, 962 F2d 20 (DC Cir 1992) | Rate-design/marginal cost pricing | Arbitrary or capricious | Denied petition for review |
| *Southwestern Public Service Co v FERC*, 952 F2d 555 (DC. Cir 1992) | Changes in estimated costs | Arbitrary or capricious | Remanded |
| *Tennessee Gas Pipeline Co v FERC*, 926 F2d 1206 (DC Cir 1991) | Ratemaking | Arbitrary or capricious | Remanded |
| *American Gas Ass'n v FERC*, 912 F2d 1496 (DC Cir 1990) | Ratemaking | Arbitrary or capricious | Remanded in part |
| *Duquesne Light Co v Barasch*, 488 US 299 (1989) | Ratemaking | Arbitrary or capricious | Affirmed |
| *Wisconsin Gas Co v FERC*, 770 F2d 1144 (DC Cir 1985) | Ratemaking | Arbitrary or capricious | Remanded |
| *Associated Gas Distributors v FERC*, 824 F2d 981 (DC Cir 1987) | Ratemaking | Arbitrary or capricious | Remanded in part |

# 6

# The Institutional Response

## Judicial Scrutiny of Economic Evidence at the UK Competition Appeal Tribunal

### 6.1 Introduction

While the US reaction to the challenges posed by economic evidence was a product of inadvertence, the UK's response represents a choice of institutional design. Legislative developments followed two parallel routes. On the one hand, the introduction of statutory appeals led to the marginalisation of judicial review as a primary means to challenge the regulatory agencies' decisions. On the other hand, the establishment of the specialist CAT largely replaced the High Court as the primary venue for hearing such challenges. Of course, as highlighted in Chapter 3, the specialist Tribunal was primarily set up as a competition tribunal, with the regulatory functions added because of its expertise and specialised knowledge. But still, these developments, taken together, signal a self-conscious repudiation of judicial review, as performed by the generalist High Court during the early days of the British regulatory state, in the realm of utility regulation.

How do these important developments affect the scrutiny of economic evidence? What is the impact of a specialist court on the intensity of review of economic evidence? What room is there for deference to agency's economic expertise when expert regulatory agencies' decisions are being reviewed by a tribunal that enjoys epistemic competence in regulatory matters? In other words, what are the limits of judicial scrutiny of economic evidence in a specialist adjudicative setting?

To address this question, we ought to consider the broader institutional environment in which the Tribunal is embedded. This would entail a thorough examination of the interplay of the following two situations: the 'specialist/specialist situation', which refers to the interactions between the expert CAT and the expert regulators and the 'generalist/specialist situation', which refers to the interactions between the generalist Court of Appeal (and the UK Supreme Court) and the specialist CAT. The former model of specialists reviewing specialists often assumes a more intensive substantive review, while the latter paradigm akin to that of conventional judicial review seems to focus on procedural aspects of agency decision-making. However, a closer look at the CAT's workings suggests that the story is far more complicated than what this paradigmatic scheme might suggest. It will be made apparent throughout the chapter that the *tripartite* relationship between the expert regulators, the specialist CAT, and the generalist Court of Appeal gives rise to a varying intensity of review better understood as a continuum. On one end of the continuum lie judgments over the review of agencies' interpretive discretion[1] where the Tribunal exercises its self-proclaimed

[1] For the distinction between interpretive and operational discretion, see Chapter 4.

*Courts, Regulators, and the Scrutiny of Economic Evidence.* Despoina Mantzari, Oxford University Press.
 DOI: 10.1093/oso/9780198851608.003.0006

'profound and rigorous'[2] scrutiny. To the above, one should also add the substantive decisions that involve rights and liabilities of the parties, such as in cases involving the liability for competition law infringements under the concurrency regime. On the other end of the continuum lie multifaceted policy considerations, which depend on inferences drawn from the evidence, and polycentric decisions. In such cases the CAT is prepared to afford a significant margin of appreciation to the discretionary assessments of utility regulators predicated upon institutional competence considerations and larger systemic considerations. This is crucial, as it demonstrates that there are limits to the pursuit of 'correctness' even in the context of a specialist adjudicative body. These limits are exposed in the 'generalist/specialist' interaction: While the generalist Court of Appeal, has acknowledged the specialist expertise of the CAT and the need for some restraint on its part when reviewing its decisions, nonetheless it has not hesitated to 'discipline' the CAT when the latter overreaches into the expert agencies' arena of discretion in multifaceted and polycentric regulatory decisions. Crucially, CAT's specialist expertise has also been acknowledged by the Supreme Court which has, on one occasion, 'disciplined' the Court of Appeal for not upholding the 'careful analysis' of the expert Tribunal.[3]

Section 2 briefly ventures into the evolution of the role of the UK courts in utility regulation. Section 3 discusses the specialist/specialist interaction. Section 4 discusses the determinants of judicial scrutiny of economic evidence as emanating from the interplay generalist/specialist situations. Section 5 concludes.

## 6.2 The Evolution of the Role of the Courts in Utility Regulation

To appreciate the distinct contribution of the specialist CAT in the realm of utility regulation, one should first briefly venture into the evolution of the role of the courts in the realm of utility regulation, as the latter has been shaped by the distinction between judicial review, which, in principle, focuses on formal matters and the validity of the administrative decision, and appeal, which focuses on the merits of the decision and is therefore also described as 'merits review'.[4]

The early case law, following the privatisation of utilities, suggests that a low intensity rationality review applied to the regulators' discretionary assessments, which was informed by constitutional considerations as well as by the apparent incapacity of the courts to deal with the complexity of economic appraisals. Consonant with a formalist conception of judicial review,[5] the fundamental mission of the courts was to carry out the legislative will by policing the boundaries set in the enabling statute. The

[2] See *Hutchison 3G UK Ltd v OFCOM* [2008] CAT 11 [164]; *Vodafone Ltd v OFCOM* [2008] CAT 22 [46]; and *TalkTalk Telecom Group Plc v OFCOM* [2012] CAT 1 [71].

[3] *British Telecommunications plc v Telefónica O2 UK Ltd and others* [2014] UKSC 42 [51].

[4] Paul Craig, *Administrative Law* (7th edn., OUP 2012) 6–7; Peter Cane, 'Judicial Review and Merits Review: Comparing Administrative Adjudication by Courts and Tribunals' in Susan Rose-Ackerman and Peter Lindseth (eds), *Comparative Administrative Law* (Edward Elgar 2010) 433–34.

[5] Michael Taggart, 'Reinventing Administrative Law' in Nicholas Bamforth and Peter Leyland (eds), *Public Law in a Multi-Layered Constitution* (Hart 2003) 312–13.

doctrine of *ultra vires* allowed the courts to keep the exercise of administrative powers within these statutory limits. Review of the substance of administrative action would apply only in cases where the demanding threshold of *Wednesbury* 'unreasonableness' was met.[6] Under this test of review courts could set aside the conclusion reached by a public authority entrusted by Parliament with discretion on a matter if this decision was wholly absurd, that is a '... decision which is so outrageous in its defiance of logic or of accepted moral standards that no sensible person who had his mind to the question to be decided could have arrived at it'.[7] It was thought that limiting substantive review in this way would prevent courts from entering into a constitutionally forbidden territory.

The deferential posture was further justified by the regulator's specialised knowledge and expertise in regulatory matters.[8] Thus, in the *Cellcom*[9] case concerning licence modifications in telecoms, Lightman J strongly suggested that:

> Where the Act has conferred the decision-making function on the Director, it is for him, and him alone, to consider the economic arguments, weigh the compelling considerations and arrive at a judgment ... If (as I have stated) the court should be very slow to impugn decisions of fact made by an expert body and experienced decision-maker, it must surely be even slower to impugn his educated prophesies and predictions for the future.[10]

The judicial reluctance extended to the regulator's findings of fact, which formed the basis of its discretionary judgement. In a number of cases, English courts have held that the existence or non-existence of fact should be left to the judgement or discretion of the decision-maker.[11] Furthermore, the absence of a proportionality test for substantive review that would require the courts 'to assess the balance the decision-maker has struck'[12] paying attention to the 'relative weight of interests and considerations'[13] subjected the regulatory agencies' decisions only to the 'monolithic' *Wednesbury* test of extreme unreasonableness, a test that is very difficult for the claimant to satisfy.[14] The economic evidence enshrined into regulatory decisions was largely immune from judicial scrutiny giving rise to a controversy over limited regulatory accountability. The judicially created boundaries of 'no-go' areas of review allowed regulators to operate largely unchecked; rarely did they state reasons or provide clear criteria for their decisions.[15]

[6] *Associated Provincial Picture Houses Ltd v Wednesbury Corporation* [1948] 1 KB 223 at 234.

[7] *Council of Civil Service Unions (CCSU) v Minister for the Civil Service* [1985] AC 374.

[8] *R (London and Continental Stations and Property Ltd) v The Rail Regulator* [2003] EWHC 2607 (Admin); *R v Independent Television Commission (ITC), ex p TSW Broadcasting Ltd* [1996] EMLR 291, HL.

[9] *R v Director General of Telecommunications, ex p Cellcom Ltd and others case* [1999] ECC 314 [29].

[10] ibid [26].

[11] *R v Independent Television Commission (ITC), ex p Virgin Television Ltd* [1996] EMLR 31.

[12] *R (Daly) v Secretary of State for the Home Department* [2001] UKHL 26 [2001] 2 AC 5.

[13] ibid.

[14] *R v Trade and Industry Secretary, ex p Lonrho plc* [1989] 2 All ER 609, [1989] 1 WLR 525 [1989] BCC 63; *Cityhook Ltd and another, R (on the application of) v Office of Fair Trading and others* [2009] EWHC (Admin) 57 [136] and [165].

[15] Cento Veljanovski, 'The Regulation Game' in Cento Veljanovski (ed), *Regulators and the Market* (The Institute of Economic Affairs 1991) 17.

The force, however, of low intensity rationality review seems to have dwindled in recent years, especially in light of constitutional and jurisprudential developments that have allowed a more demanding judicial scrutiny than traditional *Wednesbury* review. Such developments are better captured in the notion of a 'multi-streamed jurisdiction',[16] a term employed to denote that judicial review now encompasses not only common law principles, but also relevant applications of retained EU law and of the European Convention on Human Rights (ECHR).[17] Hence, claimants wishing to challenge the regulators' economic assessments can demand a more stringent review of agencies' discretion based, *inter alia*, on the 'European' proportionality head of review.[18] *BT v OFCOM*[19] is a case in point. The claimants argued that judicial review of the CMA's price control determinations under s 193(7) of the Communications Act should encompass a 'European' proportionality head of review, which would be more stringent than the 'English' standard of review. The CAT, however, refused to do so in 'the absence of an authoritative statement made that as a general proposition, English law has adopted proportionality as an independent ground of review'.[20] Similarly, in the *T-Mobile*[21] case the general principle of EU law relating to effective judicial protection was successfully invoked by OFCOM in litigation concerning auction of spectrum licences. The incumbents tried to substitute judicial review proceedings before the High Court with the lengthier proceedings before the CAT, relying on the requirement of the Framework Directive for electronic communications for an 'effective appeals mechanism'.[22] The Court of Appeal stressed the obligation on a national court 'to adapt its procedures as far as possible to ensure Community rights are protected'[23] and ruled that the High Court could also adapt its procedure to ensure a variable intensity of review.[24]

As Paul Craig has suggested, all the different tests for substantive review entail some consideration of the merits[25] and can be placed along a spectrum with classic *Wednesbury* review at the one end and judicial substitution of judgement on a correctness standard at the opposite end;[26] although the distinction from merits review has been reiterated on multiple occasions. Despite these recent developments, the default position of regulatory review under conventional judicial review is captured well in the image of a long-lived harmonious relationship between the judges and the regulatory

[16] Richard Rawlings, 'Modeling Judicial Review' (2008) 61 Curr Leg Probl 95, 96.
[17] See the discussion in Chapter 3, section 3.3.4.
[18] See *R (On the Application of Lumsdon and Others) v Legal Services Board* [2015] UKSC 41.
[19] *BT v OFCOM* [2012] CAT 11.
[20] ibid [128].
[21] *T-Mobile (UK) Ltd v Office of Communications* [2008] EWCA Civ 1373.
[22] ibid. The principle of effective judicial protection is elaborated in Case C-432/05, *Unibet v Justitiekanslem* [2007] ECR I-2271.
[23] ibid [22].
[24] ibid [23].
[25] In both judicial review and appellate review, the merits of the decision can be taken into account. To this effect, see *Wilkinson v Broadmoor Special Authority* [2002] 1 WLR 419 ('there can be, if necessary, a full merits investigation on a JR application') and *R (JB) v Haddock* [2006] EWCA Civ 961. See also Carnwath J opinion in *E v Secretary of State for the Home Department* [2004] EWCA Civ 49; [2004] 2 WLR 1351 [42] and [50].
[26] Craig (n 4) 643.

agencies predicated upon a division of labour: the judges would focus on the process of regulatory decision-making, whereas the agencies would focus on the substance thereof. The advent of the specialist CAT, enjoying both statutory appeal and statutory review jurisdiction, as well as subject-matter and professional background specialisation, disrupted this well entrenched division of labour between courts and agencies in the realm of utility regulation.

## 6.3 The Specialist/Specialist Situation: The CAT–Regulators Interactions

The section will discuss the CAT's 'profound and rigorous' scrutiny of economic evidence in two key areas emanating from the case law: (a) review of OFCOM's interpretive discretion; and (b) liability for competition law infringements under the concurrency regime. Table 6.1 includes a review of all relevant appeals from OFCOM between 1998 and November 2021. It is useful to pause here for a second and remind ourselves of the Tribunal's institutional features that allow the exercise of such a heightened review.[27] These include its membership and composition, its limited jurisdiction over regulatory and competition law disputes, and the judges' perception of their role. To these features one should also add the CAT's dual (appellate and review) jurisdiction over regulatory disputes and its procedural rules.

Notwithstanding the expansion of the English courts' supervisory jurisdiction, the CAT's dual jurisdiction allows it to exercise a higher degree of scrutiny over the merits of the decision than would normally be appropriate in judicial review proceedings. In fact, the CAT's statutorily defined merits review allows the Tribunal to review any error of law, fact, and discretion.[28] In competition cases, in particular, whether brought by the CMA or a regulator, the quasi-criminal aspect makes the possibility of a full merits appeal with examination of the evidence necessary, as reflected in Article 6 of the Human Rights Act. This however does not apply to reviews of CMA market and merger decisions, and (now) not to purely telecoms regulatory appeals either. The reader should be reminded here that the position has changed for Communications Act cases since the enactment of the Digital Economy Act 2017, which has substituted merits review for judicial review, albeit still subject to the retained Framework Directive.[29] Only three cases have been decided so far under the revised standard. We shall consider these in section 6.4.

The Tribunal has interpreted the reference to an appeal 'on the merits' to mean that it has 'full jurisdiction to find facts, make its own appraisals of economic issues, apply the law to those facts and appraisals, and determine the amount of any penalty'.[30] The scope of the CAT's appeal jurisdiction is limited, however, to the Grounds of Appeal. The following passage illustrates the expansive terms in which the CAT

[27] See Chapter 3, section 3.3.1.3.
[28] See Competition Act 1998, Schedule 8.
[29] See Chapter 3, section 3.3.2.1.3.
[30] *Freeserve v DGT* [2003] CAT 5 [107].

has expressed its approach to its appellate jurisdiction vis-à-vis the CMA and sector-specific regulators:

> It is in our view inevitable that matters will often be gone into in more detail on appeal than was possible at the administrative stage, particularly since at that stage the OFT [now CMA] has no power to compel witnesses or to cross-examine. As a matter of general approach, we do not think we should seek artificially to limit or inhibit a deeper development of the case at the appeal stage, always provided that the basic procedural framework, and the overriding principle of fairness, are respected.[31]

However, in considering whether the regulator's decision on a specific issue is wrong, the Court of Appeal has emphasised institutional competence and institutional legitimacy considerations that should guide the intensity of review:

> ... the Tribunal should consider the decision carefully and attach due weight to it, and to the reasons underlying it. This follows not least from the fact that this is an appeal from an administrative decision not a de novo rehearing on the matter, and from the fact that Parliament has chosen to place responsibility for making the decision on Ofcom.[32]

Its remedial powers are also very wide. The CAT may not only remit a decision to the CMA or to a sectoral regulator but may also take any decision these bodies could themselves have taken. Finally, although the CAT is first and foremost an appellate tribunal and not the primary fact-finder, the information record is enhanced through its discretion to permit oral cross-examination of witnesses, especially when the primary facts are in dispute.[33]

After a brief consideration of the CAT's institutional features, we can turn now to examine the Tribunal's rigorous scrutiny of OFCOM's interpretive discretion. It should be noted that the cases discussed below were decided before the change in the standard of review brought about by the Digital Economy Act 2017. But, as will be shown later in the chapter the impact of the revised standard of review has been 'minimal',[34] primarily because of the CAT's procedural rules regarding the cross-examination of witnesses that still allow the Tribunal to exercise a rigorous assessment of the economic evidence underpinning the dispute in question.

[31] *Aberdeen Journals Ltd v DGFT* [2002] CAT 4 [61].

[32] *BskyB v OFCOM* [2012] CAT 20 [84], endorsed by the Court of Appeal in *BT v OFCOM* [2014] EWCA Civ 133 [88].

[33] See Competition Appeal Tribunal, Guide to Proceedings (2015), section 3.5. See also *Hutchison 3G* (n 2): 'None of these witnesses was cross-examined and accordingly their evidence was unchallenged so far as it related to primary factual matters' ([56]); *BT v OFCOM* (PPC) [2011] CAT 5 (PPC case) [139]: 'What he omitted to say until he was cross-examined on the point by Ms Rose ... '; *BT (Termination Charges: 080 calls) v OFCOM* [2011] CAT 24 [84]: 'a number of BT witnesses were cross-examined on the meaning and scope of the NTS Call Origination Circuit ... '; *TalkTalk* case (n 2): '... Talk Talk indicated that it wished to cross-examine Mr Clarkson on a discrete and short point, and Mr Clarkson was duly called as a witness and cross-examined'.

[34] *TalkTalk and Vodafone v OFCOM* [2020] CAT 8 [134].

### 6.3.1 Review of OFCOM's Interpretive Discretion

You may recall from Chapter 4 that much of statutory interpretation is done, at least in the first instance, by regulatory agencies. This is because the legislature allows such an expansive role for regulators by drafting vague statutory language. In turn, regulators enjoy a large degree of interpretive freedom and discretion that is not only observed internally but is also externally recognised by the courts. Moreover, because the judicial interpretation of economic concepts cannot be meaningfully achieved by recourse to the traditional tools of statutory construction, but often requires an economically oriented interpretation, courts are prepared to defer to agencies' interpretation of their governing statutes. However, unlike the US courts, who under the *Chevron* doctrine consistently defer to agencies' reasonable interpretation of economically informed concepts, the expert CAT exercises a rigorous review thereof, constraining to a considerable degree OFCOM's interpretive discretion. This is particularly evident in the early set of cases reaching the Tribunal.

A telling example that illustrates our point comes from the Tribunal's assessment of OFCOM's dispute resolution jurisdiction. Enshrined in Article 20 of the 'Framework' Directive 2002/21/EC and Article 5 of the 'Access' Directive 2002/19/EC, the dispute resolution has been described as a 'third regulatory restraint':[35] another piece, together with *ex post* competition law and *ex ante* regulation of undertakings with SMP, of the telecommunications regulation puzzle. But, unlike the *ex ante* remedies that flow from a finding of SMP, and though disputes may arise within the framework of *ex ante* remedies, dispute resolution does not require such a finding of SMP.[36] Such disputes arise in the context of an overall expectation that operators should negotiate in good faith to provide interconnection so that customers benefit from end-to-end connectivity. Thus, at the core of the dispute resolution lies the interpretation of the so called 'end-to-end connectivity obligation'. The test applied is whether interconnection terms are 'fair and reasonable' in the sense of 'appropriate having regard to the regulatory objectives'.[37] In such cases, the CAT has scrutinised in great detail OFCOM's operationalisation of the 'fair and reasonable' test, overturning in half of the cases the expert regulator's analytical framework. This is despite the Tribunal endorsing Jacob LJ's pronouncement in the *T-Mobile*,[38] case that the function of the Tribunal is not to act as 'a fully equipped duplicate regulatory body waiting in the wings just for appeals', and also that it may be very difficult for it to interfere 'if all that is impugned is an overall value judgment based upon competing commercial considerations in the context of a public policy decision'.[39]

[35] *T-Mobile (UK) Ltd, British Telecommunications plc, Hutchison 3G UK Ltd, Cable & Wireless UK and others v OFCOM* [2008] CAT 12 (*T Mobile* case) [83]–[84].

[36] A point the CAT made clear in *Hutchison 3G v OFCOM* [2005] CAT 39 [129]–[130].

[37] *T-Mobile* case (n 35).

[38] See *T-Mobile* (n 21) [31].

[39] ibid. See also *Telefónica UK Ltd v OFCOM* [2012] CAT 28; *Telefónica O2 UK Ltd v BT* (the 08 Numbers case) [2012] EWCA Civ 1002.

For instance, in the *08x numbers* saga,[40] which concerned a dispute between BT, as a fixed network operator, and four principal mobile network operators (MNOs) about the charges payable by them to BT in respect of the termination on BT's network of calls to 08x numbers, the Tribunal conducted a detailed analysis of the evidence, and a wide-ranging assessment of OFCOM's role and in the end overturned the Tribunal's judgment. The Supreme Court, the sole judgment of Lord Sumption being endorsed by all other members of the Court, upheld the 'careful analysis' of the CAT and overturned the decision of the Court of Appeal,[41] which had previously reversed the CAT's decision.[42] It shouldn't come as a surprise that specialised adjudicative expertise attracts deference, as it combines the benefits of legal accountability with the professional expertise of its lay members. In the seminal decision *Everything Everywhere Ltd v Competition Commission and others*,[43] the Court of Appeal went as far as to argue that the assessments of the expert CAT carry a presumption of correctness:

> If that context and all those factors are given their due weight, the caution which Baroness Hale and others have urged should be taken in any appeal from or judicial review of the decisions of expert tribunals, or in granting permission to appeal, needs to be underlined and underlined in red. Where a tribunal has particular expertise in a highly specialised area of law it is 'quite probable' that that tribunal will have got it right. A reviewing court, amongst which can be counted the expert Competition Appeal Tribunal, should not be astute to find an error of law (Cooke v Secretary of State for Social Security [2002] 3 All ER 279, paras 15-17, AH (Sudan) v Secretary of State for the Home Department [2008] 1 AC 678 para 30 and R (Cart) v Upper Tribunal(SC(E)) [2012] 1 AC 663 paras 49-50).[44]

To offer a bit of helpful context to the dispute, 08x numbers are non-geographic numbers, part of the Number Translation Services (NTS), which essentially allow non-geographic calls to be switched to geographic numbers hosted on the network of providers like BT. BT provided termination of these calls to the mobile operators on the terms of its Standard Interconnect Agreement. That contract permitted BT to vary the charges subject, in a reflection of the Framework Directive, to a determination by OFCOM in the event of dispute. MNOs charged significantly more for all these numbers when calls are originated on a mobile telephone earning attractive margins. Hence, in 2009 BT decided that it would like to share in those attractive margins by devising termination rates that varied in accordance with the rates charged to their customers by the mobile operators, the so-called 'ladder pricing'. This ladder pricing

[40] *T-Mobile* case (n 35) [main subject] reported at [2011] CAT 24, 4 reported at [2012] EWCA Civ 1051; *British Telecommunications plc v Telefónica O2 UK Ltd and others* [2014] UKSC 42. There had been two determinations covering, in all, seven disputes; the appellants were BT, T-Mobile, Hutchison 3G UK, and a group of fixed network operators led by Cable & Wireless. Those cases led to a preliminary judgment on what were called the core issues, [2008] CAT 12.

[41] See [2012] EWCA Civ 1051.

[42] See [2014] UKSC 42 (n 3).

[43] [2013] EWCA Civ 154 (*EE*).

[44] ibid [38].

was somewhat 'novel'.[45] It essentially meant that the more that the MNOs charged their customers for calls to 08x numbers, the more BT charged that MNO for actually terminating the call on the MNO's behalf to that 08x number. To avoid competition issues, the system was designed in a series of pricing stages (ladders) in order to ensure that competing MNOs would not know the precise price any other MNO was charging for the call. When BT notified the MNOs that it was introducing this ladder pricing, as BT was permitted so to do by the contract it had with the MNOs (ie the Standard Interconnect Agreement), each of the MNOs raised a dispute with OFCOM under s 185(1) of the Communications Act 2003 on the basis that the charges were not fair and reasonable.[46] BT's ability to introduce price changes for these services was not subject to any SMP regulation.

In resolving the dispute, OFCOM applied the test outlined in the *T-Mobile* case[47] to assess whether the changes were 'fair and reasonable'. In making this assessment, the regulator put forward an analytical framework, that is, the welfare test, consisting of three principles:[48] Principle 1 related to the ability of mobile operators to recover their efficient costs of originating calls. Principle 2 envisioned that new charges should provide benefits to consumers, considering the impact of the price change on retail call prices (the direct effect), the impact of the price changes on service providers offering NTS call services (the indirect effect) and the impact of the price changes on mobile tariffs overall (the mobile tariff package effect). Finally, Principle 3 envisioned that the implementation of new charges should be reasonably practicable. All three principles can be related to objectives set out in Article 8(2) of the 'Framework' Directive. These three principles were suggested to emanate from six principles of pricing and cost recovery, which OFCOM had previously employed.[49]

OFCOM reached different conclusions in the two different determinations, the 08040, and the 0845/0870 as to whether the principles were met. In the case of the 08040 Determination, OFCOM found that neither Principle 1 nor Principle 2 were satisfied, but that it should be possible to satisfy Principle 3. In the case of the 0845/0870 Determination, OFCOM found that although Principle 1 was satisfied, Principle 2 was not demonstrated and therefore not satisfied and Principle 3 was not satisfied.[50] In both cases, therefore, OFCOM found that BT had not justified its price changes and that they were therefore not fair and reasonable. In other words, what OFCOM

45 [2011] CAT 24 (n 33) [215].

46 See OFCOM, 'Determination to resolve a dispute between BT and each of Vodafone, T-Mobile, H3G, O2, Orange and Everything Everywhere about BT's termination charges for 0845 and 0870 calls', 10 August 2010 <https://www.ofcom.org.uk/__data/assets/pdf_file/0026/82961/final_determination.pdf> accessed 6 June 2022.
and 'Dispute between BT and each of Vodafone, T-Mobile, 02 and Orange, about BT's termination charges for 080 calls', 19 April 2010 https://www.ofcom.org.uk/about-ofcom/latest/bulletins/competition-bulletins/all-closed-cases/cw_01036 accessed 6 June 2022.

47 *T-Mobile* case (n 35).

48 The principles were articulated differently in the 080 determination and the 0870 determination, but the generic approach described in this paragraph identifies the key aspects of the three principles.

49 See [2011] CAT 24 (n 33) [161].

50 See OFCOM, 'Determination to Resolve a Dispute between BT and each of Vodafone, T-Mobile, H3G, 02, Orange and EE about BT's termination charges for 0845 and 0870 calls', final determination (n 46) at para 1.18.

decided was that although the direct and indirect effect of BT's proposed changes could be expected to result in lower prices for consumers, BT should not be allowed to make the changes because it was not possible to forecast how far mobile network operators would be able to compensate themselves by increasing other charges.

OFCOM and the Tribunal agreed that the welfare test was inconclusive and the difference in the consequence flowed from a difference in how uncertainty should be handled in such cases. Each approach has risks. On the one hand one can prevent change that might turn out to be beneficial to consumers, on the other hand one can allow change that might disbenefit consumers. The Tribunal conducted a detailed analysis of the evidence, and a wide-ranging assessment of OFCOM's role. In doing so, it relied heavily on the provision of external economic expertise, that is, economists acting as expert witnesses or witnesses of fact. All eleven witnesses provided their evidence in the form of witness statements or expert reports. In total, some forty-nine witness statements and expert reports were adduced in evidence. The conclusions about this evidence were dealt with at various stages throughout the judgment of the Tribunal. For the most part, expert economists relied on economic theory alone, which was not accompanied by supporting data. Some of the models were based upon assumptions, which may or may not hold good in the 'real world' and which could not be proved or disproved because of the absence of empirical evidence.[51]

In respect to Principle 2, the CAT considered eleven 'potentially relevant factors'.[52] It dealt with other factors in some considerable depth, for example the precise magnitude of the direct effect, which it held could not be ascertained,[53] and the precise nature of the 'waterbed effect', the size of which it was again held could not be ascertained.[54] The CAT essentially agreed with OFCOM's analysis save in respect of three specific issues:[55] (i) BT's rights to change the agreement, (ii) the regulatory obligations and duties on the parties; and (iii) the effect on competition.[56]

The fact that OFCOM found the whole of the 'welfare assessment' to have been inconclusive should not have prevented the pricing change introduced by BT in light of BT's private law rights and the finding that disallowing the price change might act as a fetter on competition. What the Tribunal recognised was that an undue fetter on commercial freedom is itself a disbenefit to consumers. Based on this the CAT found that all the factors in the case, when properly assessed, led to the opposite conclusion to that which OFCOM had reached and the CAT reversed OFCOM's determinations allowing BT's appeal.

The judgment is an important one for the following two reasons. First, it demonstrates that even in the specific adjudicative *topos* of a specialist Tribunal, there are limits to the import of economics in the adjudicative process. When assessing the body of economic evidence presented before it, the CAT adopted the 'as if' mode of reasoning, discussed in Chapter 2, deferring to the expert economists' assessments

[51] See, eg the discussion on Professor Dobbs' model [2011] CAT 24 (n 33) [297]–[346].
[52] See [2011] CAT 24 (n 33) [198].
[53] ibid [344].
[54] ibid [364].
[55] ibid [418].
[56] ibid [444].

only if the latter were carefully and fully explained. The CAT scrutinised the economic models employed, their underlying methodology, and how these work, and through a series of cross-examinations sought to ascertain why those models or methods were suited to the specific welfare analysis and how those methods or models supported particular conclusions drawn on the basis of the facts of the case:[57] why the suggested models were more appropriate than the competing models, why they were more consistent with the facts of the case or economic literature and so on. Secondly, the judgment reflects upon the limits of expert economic knowledge in certain areas, as reflected in the discussion of the 'waterbed effect'; something that was impossible for both OFCOM and the expert witnesses to quantify.[58]

In the related *T-Mobile* case,[59] the Tribunal scrutinised OFCOM's interpretation of its statutory mandate when determining disputes and found that OFCOM had made a number of errors of law. First, the Tribunal found that OFCOM failed to properly exercise its powers for determining disputes. OFCOM should approach its dispute resolution having regard to all its statutory obligations and not focus unduly on the existence of other regulatory constraints imposed on one or other of the parties to the dispute, such as BT's end-to-end connectivity obligation. The Tribunal noted that the regulator failed to recognise that dispute resolution is itself a third potential regulatory restraint that operates in addition to other *ex ante* obligations and *ex post* competition law. Secondly, the Tribunal also found that OFCOM erred in drawing too rigid a boundary between the exercise of its dispute resolution powers and its SMP-related powers. Thirdly, and most relevant to our purposes here, the Tribunal held that OFCOM was wrong to reject entirely a cost-based analysis when assessing whether the proposed prices were reasonable.

To explain this further, in interpreting its duty to ensure end-to-end connectivity OFCOM rejected setting 'a strictly cost based charge' as unnecessary and disproportionate to achieve the purpose of end-to-end connectivity obligation and secondly, because it was not appropriate as a matter of policy to use the dispute resolution process as a substitute for decisions already taken under the appropriate regulatory processes for addressing the question of SMP; hence drawing a strict boundary between *ex ante* regulation and dispute resolution. The Tribunal criticised this approach by saying that there is a middle ground between eschewing analysis of the relationship of price to cost completely on the one hand and a full investigation of the costs of the kind carried out as part of the SMP review on the other:

> The Tribunal does not accept that there is such a strict dichotomy. It should be possible to carry out some investigation of costs to form a broad idea of what that relationship is. Such an assessment may or may not give rise to a cost-based price'. It may simply result in Ofcom concluding that the price proposed is a reasonable one even though that price was not arrived at on a cost basis. The costs are not only relevant when setting a 'strictly cost based price' but are likely to be a factor to a greater or lesser extent in most cases where the dispute between the parties concerns price.[60]

[57] See Chapter 2, section 2.4.
[58] ibid [363]–[364].
[59] *T-Mobile* case (n 35).
[60] ibid [104].

At the heart of the dispute lay an economic assessment, that of the 'gains from trade' test, which meant determining whether BT would be making a profit (relative to incremental cost) when providing fixed to mobile calls to the MNO in question at the proposed disputed charges. If it could be shown that BT would be making a profit at the proposed disputed charges, then OFCOM considered that the charges should be upheld as reasonable. If, however, BT made no profit, or a loss, then it would appear that BT would derive no gains from trade with the MNO in question. In that situation, OFCOM would have to consider whether BT could pass through the increased charges to its customers and make a gain from trade from such higher prices. As well as applying the gains from trade test OFCOM considered whether there were any benchmarks against which it could measure the reasonableness of the proposed charges. Given that the charges of all five MNOs were in dispute it was not possible to compare the charges of one against the other.

The CAT criticised the methodology on several grounds. First, the Tribunal criticised the complete lack of cost analysis. Second, it criticised OFCOM's methodology for assessing the reasonableness on the basis that the regulator did not take into account the information available from its extensive review of mobile call termination charges and to ignore what it concluded were the appropriate process as a result of that review was a serious error approach.[61] The Tribunal also held that OFCOM had placed too much weight on the need for consistency and erred in relying on the conclusions in its statement dated 1 June 2004 on Wholesale Mobile Call Termination without properly weighing the factors, which the appellants argued meant that these conclusions were no longer valid.[62]

Crucially, not only did the Tribunal provide guidance on how OFCOM should approach the task of resolving disputes in future, but also interpreted itself the concept of reasonableness laying down the test to be applied:

> That test can be expressed as requiring Ofcom to determine what are reasonable terms and conditions as between the parties. The word 'reasonable' in this context means two things. First it requires a fair balance to be struck between the interests of the parties to the connectivity agreement. It therefore requires the same kind of adjudication that any arbitrator appointed by the parties to determine a dispute about the reasonable rate would carry out. But secondly, because Ofcom is a regulator bound by its statutory duties and the Community requirements it also means reasonable for the purposes of ensuring that those objectives and requirements are achieved. Ofcom did not approach resolving these disputes on this basis and it therefore committed an error of law.[63]

In doing so, the Tribunal significantly constrained OFCOM's interpretive discretion. It held that OFCOM's interpretation of the purpose of the end-to-end connectivity obligation was too narrow. The purpose of that obligation was not just to achieve

[61] ibid [150].
[62] ibid [99].
[63] ibid [101].

interconnection, but to do so in a manner which promotes, or at least is not inconsistent with, other regulatory objectives:

> In any event we do not consider that it is right to interpret the use of the term 'reasonable' as it is used in the end-to-end connectivity obligation in such a narrow sense as to mean the highest price which could be charged which would still result in BT not making a loss. There is no reason to give the word anything other than its ordinary meaning; the price that it is fair should prevail as between the parties taking into account all the circumstances including in particular the arguments put forward in the dispute by the parties, Ofcom's statutory duties and the Community requirements set out in the 2003 Act.[64]

Similarly, in the *Ethernet Determinations*[65] case, the CAT also scrutinised in detail the cost-orientation requirement laying down its own approach. This case is distinguishable from the *T-Mobile* case in that there had been a finding of SMP from which followed a requirement that prices be cost-oriented. The CAT delivered its judgment in five related appeals from OFCOM's Ethernet Determination of 20 December 2012.[66] The Determination itself resolved a number of regulatory disputes between BT, the provider of a particular subset of Ethernet services,[67] and various communications providers that purchase wholesale Ethernet services from it by (i) finding that BT had breached an SMP Condition requiring it to charge cost orientated prices for the relevant wholesale Ethernet services; and (ii) requiring BT to repay the resultant overcharge to its wholesale customers without interest.

Again, a bit of context is helpful in navigating these complex disputes. In its 2004 Leased Lines Market Review (LLMR),[68] OFCOM determined that BT held SMP on the market for wholesale AISBO services at all bandwidths in the UK (excluding the Kingston-upon-Hull area). The regulator reviewed that determination in the context of its 2008 Business Connectivity Market Review (BCMR)[69] and found that BT had SMP in the wholesale market for low bandwidth AISBO services in the United Kingdom excluding Hull, but neither BT nor any other provider had SMP on the wholesale market for high bandwidth AISBO services in the United Kingdom. Following each of the findings of SMP in a relevant wholesale AISBO market, OFCOM imposed

[64] ibid [117].

[65] *BT v OFCOM* (Ethernet Determinations) [2014] CAT 14.

[66] OFCOM, 'Disputes between each of Sky, TalkTalk, Virgin Media, Cable & Wireless and Verizon and BT regarding BT's charges for Ethernet services: Determinations and Explanatory Statement', 13 March 2013 <https://www.ofcom.org.uk/about-ofcom/latest/bulletins/competition-bulletins/all-closed-cases/cw_01052> accessed 6 June 2022.

[67] Ethernet is an international standard for the transmission of data. The subset of Ethernet services is known as alternative interface symmetric broadband origination (AISBO). AISBO services can be used by communications providers to supply their customers with high bandwidth data connectivity. AISBO services provided dedicated capacity between two points and are referred to as 'symmetric' because they allow data traffic to be carried in both directions along the circuit at the same rate.

[68] See OFCOM, 'Review of the retail leased lines, symmetric broadband origination and wholesale trunk segments markets: Final Statement and Notification', 24 June 2004: <https://www.ofcom.org.uk/__data/assets/pdf_file/0022/37444/state_note.pdf> accessed 6 June 2022.

[69] See OFCOM, 'Business Connectivity Market Review: Review of the retail leased lines, symmetric broadband origination and wholesale trunk segments markets—Statement and Consultation', 13 January 2009 <https://www.ofcom.org.uk/__data/assets/pdf_file/0019/33823/bcmr08.pdf> accessed 6 June 2022.

SMP access and cost-orientation obligations on BT pursuant to its powers under ss 87–88 of the Communications Act 2003. In each case, the relevant cost-orientation obligation (Condition HH3.1) on the dominant provider, BT, provided that the dominant provider, BT, should be able to demonstrate that every charge for network access for AISBO services is reasonably derived from the costs of provision based on a forward looking long run incremental cost approach and allowing an appropriate mark up for the recovery of common costs including an appropriate return on capital employed. A number of BT's wholesale AISBO customers (Sky, TalkTalk, Virgin, Cable & Wireless, Verizon) referred disputes to OFCOM under s 185(3) of the 2003 Act alleging that BT had charged prices in breach of its cost-orientation obligation for certain wholesale AISBO services at various bandwidths. OFCOM found that BT had breached its cost-orientation obligation and therefore overcharged for a number of WES and BES at various bandwidths over certain periods between 2006 and 2011.

The CAT had to address, *inter alia*, the correct approach to the assessment of cost-orientation. BT's argument that whether services were cost-oriented ought to be assessed in aggregate, rather than by way of assessment of the individual charge (which would have reduced the level by which BT had overcharged), was rejected. Sky and TalkTalk's appeal on the basis that a different measure of cost ought to have been adopted by OFCOM and not on the basis of the distributed stand alone cost measure (DSAC), which would have increased the level of overcharge, was also rejected. The CAT, manifesting its specialist expertise, laid down in detail the relevant measures of cost which in turn reflected the different bases on which a cost obligation could be evaluated, constraining the regulator's interpretive discretion. The Tribunal acknowledged that there are various methods by which such costs can be allocated and there is no 'correct' method of allocating costs, nor is one method inherently superior to the others. Rather, the appropriate allocation of common costs is dependent on the purpose for which the cost information will be used.[70] Emanating from this principle, it then engaged closely with the relevant cost standard. Both the DSAC and the FAC measures take into account the incremental and the fixed common (overhead) costs of providing a given service. However, whilst the FAC measure distributes the common costs of a firm across all of the services that the firm provides, the DSAC distributes those common costs across a particular group of related services provided by the firm in a given market.[71] In defending its use of the DSAC test as the benchmark of cost-orientation, OFCOM relied on the Court of Appeal's approach in *Partial Private Circuits*[72] and considered that the 'appropriate' mark-up depended on the purpose for which the cost-orientation obligation was imposed.[73] The Tribunal considered that pricing up to DSAC was consistent with OFCOM's objective of stimulating competition and new entry on the wholesale market—as DSAC is the measure of cost that would allow a new entrant providing the same package of either WES or BES as BT to recover its common costs.[74] By contrast, the application of a FAC-based

[70] *Ethernet Determinations* (n 65) [155].
[71] Ibid [158].
[72] *BT v OFCOM (Partial Private Circuits)* [2012] EWCA Civ 1051.
[73] *Ethernet Determinations* (n 65) [171]–[172].
[74] Ibid [177].

test of cost-orientation would only encourage new entry of firms that could replicate the entirety of BT's AISBO offering.[75] This would contravene OFCOM's objectives in imposing the cost-orientation obligation which include not only an increase in competition on downstream retail markets for Ethernet services, but also the stimulation of new entry in the wholesale AISBO market.[76] In light of the above, the Tribunal considered that OFCOM was entitled to exercise its regulatory judgment to balance the objectives of stimulating wholesale competition on the one hand and retail competition on the other. In other words it afforded discretion to OFCOM to balance various different forms of economic efficiency and to determine the appropriate trade-off between the benefits of increased access-based competition in downstream markets and the potential for more competition in the wholesale AISBO market.[77] Echoing the Supreme Court's guidance, the Court of Appeal did not interfere in OFCOM's regulatory judgement as to what cost-orientation obligations to impose in any particular situation nor in the CAT's factual judgement on the issue.[78]

These judgments demonstrate that the expert Tribunal does not shy away from scrutinising OFCOM's statutory interpretation of economically informed concepts and substituting in some cases its own view for that of OFCOM. However, as the section hinted, CAT's propensity of regulating the regulators is constrained by the underlying important value judgements that the latter are called upon to perform in forming a judgment which even a specialist Tribunal should respect. In other words, there are limits to the judicial scrutiny of economic assessments and these limits are predicated upon relative institutional competence considerations relating to OFCOM's superior institutional legitimacy in matters relating to regulatory policy. We shall return to this point shortly in section 6.3.

### 6.3.2 Liability for Competition Law Infringements

This section will consider the CAT's exercise of rigorous review of economic evidence in cases involving the assessment of liability for competition law infringements under the concurrency regime. As it will be made apparent, there is little room for epistemic deference. On the contrary, it can be argued that the CAT emerges as the regulator of the regulators. This section will focus on two important cases: (i) the *Albion saga*,[79] and (ii) the Royal Mail infringement decision in the postal sector,[80] which was upheld by the CAT.[81] Both cases can be regarded as prime manifestations of the specialist/

[75] Ibid [178].
[76] Ibid [182].
[77] Ibid [183].
[78] [2017] EWCA Civ 330 [186].
[79] The Albion saga is long and complicated. Emphasis is placed primarily upon the following judgments: [2008] CAT 31 (hereinafter, 'Albion unfair pricing judgment'); [2006] CAT 23 (hereinafter 'Albion Main Judgment'); [2006] CAT 36 ('Albion Further Judgment'); 2008 EWCA Civ 536 (hereinafter 'Albion Court of Appeal judgment'); [2009] CAT 12 (hereinafter 'Albion remedies').
[80] OFCOM, 'Discriminatory pricing in relation to the supply of bulk mail delivery services in the UK, CW/01122/01/14, 26 October 2018, <https://www.ofcom.org.uk/__data/assets/pdf_file/0022/124591/01122-infringement-decision.pdf> accessed 6 June 2022.
[81] *Royal Mail plc v OFCOM* [2019] CAT 17.

specialist situation. One may ask, however, why competition law appeals from the two remaining regulators OFCOM and OFGEM are not discussed. The reason is that there have only been a handful of competition law appeals from OFCOM and OFGEM. All OFCOM's Competition Act 1998 decisions in the telecom sector, except for the abovementioned Royal Mail infringement decision, are non-infringement decisions. There has been only one appeal to the CAT against OFGEM's infringement decision in the *National Grid*,[82] where the CAT upheld OFGEM's finding that National Grid had abused its position of dominance in the market for the provision of domestic gas meters. It is outside the scope of this study to explore why there has been such a profound underenforcement on the part of the regulators of their competition law powers. Pietro Crocioni offers an insightful analysis of OFCOM's record as a competition authority and argues that it reflects a formalistic understanding of competition law rules and enforcement.[83] The poor record does have implications for the institutional design of the regulatory regime in the UK and the future of the concurrency regime. It might also imply that when exercising their competition law powers sectoral regulators face an epistemic asymmetry vis-à-vis the Competition Appeal Tribunal on competition law matters that affects their propensity to resort to competition law enforcement.

#### 6.3.2.1 The *Albion Saga*

The *Albion saga* is a unique case in its combination of the facts, the regulatory regime, and the framework of the UK Competition Act 1998 Chapter II prohibition and Article 102 TFEU. It is, however, discussed extensively here as it exemplifies the Tribunal's tougher scrutiny of the merits of the regulatory decisions. All the tools available to the CAT that enable it to perform an intensive review of economic evidence were put into play: The Tribunal determined disputes over primary facts, held extensive case management conferences, cross-examined expert witnesses, and finally substituted its decision for that of the authority on the appropriate pricing methodology. Crucially, the Tribunal was not prepared to afford 'substantial deference'[84] on the basis of the regulators' superior epistemic competence in regulatory matters.

The litigation concerned the lawfulness of the price offered by Dwr Cymru (DC), an incumbent water undertaker, for the partial treatment and transmission of non-potable water through a pipeline to a paper factory. Albion, a new entrant statutory water undertaker since the privatisation of the water industry in England and Wales, claimed that the price quoted to it by DC for 'common carriage' across part of DC's network (Ashgrove system) was excessive and gave rise to a margin squeeze in violation of Chapter II of the Competition Act 1998.[85]

No statutory provision for common carriage was in place at the time of the complaint, although both OFWAT and the then competition authority, OFT, recognised

[82] *National Grid v OFGEM* [2009] CAT 14.
[83] P Crocioni, 'Ofcom's Record as a Competition Authority: An Assessment of Decisions in Telecoms' (2021) 9 JAE 505 <https://doi.org/10.1093/jaenfo/jnaa057>.
[84] Aileen Kavanagh, 'Deference or Defiance' in Grant Huscroft (ed), *Expounding the Constitution: Essays in Constitutional Theory* (CUP 2008) 191. See Chapter 1, section 1.4.
[85] Albion was granted an inset appointed under the Water Industry Act 1991, s 6.

that if an undertaker refused a request for common carriage or imposed an unreasonable price this would constitute a breach of the Competition Act 1998 rules.[86] Following an investigation, OFWAT found that the common carriage price was justified on their application of the ECPR methodology.[87] Albion appealed to the CAT against OFWAT's non-prohibition decision, arguing that DC had abused its dominant position by (i) demanding excessive prices and (ii) causing a margin squeeze. The CAT upheld the appeal finding that the undertaking had engaged in margin squeeze practices.

The Tribunal delivered several judgments on this matter, scrutinising several aspects of the regulatory decision in detail, including the relevant 'imputation' test. There are two main 'imputation tests' for the assessment of an abusive margin squeeze: the 'as efficient competitor' test (AEC) and the 'reasonable efficient competitor' test' (REC). The AEC test focuses on the costs of the dominant undertaking's own downstream operation, while the REC pays more attention to the costs of an actual or potential competitor, even one less efficient than the incumbent, in the downstream market. Both feature in EU soft law. Nonetheless, the CAT followed the AEC test which has been adopted by the EU courts.[88] Crucially, the CAT ruled on the appropriateness of the ECPR test to determine margins and any alleged squeeze; hence signalling that pricing methodologies are not immune from strict scrutiny, nor do they form part of the regulator's margin of appreciation, as the EU Courts have ruled in a number of preliminary rulings delineating the NRA's arena of discretion.[89] The application of the ECPR rule was one of the choices lying in the regulator's arena of discretionary power. There was no legal constraint to applying the ECPR in support of OFWAT's application of an average accounting cost methodology. Whether it promotes more or less competition is a different story. However, the CAT felt confident to decide whether the application of such a controversial rule should be accepted or not. Engaging in an academic discussion on the ECPR and examining its application in different countries around the globe,[90] it clearly rejected the use of the ECPR: 'it cannot be assumed that [the incumbent's] upstream price is reasonable ... [t]he margin squeeze in question cannot be justified on the basis of an ECPR approach which is itself unsound.'[91]

[86] See OFWAT, Guidance on Access Codes (March 2002): 'Companies risk infringing CA98 if they refuse access to their facilities without objective justification, or if they offer access on unreasonable terms' (para 4); see OFT 422, 'Competition Act 1998: Application in the water and sewerage sectors': 'under the [Competition] Act ... a refusal by a dominant undertaking to grant access to facilities may be an abuse of a dominant position. Similarly, the imposition of unreasonable price or non-price terms for access would infringe the Chapter II prohibition'.

[87] On the ECPR methodology, see Chapter 4, section 4.4.2.3.

[88] The Commission has applied the AEC test since its 1998 decision in Napier; see 88/518/EEC: Commission Decision of 18 July 1988 relating to a proceeding under Article 86 of the EEC Treaty (Case No IV/30.178 Napier Brown—British Sugar). In 2000, the Court of First Instance reaffirmed the AEC test in Case T-2/95 *Industrie des Poudres Sphériques v Council* [1998] ECR II-3939 and in 2007 in case T-271/03 *Deutsche Telekom v Commission* [2008] ECR II-477.

[89] See Chapter 3, section 3.3.3.

[90] The ECPR rule was banned in the New Zealand Telecommunications sector following the *Clear* case and it was rejected by the US Supreme Court in the *Verizon* case. See cases *Telecom Corporation of New Zealand Ltd v Clear Communications Ltd* [1995] 1 NZLR 385 and *Verizon v FCC*, 535 US 467 (2002).

[91] Albion Main Judgment (n 79) [873].

It may be argued that the CAT sought to align the access-pricing regime with orthodox regulatory practice. Notwithstanding the value of the academic criticism advanced against the ECPR, the CAT advanced competition over any other objective that the regulator could have considered when deciding to apply the ECPR. The Tribunal judged that an economic approach which requires new entrants to be 'super-efficient' effectively eliminates the development of competition and is not consonant with the government's policy goal in regulated industries. At the same time, the CAT was unable to offer any alternative to the regulator as the other solution advanced in the economics literature to the issue of access pricing, known as the Ramsey pricing rule, had also been discarded.[92]

#### 6.3.2.2 The Royal Mail Case

On 12 November 2019, the CAT published its judgment rejecting Royal Mail's appeal against a £50 million fine imposed by OFCOM for abuse of a dominant position in bulk mail delivery following a complaint from Whistl, Royal Mail's only competitor in the market for delivery of business letters, known as 'bulk mail'. OFCOM found that Royal Mail, the formerly state-owned monopoly provider of mail services in the UK, had abused its dominant position by issuing contractual notices to change its whole-sale prices for other operators to access its delivery network which discriminated against its competitors who also undertook deliveries of bulk mail.[93]

A central issue before the CAT was the extent to which competition law prevents a dominant firm from introducing pricing structures that might exclude competitors less efficient than itself, which in turn affects the appropriate evidential weight to be placed on the as-efficient-competitor test (AEC test) submitted by Royal Mail's expert economist.[94] Another issue was whether evidence from an AEC 'could over-ride actual evidence of exclusionary intent and activity'.[95] The CAT issued a remarkable opinion both on the proper role of the AEC test in establishing anticompetitive foreclosure in exclusionary price-based conduct and on the relevance of the test given the specific facts of the case.[96] CAT's decision involved detailed consideration of economic evidence on the levels of efficiency required for successful entry[97] and the effect of Royal Mail's Universal Service Obligation (USO) and other incumbency advantages and disadvantages.[98] CAT's analysis was strongly endorsed by the Court of Appeal,[99] which concluded that: 'Ofcom was not required as a matter of law to treat the AEC test [the as-efficient-competitor test relied upon by Royal Mail] as either determinative or highly relevant. In those circumstances Ofcom gave adequate consideration to the AEC test, and the Tribunal did not err in law in so concluding'.[100] But let's take a closer look at the judgment.

[92] See generally Jean-Jacques Laffont and Jean Tirole, *Competition in Telecommunications* (MIT Press 2000).

[93] See also OFCOM's infringement decision in Royal Mail, CW/01122/01/14, 'Discriminatory Pricing in Relation to the Supply of Bulk Mail delivery services in the UK' (14 August 2018) <https://www.ofcom.org.uk/__data/assets/pdf_file/0022/124591/01122-infringement-decision.pdf> accessed 6 June 2022.

[94] *Royal Mail* (n 81) [455]–[465].

[95] ibid [6].

[96] ibid [470]–[548].

[97] ibid [505]–[521].

[98] ibid [194]–[204].

[99] *Royal Mail v OFCOM* [2021] EWCA Civ 669.

[100] ibid [70].

The CAT adjudicated Royal Mail's appeal in light of the EU case law which emphasises the requirement to undertake an 'effects' analysis.[101] These cases were decided following the European Commission issuing its 2009 enforcement priorities guidance (Guidance paper) on abusive exclusionary conduct by dominant firms;[102] the latter being rather clear in its support of the AEC test for exclusionary price-based practices. With a view to preventing anticompetitive foreclosure, the Commission 'will normally only intervene where the conduct concerned has already been or is capable of hampering competition from competitors which are considered to be as-efficient-as the dominant undertaking'.[103] Inspired by economic efficiency considerations, the AEC test, originating in the US,[104] focuses on the effects of the conduct: it is deemed exclusionary if it is likely in the circumstances to exclude from the defendant's market an equally or more efficient competitor. For example, below-cost pricing by a dominant firm is considered exclusionary because an as-efficient rival could not match the dominant firm's pricing without incurring a loss on each unit produced. The test is particularly apt in relation to price abuses. As the CAT put it, it reflects 'an economic implementation of the legal concept of competition on the merits'.[105] The test itself does not constitute a *sufficient* condition for finding an abuse however: if the Commission does establish exclusion on the basis of an as-efficient-competitor analysis, it will then 'integrate this in the general assessment of anti-competitive foreclosure'.[106] The Guidance also adopts *AKZO*'s price–cost analysis approach in the broader context of price-based conduct, explaining both prongs of the test by reference to, *inter alia*, the exclusionary effect on an as-efficient competitor.[107]

Although the Commission in its Guidance Paper gave the impression that the AEC test would take centre stage in the assessment of exclusionary pricing abuses, in practice both the Commission and the EU courts seemed unwilling to do so. In fact, they have both disregarded and downgraded the test's significance, indicating not only that the test is not a *sufficient* condition for finding an abuse but also that it is not a *necessary* condition, at least for some exclusionary pricing conduct.[108]

The EU courts have also sent contradictory signals. In *Tomra*,[109] which was the first conditional rebates case in which the CJEU ruled of substance following the Guidance Paper, the Court considered the Guidance to be of no relevance to the legal assessment of the contested decision since it post-dated the Commission's decision

[101] Case C-209/10 *Post Danmark A/S v Konkurrencerådet*, EU:C:2012:172 (*Post Danmark I*); Case C-23/14 *Post Danmark A/S v Konkurrencerådet*, EU:C:2015:651 (*Post Danmark II*); Case C-413/14 P *Intel Corp v European Commission*, EU:C:2017.

[102] Guidance on the Commission's enforcement priorities in applying Article 82 of the EC to abusive exclusionary conduct by dominant undertakings [2009] OJ C45/7 at para 24 (Guidance paper).

[103] ibid at para 23.

[104] See RA Posner, *Antitrust Law* (Univ Chicago Press 2001) 195. For a discussion see Martin Mandorff and Johan Sahl, 'The Role of the Equally Efficient Competitor in the Assessment of the Abuse of Dominance' (2013) 12 Compet LJ 221, 223–26.

[105] *Royal Mail* (n 81) [497](3).

[106] Guidance paper, at para 27. The general assessment could include, inter alia, the position of the dominant undertaking, the degree of foreclosure (share of the relevant market foreclosed by the conduct), evidence of actual foreclosure, and direct evidence of any exclusionary strategy, at para 20.

[107] ibid at para. 26. The Commission refines the cost measures used in *AKZO*, substituting average avoidable cost for average variable cost and long-run average incremental cost for average total cost.

[108] *Prokent-Tomra* (Case COMP/E-1/38.113) Commission Decision of 29 March 2006; *Post Danmark II* (n 101).

[109] Case C-549/10 P *Tomra Systems ASA and others v Commission*, EU:C:2012:221.

in that case,[110] and thus rejected the relevance of a price–cost test in the context of rebates. However, in *Post Danmark I*, the CJEU took several steps to endorse the AEC principle, this time more broadly than ever before.[111] Against that backdrop, the Court considered that selective pricing, or price discrimination, cannot of itself amount to an exclusionary abuse.[112] The Court further affirmed the AEC test, as it went on to state that some of the prices concerned in the case were above Post Danmark's average total cost and, as such, 'cannot be considered [to] have anticompetitive effects'.[113]

But then in *Post Danmark II*, the Court held that in the context of conditional rebate practices pricing below cost is not a prerequisite of a finding of an abuse, albeit it might be one tool 'amongst others'.[114] In other words, the Court refused to consider it necessary to perform a price–cost test in order to determine if the excluded competitors were as efficient as the dominant undertakings. Does this mean that the AEC test is rejected outright by the CJEU? Apparently not, as the Court states that its conclusion with regard to the relevance of the test in this case 'ought not to have the effect of excluding, on principle, recourse to the as-efficient-competitor test in cases involving a rebate scheme for the purposes of examining its compatibility with Article [102 TFEU]'.[115] It is the facts of the specific case in which the dominant undertaking has a very large market share and benefitted from structural advantages and the scope of the rebate scheme that led the CJEU to conclude that 'the as-efficient-competitor test is of no relevance inasmuch as the structure of the market makes the emergence of an as-efficient competitor practically impossible'.[116] Finally in its *Intel*[117] judgment, whilst the CJEU expressed the need to consider the AEC test as a procedural obligation on the part of the authority, when the undertaking under investigation relies upon an AEC test as rebutting the contention that the pricing practice in issue is anticompetitive, it created in fact a substantive rule to this effect.

This brief venture into the EU case law on the topic is necessary in order to fully appreciate the CAT's remarkable judgment. The CAT offered its own interpretation of the EU case law and concluded that 'whether as a matter of law or economics it is not necessary to conduct an AEC test in all pricing cases'.[118] First, the CAT noted that the relevant law has not changed since its decision in *British Telecom*,[119] so that there is no requirement to establish anticompetitive foreclosure by means of an AEC test in all pricing cases.[120]

The CAT also found that as a matter of economics 'there are no compelling reasons of economic principle that mandate such a test'.[121] Royal Mail put forward an AEC

[110] ibid [81].
[111] *Post Danmark I* (n 101) [21]–[22].
[112] ibid [30].
[113] ibid [36].
[114] ibid [61].
[115] ibid [59].
[116] ibid.
[117] *Intel* (n 101).
[118] *Royal Mail* (n 81) [522].
[119] ibid [471]–[474].
[120] ibid [490].
[121] ibid [495].

test that involved checking whether an operator with Royal Mail's delivery costs could profitably operate in some areas while having to rely on Royal Mail for delivery in other areas. The CAT was not persuaded by Royal Mail's expert economist's argument that entry by higher variable cost firms may reduce the industry's productive efficiency[122] and thereby risk consumer welfare. Rather the CAT considered that there is nothing inevitable about a price rise because entry may drive down the dominant firm's prices, even if the entrant is inefficient, and concluded that more work would be required to sustain the argument that prices may rise convincingly.[123]

The CAT dismissed one of the main arguments in favour of the AEC test, that is, a method that improves legal certainty. As with any rule for assessing whether conduct is anticompetitive, the AEC test is subject to both false positives and false negatives. Proponents of consistent enforcement across all pricing conducts argue that the test strikes the right balance between protecting entrants from abuse of dominance and giving the dominant firm freedom to respond aggressively to entry. It is also argued that the AEC test provides legal certainty to a dominant firm because by using the dominant firm's prices and costs, it allows 'self-assessment' of conduct using information in the possession of the dominant firm providing a 'safe harbour' for the dominant firm if the test is passed. The CAT found that there are no such benefits in practice since 'the design and methodology of an AEC test are not fixed or universal'[124] so the competition authority might deem the dominant undertaking's test to be flawed in some way, or run its own test and reach a different conclusion.[125] While the CAT was critical of the AEC test, it nevertheless conducted an extensive analysis of Royal Mail's proposed AEC test, implying that the exercise was not wholly without merit.

Finally, the CAT turned to consider whether there is a clear class of cases where an AEC test should be used and, if so, whether this case fell into that class, concluding that 'there is no well-defined class of cases in which the use of an AEC test is the appropriate way of identifying anticompetitive behaviour. Trying to determine whether an AEC test should be performed by attaching a label to a practice in an attempt to place it in a particular class of eligible cases is not a sensible approach.'[126] Thus while the CAT acknowledged that the AEC test can be 'a critical element',[127] it found in the case law of the EU courts neither a legal requirement to apply the AEC test nor a well-defined category of cases where the test could or should be applied. Moreover, the specific circumstances of this case—a recently liberalised sector, characterised by significant economies of scale and high fixed costs, and in which Royal Mail had accrued advantages and disadvantages by virtue of its universal service provider status made the AEC test inappropriate.[128]

The section discussed the CAT's rigorous scrutiny of economic evidence in two key areas emanating from the judicial record: (a) review of OFCOM's interpretive

[122] ibid [509].
[123] ibid.
[124] ibid [514].
[125] ibid [516].
[126] ibid [529].
[127] ibid [487](1).
[128] ibid [532]–[548].

discretion; and (b) liability for competition law infringements. It was made apparent that the expert Tribunal has on many occasions constrained OFCOM's interpretive discretion and has not hesitated to lay down its own economic test to operationalise the objectives of the statutory regime. The Tribunal's assessment of liability for competition law infringements exemplifies its tougher scrutiny of the merits of regulatory decisions. The next section will explore the circumstances under which the CAT's propensity towards a heightened review has been constrained by the generalist Court of Appeal.

## 6.4 The Generalist/Specialist Situation: The Court of Appeal–CAT Interactions

We can now turn to consider how the preferences of the generalist Court of Appeal shape and ultimately constrain the CAT's propensity towards a heightened review of multifactorial regulatory decisions adopted in the exercise of operational discretion. It will be argued that the Court of Appeal regulates the institutional interactions of the CAT with the regulatory agencies based on relative institutional competence considerations. Those primarily refer to the regulatory agency's superior institutional legitimacy in deciding cases involving multifaceted policy considerations. As will be shown, whilst in the early cases the Court of Appeal was primarily concerned with striking an institutional balance between the CAT and the regulators, it gradually emerged as the 'regulator' of the CAT's decision-making process. We shall begin our discussion with an overview of the Court of Appeal's early interaction with the specialist Tribunal in the context of regulatory disputes and will then move on to consider the CAT's exercise of self-restraint in the context of OFCOM's regulatory remedies in telecoms, which is predicated on institutional competence considerations. We shall conclude with an analysis of how broader systemic considerations affect the Tribunal's scrutiny of economic evidence.

Institutional balance considerations were prominent in the Court of Appeal's reasoning in the early days of the CAT when the Court of Appeal sought to strike what it perceived to be as 'the right balance' between the expert CAT and the expert regulators. Hence in the *Floe I* case[129] the Court of Appeal considered that the Tribunal had gone too far in requiring OFCOM to reach a conclusion, either finding an infringement or a decision to issue a statement of objections within five months.[130] In the opinion of Lloyd LJ, while it was entitled to 'express its own view as to how urgently the case should be dealt with', it is not 'able to give directions to the regulator in relation to the conduct of further investigation'.[131] In the same vein in the *Floe II* case,[132] the Court of Appeal remarked on the potential for specialist adjudicatory bodies to issue 'advisory opinions to litigants or potential

[129] *OFCOM v Floe Telecom Ltd* [2006] EWCA Civ 768 [35]. See CAT judgment, *Floe Telecom Ltd (in liquidation) v OFCOM* [2005] CAT 14.
[130] ibid.
[131] ibid.
[132] *OFCOM and T-Mobile (UK) Ltd v Floe Telecom Ltd* [2009] EWCA Civ 47.

litigants' and as such 'do things which they are not intended, qualified or equipped to do'.[133]

Perhaps the most important area in which the CAT has integrated into its reasoning the Court of Appeal's guidance is when assessing OFCOM's regulatory remedies in the context of market review process. In such cases, as we shall see, the Tribunal exercises a measure of self-restraint emanating from relative institutional capacity considerations. The CAT's reasoning largely echoes the Court of Appeal's guidance to the Tribunal in cases involving the assessment of multifactorial regulatory decisions. In such cases, the Tribunal maintains a respectful attitude in not substituting its own view for a tenable view of the regulator properly made on a sound factual foundation. Despite its specialist nature and its appellate jurisdiction, the CAT is prepared to allow a margin of discretion to the initial decision-maker.

As discussed in Chapter 4, the market review process consists of two distinct economic assessments: (i) the finding a Significant Market Power, and (ii) the consideration of the appropriate remedy. Regarding regulatory remedies, the Court of Appeal has repeatedly held that:

> any value judgment (of OFCOM) as between different considerations, must carry great 'weight'—the weight to be attached to different considerations in forming a value judgment is a matter for Ofcom as the NRA charged with the duty of resolving disputes, and in the absence of any misdirection by Ofcom the court will normally respect its determination, whether or not the court would itself have balanced the considerations in the same way and reached the same conclusion.[134]

Under the former regime of statutory appeals that was modified by the Digital Economy Act 2017, the CAT would consider not only whether the decision under challenge is properly reasoned, but whether it is the right decision.[135] But still this was not enough to identify some error in reasoning: the appeal could only succeed if the decision cannot stand in the light of that error.[136] Following up on the Court of Appeal's direction, the CAT has thus proclaimed that 'it may be slower to overturn certain decisions where there may be a number of different approaches which OFCOM could reasonably adopt':[137]

> It is ... common ground that there may, in relation to any particular dispute, be a number of different approaches which OFCOM could reasonably adopt in arriving at its determination. There may be no 'single right' answer to the dispute. To that extent, the Tribunal may, whilst still conducting a merits review of the decision, be slow to overturn

[133] ibid [20].

[134] *BT v OFCOM* (PPC) [2012] EWCA Civ 1051. See also *Telefónica O2 Ltd v BT* [2012] EWCA Civ 1002, from which it quoted per Lord Justice Lloyd at [67] 'if the regulator has addressed the right question by reference to relevant material, any value judgment on its part, as between different relevant considerations, must carry great weight', and at [90] 'the Tribunal ought to respect the policy decisions and matters of judgment involved in Ofcom's decisions'.

[135] *Hutchison 3G UK Ltd v OFCOM* [2008] CAT 11 [164].

[136] *EE* case (n 43), Moses LJ.

[137] *Vodafone and others v OFCOM* [2008] CAT 22 [46].

> a decision which is arrived at by an appropriate methodology even if the dissatisfied party can suggest other ways of approaching the case which would also have been reasonable, and which might have resulted in resolution more favourable to its cause.[138]

This is because the Tribunal essentially recognises the polycentricity of regulatory remedies, such as price controls. In such cases, the Tribunal exercises a measure of self-restraint emanating from relative institutional capacity considerations. This is despite the CAT's epistemic competence and despite the wide possibility for third party interventions under its procedural rules that allow the representation of a greater number of interests. In such cases, the institutional choice of deferring to the regulator is more of a recognition that the 'proper limits of adjudication have been reached',[139] rather than an admission on the part of the expert court of its incapacity to deal with price-setting. This finding is further supported by the similar standard of review adopted by the CAT's partner in the resolution of regulatory disputes, the CMA, when determining the correctness of the price control adopted by OFCOM. Only an error of 'sufficient importance' is capable of vitiating the regulator's determinations. For example, an error will not be of sufficient importance where it has only an insignificant or negligible impact in relative terms on the overall level of price control that has been set by OFCOM; that would fall within an acceptable margin of error for a regulator.

> We have also kept in mind the point made by the Interveners that Ofcom is a specialist regulator whose judgment should not be readily dismissed. Where a ground of appeal relates to a claim that Ofcom has made a factual error or an error of calculation, it may be relatively straightforward to determine whether it is well founded. Where on the other hand a ground of appeal relates to the broader principles adopted or to an alleged error in the exercise of discretion the matter may not be so clear. In a case where a number of alternative solutions exist to a regulatory problem with little to choose between them, we do not think it would be right for us to determine that Ofcom erred simply because it took into a course other than the one that would have taken. On the other hand, if, out of alternative options, some clearly had more merits than others, it may more easily be said that Ofcom erred if it chose an inferior solution. Which category a particular choice falls within can necessarily only be decided on a case-by-case basis.[140]

But the specialist Tribunal's deferential stance towards the assessment of multifaceted policy decisions may also suggest that in cases involving multifactorial policy considerations there may be no single right answer, but several 'right' answers. This is true both for decisions relating to the setting of price controls and more general policy decisions. To put it otherwise, such cases render redundant the pursuit of 'correctness':

[138] *T-Mobile* case (n 35) [82]–[83].

[139] Lon Fuller (1978), 'The Forms and Limits of Adjudication' 92(2) Harvard Law Rev 353, 398.

[140] *Everything Everywhere Ltd v OFCOM* (Case 1181/3/3/11); *Hutchison 3G UK Ltd v OFCOM* (Case 1182/3/3/11); *Vodafone Ltd v OFCOM* (Case 1183/3/3/11) and Telefónica UK Ltd, Determination, 9 February 2012 <https://www.gov.uk/cma-cases/bt-everything-everywhere-hutchison-3g-and-vodafone-v-ofcom-wholesale-mobile-voice-call-termination-price-control-appeals> at 1.33 accessed 6 June 2022.

> We consider questions of policy preference to be, par excellence, the sort of question where there is no single 'right answer', and we agree with the Tribunal's statement in T-Mobile that the Tribunal should be slow to overturn such decisions. This is particularly the case here, where OFCOM is seeking to articulate policy preferences that are compliant with its statutory duties under the 2003 Act. We remind ourselves that these duties, which are broadly framed and clearly give OFCOM a measure of discretion, are duties imposed upon OFCOM itself and not on this Tribunal.[141]

Where there are a number of competing, legitimate views, the CAT will not interfere in a regulator's decision unless it is clearly wrong. One wouldn't be mistaken to think that the CAT's standard of review of polycentric assessments is very close to the EU courts' standard of review of complex economic assessments. The Tribunal is prepared to test whether the regulators' findings withstand its 'profound and rigorous' scrutiny, while at the same time allowing a margin of appreciation in cases involving policy judgments.

The 'margin of appreciation test,' which has entered English domestic jurisprudence,[142] features prominently in the case law of the Court of Justice, involving review of complex economic[143] or technical[144] appraisals. Despite the calls to 'marginalise' its application,[145] this judge-made doctrine still survives as a doctrinal constraint upon the appreciation of economic evidence enshrined in the European Commission's decisions. The concept of a margin of appreciation suggests an ambit of discretion, a 'latitude in the factual assessment'[146] left to the Commission by the Treaty or legislative provisions. However, its wide application renders its 'properties' uncertain.[147] The courts have applied the doctrine in areas as diverse as mergers[148] and abuse of dominance cases,[149] as well as in fields where the Commission enjoys discretion of a political nature, such as state aid,[150] when reviewing administrative or legislative acts

[141] *British Telecommunications plc v OFCOM* (080) [2011] CAT 12 [230].

[142] Vivien Rose, 'Margins of Appreciation: Changing Contours in Community and Domestic Case Law' (April 2009) 5 Compet Policy Int J.

[143] See, eg, Case C-42/84 *Remia v Commission* [1985] ECR I-2545 [35]; C-56/64 and 58/64, *Consten and Grundig* [1996] rec 279; Case C-194/99 P *Thyssen Stahl v Commission* [2003] ECR I-10821 [78]; Case T-170/06 *Alrosa v Commission* [2007] ECR II-2601 [108].

[144] See Case T-201/04 *Microsoft v Commission* [2007] ECR II-3601 [88]; Case T-321/05 *AstraZeneka v Commission* [2010] ECR II-02805 [32]; Case C-269/90, *Technische Universität v Hauptzollamt München-Mitte* [1991] ECR I-5469 [14].

[145] See, eg, Marc Jaeger, 'The Standard of Review in Competition Cases Involving Complex Economic Assessments: Towards the Marginalization of the Marginal Review?' (2011) 2 J Eur Compet L Pract 295.

[146] David Bailey, 'The Scope of Judicial Review under Article 81 EC' (2004) 41 Common Market L Rev 1237.

[147] See Andriani Kalintiri, 'What's in a Name? The Marginal Standard of Review of "Complex Economic Evaluations" in EU Competition Enforcement' (2016) 53 Common Market L Rev 1283, 1290–94.

[148] Joined Cases C-68/94 and C-30/95 *French Republic and Société commerciale des potasses et de l'azote (SCPA) and Enterprise minière et chimique (EMC) v Commission* [1998] ECR I-1375; T-342/99 *Airtours v Commission* [2002] ECR II 2585; Case T-351/03 *Schneider Electric v Commission* [2002] ECR II-4071; Case T-5/02 *Tetra Laval v Commission* [2002] ECR II-4381 [119].

[149] See, eg, Case T- 65/96 *Kish Glass v Commission* [2000] ECR II -1885 [64] upheld by appeal by an order of the CJEU in Case C-241/00 *P Kish Glass v Commission* [2001] ECR I- 7759; Case T -301/04 *Clearstream v Commission* [2009] ECR II 3155 [47]; Case T-57/01 *Solvay v Commission* [2009] ECR II 4621 [250].

[150] Case C-333/07 *Société Régie Network v Direction de contrôle fiscal Rhône-Alpes Bourgogne* [2009] ECR I-10807 [78].

of institutions required to balance different interests and policies,[151] and decisions of independent expert committees.[152]

The courts' recognition of a margin of appreciation triggers, in turn, a limited standard of review.[153] Although, as a general rule, in actions for annulment the EU courts exercise a comprehensive, full review of legality[154] of an allegation of error of law, fact, or procedural impropriety,[155] review is limited when faced with complex economic assessments. This is thought to be a less strict standard of judicial control, which allows the Commission some latitude and entails checking 'whether the rules on procedure and on statement of reasons have been complied with, whether the facts have been accurately stated, and whether there has been any manifest error of appraisal or a misuse of powers'.[156] That said, however, the EU Courts have on several occasions explained that despite the Commission's appreciation in relation to economic matters, they will not 'refrain from reviewing the Commission's interpretation of information of an economic nature'.[157] By contrast, they will carefully examine 'whether the evidence relied on is factually accurate, reliable, and consistent, but also whether that evidence contains all the information which must be taken into account in order to assess a complex situation and whether it is capable of substantiating the conclusions drawn from it'.[158]

Finally, broader systemic considerations also affect the degree of judicial scrutiny at the CAT. The first one is enforcement related. Regulatory disputes had never been tested before in a specialist adjudicatory body. By integrating institutional competence considerations into its reasoning, the CAT can avoid institutional conflict with the regulatory agencies and ensure that its rulings will be carried out by the regulators. The second consideration reflects a legitimacy-building assumption. Adherence to the Court of Appeal's guidance not only weakens the possibility of a costly reversal of its judgments, but further contributes to its legitimacy-building exercise vis-à-vis the regulators and the other actors of the regulatory space. Finally, the third consideration relates to the scope of the Tribunal's judicial power. One could hypothesise that the establishment of a complementary relationship between the CAT and the regulators will reduce the chances of legislative interference with the CAT's statutory mandate that could result in stripping off or limiting the scope of its mandate. However, this

[151] See, eg, C-225/91 *Mantra SA v Commission* [1993] ECR-I 3203 [24-25]; C-372/97 *Italy v Commission* [2004] ECR I-3679.

[152] See, eg, Cases T-13/99, *Pfizer Animal Health SA v Council of the European Union* [2002] ECR II-3305 [170]–[172]; Case T-70/99 *Alpharma Inc v Council of the European Union* [2002] ECR II-03495 [177]–[180]; Joined Cases T-74/00, T-76/00, T-84/00, T-85/00, T-137/00 and T-141/00 *Artegodan GmbH a.o. v Commission* [2002] ECR II-4945.

[153] See Case T-21/05, *Chalkor v Commission* [2010] ECR II-1895 [62].

[154] See H Legal, 'Standards of Proof and Standards of Judicial Review in EU Competition Law' in Barry Hawk (ed), *Annual Proceedings of the Fordham Corporate Law Institute* 2005, vol 32 (Juris Publishing 2005) 107.

[155] Case T-41/96 *Bayer AG v Commission* [2000] ECR II-3383 [67]–[69], [71].

[156] See Case C-7/05 P *John Deere v Commission*, [1998] ECR I-3111 [34]–[36]; Case 42/84 *Remia v Commission* [1985] ECR I-2545 [34]–[35]; Case C-194/99 P *Thyssen Stahl v Commission* [2003] ECR I-10821 [78].

[157] Case C-12/03 P *Tetra Laval v Commission* [2005] ECR 1-987 [39].

[158] C–386/10 P *Chalkor v Commission* [2011] ECR I–0000 [54].

does not hold true; the change in the standard of review of appeals from OFCOM being a telling example in this regard. OFCOM argued over the years that statutory appeals were being strategically deployed by market players with deep pockets;[159] an argument that eventually led to scaling back the standard of review to that of a judicial review by the Digital Economy Act 2017.[160] OFCOM nevertheless recognised the continuing effect of the Framework Directive which requires the appeal body duly to take account of the merits in any individual case.[161]

The revised standard of review was discussed in greater detail in *Virgin Media*,[162] where the Tribunal emphasised that its role is not one of rehearing the case on its merits and underlined OFCOM's superior expertise as a specialist regulator that invites deference on the basis of institutional competence considerations:

> Proper respect must be accorded to Ofcom's role as a specialist regulator, and the expertise of Ofcom's staff. As explained by Green J in R (Hutchison 3G UK Ltd) v Office of Communications [2017] EWHC 3376 (Admin) ('Hutchison') at [40], the focus is Ofcom's decision and whether Ofcom got their decision materially wrong. It is that decision that is being challenged. The question is not what decision the appellate body might itself have reached if it had started afresh.[163]

In *TalkTalk v OFCOM*,[164] the CAT also discussed extensively the impact of the new standard of review. Despite the possible uncertainty arising from the change from 'full merits appeal' to 'the principles of judicial review', the appellants in this case argued essentially that 'nothing had changed'.[165] The Tribunal further emphasised the margin of appreciation to the regulator's expert assessment in complex assessments, 'in which the knowledge and experience of a specialised sectoral regulator are heavily engaged'.[166]

So far, only three cases have been decided under the new standard of review.[167] But the remedial powers associated with judicial review may prolong the end-to-end decision-making process: where a decision would be successfully challenged by judicial review the reviewing court would typically remit the quashed decision back to the regulator to remake it in the light of the court's findings. This involves a fresh consultation and evidence gathering by the regulator which can prolong decision-making with negative implications for the fast-moving electronic communications markets.

159 See Department for Business, Innovation and Skills (BIS), 'Streamlining Regulatory and Competition Appeals: Consultation on Options for Reform' 19 June 2013, available at: <https://assets.publishing.service.gov.uk/government/uploads/system/uploads/attachment_data/file/229758/bis-13-876-regulatory-and-competition-appeals-revised.pdf> accessed 6 June 2022.

160 For a discussion, see Chapter 3, section 3.3.

161 Ofcom Response to BIS Consultation on regulatory appeals reform, para 21 <https://assets.publishing.service.gov.uk/government/uploads/system/uploads/attachment_data/file/252842/regulatory-and-competition-appeals-consultation-responses-i-z.pdf> accessed 6 June 2022.

162 *Virgin Media Ltd v OFCOM* [2020] CAT 5.

163 ibid [57].

164 *TalkTalk* (n 34).

165 ibid [138].

166 ibid [139].

167 *Viasat UK Ltd v OFCOM* [2018] CAT 18, *Virgin Media Ltd v OFCOM* [2020] CAT 5, and *TalkTalk* (n 34).

## 6.5 Conclusion

This chapter examined the determinants of judicial scrutiny of economic evidence at the specialist CAT. In doing so, it highlighted the interplay of two different situations. The first one is the specialist/specialist situation and concerns the Tribunal's scrutiny of the economic evidence enshrined in regulatory agencies' decisions. The second one is the generalist/specialist situation and concerns the Court of Appeal's review of the CAT's determinations. The chapter showed that the specialist/specialist situation mostly manifests itself in the context of appeals involving the assessment of liability for competition law infringements. In those cases, the CAT is not only seen to exercise an intensive scrutiny of the merits of the regulatory agencies' decisions, but it has in some cases not hesitated to substitute its decision for that of the authority on issues which have been traditionally considered as 'no-go' areas for generalist courts (eg pricing methodologies). The chapter attributed this intensity of review to a number of institutional features of the Tribunal, such as its membership and subject-matter expertise.

The chapter then turned to consider the generalist/specialist situation and the role of the Court of Appeal in constraining the CAT's propensity towards a more intensive review. It was shown that the Court of Appeal regulates the institutional interactions of the CAT with the regulatory agencies on the basis of considerations of relative institutional competence. Those primarily refer to the agency's superior institutional expertise and legitimacy in deciding cases involving multifaceted policy considerations. Thus, the CAT, in reviewing OFCOM's decisions involving the assessment of SMP remedies in electronic communications, essentially disputes of a 'polycentric' nature, exercises a measure of self-restraint predicated upon considerations of relative institutional competence. The chapter shows that there is scope for a specialist tribunal conducting a merits review of regulatory decisions to confer 'a margin of appreciation' to the discretionary assessments of the regulatory authority. It also pointed to a number of other micro-level considerations and broader systemic considerations that affect the degree of judicial scrutiny at the CAT (ie enforcement-related, legitimacy building).

In conclusion, the status of the reviewing court and its access to epistemic competence is an important factor, but not a dispositive one, in determining the degree of judicial scrutiny of economic evidence. This is mostly attributable to the polycentric nature of the regulatory disputes. In such cases, the functional limits of adjudication are reached, irrespective of the status of the tribunal as a specialist one. Even specialist tribunals are limited in their ability to decide on regulatory remedies, which involve the representation of diverse interests, the balancing of a variety of goals, and prospective analysis.

# Appendix to Chapter 6

**Table 6.1** Appeals from OFCOM

| Case Name | Nature of Decision Appealed | Type of Review | Outcome/ Remedy | Court of Appeal Decision | Supreme Court Decision |
|---|---|---|---|---|---|
| *BT v DGT* [2004] CAT 8 | Dispute resolution | Merits review | Remitted to OFCOM | | |
| *BT v OFCOM* [2004] CAT 23 | Dispute resolution | Merits review | Upheld OFCOM's determination | | |
| *Hutchison 3G (UK) Ltd v OFCOM* [2005] CAT 39 (H3G1) | *Ex ante* regulation SMP | Merits review | Remitted to OFCOM | | |
| *T-Mobile (UK) and others v OFCOM* [2008] CAT 12 (core issues) and [2008] CAT 19 | Dispute resolution | Merits review | Remitted to OFCOM | | |
| *Hutchison 3G UK Ltd v OFCOM* [2008] CAT 11 (H3G2) | Dispute resolution and *ex ante* regulation/SMP | Merits review | Dismissed appeal/ upheld OFCOM | [2009] EWCA Civ 683: dismissed appeal | |
| *Vodafone v OFCOM* [2008] CAT 22 | Cost-benefit analysis | Merits review | Remitted to OFCOM | | |
| *The Number UK Ltd v OFCOM* [2008] CAT 33 | Dispute resolution | Merits review | Reference to ECJ | [2009] EWCA Civ 1360 | |
| *BT v OFCOM* [2009] CAT 11 | Disposal of appeals/price control matter | Judicial review | Rejected the challenges against CC's determinations | [2010] EWCA Civ 391: allowed appeal | |
| *BT v OFCOM* [2011] CAT 5 (PPC) | Dispute resolution | Merits review | Upheld OFCOM's determination | [2012] EWCA Civ 1051: dismissed appeal | |
| *BT v OFCOM* [2011] CAT 15 | Dispute resolution | Merits review | Upheld OFCOM's determination | | |
| *BT v OFCOM* [2011] CAT 24 (termination charges) | Dispute resolution | Merits review | Remitted to OFCOM | [2012] EWCA Civ 1002: reversed CAT | |

*(continued)*

**Table 6.1** Continued

| Case Name | Nature of Decision Appealed | Type of Review | Outcome/ Remedy | Court of Appeal Decision | Supreme Court Decision |
|---|---|---|---|---|---|
| *TalkTalk Telecom Group plc v OFCOM* (WAB charge control) [2012] CAT 1 | *Ex ante* regulation/SMP | Merits review | Upheld OFCOM's decision | [2013] EWCA Civ 1318: dismissed appeal | [2014] UKSC 42: upheld CAT |
| *BT v CC and OFCOM* [2012] CAT 11 (Mobile call termination) | *Ex ante* regulation/SMP | Judicial review | Remitted to OFCOM | [2013] EWCA Civ 154: dismissed appeal | |
| *Telefónica UK Ltd v OFCOM* [2012] CAT 28 | Dispute resolution | Merits review | Dismissed appeal | | |
| *BT and others v OFCOM* [2014] CAT 14 (Ethernet Determinations) | Dispute resolution | Merits review | Dismissed appeal | [2017] EWCA Civ 330 | |
| *BT v OFCOM (VULA)* [2016] CAT 3 | *Ex ante* regulation/SMP | Merits review | Dismissed appeal | | |
| *BT v OFCOM* [2016] CAT 22 (APPCs) | Dispute resolution | Merits review | Dismissed appeal | | |
| *BT v OFCOM* [2017] CAT 25 | *Ex ante* regulation/SMP | Merits review | Remitted to OFCOM | [2018] EWCA Civ 2542 (costs) | |
| *TalkTalk and Vodafone v Ofcom* [2020] CAT 8 (BCMR) | *Ex ante* regulation/SMP | Judicial review (s 194A CA 2003) | Upheld OFCOM's decision | | |
| *Virgin Media Ltd v OFCOM* [2020] CAT 5 | Breach of general conditions of entitlement | Judicial review (s 194A CA 2003) | Dismissed appeal | | |

# 7

# Towards a Complementary Relationship between the Court and the Regulatory Agency in the Realm of Utility Regulation

## 7.1 Introduction

In the introduction to this study, we argued that judicial review of economic evidence enshrined in the regulatory agency's discretion should become attentive to institutional competencies considerations if the challenges posed by economic evidence are to be effectively met. As we saw in Chapter 3, the pluralistic nature of the regulatory and adjudicative processes, where various imperfect alternative decision-makers interact, coupled with the polycentric element of regulatory disputes, bring to the forefront several factors, such as fact-finding competence and evidence gathering tools, that should inform the scope of review. Through the lenses of comparative institutional analysis, the regulatory and adjudicative processes emerge as interdependent complements, as they may both be equally defective in some respects in ensuring the soundness of regulatory decisions. Hence, deference emerges as the institutional choice of the least imperfect alternative; an essentially competence-assessment exercise. This chapter will delve deeper into this analytical exercise. Drawing on insights from political science and economics, it will illuminate the institutional disadvantages of the courts that may warrant a high degree of deference. At the same time, it will also highlight several institutional realties and procedural developments that may attenuate the weight of such comparative institutional disadvantages. This exercise not only furnishes valuable insights regarding the scope of review, but also the optimal institutional response to the pervasiveness of economic evidence in regulatory decisions.

## 7.2 The Comparative Institutional Disadvantages of Courts

As compared to the regulatory agencies, generalist courts suffer from a number of institutional disadvantages in assessing the different manifestations of economic evidence in regulatory disputes. These include: (i) lack of economic expertise; (ii) limited access to information; (iii) lack of requisite institutional legitimacy, especially in addressing polycentric disputes; and, finally, (iv) susceptibility to 'minoritarian' bias. These disadvantages, of course, vary according to the nature of the decision being challenged. Some decisions may turn upon a narrow category of clear and certain facts

*Courts, Regulators, and the Scrutiny of Economic Evidence.* Despoina Mantzari, Oxford University Press.
 DOI: 10.1093/oso/9780198851608.003.0007

and involve little by way of judgement call or by way of economic expertise. Other decisions, however, might require the regulator to consider a wide range of facts which may themselves be characterised by their polycentric element.

### 7.2.1 Lack of Economic Expertise

One of the most obvious institutional disadvantages of ordinary courts relates to their lack of economic expertise. One cannot possibly expect judges sitting on such courts to have acquired cross-disciplinary expertise in economics, business, or accountancy, as members of the specialist CAT. Nor can one anticipate judges sitting in ordinary courts to have developed subject-matter expertise, when they are exposed to a very wide spectrum of disputes, not limited to sectoral regulation.

The regulatory agencies, on the other hand, have in recent years invested heavily in economic expertise. On both sides of the Atlantic, professional experts drawn from the field of economics, statistics, and finance form part of the regulatory agencies' in-house expertise. Furthermore, economists often hold key positions in the agencies and most utility regulators have a panel of external economic consultants to complement the in-house economic skills. Moreover, because the regulatory agencies are endowed by statute with primary responsibility for the regulation of the sector in question and need to pay due regard to the legislative requirement of evidence-based policymaking, their incentives to employ and rely on economic expertise are further strengthened.[1]

Those economic experts, the so-called 'specialists', are proficient in a body of knowledge that is in form and content largely opaque to the generalist judge. This comparative imbalance in epistemic competency provides a basis for judicial deference to the agency's economic assessments grounded on the latter's 'epistemic authority'.[2] In such a case, the judge acknowledges her 'epistemic deficit'[3] in evaluating the economic evidence enshrined in regulatory decisions and accords greater weight to the judgment of the agency, which is closer to the facts on the ground. Aileen Kavanagh refers to this kind of deference as 'substantial'[4] deference, in the course of which the judge recognises her 'institutional shortcomings'[5] in respect of an issue. It follows that failure on the part of the court to afford substantial deference to the regulator will lead to the court giving a wrong pronouncement on the issue at stake. Seen this way, substantial deference is reflected in 'thin rationality' review that has been adopted by the US courts. Crucially, it differs from the 'minimal' deference that is owed to the agency because of constitutional reasons.[6]

The claim that agency expertise in regulatory matters is a good ground for showing judicial restraint is by no means a suggestion for blanket deference to the economic

[1] Rufus C Taylor, *Embedding Evidence Based Policy Making in Regulatory Organisation: A Case Study of the UK Office of Communications—OFCOM* (PhD thesis, Univ of Oxford 2009) 125 .

[2] See Paul Horwitz, 'Three Faces of Deference' (2008) 83 Notre Dame L Rev 1061, 1079–90.

[3] Scott Brewer, 'Scientific Expert Testimony and Intellectual Due Process' (1998) 107 Yale LJ 1535, 1586.

[4] Aileen Kavanagh, 'Deference or Defiance' in Grant Huscroft (ed), *Expounding the Constitution: Essays in Constitutional Theory* (CUP 2008) 191.

[5] ibid 139, 192.

[6] ibid.

assessments of expert regulators whatsoever. The reason why judges are prepared to defer to expert economic assessments is because we have accepted within adjudication a trade-off between the need for expertise and the need for control over arbitrary exercise of power.[7] Indeed, as we discussed in Chapter 5, the tension between deference to expertise and democratic oversight was among the greatest issues confronting the US in the wake of the New Deal Policies with scholars advocating an enhanced role for the courts in evaluating the value-laden determinations of regulatory agencies. But the situation is somewhat complicated here. As has been discussed throughout the book, while regulatory agencies are entrusted with technical decisions, at the same time these decisions are explicitly policy-laden. It is helpful to briefly introduce here the distinction between 'discretion of a technical nature',[8] and 'discretion of a political nature',[9] which was originally introduced by the EU courts in their effort to domesticate the European Commission's wide discretionary power.[10] Broadly, discretion of a political nature is 'justified by the fact that the institutions must generally reconcile divergent interests and thus select options within the context of the policy choices which are their responsibility'.[11] Discretion of a technical nature is defined as 'the discretion allowed to the institutions ... justified by the complexity of the technical, economic, and legal situations they have to examine and of the assessments which they have to make'.[12] As discussed in Chapter 4, the layer of discretionary power inserted by economics into the realm of utility regulation is not limited to what has been described as 'discretion of a technical nature', but further invades the realm of 'discretion of a political nature', thus blurring their boundaries. In such situations the argument for a strong judicial oversight on grounds of democratic deficit is weakened. Great weight should be and typically is given, as evidenced in the preceding discussion, to expertise for epistemic reasons detailed above. The comparative imbalance in epistemic competency and the fact that such bodies generally set policy for a large class of consumers, skews the accountability trade-off towards deference to expertise.

Does this mean the end of judicial review of economic evidence? Certainly not. Even in situations where a policy or value dimension arises, the role of the judge remains relevant. In such situations, though not constrained by the need to defer to expertise, judges have an important contribution to make in invigorating the democratic elements of the regulatory decision-making process and ensuring the decision's 'thick' legality. For instance, a court might enforce procedural rights to facilitate greater transparency and consideration of different views. This is even more so when expert assessments are polycentric in nature. Indeed, procedural rights offer the promise of presenting a range of tools that courts can use to bring the benefits of affected parties' participation in polycentric disputes, without imposing undue finality over agencies' policy-making discretion. There are various procedural rights that the courts

[7] For a discussion, see Jeff King, Judging Social Rights (CUP 2012) ch 8.

[8] See AG Léger, Opinion in Case C-40/03P *Rica Foods (Free Zone) NV v Commission* [2005] ECR I-68 II [45]–[56].

[9] ibid.

[10] ibid. See also Alexander Fritzche 'Discretion, Scope of Judicial Review and Institutional Balance in European Union' (2010) 47 Common Mark L Rev 361, 368.

[11] See AG Léger Opinion (n 8) [45].

[12] ibid [46].

may decide to activate to enhance the robustness of the regulatory decision-making process, such as, (i) reasonable access to information; (ii) mandatory consideration of a particular interest or factor; (iii) duty of consultation; and (iv) right to be provided with reasons. The range of procedural rights also show how judges can deploy various techniques depending on the case before them in order to adjust the intensity of judicial review of final decision-making. An interesting case that exemplifies this point is *Vodafone v OFCOM*.[13] Vodafone brought an appeal against a decision by OFCOM to modify the system of telephone number portability. Vodafone alleged that OFCOM had breached several of its obligations including the obligation to correctly evaluate the likely benefits and detriments arising from the implementation of its proposed decision due to various procedural flaws during the public consultation process. The CAT noted that the decision had followed a lengthy process, but that mere consultation and transparency alone were not sufficient grounds to save the decision: 'The purpose of the consultation is to seek the informed views of, and best available information from, industry and, with the benefit of the expertise inherent in a specialised adjudicative body apply those views and information to the perceived industry failings.'[14] Citing *Coughlan*,[15] the Tribunal found unanimously that 'the process undertaken by OFCOM had not fully allowed stakeholders 'to provide intelligent and realistic responses as to the likely costs of adopting the proposed modifications ... [I]n the absence of a provisional technical specification on which consultees could provide useful data, OFCOM deprived themselves of the opportunity properly to inform their analysis of the potential costs of their proposals'.[16] The Tribunal chose an interesting remedy: it remitted the whole matter back to OFCOM for reconsideration directing the agency to 'seek the fresh views of the industry on the issue of altering the current arrangements in the UK for fixed and mobile porting, on the basis of appropriate evidence and analysis in light of the findings set out in this judgment'.[17]

Another case in point comes from the High Court this time. In *British Gas Trading Ltd v GEMA*,[18] British Gas successfully challenged the level of the price cap set by OFGEM on certain tariffs for the retail supply of domestic energy, on the basis that the regulator had based its calculations on an incorrect assumption, which had led to an unfair consultation and amounted to a mistake of fact. British Gas challenged the assessment of the sufficiency of the wholesale energy cost allowance, which was used to calculate the price cap, arguing that the regulator had relied on an incorrect assumption about the behaviour of a 'typical' supplier in respect of the supplier's hedging strategy in relation to purchasing wholesale energy that the suppliers did not have an opportunity to comment upon. British Gas sought declaratory relief.

In her judgment, Mrs Justice Andrews while recognising the complexity of the task of setting the price cap at the appropriate level, concluded that the assumption was not communicated to the consultees before making the decision, despite the

[13] *Vodafone Ltd v OFCOM* [2008] CAT 22.
[14] ibid [94].
[15] *R v North and East Devon Health Authority, ex p Coughlan* [2001] QB 213.
[16] *Vodafone Ltd v OFCOM* (n 13) [95].
[17] ibid [159].
[18] *R (on the application of British Gas Trading Ltd) v Gas & Electricity Markets Authority and others* [2019] EWHC 3048 (Admin).

assumption being a 'critical factor in' and 'underpinned' the regulator's assessment.[19] According to well-established standards governing consultations, the process must be fair to allow the consultees to address the issue in question before a final decision is made. Particularly relevant here was the requirement to provide consultees with sufficient information to enable them to put forward an intelligent response.[20] As a consequence of the above, the Court found that OFGEM's reasoning in reaching is decision had been insufficiently transparent, the aspect of the consultation process that related to the assumption was unfair, and British Gas was entitled to relief on that basis. Interestingly, although it was not necessary for the granting of relief, the Court contended that OFGEM's assumption was wrong insofar as large suppliers had in fact adopted different purchasing strategies such that the allowance was vitiated by an error of fact.[21] This is indeed one of the rare occasions the generalist High Court declared OFGEM's decision unlawful and directed it to reconsider the relevant wholesale costs allowance. Typically, any ground based on factual 'error' is perceived as a question going to the weight given to a particular set of facts or analysis, and this is a matter of administrative discretion beyond the remit of a court in a judicial review, which demonstrates the severe limitations of judicial review in this field. The regulator typically responds invoking its specialist expertise in the sector it regulates and successfully, most of the times, argues that a court should be slow to impugn its judgment. In this case OFGEM might indeed be considered to be 'expert' in issues relating to imposition of a retail price cap (which was not quashed and remains in place), however in carrying out the setting of a retail price cap, Ofgem had not grappled with the relevant information, and this was ultimately framed by the judge as a failure to consult.[22]

There are however a set of situations where judicial deference to agency expertise is inappropriate. One can distinguish between two categories of situations where this occurs. First, when the regulatory agency has not applied its expertise to the problem. Secondly, in situations of agency capture. Each will be examined in turn.

The fact that the regulatory agency possesses expert knowledge does not necessarily mean that it will employ its expertise in every case. The case law demonstrates that there are instances where the regulator has not applied his economic expertise to the problem. For example, the regulatory agency may have disregarded a relevant factor or may have failed to consider a relevant consideration. In fact, a failure of expertise is a well-recognised principle in the US case law: 'Deference to the administrator's expertise is inapplicable where the administrator has failed to apply his expertise to a particular decision.'[23] There are a number of cases where courts have compelled the regulator to apply itself to a particular problem. For example, in *Hutchison 3G (UK) Ltd v OFCOM*,[24] the CAT partially upheld the appeal against

[19] ibid [73].

[20] See *R (Help Refugees Ltd) v SSHD* [2018] EWCA Civ 2098 cited.

[21] As set out in *E v Secretary of State for the Home Department* [2004] EWCA Civ 49.

[22] See also *R (on the application of Gwynt-y-Môr Offshore Wind Farm Ltd) v Gas and Electricity Markets Authority* [2019] EWHC 654 (Admin) (Ofgem was said to have only taken a 'high level' approach to evidence (including evidence by actual experts) and so 'failed to grapple with the material before it' [156] such that the decision was overturned).

[23] *Gilbertson v Allied Signal, Inc* 328 F3d 625 (10th Cir 2003).

[24] [2005] CAT 39.

OFCOM's Wholesale Mobile Voice Call Determination and found that OFCOM had erred in its determination of SMP because it had not carried out a full assessment of the extent to which BT had countervailing buying power, which would negate the finding of SMP on the part of Hutchison. In essence, the Tribunal took a closer look at the observable indicators laid down in the Commission's Guidelines and adopted by OFCOM when assessing whether a mobile network operator has SMP in the market for wholesale voice call termination: (a) market share; (b) ease of market entry; (c) excessive prices and profitability; and (d) countervailing buyer power. In such situations, courts will compel the agency to apply itself to a particular problem by applying remedies.

Failure to apply expertise may be also due to non-expert bias. A telling example of refusal to apply expertise for political reasons is found in the *State Farm* case, discussed in Chapter 5. The agency at issue changed its policy regarding the necessity of mandating motor vehicle safety constraints without adequately considering certain obvious alternatives. It is said that the incoming agency chief, appointed by President Reagan, intended to apply party ideology to the issue and disregard the alternatives.[25] In our context, non-expert bias is also reflected in structural and ideational constraints to which regulators may become vulnerable, as the case of OFGEM paradigmatically reveals. As discussed in Chapter 4, sound economic analysis was sidelined and the role of economic expertise within the organisation was undermined because of political influence and considerations.

Secondly, overreliance on agency's expertise may not account for the possibility of agency capture. Regulatory agencies are under the continuous threat of interest group capture because of the very essence of the deregulatory process. Deregulation is not only limited to the abolishment of complex rules designed to curb state-sanctioned monopolies' power, but further entails their replacement with a new set of rules subject also to government oversight. Unlike free market competition, deregulation requires a continuous regulatory and governmental 'hand' to 'manage'[26] the emerging competition. Though agency capture has not arisen to the same degree in Great Britain compared to the US, one cannot exclude the possibility and assume that agencies are immune from it.

### 7.2.2 Limited Access to Information

Another comparative institutional disadvantage of the courts is their limited access to information that is relevant to the dispute in question. Judges depend for their information on the evidence that is put before them in a case. In other words, they are situated decision-makers, called to decide upon regulatory disputes on an *ad hoc* basis. This is especially the case in the context of adversarial proceedings (that characterise

[25] See King (n 7) ch 8.

[26] See Gregory Sidak and Daniel Spulber, 'Deregulation and Managed Competition in Network Industries' (1998) 15 Yale J Reg 117, 118 and Dale Lehman and Dennis Weisman, *The Telecommunications Act of 1996: The Costs of Managed Competition* (Kluwer 2000).

both the generalist and the specialist courts examined in the book), whereby the adjudicator is informed solely by the litigating parties and thus she is significantly insulated from the whole spectrum of relevant information. The regulatory agency, on the other hand, has a continuous involvement in the administration of the sector it supervises and enjoys broad access to information regarding the problems and characteristics thereof. This in turn may warrant a high degree of deference to the regulators' assessments because of their superior institutional capacity in gathering and assessing relevant information.

There are several ways by which the regulatory agency can acquire such information. First, during the consultation period that precedes the promulgation of a new rule. All UK utility regulators enjoy statutory information gathering powers,[27] which they may use if they believe it is appropriate to do so. Both the consultation and the pre-consultation processes allow the gathering of relevant market data, the exchanges of view with affected interests, and therefore enable epistemic communities representing different values to be represented in the regulatory process. This in turn allows a broader representation of the diverse set of consumer preferences, which strengthens the agency's capacity to assess the effects of its interventions. In the case of the US, the main mechanism for the provision of relevant information is the 'notice and comment' rulemaking process. The FERC, for example, frequently solicits comments from regulated industries, competitors, and interested citizens and organisations, collectively referred to as interest groups.[28]

Secondly, the regulatory agency collects relevant information during the enforcement stage. Evidence gathering tools are important in this respect. For example, in the US context, the APA has endorsed fairly liberal standards for the admissibility of evidence in formal proceedings,[29] whereas agencies are free to complement the standards of the APA with those found in the Federal Rules of Civil Procedure or in the Federal Rules of Evidence. Additionally, trial staff that participate in the administrative litigation process enjoy a wide array of tools, from data requests and dispositions to inspections and interrogatories to collect relevant information and ensure that the evidentiary record developed is adequate for decision-making by the Administrative Law Judge and the Commission. In the UK context, utility regulators and the CMA also possess wide evidence collection tools. OFCOM, for example, makes frequent use of its statutory information-gathering powers when exercising its regulatory functions.[30] To take another example, the CMA has the power to require the submission of additional information and clarification of the evidence during energy licence modification appeals. It may also commission expert evidence to help it interrogate evidence submitted by the appellant and by OFGEM. Parties are permitted

[27] See, eg, Communications Act 2003, ss 135 and 136.

[28] Susan W Yackee, 'Sweet-Talking the Fourth Branch: The Influence of Interest Groups Comments on Federal Agency Rulemaking' (2006) 16 J Public Adm Res Theory 103.

[29] APA, 5 USC § 556(d).

[30] Communications Act 2003, s 145.

to introduce new evidence in so far as the appeal body considers it is relevant to the issue before it.

### 7.2.3 Lack of Requisite Institutional Legitimacy

As compared to regulatory agencies, both generalist courts and specialist tribunals lack the requisite institutional legitimacy to address cases involving broad policy considerations and value-laden determinations. As already discussed in detail in Chapters 4 to 6, in many contexts, regulatory agencies are required to trade off efficiency with equity considerations. This is because utility regulation has diverse legitimate aims that are not solely guided by economic efficiency. For example, as we saw in Chapter 5, conditions for access to bottleneck services for new entrants are mainly driven by efficiency considerations related to the creation of a competitive marketplace. The provision of universal service, however, seeks to create equality of outcome by supporting the service to a legislatively defined category of users. This may involve the provision of a set of services to end users at prices that depart from those resulting from normal conditions. In such cases, a trade-off may arise in meeting the objective of promoting competition, while at the same time ensuring universal access to a set of services.

The regulatory agency may be said to enjoy superior institutional legitimacy in resolving such trade-offs deriving in turn from her political accountability. This is acknowledged by the US DC Circuit, when reviewing the scope and funding mechanisms of universal service. The agency is undoubtedly more informed on current political preferences than the judiciary, which makes it 'more likely to accurately reflect current enactable preferences than judicial estimates about what political forces would enact'.[31] The judiciary, on the other hand, is a 'counter-majoritarian'[32] institution composed of unelected judges who should not use their power of review to act contrary to the 'majority will' as expressed by representative institutions. Hence, an increased judicial interference with policy choices jeopardises the legitimacy of the institution. Especially in the UK context, institutional legitimacy considerations are strongly pronounced, considering the principle of parliamentary sovereignty. Minimal deference, thus, becomes relevant because there are constitutional reasons for granting authority over the judiciary to the agency. The judge, however, will still have to assess the economic methodologies and considerations employed to support the agency's policy decision as well as the factors relevant to the regulators' determinations. But as Chapter 6 demonstrated, the more expert the court or the tribunal in economics the greater the scrutiny that will be applied. But the court cannot pronounce on the right policy to be pursued because the agency has the legitimate authority to decide on this.

[31] Einer Elhauge, 'Preference-Estimating Statutory Default Rules' (2002) 18 Colum L Rev 2027, 2129.

[32] Alexander Bickel, *The Least Dangerous Branch* (Yale Univ Press 1962); Barry Friedmam. 'The Birth of an Academic Obsession: The History of the Countermajoritarian Difficulty, Part Five' (2002) 112 Yale LJ 153.

### 7.2.4 Courts' Susceptibility to 'Minoritarian Bias'

Contrary to what intuition would suggest, courts, and not solely regulatory agencies, can be susceptible to 'rent seeking' influences. While the initial wave of public choice scholars addressed judges as operating outside the world of special interests,[33] the 'new school of public choice theory' increasingly brings the courts into the framework of public choice analysis.[34] For example, Frank Cross argues that '[c]ourts are simply another venue in which influence may be brought to bear upon government policy'.[35] He further discusses the variety of forms that the lobbying of courts can take, including 'text cases and forum shopping, amicus curiae participation, provision of expert witnesses, selective settlement and other techniques'.[36] Therefore, the Olsonian tenets of interest group theory can also be ratified in the context of litigation, as narrow groups with greater economic stakes in regulatory issues will be more willing to devote time and resources to hiring the best lawyers and economic experts for their case, so as to be effectively represented in expensive litigation over regulatory disputes.[37] Ultimately, the judge might end up being captured by special interests.

Most worryingly, courts' susceptibility to 'minoritarian bias' might exacerbate the instances of tactical litigation. In other words, narrow groups may be encouraged to bring unmeritorious appeals with a view to hampering or obstructing the regulators' functions. In the UK, OFCOM has advanced concerns about tactical litigation in the context of spectrum policy where incumbent mobile operators allegedly attempted to hold up by the threat of litigation the auction for the 800MHz/2.6GHz spectrum. Strategic litigation may also be encouraged in the aftermath of the *Infinis*[38] judgment in the UK, which, as already discussed in Chapter 3, introduced a novel action for damages for unlawful state actions in violation of the ECHR rights. Companies may be willing to use human rights claims to seek more favourable forms of redress in judicial review proceedings.

## 7.3 Implications for Polycentric Disputes

The case of polycentric disputes epitomises the balance of institutional competencies approach in determining the appropriate scope of review of economic evidence. As

[33] William Landes and Richard Posner, 'The Independent Judiciary in an Interest Group Perspective' (1975) 18 J L Econ 875.

[34] Daniel Farber and Anne Joseph O' Connell, 'Introduction: A Brief Trajectory of Public Choice and Public Law' in D Farber and A O' Connell (eds), *Research Handbook in Public Law and Public Choice* (Edward Elgar 2010) 4.

[35] Frank Cross, 'The Judiciary and Public Choice' (1998) 50 Hastings LJ 355, 360.

[36] ibid.

[37] See Mancur Olson, *The Logic of Collective Action: Public Goods and the Theory of Groups* (Harvard Univ Press 1971); Susan Olson, 'Interest Group Litigation in Federal District Courts: Beyond the Political Disadvantage Theory' (1990) 52 J Pol 854, 859; Donald Songer and Reginald Sheehan, 'Who Wins on Appeal: Upperdogs and Underdogs in the United States Courts of Appeals' (1992) 36 Am J Pol Sci 235.

[38] *R (on the application of Infinis Plc) v GEMA* [2011] EWHC 1873 (Admin). See further *R (on the application of Gravis Solar 1 Ltd and another) v GEMA* [2021] EWHC 490 (Admin).

you may recall, such disputes do not solely involve the assessment of complex economic appraisals, but further the difficulty of distinguishing who will be affected in the complex web of interdependent relationships. Concealed polycentric elements are present in all problems resolved by adjudication. The more polycentric a dispute is, the more flexible the decision-maker should be, and the more 'liberally' judicial precedents would be interpreted and subject to reformulation, as problems not originally foreseen arise.

Of course, courts in the realm of economic regulation enjoy a strong judicial mandate to adjudicate polycentric issues deriving from the agencies' governing statute. One can think of the judicial interpretation of vague terms such as 'just and reasonable' rates. In such cases the legislators no doubt knew that courts would adjudicate highly polycentric disputes and balanced that cost against the harm of allowing powerful firms to abuse their power. But relative institutional competence considerations highlight the fact that courts lack the access to information that specialist regulators enjoy which is crucial in acquiring an informed view of the diverse and heterogeneous interests at play. The regulator on the other hand through negotiation and consultation can acquire such a view. For instance, in the course of designing the Revenue = Incentives + Innovation + Outputs (RRIO) price control mechanism OFGEM sought to enhance the engagement of heterogeneous interests, such as consumer representatives, network users, and companies. The authority also set up a Consumer Challenge Group for the RRIO-ED1 network price control to act as a 'critical friend' to OFGEM to help ensure that the price control settlement is in the best interests of existing and future consumers.[39] Moreover, the regulatory process may be better at ensuring the adequate representation of those groups that have been traditionally deemed vulnerable to 'majoritarian bias', such as the disabled, the elderly, or the chronically sick. You may recall from Chapter 4 that UK utility regulators have a specific objective to promote the interests of such groups.[40] The adjudicative process, however, cannot consider, to the same extent, the complex repercussions that may result from the establishment of a price control mechanism nor secure the meaningful participation of all affected interests in court. Hence, it is the polycentric dimension of such disputes rather than the difficulty of courts in general to deal with price setting, which may warrant a greater flexibility to the regulatory agency to assess the weight of the relevant issues at stake.

Despite the inherent weakness of using the judicial process for evaluating polycentric regulatory decisions, one can think of certain mechanisms to adjust the adjudicative process to polycentric questions, such as the possibility for third party interventions that allow the representation of a greater number of interests in court. For example, the CAT's rules of procedure allow third parties, who are sufficiently interested in the outcome of proceedings, the right to be heard and assist the Tribunal.[41] But the CAT cannot invite or require parties to intervene if they do not wish to. We shall return to this point shortly (in section 7.4.2), where we will explore how the rules of procedure

[39] OFGEM, Consumer Challenge Group available at: <http://www.ofgem.gov.uk/network-regulation-%E2%80%93-riio-model/riio-forums-seminars-and-working-groups/consumer-challenge-group> accessed 6 June 2022.

[40] The Electronic Communications (Universal Service) (Amendment) Order 2011 (SI 2011/1209); Gas Act 1986, s 4AA(2); Electricity Act 1989, s 3A2.

[41] CAT Rules 2015 (SI 2015/1648), 19c.

may enhance the information record of the courts concerning the dispute in question and allow for a better representation of affected interests. These procedural rules may in turn serve to attenuate the courts' comparative institutional disadvantages in considering polycentric disputes.

## 7.4 Factors Attenuating the Comparative Institutional Disadvantages of Courts

While institutional competence considerations are an influential factor in determining the appropriate scope of review of economic evidence, they are not decisive. The presence of several institutional realities may significantly attenuate the comparative institutional disadvantages of courts and hence the degree of deference accorded to the regulatory agency's economic assessments. This section will discuss a non-exhaustive list of such realities. Broadly, those relate to (i) the courts' specialisation in regulatory matters and (ii) the courts' rules of procedure.

### 7.4.1 Courts' Specialisation in Regulatory Matters

In the presence of a specialist tribunal, like the CAT, the deference afforded to the regulatory agency's economic determinations may be lower in comparison to where the assessment is made by a generalist court without any direct access to epistemic competence. The CAT itself has acknowledged that its familiarity with the statutory regime as well as 'the relevant expertise in its disposal may render the Tribunal a more demanding and/or less deferential tribunal than might otherwise be the case where a court is called upon to review a decision of a specialist regulator'.[42] One should also add that the legislative provision of the appeal rights on the merits also encourages the appellate institution to engage with economic arguments, within the limits of the Grounds of Appeal. As discussed in Chapter 6, in a number of cases, judges have not hesitated to engage in a forensic review of complex regulatory issues, to delve into the detail of the regulator's reasoning and eventually overturn her decision.

The court's specialisation in economic expertise, through its repeated exposure to regulatory disputes may also enhance its relative epistemic competence vis-à-vis the agencies. For example, you may recall that the US DC Circuit's members achieve a certain degree of specialisation through their repeated exposure to regulatory cases. This kind of specialisation, owing to rules of venue and geographical patterns in litigation, is better captured in the notion of 'subject-matter' specialisation. The mechanisms of opinion specialisation and case assignment may also ameliorate the institutional disadvantages of courts with respect to their lack of economic expertise.

Finally, judges' prior educational background or training in economics or, possibly, their prior experience in a regulatory agency of some kind may strengthen their capacity to deal with economic evidence. Except for CAT Panel Members, this

[42] *BSkyB v CC* [2008] CAT 25 [61].

is extremely rare if not completely absent in the UK. In sharp contrast, US judges have proven to be particularly receptive to economic authority in regulatory disputes. Although US justices are largely self-perceived as generalists, they have often taken a variety of career paths before their judgeship. For example, they may have engaged in private practice of law, academia, legal government practice, or they might have held executive policy positions in a regulatory agency of some kind. Consider, for instance, Justice Breyer of the US Supreme Court, who had extensive experience in policymaking before joining the bench. He served, *inter alia*, as Assistant to the Attorney General of the US Department of Justice and was instrumental in drafting the 1975 report that made possible the passage of the Airline Deregulation Act. It is safe to argue that judges' prior experience in the regulatory process makes them more attentive to the underlying policy issues of regulatory disputes.

Another rationale affecting the US courts' openness to economic authority as an external source of wisdom is a less obvious one and it derives from two jurisprudential movements that originated in the US, that of sociological jurisprudence[43] and legal realism.[44] Both movements developed as a reaction against formalism (otherwise known as 'mechanical jurisprudence')[45] that largely characterised traditional legal theory in the latter half of the nineteenth century. The formalists applied the 'logic' of 'hard sciences' to the law in an effort to produce unique and correct answers to cases under consideration. On the contrary, scholars such as Pound, Brandeis, and Cardozo attempted to recast their decisions in the light of the social and economic facts upon which they were adjudicated. The famous 'Brandeis brief',[46] the first in the Unites States legal history to rely on the combination of scientific and social science data epitomised the advent of sociological jurisprudence in the US courts. A closer examination of judicial discourse today will reveal that judges often engage in a judicial debate over substantive policy issues, while individual opinions take the form of discursive essays that frequently employ a variety of legal and non-legal arguments to justify their decisions.[47]

### 7.4.2 The Courts' Rules of Procedure

The courts' rules of procedure may enhance the information record of the court concerning the dispute in question and allow for the better representation of affected interests. This in turn strengthens the institutional capacity of the court to deal with polycentric disputes. For instance, the CAT's procedural rules favour an extensive, often forensic in nature, examination in respect of each aspect of the regulators'

[43] See, eg, Roscoe Pound, 'The Scope and Purpose of Sociological Jurisprudence' (1911) 24 Harvard L Rev 591.

[44] Defining Legal Realism with precision is not easy. It mostly refers to a body of legal thought produced for the most part by law professors at Columbia and Yale Law Schools during the 1920s and the 1930s. See the movement led by Karl Llewellyn in William Twining, *Karl Llewellyn and the Realist Movement* (Weidenfeld and Nicolson 1973).

[45] See Roscoe Pound, 'Mechanical Jurisprudence' (1908) 8 Colum L Rev 605.

[46] *Muller v Oregon*, 208 US 412 (1908).

[47] Mitchel de S-O-l'E. Lasser, *Judicial Deliberations-A Comparative Analysis of Judicial Transparency and Legitimacy* (OUP 2010) 16.

findings of fact and expert analysis.[48] Prominent amongst these is the obligation on the part of the Tribunal to ensure case management through active intervention.[49] Unlike the narrow scope of the duty of case management on the High Court, there is wide scope for case management under the CAT's Rules of Procedure.[50] Those rules, which are partly based upon those of the EU General Court as well as on the Civil Procedure Rules,[51] crucially reserve to the CAT a central role in controlling the process, which is not inquisitorial but adversarial. During the case management conference, which consists of a pre-hearing review serving a variety of functions (eg evidence gathering and fact-finding), the Tribunal may order the disclosure of documents or require the parties to particularise their pleadings. There also exists an enforcement mechanism in the form of penalties for non-compliance with the court orders. Indeed, active case management is key to the CAT's way of working, as is the 'single docket' approach where one judge/panel handles the case from the start.

Crucially, one of the 'unusual'[52] powers the CAT enjoys is that it can direct under its rules the evidence that it considers necessary or useful for the determination of a dispute.[53] This flexible approach to evidence includes the discretionary power to admit or exclude new evidence in appeals, that is, evidence that was not put forward by the parties during the investigatory phase. Enunciated in rule 21(2) of the CAT's Rules of Procedure 2015, this power applies to both statutory appeals and reviews and it attempts to guide the Tribunal's exercise of discretion by enumerating, on a non-exclusive basis, factors that the Tribunal is required to take into account in its determination, such as 'the statutory provision under which the appeal is brought'[54] or 'the question of whether the evidence was available and the reasons why it wasn't made available'.[55] The former reflects the qualitative differences that exist between competition law appeals and the criminal nature of the infringement decision and appeals against a dispute determination by OFCOM under the 2003 Communications Act and applications for judicial review.[56] The latter reflects the concern that litigants may deliberately withhold evidence during the investigatory phase, only to produce it at the appeal phase. Indeed, rule 21(2) embodies a fundamental tension between on the one hand safeguarding the rights of the defence by allowing an appellant to adduce new evidence in appeal, and on the other hand that of the effective enforcement of the law that could be severely undermined if the undertakings tactically hold on to evidence without a proper reason only to deploy it later in appeal. Recourse to the legislative history of the Rule reveals that the adequacy of the reasons why the evidence was not submitted during the administrative phase is crucial in determining the admission or exclusion of evidence.

[48] See, eg, *Everything Everywhere Ltd v CC* [2012] CAT 11.

[49] CAT, Guide to Proceedings (2015), section 7.

[50] CAT Rules 2015 (n 41).

[51] Civil Procedure Rules (SI 1998/2123).

[52] In *British Telecommunications v OFCOM* [2011] EWCA Civ 245 [21], Toulson LJ.

[53] For an analysis see, Renato Nazzini and Despoina Mantzari, 'The Ruling of the UK Competition Appeal Tribunal in *Ping v Competition and Markets Authority*' (2018) 6 JAE 281.

[54] CAT Rules 2015 (n 41), rule 21(2)(a).

[55] ibid rule 21(2)(c).

[56] To this effect, see CAT Guide to Proceedings (n 49), section 7.78 (a).

Regarding rule 21, the Tribunal may consider, for example, an econometric study that had not yet been conducted when the regulatory agency was forming its decision. *Vodafone v OFCOM*,[57] discussed earlier, is a case in point. On the basis of the witness statement submitted on behalf of the intervener H3G the CAT decided that OFCOM's decision to mandate direct routing of calls to ported numbers was not robust and should be overturned. The CAT considers its ability to consider new evidence as conferring 'a broad discretion to the Tribunal regarding the admission or exclusion of evidence which discretion is colored by the nature of the appeal that is being heard'.[58] The circumstances under which the CAT should admit fresh evidence were elucidated in principle by the Court of Appeal in *BT v OFCOM*.[59] It was stressed that OFCOM is not only an adjudicative but an investigative body, and the appellant should be able to produce material to rebut OFCOM's conclusions from its investigation. But it was also made clear that no party should enjoy an unfettered right to adduce fresh evidence on appeal and that parties should present their cases during the administrative phase as fully as the circumstances permit. Rather, in the event of a dispute about its admission, precisely because the introduction of fresh evidence is not a matter of right, it should be regarded 'as a possibility of the party who wants to introduce it to show why the CAT should admit it'.[60] The question for the CAT would be whether in all the circumstances it considers that it is in the interests of justice for the evidence to be admitted. In sharp contrast, a High Court judge will typically refuse to allow a decision-maker to adduce evidence to justify its original decision or to allow a party to challenge a decision on the basis of material that was not available to the decision-maker when the original decision was made. In such cases, the High Court will normally remit the decision for reconsideration by the original decision-maker on the basis of the new evidence. The rationale for that restrictive approach is that the reviewing court should normally be directing its attention to the material available to the body whose decision is being reviewed rather than deciding the merits of the case *de novo*.[61]

Finally, although the CAT is first and foremost an appellate tribunal and not the primary fact-finder, the information record is enhanced through its discretion to permit oral cross-examination of witnesses, especially when the primary facts are in dispute.[62] In fact, the Tribunal has gone as far as to argue that a merits appeal 'provides ... a right to call and cross examine witness[es]'.[63] Although the CAT disfavours 'prolonged cross-examination sessions that last for days and days and days',[64] in a number of regulatory disputes it has ordered the cross-examination of witnesses. In the *PPC*[65] case, for instance, which involved a challenge against OFCOM's determination to resolve disputes between BT and other communications providers regarding BT charges for Partial Private Circuits (PPCs), four witnesses were cross-examined on the economic

[57] See n 13.

[58] *BT (British Telecommunications plc (Termination Charges: 080 calls) v OFCOM* [2010] CAT 17 [83].

[59] See *BT v OFCOM* [2011] EWCA Civ 245 [72], Toulson LJ.

[60] ibid.

[61] This was the reason behind the court's refusal to admit fresh expert evidence in relation to the provision of public sewers in *Dwr Cymru Cyfyngedig v Environment Agency of Wales* [2003] EWHC 336 (Admin).

[62] See CAT Rules 2015 (n 41), rule 55(h).

[63] *VIP Communications Ltd v OFCOM* [2007] CAT 3 [43].

[64] *Argos Ltd & Littlewoods Ltd v OFT* [2003] CAT 10.

[65] *BT v OFCOM* (PPC) [2011] CAT 5.

assessments underlying BT's cost-orientation obligation. To take another example, in the *08-numbers* case[66] involving two appellants (BT plc and Everything Everywhere Ltd), OFCOM as a defendant and five interveners, forty-nine witness statements and expert reports were adduced in evidence, thirteen witnesses of fact provided evidence, and seven economic experts were cross-examined on the twenty-four reports analysing the impact of BT's proposed price charges. Cross-examination can be a powerful mechanism in exposing witnesses whose evidence is not empirically supported, contradictory, or misleading.

Most interestingly, the CAT recently implemented the 'hot tub' approach.[67] A 'hot tub' refers to the mechanism by which expert witness evidence is taken concurrently with the relevant tribunal taking the lead in questioning the experts, usually with counsel then having the opportunity to ask supplementary questions of the expert called by the other side. 'Hot tubs' seek to identify areas where experts are in agreement and flag up those where there is disagreement. The judge is not confined to the opinion of one advisor but has the benefit of multiple advisors who are rigorously examined in public. Hot tubbing works best when the relevant experts agree on the basic economic principles that are in play but disagree on their interpretation and application to the case.[68] The CAT normally asks the experts to also agree a reasoned schedule of issues on which they agree/disagree for use at the trial.

The Civil Procedure Rules contemplate that there can be a 'conversation' between the parties' experts, and that the court can also ask the defendant's expert to comment on what the claimant's expert has just said about an issue.[69] Surprisingly, hot tubbing in a competition law case was used for the first time in the High Court in *Streetmap. EU Ltd v Google Inc*,[70] a dispute concerning the alleged abuse of dominant position by Google regarding online streetmapping. The economist experts were hot tubbed concerning measuring searches for online maps or online mapping websites. Mr Justice Roth gave permission for the economist experts in the 'hot tub' to respond to each other's questions directly on areas where they were in dispute. But this should be considered an exception. 'Hot tubbing' is obviously only possible when you have witness evidence. The High Court rarely hears witnesses or expert witnesses in a judicial review case. Indeed, the evidentiary constraints of judicial review before the High Court are highlighted in *BT v Secretary of Business, Innovation & Skills*,[71] involving BT's challenge by way of judicial review to the implementation of the Digital Economy Act 2010. The following extract from the judgment of Justice Kenneth Parker recognises that although economic evidence was adduced, the constraints of judicial review and the High Court's case management rules, meant that it was not possible to scrutinise the volume of the material submitted to the Court:

[66] See *BT and others v OFCOM* [2012] EWCA Civ 1002.

[67] *British Telecommunications Plc v OFCOM* [2017] CAT 4; *Socrates Training Ltd v The Law Society of England and Wales* [2017] CAT 12.

[68] *TalkTalk and Vodafone v OFCOM* [2020] CAT 8.

[69] See Civil Procedure Rules, PD 35, 11.4(1)

[70] [2016] EWHC 253 (Ch).

[71] *R (on the application of British Telecommunications Plc and another) v Secretary of State for Business, Innovation & Skills and Others (Open Rights Group and another, intervening)* [2011] EWHC 1021.

> In a case of this nature, there are real limits on the process of adjudication. Although I was confronted with 11 files of evidence, I cannot be entirely confident that all relevant material was before me, nor can the sheer constraints of judicial review proceedings afford the time that would be necessary critically and rigorously to evaluate the volume of material that was submitted. For example, a number of expert economists were deployed on each side, putting forward with equal conviction and rigour their rival cases. Experience in the Restrictive Practices Court, now extinct, suggests that a thorough exploration and assessment of such evidence could be likely to take many days of detailed cross-examination.[72]

The chapter has so far put forward the institutional disadvantages of the courts that may warrant a high degree of deference and has highlighted several institutional realties and procedural developments that may attenuate the weight of such comparative institutional disadvantages. This is not only a normative exercise informing the appropriate scope of review of economic evidence, but it is also grounded in the case law of the US and UK courts. Indeed, both the US and the UK courts do assess their relative institutional competence vis-à-vis the regulators in regulatory disputes. We saw in Chapter 5 that the DC Circuit has been attentive to a large extent to institutional competence considerations, especially in ratemaking cases. In the UK, as we discussed in Chapter 6, in the adjudication of regulatory disputes that involve polycentric elements the CAT nearly always affords a considerable degree of deference to the regulators, despite its epistemic competence and the wide possibility for third party interventions that allow the representation of a greater number of interests. For instance, in the *Albion*[73] case, when the Tribunal was asked to specify a minimum retail margin, it refrained from doing so:

> How can the Tribunal [or a competition authority] determine this margin without examining costs and demands, indeed without acting as a price-setting regulator, the determinations of which often last for several years (and are themselves subject to appeals)? … (H)ow [should] the Tribunal, or the Authority, … respond when costs or demands change over time, as inevitably they will. The efficient margin fixed today may, through economic and business changes, become the inefficient margin of tomorrow. We do not say that these questions are unanswerable, but we have said enough to show why courts normally avoid direct price administration, relying on more appropriate methods.[74]

In fact, the Tribunal engaged in an implicit comparative institutional analysis of the relative merits of the adjudicative and regulatory process when presented with polycentric disputes. At the same time the CAT avoided entering into the realm of a price-regulator, setting prices or margins.[75]

[72] ibid [213]–[215].
[73] *Albion Water Ltd v Water Services Regulation Authority* [2006] CAT 23 [31].
[74] Ibid [55].
[75] See also *Flynn Pharma Ltd and Flynn Pharma (Holdings) Ltd v Competition and Markets Authority* [2018] CAT 11.

## 7.5 Lessons for Institutional Design

We can now turn from the allocation of decision-making power across institutions, to the design of the institutions themselves. It will be argued that specialist courts, enjoying both subject-matter specialisation and professional background specialisation in economics, could be the optimal solution for addressing the epistemic asymmetry that exists between the judge and the expert agency in regulatory disputes and could minimise the likelihood of error. The examination of the UK's CAT undertaken in the previous chapter yields some interesting insights on the value of epistemic diversity on the bench. The CAT's bench combines legal and non-legal expertise together with subject-matter specialisation in regulatory and competition law disputes. It further provides an institutional forum where the dialectic relationship between the legal and economic rationalities can develop and flourish. Recent theoretical work on decision-making theory and the law underscores the epistemic benefits of cognitive diversity in institutional design and suggests that a court with at least some lay justices will minimise judicial error across a total number of cases compared to a court with zero lay justices in areas in which the law draws upon non-legal specialised knowledge, such as economics.[76] Furthermore having lay members participating in the deliberation provides an institutional foundation for economic expertise, one that cannot be replicated, as we shall see below, through case-by-case mechanisms for incorporating expert economist's views. It further avoids the situation of, what Adrian Vermeule calls, an 'epistemic bottleneck'.[77] An 'epistemic bottleneck' arises when only a small group of judges trained in law decide whether and how to incorporate non-legal expertise. But to substantiate our claim, we need to consider the institutional alternatives to a specialist court when it comes to the incorporation of economic expertise in the courtroom. Drawing on transaction costs economics, these alternatives can either exist within the boundaries of the 'judicial firm'[78] (eg law clerks) or 'can be contracted out' (eg expert witnesses, court-appointed experts).[79] The remainder of this section will take us through these various options.

### 7.5.1 Expert Witnesses

Expert witnesses differ from ordinary witnesses. While the latter offer evidence which is factual (eg how a business functions in practice), an expert possesses specialist knowledge and is entitled to give evidence of opinion of facts which others have adduced before the court (eg how the business's actions and interactions result in certain market outcomes) and can often measure these effects quantitatively. While expert witnesses have been the dominant method of providing expertise in common law jurisdictions, there are risks stemming from the partisan character of expert witnesses,

[76] Adrian Vermeule, *Law and the Limits of Reason* (OUP 2009) 127.
[77] ibid 50–53.
[78] ibid 152
[79] Oliver Williamson, *Market and Hierarchies: Analysis and Antitrust Implications* (Free Press 1975).

not least because expert witnesses are put forward by the respective parties.[80] There is therefore the risk that the expert will take a specific position to please one of the litigants. The CAT is particularly vigilant on this, and some experts have been criticised for being too partisan.[81]

A second issue that arises is that experts are dependent on the parties to collect economic data and such parties might in turn exhibit a selection bias in favour of the experts that reflect a position that is close to them. As discussed in Chapter 2, economics is far from an objective source of knowledge. The assumptions made, methodology used, variables picked, and data selected will inescapably reflect the economists' personal values and views. The selected data and omitted data may be used in such a way that furthers the parties' outcome and serve to obtain a predetermined result. These features may render the expert witness a 'hired gun' instead of representing a neutral opinion.

This brings us to a third issue, that of the possibility of conflicting expert opinions and testimony. This is especially true in economics where 'virtually every economic proposition is characterized as creating meaningful expert disagreement'.[82] Hence judges cannot merely defer to the discipline of economics as a neutral source for unambiguous factual inputs to a rule or decision.

Some of these issues have been highlighted by Lord Woolf in his report on the civil justice system in England and Wales.[83] He pointed out the excessive cost and the delays associated with each party appointing their own experts and recorded concerns expressed about the failure of experts to maintain their independence from the party by whom they had been instructed. The report led to the adoption of strict rules in Part 35 of the Civil Procedure Rules to regulate the giving of expert evidence promoting at the same time fairness and efficiency considerations. The Rules empower the court to regulate the process by providing that parties must have the permission of the court to call an expert or put in evidence an expert's report. Efficiency is promoted by imposing as a general rule that expert evidence is to be given in a written report, by regulating the written questions which another party may ask of the expert, by providing opportunities for experts to discuss and, if possible, agree the expert issues in the proceedings. Fairness is promoted by regulating the content of the expert's report and requiring the disclosure of the substance of the instructions on which the expert has written the report. Part 35.3 of the CPR enshrines the concept of the independent expert by providing that it is the duty of experts to help the court on matters within their expertise and that that duty overrides any obligation to the person who has instructed them or by whom they are paid. It further provides protection to the expert against, among other things, improper pressure by enabling the expert to seek directions from the court.

[80] Richard A Posner, 'The Law and Economics of the Economic Expert Witness' (1999) 13(2) J Econ Perspect 91.

[81] See, eg, *Sainsbury's Supermarkets v MasterCard* [2016] CAT 11 [27], 3.

[82] Rebecca Haw Allensworth, 'Adversarial Economics in Antitrust Litigation: Losing Academic Consensus in The Battle of the Experts' (2012) 106 Northwestern Univ L Rev 1261, 1264.

[83] Lord Woolf, Access to Justice, Final report to the Lord Chancellor on the civil justice system in England and Wales, June 1996, Ch. 13, available at: <https://webarchive.nationalarchives.gov.uk/ukgwa/+/http:/www.dca.gov.uk/civil/final/contents.htm> accessed 6 June 2022.

Another innovation brought by the UK Civil Procedure Rules (CPR) following Lord Woolf's report has been the concept of the single joint expert. If the issue is not contentious, the parties are encouraged to use a single joint expert (SJE). A SJE is, as the name suggests, one expert instructed by both parties with instructions to report on a particular issue. Part 35.7 of the CPR endorses Lord Woolf's suggestions: '[W]here two or more parties wish to submit expert evidence on a particular issue, the court may direct that the evidence on that issue is to be given by one expert only'. Where the instructing parties cannot agree on who the expert should be, the court may either select the expert from a list prepared by the instructing parties or may devise a different procedure to select the expert. The main rationale for using a SJE is to reduce the costs and delays associated with using expert witnesses on behalf of each of the parties in litigation. This has been in place for a number of years, but experience of SJE appointments confirms that new issues are raised and can actually lead to increased costs and delays. This is most commonly the case when the SJE produces a report which contains conclusions adverse to one party which then seeks to obtain, and put into evidence, a second opinion that is more favourable.

### 7.5.2 Court-appointed Experts

In the US, Rule 706 of the Federal Rules of Evidence empowers a trial judge to appoint his own neutral expert witnesses.[84]A court-appointed expert can mitigate the risk of impartiality (because of the financial bias) that undermines the option of expert witnesses, but may, however, reduce the adversarial character of the procedure and increase the risk of erroneous decisions. There are also increased 'search costs' when deciding to resort to a court-appointed neutral expert. As Judge Posner notes, not only does 'finding, interviewing, and appointing'[85] the neutral expert take time, but the neutral expert does not have a lawyer 'to shepherd and protect'[86] him. Consequently, either the judge must assume that role or the court must find another lawyer to represent the neutral expert pro bono. Court-appointed experts further present a higher risk of error as the judge cannot always be confident that the picked expert is in fact neutral. Ioannis Lianos adds another important and underexplored dimension by highlighting that 'the system of court-appointed experts will tend to maintain the *status quo*, represented by mainstream and well-accepted economic theories, and will reduce the opportunity for minority views to gain access to the courtroom'.[87]

Do the above mechanisms of external economic expertise (expert witnesses, court-appointed experts) provide adequate substitutes for having economists on the bench? Expert witnesses do not address the inherent difficulty of a non-specialist judge to monitor the performance and the reliability of the expert. A hyper specialist tribunal,

[84] For an analysis, see Gregory Sidak, 'Court-Appointed Neutral Economic Experts' (2013) 9(2) J Compet L Econ 359.

[85] Richard Posner, *Reflections on Judging* (Harvard Univ Press 2013) ch 9.

[86] ibid.

[87] Ioannis Lianos, 'Judging Economists': Economic Expertise in Competition Law Litigation: A European View' in Ioannis Lianos and Ioannis Kokkoris (eds), *The Reform of EC Competition Law: New Challenges* (Kluwer Law International 2010) 256.

such as the CAT, on the other hand will be able to cross-examine witnesses and expose misleading evidence and vexatious elements in the proceedings more effectively. This would ensure that in adversarial proceedings, where both parties offer meritorious interpretations of the factual, legal, and economic circumstances, the party with the more complex and sophisticated analysis will not necessarily have a better chance of winning the case simply by resorting to technical wizardry. Procedural innovations such as hot tubbing may also deliver more promise in the context of a specialist court. Because hot tubbing requires the court to take the lead role in questioning the expert witnesses, this naturally requires that the court must have a good grasp of the expert witnesses' written testimony, and of the differences of opinion among the experts, before the hearing commences. Of course, in situations where the expertise/information-gathering function is integrated into that of the adjudication, that is, the expert is an assessor or the judge is an expert himself or has developed expertise in the area, the 'transaction' costs associated with resorting to the provision of external economic expertise are reduced. These represent sources of internal economic expertise to which the next section turns to.

### 7.5.3 Assessors

Following the recommendations of Lord Woolf, Part 35.15(2) of the UK Civil Procedure Rules gives the courts authority to appoint an assessor, with the aim to assist the court in dealing with a matter in which the assessor has skill and expertise. Assessors (or technical advisors, as they are called in the US) are only appointed to assist the court to fulfil its obligations. Contrary to court-appointed experts, they are not strictly subject to the adversarial process. However, because of the *ad hoc* nature of the external appointment, assessors cannot develop an institutional *ethos* in the way a member of the specialist tribunal, who can associate with a public institution with clear statutory responsibilities, does.

### 7.5.4 'Teach-in'

Another less explored option to deal with expert issues is that of the 'teach-in' approach employed for the first time in the UK in the *Electromagnetic Geoservices ASA v Petroleum Geo-Services*,[88] a patents dispute case which involved physics and mathematics. Although the parties eventually settled, Justice Birss explained how the court had appointed a 'neutral scientific advisor' to provide a tutorial, or 'teach-in', on the technical issues arising in the case. The advisor's instructions were settled by the court; she was not informed about the specific issues in the case, but gave 'high-level' assistance; she was asked to prepare materials to educate the court on five topics; and she met with the judge for one day, for a 'candid discussion'.[89] The parties and their representatives were not present during the 'teach-in', but were provided with a copy of the

[88] [2016] EWHC 881 (Pat) (19 April 2016).
[89] ibid [4].

relevant papers afterwards, in the interests of transparency. The advisor did not sit in court for the trial itself either. Justice Birss described the process as a 'useful one'[90] in this case:

> No doubt, in the end, the court might have reached the same level of understanding of the issues eventually, but speaking personally, I would have needed much more time to read into the case in advance without this assistance, and the trial itself would have had to be conducted more slowly. The teach-in allowed the speeches and cross-examination to proceed more briskly than would have been possible without it. So time, and therefore costs, has been saved and the court's comprehension of the issues was significantly improved.[91]

One could envisage a scenario in which it could be valuable where the underlying economics of the case was so complicated that the judge would benefit from a tutorial on the general area. Of course, in the context of a specialist tribunal, such as the CAT, in a case where there may be difficult economic issues, it would be customary to include an economist on the panel, who could explain the technical issues, insofar as was necessary, to the other panel members. Hence the very institutional make-up of a specialist Tribunal may obviate the need for a 'teach-in' in that scenario. The CAT will normally seek technical advice from the parties rather than from outside.[92]

### 7.5.5 Amicus Curiae

Amicus curiae refers to a non-party with an interest in the outcome of a pending lawsuit who argues or presents information in support of or against one of the parties to the lawsuit and attempts to draw the court's attention to arguments or information that the parties may not have presented, such as the effects of a particular court ruling on the interests of certain third parties. One could imagine economists or antitrust and economic associations to act as amicus curiae if court's procedural rules allow for the possibility.

### 7.5.6 Law Clerks and Référendaires

Between soliciting the views of outside experts, on the one hand, and appointing experts to the court on the other, there is a middle ground: experts might be employed as law clerks, either for a particular case or as more permanent personnel. One might imagine a justice preferring law clerks with joint degrees in law and economics or keen to recruit economists as law clerks. The CAT, inspired by the EU courts, relies on référendaires in its workings.

[90] ibid [6].
[91] ibid.
[92] See technical briefing in *TalkTalk v OFCOM* (n 68).

Surely sources of internal expertise, discussed above, minimise transaction costs and the likelihood of error, which results from the difficulty of assessing conflicting expert testimony or from appointing a neutral expert. Under conditions of high transaction costs, sources of internal expertise are superior to relying on a case-by-case incorporation of expert knowledge. But are the above sources of internal expertise superior to a specialist court? The specific attraction of a specialist court is that it incorporates expert knowledge 'within the boundaries of the judicial firm'.[93] Furthermore, having epistemic diversity on the bench improves deliberation in the sense that '[d]ifferences in perspective often improve both the collective reasoning process and the outcomes'.[94] Although differences in perspective can also be communicated via expert witnesses, they still need to be evaluated by members of the court during deliberations. If differing views and perspectives are not heard and/or represented during internal deliberations, important points and ideas might be mishandled due to the cognitive limitations of generalist judges. Of course, judge's specialisation in regulatory economics alone cannot address the polycentric element of regulatory disputes and the value-laden economic assessments, but still needs to be accompanied by procedural rules that will ensure the representation of affected interests.

One needs to engage with two main risks of specialization which are well-documented in the literature. The first relates to 'tunnel vision', in other words the risk that a judge's immersion into a narrow field may lead to the loss of a broader perspective that generalist judges may bring to bear on their judgments.[95] But, the risk of insularity would be much less of a concern in the case of the CAT since it is a hybrid body that brings together High Court judges and practicing lawyers as well as former practitioners (ie non-judicial experts). The second risk refers to the specialist court usurping the function of the agencies and 'second guessing' their positions on policy issues.[96] But the 'interaction' of specialist Tribunals with generalist appeal courts can safeguard against the former 'going native'.[97]

Now, how does our institutional claim interact with the normative proposals on deference to regulatory agencies' superior economic expertise discussed above? Would increasing the epistemic diversity of the court dilute the epistemic superiority of regulatory agencies when it comes to economic expertise? To a certain extent yes, save for polycentric disputes, where even a specialist tribunal encounters the 'proper limits' of adjudication. But a specialist court cannot substitute agencies' superior institutional legitimacy in policy considerations. However, this does not mean that we must choose between the two claims altogether. The approach advanced emphasises interinstitutional collaboration between courts and regulatory agencies who find

[93] Vermeule (n 76) 127.

[94] Peter Strauss and Cass Sunstein, 'The Senate, the Constitution, and the Confirmation Process' (1992) 100 Yale LJ 1491, 1511.

[95] Douglas H Ginsburg and Joshua D Wright, 'Antitrust Courts: Specialists versus Generalists' (2013) 36(4) Fordham Int LJ 788, 802–04; Lawrence Baum, 'Probing the Effects of Judicial Specialisation' (2009) 58 Duke LJ 1667, 1677–78; Stephen Legomsky, *Specialised Justice* (Clarendon Press 1990).

[96] See, eg, Richard L Revesz, 'Specialized Courts and the Administrative Lawmaking System' (1990) 138 Univ Pennsylvania L Rev 1111, 1151–53 (1990).

[97] Peter Freeman, 'Competition Decision-Making and Judicial Control—The Role of the Specialised Tribunal', Centre for Competition Policy, UEA Annual Conference, Norwich 6–7 June 2013, available at: <https://www.catribunal.org.uk/sites/default/files/2018-01/Competition_Decision_Making_and_Judicial_Control-The_Role_of_the_Specialised_Tribunal_06-070613.pdf> accessed 6 June 2022.

themselves in an essentially complementary relationship in the regulatory space. The optimal solution might require a balance to be struck, in which deference is accorded to agencies on institutional competencies grounds and some epistemic diversity is introduced in courts as an institutional foundation for economic expertise.

## 7.6 Conclusion

Comparative institutional analysis should inform the choice of the appropriate standard and intensity of review by requiring that any determination of the standard of review should follow and not precede that of institutional choice. Institutional choice should be comparative and include an assessment of the comparative institutional competence of all institutions engaging in the review of regulatory decisions, as discussed in this chapter. In doing so, this approach rejects those normative prescriptions on deference that are informed by single-factor explanations (ie that a judge does not possess expertise in economics) in favour of a richer set of macro-level (eg cultural and environmental factors) and micro-level (eg court's rules of procedure) institutional factors that may determine the degree of deference owed to the regulators' economic assessments. Epistemic asymmetry is a matter of degree. Whether courts can minimise the likelihood of error depends on a number of institutional factors, such as the nature of the proceedings (administrative or court proceedings), the degree of specialisation of the authorities and courts, and the adversarial or inquisitorial character of the proceedings. The relevance of these factors varies depending on the institutional context and the legal issue at hand. The different institutional arrangements that exist in the US and the UK for the review of economic evidence, each reflecting the constellation of a particular constitutional and socio-political context, allowed the appreciation of the role of a rich set of factors in judicial scrutiny of economic evidence. It is useful to bring these factors together in this part of the book. Those include the following:

(1) the institutional design of the regulatory decision-making process and the incentives it creates;
(2) institutional capacity considerations;
(3) the standard of review;
(4) the judge's perception of his role;
(5) the broader socio-political context that shapes the role-orientation of the actors within the regulatory space;
(6) the status of the reviewing court or tribunal (ie generalist or specialist);
(7) the nature and the processes of the review body (eg whether the proceedings are adversarial or are more investigative);
(8) the relationship between the court of first instance and the appellate court;
(9) the court's rules of procedure;
(10) the form the delegated power takes;
(11) the nature of the regulatory decision being made and the number of persons affected by it (polycentricity).

Table 7.1 offers an analysis of these factors.

**Table 7.1** The Determinants of Judicial Scrutiny of Economic Evidence

<table>
<tr><td></td><td>US</td><td>UK</td></tr>
<tr><td>1</td><td colspan="2">Institutional Design of the Regulatory Regime</td></tr>
<tr><td></td><td>Internal Model of Review of Economic Evidence</td><td>External Model of Review of Economic Evidence</td></tr>
<tr><td></td><td><u>Administrative Litigation Model</u><br>• Fact-finding and economic assessments undertaken by the ALJ<br>• Trial staff possess wide array of tools<br>• FERC/FCC enjoy discretion to choose from a wide set of policymaking tools</td><td><u>Competition and Markets Authority</u><br>• Price controls/licence modification references<br>• No legislative document close to the US APA, thus no development of a uniform procedural framework governing appeals</td></tr>
<tr><td></td><td><u>APA</u><br>• Regulates the decision-making process<br>• Endorses liberal standards for the admissibility of evidence<br>• Judicialises the agency's decision-making process thus facilitating and constraining judicial review</td><td><u>CMA's Rules of Procedure</u><br>• Active case management<br>• Mixture of merits-based and judicial review<br>• Broad representation of affected interests<br>• Admissibility of new evidence<br>• Access to epistemic competence<br>• Utilities Panel</td></tr>
<tr><td>2</td><td colspan="2">Institutional Capacity Considerations</td></tr>
<tr><td></td><td colspan="2"><u>Rationales for Deference</u><br>• Regulatory agency's superior expertise and access to information<br>• Regulatory agency's superior institutional legitimacy deriving from its political accountability<br>• Courts suffer from informational limitations and political insulation<br>• Court's susceptibility to minoritarian bias</td></tr>
<tr><td>3</td><td colspan="2">The Standard of Review / Grounds of Review</td></tr>
<tr><td></td><td>Federal Courts</td><td>High Court</td></tr>
<tr><td></td><td><u>Judicial Review</u><br>• Refrain from a de novo examination of facts<br>• Arbitrary and capricious test<br>• Substantial evidence standard (rules made 'on the record'—factual findings)<br>• Increased convergence of the two tests in informal rulemaking</td><td><u>Judicial Review</u><br>• Illegality, irrationality, procedural impropriety<br>• Serious factual error<br>• Proportionality</td></tr>
<tr><td></td><td></td><td>CAT</td></tr>
<tr><td></td><td></td><td>• Statutory review and statutory appeal</td></tr>
</table>

**Table 7.1** Continued

| | US | UK |
|---|---|---|
| 4 | **The Judge's Perception of his Role** | |
| | 'Hard Look' Review<br>• Judge confident in second-guessing the policy choices of agencies<br>• Judge assumes a corrective role for the alleged failures of the legislative and regulatory processes caused by interest group activity | *Wednesbury* Review<br>• 'ill suited' judge to assess the agencies' discretionary assessments<br>• No reasonableness test for errors of law |
| | | CAT |
| | | The institutional identity of the specialist tribunal has a direct impact on judicial behaviour |
| 5 | **The Broader Socio-Political and Constitutional Context that Shapes the Role-Orientation of Judges** | |
| | **Federal Courts** | **High Court** |
| | • Federalism | • Constitutional structure of the separation of powers in the UK minimised institutional conflict between the Executive and the regulatory agencies<br>• Post-privatisation design of the British regulatory state reserved a minor role for judges |
| 6 | **The Status of the Reviewing Court/Tribunal** | |
| | **Generalist Federal Courts** | **Specialist CAT** |
| | Resist Specialisation<br>However:<br>• Subject-matter specialisation (DC Circuit)<br>• Case assignment<br>• Opinion specialisation<br>• Specialist Washington 'uptown bar'<br>• Judge's prior education and professional background<br>• Influence of jurisprudential movements/ideas from the legal academy (sociological jurisprudence/legal realism) | • Cross-disciplinary expertise in law/economics/accountancy<br>• Limited jurisdiction over regulatory and competition law disputes |
| 7 | **The Nature and the Process of Review** | |
| | **Federal Courts** | **High Court** |
| | Adversarial | Adversarial |

*(continued)*

**Table 7.1** Continued

| | US | UK |
|---|---|---|
| | | CAT |
| | | Adversarial |
| 8 | **Relationship between the Court of First Instance and the Appellate Court** | |
| | **DC Circuit—Supreme Court** | **CAT—Court of Appeal** |
| | • *Certiori* jurisdiction of the Supreme Court<br>• Allows policy statement | Court of Appeal 'regulates' the CAT on the basis of relative institutional competence considerations |
| 9 | **The Courts' Rules of Procedure** | |
| | **DC Circuit—Supreme Court** | **High Court** |
| | • Case assignment<br>• Opinion specialisation | • The authority is not allowed to adduce new evidence<br>• Limited use of assessors/access to epistemic Competence |
| | | CAT |
| | | • Active case management<br>• Admission of new evidence<br>• Third party interventions<br>• Cross-examination of witnesses<br>• 'Hot tubbing' |
| 10 | **The Form the Delegated Power Takes** | |
| | Standards (rather than rules) that encompass a plurality of economic and non-economic objectives | |
| 11 | **The Nature of the Regulatory Decision being made, and the number of persons affected by it** | |
| | Polycentric regulatory disputes<br>Price controls versus universal service obligations | |

## Acknowledgements

Reproduced with permission from Oxford University Press. Mantzari, D, 'Economic Evidence in Regulatory Disputes: Revisiting the Court-Regulatory Agency Relationship in the US and the UK' (2016) 36 Oxf J Leg Stud 565–94 (doi: <https://doi.org/10.1093/ojls/gqv035>) © 2015, Oxford University Press.

# 8
# Epilogue

## 8.1 Introduction

This concluding chapter will draw together some of the common threads which have been woven throughout the preceding chapters and highlight the principal issues lying at the heart of this inquiry. It will also explain the distinct contribution of this work to public law and regulation as well as competition law scholarship more generally. But in doing so the aim is not solely to retrace our steps; the chapter will also look ahead to the future by briefly considering the implications of this research for the regulatory state in the era of informational capitalism.

## 8.2 Summary

This section stands as a summary of the entire book. It is helpful to retrace the steps traversed to see the conclusion to which they all lead. Chapter 1 introduced the idea that the manifestation of economic evidence in regulatory disputes challenges the error-correction function of judicial review because of the profound epistemic asymmetry between the expert regulatory agency and the generalist judge. At the same time, regulatory implementation entails matters of significant complexity, requiring consideration of diverse, disparate, and often conflicting interests. The decisions that regulators may be required to make do not throw up obvious, simple solutions. Furthermore, what might be perceived as a 'right' decision in the economist's universe may not coincide with what is 'legal' in the lawyer's kingdom; and by legal we do not simply refer to a decision that is authorised by law ('thin' legality), but a decision that reflects substantive (eg rationality) and procedural (eg due process requirements) values drawn from a largely formal conception of the rule of law. The question therefore that arises is what the limits of the error-correction function of judicial review are following the greater recourse to expert economic evidence and analysis. The increased presentation of economic evidence in regulatory disputes naturally leads us to consider both the jurisprudential question of the appropriate scope of review of discretionary economic assessments and the institutional question regarding the optimal institutional forum for regulatory disputes. The chapter argued that these questions cannot be meaningfully addressed without a deep appreciation of how the institutions comprising the regulatory and adjudicatory processes work, and without being sensitive to considerations of those institutions' capacities. Comparative institutional analysis was therefore introduced as both a methodological avenue for the research question advanced, but also as a normative prescription for adjudicating economic evidence; its appeal being that it embraces a richer set of considerations that help to

*Courts, Regulators, and the Scrutiny of Economic Evidence*. Despoina Mantzari, Oxford University Press.
 DOI: 10.1093/oso/9780198851608.003.0008

understand the norms, structures, and processes that shape the relationship between the court and the regulatory agency in the realm of utilities regulation. The chapter explained why a comparative analysis between the US and the UK is particularly fertile in this endeavour.

Chapter 2 delved deeper into the use of economics as an external source of wisdom and authority in the realm of utility regulation, demonstrating at the same time the contested nature of the economics discipline. The chapter elaborated on the different points of entry of economics in rulemaking and adjudication and the specific challenges raised. Economic evidence and analysis inform both technical aspects and value judgements. It transcends both questions of law and questions of fact and policy, thus blurring their boundaries. The chapter also introduced the concept of polycentric disputes and argued that such disputes invite a case-by-case assessment of the factors that may attenuate the polycentric dimension of the dispute in question thus making it amendable to the adjudicative process; a task that was undertaken in Chapter 7. Finally, the chapter elaborated on the limits of the import of economic evidence in courts, which stem from the distinct rationalities of the legal and scientific/economic process.

Chapter 3 set the scene for the comparative institutional analysis by introducing all actors and processes of review in the two comparator jurisdictions. The imperfect alternatives discussed allowed us to appreciate the different mechanisms that exist for the review of economic evidence and the varying types of scrutiny applied to regulatory agencies' actions. At the same time, the chapter hinted at an array of institutional and larger environmental factors that affect the scope of judicial review of economic evidence in the US and the UK, foreshadowing to a large extent the discussion in Chapters 5 and 6.

Chapter 4 zoomed into the workings of the UK regulatory agencies. Relying on semi-structured interviews with sectoral regulators it opened the 'black box' of the regulatory decision-making process and explored the influence of economic evidence and analysis on the regulators' discretionary economic assessments. It studied closely the outputs of economic evidence and the findings were derived inductively from the observations of economists themselves. The chapter did not seek to establish whether the right economic model was used, or criticise the approach undertaken—this arguably being the job of an economist and not that of a lawyer—but rather to expose the interaction of two distinct rationalities—economic and legal—and how they play out in the regulatory and adjudicative decision-making process. It thus provided a context-specific understanding of how regulators perceive and exercise their discretionary powers, which can inform our normative prescriptions regarding judicial review of economic evidence. The chapter offered three key findings: firstly, that economic evidence informs a wide array of discretionary assessments and the trade-off between efficiency and equity which has been more pronounced in the last two decades due to the broadening of regulatory objectives. Secondly, that while economists enjoy formal discretionary powers, they are in fact constrained by structural, institutional, and ideational factors. Structural constraints emanate from the need to cater for social and environmental objectives, arguably more fitted to the role of the government. The upshot, however, of this development is that sound economic evidence and analysis may be sidelined, as the case of OFGEM revealed. Economists are also constrained by institutional factors, including the desire to produce substantively fair decisions, and this may increase the quality of economic evidence, especially when their decisions are challenged on the merits by the specialist CAT. However, when specialist courts, such as the CAT, exercise too much zeal in second-guessing the regulators' expert assessments, the latter become more legalistic in their approach, as the case of OFCOM reveals, which may in turn undermine both sound economic analysis and the agency's overall statutory objective of promoting the interests of consumers. Finally, economists are constrained by ideational factors, such as scrutiny by the academic community, as the case of OFGEM and OFWAT revealed. The chapter demonstrated that although the effective achievement of policy outcomes is appropriately given prominence considering the instrumentalist nature of the regulatory enterprise, there are values and considerations other than economic efficiency that have an important role in moulding the use of economic evidence in the pursuit of regulatory goals. And institutional constraints, both legal (eg threat of judicial review) and quasi-legal (eg organisational factors, norms), steer the agencies away from the monolithic pursuit of economic rationality towards the requirements of legal rationality reflected in both *thin* and *thick* conceptions of legality.

Chapters 5 and 6 turned to the descriptive/positive argument and explored in a systematic way the rationales and determinants of judicial review of economic evidence in the US and the UK courts respectively. In the US, federal courts, and prominently the DC Circuit, have emphasised institutional competence and historical considerations that should inform their scope of review. This has given rise to an undemanding version of rationality, referred to as 'thin rationality' review. Chapter 6 examined the institutional response to the epistemic asymmetry between the expert regulatory agency and the judge embodied in the hyper specialist CAT and discussed the limits of judicial scrutiny of economic evidence in such an institutional setting.

Chapter 7 brought together the different institutional factors emanating from the examination of judicial scrutiny of economic evidence in generalist courts (US federal courts, UK High Court) and specialist courts (UK Competition Appeal Tribunal) to bear on the normative prescriptions for the jurisprudential and institutional dilemmas. Drawing on insights from studies in political science and economics, it illuminated the institutional disadvantages of the courts that may warrant a high degree of deference. At the same time, it also highlighted several institutional realties and procedural developments that may attenuate the weight of such comparative institutional disadvantages. This exercise did not only furnish valuable insights regarding the scope of review, but also the optimal institutional response to the pervasiveness of economic evidence in regulatory decisions. The conclusion of the entire study is that due to epistemic and in some cases (eg polycentric disputes) institutional legitimacy concerns, the role of the courts ought to be one of restraint. The argument advanced is embedded in precedent: courts not only should, but for the most part in fact do adopt a deferential posture towards the agencies' discretionary economic assessments predicated upon institutional competencies considerations. The best way to promote the error-correction function of judicial review in the assessment of economic evidence requires a balance to be struck, in which deference is accorded to agencies on institutional competencies grounds and some degree of epistemic diversity is introduced in courts.

## 8.3 Contribution

One of the principal motives when embarking on this book was to shed light on the challenges that expert economic evidence and analysis presents for a neighbouring field to competition law, that of utility regulation, which has been largely underexplored by competition lawyers. As with the case of competition law, the field of utility regulation has also been defined by the rise of economic expertise as an external source of wisdom and authority. Indeed, ever since the liberalisation of essential services technocracy has emerged not only as a rule by experts, but also as an *ethos* signalling the commitment to the protection of consumers' interests, whenever appropriate, by promoting competition. Professional economists have applied their discipline-specific criteria in implementing this goal. But unlike competition law, which was, until recently at least, monocentric in nature,[1] the regulation of essential services has always been 'polycentric' in terms of the plurality of economic and societal objectives it has to serve.[2] As the book illustrated, economic evidence and analysis informs a wide array of discretionary assessments and trade-offs between efficiency and equity which have been more pronounced in the last two decades due to the broadening of regulatory objectives. Economic evidence operationalises vague statutory standards ('just and reasonable price') and gives expression to the trade-offs of the regulatory enterprise via its own tools (eg welfare analysis). When judges are asked to interpret the agency's statutory mandate or when presented with economic evidence in the courtroom, they inevitably face an epistemic asymmetry vis-à-vis the agencies.

Regrettably, however, much of the work so far has focused on human rights aspects of regulation, on issues of legitimacy and accountability in the regulatory state and has overlooked the 'outputs' of regulatory agencies, which are far from merely 'technical' assessments, but contain important value judgements, albeit expressed in economic models. Others have heavily criticised the use of economics in regulation, raising doubts as to the scientific foundations of economics, their relevance for justice, and the political implications of relying on neoclassical price theory and efficiency as normative goals. The latter jurisprudence-focused group takes an overly polemical perspective to economics, without, however, seriously engaging with the tools and philosophy of economics.

Instead of refusing to engage in a conversation with an important epistemic community, the book engaged directly with economists and economics to address the realities of the regulatory process and the adjudicative process as this is taking place. So, while existing legal scholarship attempts to locate the sphere of regulatory discretion within the confines of judicial review, this study adopted an inductive and context-sensitive approach that purports to better appreciate the inner-workings of regulatory discretion, as the latter is shaped by the power relations between the

[1] Ioannis Lianos, 'Polycentric Competition Law' (2018) 71(1) Curr Leg Probl 161.

[2] Tony Prosser, *The Regulatory Enterprise: Government, Regulation, and Legitimacy* (OUP 2010).

hybrid communities of lawyers and economists within regulatory agencies and other actors in the regulatory space. And while scholarship on judicial review is chiefly preoccupied with the interaction between democracy and expertise, the study adopted the error-correction function of judicial review as the main framework of analysis which is more attentive to the epistemic asymmetry between the judge and the regulatory agency. The study's methodology and theoretical framework is significant in the sense that it is the first of its kind in the context of utility regulation and in that it can be applied to other areas of regulation that are heavily influenced by economic evidence and analysis, such as 'pure' competition law enforcement and disputes. At the same time, the identification of macro-levels and micro-level factors that affect the reception of economic evidence in courts offers a 'recipe' for adjudication of regulatory disputes and a valuable roadmap for the institutional design of the regulatory and judicial process for those jurisdictions around the globe grappling with similar concerns.

This endeavour required to step out of one's comfort zone, not only in navigating the interdisciplinary nature of this work, but also in bringing together two fertile sources of scholarship: the competition law and regulation scholarship (which informs the substantive rules governing economic regulation) and the administrative law scholarship (which informs the procedural rules governing this area). This is no doubt challenging. But only by engaging deeply with the work of economists can we develop some mutual understanding between the two disciplinary communities of lawyers and economists to the benefit of the regulatory enterprise. It is hoped that the analysis undertaken in this book will stimulate and encourage a productive dialogue between these two communities, but also between competition law and administrative law scholars, who have tended to talk past each other despite facing common interpretive challenges.

## 8.4 Taking Stock and Looking Ahead: Courts and Economic Evidence in the Post-Industrialism Regulatory State

Since the study looked primarily in the past, it seems appropriate to conclude this book with a glimpse at the future role of economic evidence in the regulatory enterprise, considering the monumental societal and technological changes currently underway. As we shall explain, these developments not only challenge existing regulatory frameworks, but also alter the nature of economic evidence in the regulatory state, which has so far mostly been derived from industrial organisation economics. Two main challenges lie ahead. The first relates to the relatively recent advent of behavioural economics in utility regulation. This is a new source of wisdom that is slowly being incorporated in the regulatory decision-making process and creates new challenges for the error-correction function of judicial review. The second challenge relates to the rise of informational capitalism, which has already started to disrupt the prevailing paradigm of utility regulation.

### 8.4.1 The Advent of Behavioural Economics

Influenced by the neoclassical economics approach to regulation, existing regulatory frameworks, and the regulators themselves tend to see their role in classic market failure terms: monopolies and imperfectly competitive markets will typically set excessive prices. The ideal solution is to introduce more competition (see, eg, OFWAT's efforts in the retail market), but where there is a genuine natural monopoly, economic regulation is needed to ensure that prices do not rise above the level which would operate should competition exist. Much regulatory practice continues to focus on tools such as prices, taxes, subsidies, and quality standards, all flowing from the underlying assumption that consumers and producers are always rational. But investment in networks has been slower than expected and the 'losers' of liberalisation continue to have a hard time either accessing or paying for services so essential to their well-being.[3] The ever-growing segment of 'losers' in markets for essential services in many ways shows that the assumption of rationality may lead to a poor understanding of how consumers or producers actually behave in a market. Indeed, one of the main weaknesses of the prevailing normative framework for regulation has been the underestimation of the role of behavioural biases in the way producers and consumers, but also regulators behave. The advent of behavioural economics attempts to draw a map of 'bounded rationality',[4] by exploring the systematic biases that people show in their day-to-day behaviour in relation to choices a fully rational agent would have made in similar circumstances. For instance, people may make choices that could satisfy their immediate preferences, which they would have changed had they behaved as if they were fully rational agents. This new framework of analysis has slowly started to become incorporated in the regulatory decision-making process. For example, we saw in Chapter 4 how the regulatory toolkit evolved in the UK to take into account consumers' cognitive biases in the retail energy market. Behavioural economics offer a promising positive theory of consumer behaviour that has far-reaching implications as it identifies a new form of 'market failure', this time not due to externalities, but due to internalities, that is situations in which people do not internalise all consequences of their actions on themselves because of 'bounded rationality'. Its insights can thus offer us a better understanding of consumer behaviour that can in turn improve the effectiveness of regulation. Although behavioural economics does not offer a clear alternative to industrial organisation economics, it can still be an important complement.

This new source of wisdom presents new challenges for regulators and courts alike. Regarding the former, one of the biggest challenges is that of protecting individuals with less capacity for 'rational' decision-making, while taking care not to increase the costs for individuals who are less prone to 'bounded rationality' problems or biases: the legislative and policy debate on the UK energy price cap offering an ample

[3] For a discussion, see Emmanuelle Auriol, Claude Crampes, and Antonio Estache, *Regulating Public Services: Bridging the Gap between Theory and Practice* (CUP 2021).

[4] Daniel Kahneman, *Thinking, Fast and Slow* (Allen Lane 2011); Amos Tversky and Daniel Kahneman, 'Judgment under Uncertainty: Heuristics and Biases' (1974) 185 Science, New Series, 1124; Daniel Kahneman and Amos Tversky, 'Prospect Theory: An Analysis of Decision under Risk' (1979) 47(2) Econometrica 263.

illustration of this conundrum.[5] Regarding courts (and regulators), the main challenge this new source of knowledge presents relates to a common critique of its methods. Behavioural economics rely on laboratory experiments, survey experiments, and field experiments to address a wide variety of questions within economics, including whether behaviour is consistent with the predictions and assumptions of theory and how various mechanisms and institutions affect the behaviour of economic agents.[6] The primary virtue of experiments lies in their ability to isolate the causal impact of a particular independent variable, a characteristic known as 'internal validity'. But there is an ongoing debate on whether such experiments can produce 'external validity', that is whether the insights gained from such experiments can be extrapolated to the world beyond.[7] Some economists have adopted more moderate statements arguing that external validity is relatively more important for experiments searching for empirical regularities than for theory-testing experiments.[8] This is an open debate in academia, but in the meantime this new form of economic evidence, manifesting itself through randomised control trials, is already being adopted by regulatory authorities.[9] Both the regulatory decision-making process and the adjudicative one need to 'communicate' with this new manifestation of economic expertise and overcome the new set of cognitive challenges it presents. For example, judges need to understand how to test the underlying assumptions and methods of experiments, when such decisions reach the bench. Not every experiment is well designed, and the simple act of carrying out an experiment does not guarantee a high degree of internal validity. For example, experimenters may inadvertently introduce bias into the experiment if and insofar as the experimenter communicates how researchers want or expect the subjects to respond, or the design of the experiment may fail to achieve balance across the treatment and control groups. Experiments are also prone to measurement problems, and the internal validity of an experiment can be called into question by unreliable measures of experimental or outcome variables. Judges need to be aware of these threats to internal validity and assess the ways in which, and the extent to which, researchers have dealt

[5] See Maria Ioannidou and Despoina Mantzari, 'The UK Domestic Gas Electricity (Tariff Cap) Act: Re-regulating the Retail Energy Market' (2019) 82(3) Modern L Rev 488; CMA, 'Consumer Vulnerability: Challenges and Potential Solutions', 28 February 2019, available at: <https://www.gov.uk/government/publications/consumer-vulnerability-challenges-and-potential-solutions/consumer-vulnerability-challenges-and-potential-solutions> accessed 6 June 2022.

[6] See Alvin E Roth, *Laboratory Experimentation in Economics, and its Relation to Economic Theory' Scientific Inquiry in Philosophical Perspective* (Univ Press America 1987). According to Roth in experiments the economic environment is very fully under the control of the experimenter, who also has relatively unimpeded access to the experimental subjects. This distinguishes laboratory experiments from 'field' experiments, in which relatively few aspects of the environment can be controlled, and in which only limited access to most of the economic agents may be available.

[7] Steven D Levitt and John A List, 'What do Laboratory Experiments Measuring Social Preferences Reveal about the Real world?' (2007) 21 J Econ Perspect 153.

[8] Arthur Schram, 'Artificiality: The Tension between Internal and External validity in economic experiments' (2005) 12(2) J Econ Methodol 225.

[9] FCA, Applying Behavioural Economics at the Financial Conduct Authority (April 2013), available at: <https://www.fca.org.uk/publication/occasional-papers/occasional-paper-1.pdf> accessed 6 June 2022 and FCA, Encouraging Consumers to Claim Redress: Evidence from a Field Trial (April 2013), available at: < https://www.fca.org.uk/publication/occasional-papers/occasional-paper-2.pdf> accessed 6 June 2022; OFGEM, 'Insights from OFGEM's Consumer Engagement Trials (2019), available at: <https://www.ofgem.gov.uk/sites/default/files/docs/2019/09/cross_trials_paper_report.pdf> accessed 6 June 2022.

with and minimised these threats in any particular study. This is a new challenge for the adjudicative decision-making process that has for a long time relied on evidence stemming from industrial organisation economics, which despite its many imperfections can claim superior external validity.

### 8.4.2 The Rise of Informational Capitalism

The second challenge lying ahead, that of the rise of informational capitalism, has far more profound implications for the future interaction between expert regulatory agencies and courts, as it is already disrupting in many different ways the existing paradigm of utility regulation.

There is no doubt that our economies are currently experiencing a paradigmatic shift from an industrial mode of development to an informational one. This is owing to the far-reaching social, economic, and political changes due to recent advances in information and communications technologies together with the globalisation of trade. The rise of informational capitalism has created existential challenges for both the regulatory models that flourished in the era of industrialised economy and for their underlying normative foundations.[10] Indeed, the institutions and regulatory techniques that we currently have in place to oversee utilities are designed around the regulatory problems and competencies of an era in which industrialism was the principal mode of development (ie based on social labour, industrial capital, manufacturing, and bulk production). But technological developments have seriously undermined the vertical sector-specific silos of sectoral regulators and have revealed their cross-sectional nature. Energy and telecoms are already disrupted by rapid developments in automation and big data, whereas the advent of blockchain will impact retail intermediation.[11] At the same time, our data-driven economy, that allows the collection, processing, and management of massive amounts of data opens up new possibilities in terms of managing supply and meeting demand, as suppliers have come to better understand consumer needs, preferences, and patterns at unprecedented levels. It has also allowed the offering of more integrated services, as telecommunications and energy operators are gathering increasing amounts of data from users in order to compete in adjacent markets. New forms of market power are created stemming from the collection of Big Data and the use of algorithms, what Frank Pasquale refers to as 'algorithmic power': a power based on technological dependence of economic actors that consume in an increasingly complex computational environment and the capability of some actors to control the 'agenda' of decision-making.[12] This power allows such actors to exploit their superior 'algorithmic power' and/or 'manipulate' the choice and eventually the

[10] For an analysis, see Julie E Kohen, *Between Truth and Power: The Legal Constructions of Informational Capitalism* (OUP 2019).

[11] Merlinda Andoni and others, 'Blockchain Technology in the Energy Sector: A Systematic Review of Challenges and Opportunities' (2019) 100 Renew Sustain Energy Rev 143.

[12] See Frank Pasquale, *The Black Box Society: The Secret Algorithms that Control Money and Information* (Harvard Univ Press 2015) ch 2.

preferences of consumers.[13] At the same time, new markets are being created for the collection and storage of information collected by tracking behaviour.

The data-driven economy has many implications for the future of the regulatory state and the role of economic evidence therein. It affects both the institutional design of the regulatory state and the allocation of decision-making power within the agencies as it squarely introduces new disciplinary communities and thus new sources of wisdom in utility regulation stemming from data science and computer science. Identifying consumer harm and rationales for regulatory intervention will require the legal system incorporating these new sources of wisdom alongside economic wisdom and authority.

But economic wisdom might also take a different direction as essential services become increasingly 'complex' systems. Complex systems are systems which consist of interacting individuals that change their actions and strategies in response to the outcome they mutually create.[14] New frameworks of regulation are slowly emerging, stemming from adaptive systems theory and reliance on computational modelling approaches (eg agent-based models) to address such 'complex' systems. A new field has emerged within economics, that of 'complexity economics', which focuses on the emergence of structures and the unfolding of patterns in the economy and regularly dispenses with the assumptions of individual optimisation and/or systemic equilibrium usually employed in the mainstream.[15]

The developments in the wholesale energy market offer a useful illustration of the relevance of 'complexity' economics in regulation. The rise of renewable energy resources and other off-the-grid forms of energy products have rendered electricity systems far more complex, as interactions between participants become multidimensional. This creates a 'knowledge problem' for the regulator in an 'increasingly complex electricity system'.[16] The implications for network pricing are profound, as regulation needs to gradually move away from unidirectional pricing on which it has relied for over a century and adapt to a multidimensional and interdependent complex system.

Another example concerns regulatory interventions in monopolistic market segments, such as the local loop in telecoms. The limited and focused measures were useful during the era when monopolistic elements prevailed in the industry, but they prove to be increasingly less appropriate in the present framework of highly interrelated, interdependent, and complementary market segments. In such an environment, regulation also needs to systematically assess and take into account indirect effects of limited regulatory interventions on the information and communication technology systems at large, which have also become 'complex systems'. But regulators lack the systematic tools to do this and have been slow to adapt to the post-industrial informational capitalism era. Although the frameworks stemming from 'complexity

[13] John Hanson and Douglas Kysar, 'Taking Behavioralism Seriously: Some Evidence of Market Manipulation' (1999) 112 Harvard L Rev 1420.

[14] See Brian Arthur, 'Foundations of Complexity Economics' (2021) 3 Nat Rev Phys 136.

[15] See Brian Arthur, Complexity and the Economy (1999) 284 (5411) Science 107. See further John Foster, 'From Simplistic to Complex Systems in Economics' (2005) 29 (6) Cambridge J Econ 873.

[16] Fuat Oguz, 'Complexity of Electricity Markets and their Regulation: Insights from the Turkish Experience' MPRA paper 99261, University Library of Munich, Germany, available at: <https://mpra.ub.uni-muenchen.de/99261/1/MPRA_paper_99261.pdf> accessed 6 June 2022.

economics' are in many ways more appropriate for the current technological and economic environment of energy and telecoms, they are not yet fully developed and have not been translated into specific regulatory actions.[17] But their adoption can perhaps provide a better alternative to static equilibrium economics considering the dynamic evolution of the industries. Whether 'complexity economics' will prove themselves too 'complex' for generalist judges remains to be seen.

Finally, informational capitalism presents existential challenges for the institutional design of the regulatory state. We already witness several contests over the substance of regulatory mandates in both utility regulation and competition law,[18] and the shape of regulatory institutions. These are most usefully understood as moves within a larger struggle to chart a new direction for the regulatory state in the era of informational capitalism. A telling example comes from the UK, where the 'Penrose report'[19] suggests a number of radical changes to the architecture and operation of UK competition and utility regulation; changes of such magnitude and scope that if implemented would represent a major reorientation for regulated sectors and regulators in the UK. Regarding utility regulation the report suggests a sweeping away of diverse regulatory duties and the imposition of a primary duty focused on 'competition for the benefit of consumers first, regulation only as a last resort'. However, it also recognises that even after this dramatic shrinking of the scope of regulation, there will still be a need for regulation of monopoly services and networks in water and energy. On the institutional front, one of the most radical proposals is that of centralising monopoly regulation under a proposed new unit in the CMA—a Network and Data Monopolies Unit (NDMU). In time, the Report envisages the role of sectoral regulators being entirely subsumed by the CMA, with regulators' residual oversight of core network monopolies being handed to the NDMU. Finally, it suggests all appeals from decisions of sectoral regulators should be heard by the CAT (not the CMA or other courts) so as to streamline the appeals processes. This is not a straightforward issue at all, and one may be forgiven for thinking that it would be very difficult for the CAT to handle all the important and laborious work the CMA currently does in regulatory appeals without some considerable change to its procedures and composition. It is hoped that the ability of the courts to hear and test economic and other evidence will not be lost in the drive for tidiness and efficiency.

Despite the ongoing transformation of the regulatory state there is little doubt that economics and economic evidence will remain an important source of wisdom in the workings of regulatory authorities. Regulatory decisions promoting both the economic and the more redistributive goals of the regulatory enterprise will continue to be dominated by expert economic evidence and analysis, albeit taking different forms

[17] See I Lianos, 'Competition Law for a Complex Economy' (2019) IIC Int Rev Intellect Prop Compet L 643.

[18] See, eg, the Digital Markets Act in the EU or the Digital Markets Unit in the UK.

[19] In September 2020, John Penrose MP was commissioned by the UK Chancellor of the Exchequer and the Secretary of State for Business, Energy and Industrial Strategy to write an independent report on how the UK's approach to competition and consumer issues could be improved. The report was published in February 2021; see 'Power to the People: Independent Report on Competition Policy' available at: <https://www.gov.uk/government/publications/power-to-the-people-independent-report-on-competition-policy> accessed 6 June 2022.

as regulators slowly embrace new directions in academic research. Whatever the trajectory of economic evidence in the regulatory state, it is hoped that the conceptual framework developed in this work will provide a useful roadmap for tackling both old and the new challenges brought about by the era of informational capitalism. It may also allow for a more relevant discussion about any procedural or institutional reforms.

# Bibliography

## 1. Books


Adams S, *The Dilbert Future* (Harper Collins 1997).

Arancibia J, *Judicial Review of Commercial Regulation* (OUP 2011).

Auriol E, Crampes C, and Estache A, *Regulating Public Services: Bridging the Gap Between Theory and Practice* (CUP 2021).

Baum L, *Specializing the Courts* (Univ Chicago Press 2010).

Baumol W and Sidak G, *Toward Competition in Local Telephony* (MIT Press 2013).

Benjamin SM, Lichtman DG, and Shelanski H, *Telecommunications Law and Policy* (2nd edn, Carolina Academic Press 2006).

Bickel A, *The Least Dangerous Branch* (Yale Univ Press 1962).

Black J, Muchlinski P, and Walker P (eds), *Commercial Regulation and Judicial Review* (Hart 1998).

Blaug M, *The Methodology of Economics. Or How Can Economists Explain* (2nd edn, CUP 1992).

Breyer SG, Stewart RB, Sunstein CR, and Vermeule A, *Administrative Law and Regulatory Policy: Problems, Texts and Cases* (6th edn, Aspen Publishers 2006).

Buigues PA and Rey P (eds), *The Economics of Antitrust and Regulation in Telecommunication: Perspectives for the New European Regulatory Framework* (EE 2004).

Cane P, *Administrative Tribunals and Adjudication* (Hart 2010).

Craig P, *Administrative Law* (7th edn, Sweet & Maxwell 2012).

Davis KC and Pierce R, *Administrative Law Treatise* (3rd edn, Publishing Company 1994).

De S-O- l'E Lasser M, *Judicial Deliberations—A Comparative Analysis of Judicial Transparency and Legitimacy* (OUP 2010).

De Smith SA, Woolf Sir H, Jowell JL, and Le Sueur AP, *De Smith, Woolf and Jowell's Principles of Judicial Review* (Sweet & Maxwell 1999).

Drucker PF, *The Age of Discontinuity—Guidelines to Our Changing Society* (Harper & Row 1969).

Dubash NK and Morgan B (eds), *The Rise of the Regulatory State of the South-Infrastructure and Development in Emerging Economies* (OUP 2013).

Dwyer D, *The Judicial Assessment of Expert Evidence* (CUP 2009).

Ehlerman C-D and Marquis M (eds), *European Competition Law Annual 2009: The Evaluation of Evidence and its Judicial Review in Competition Cases* (Hart 2011).

Essens O, Gerbrandy A, and Lavrijssen S (eds), *National Courts and the Standard of Review in Competition Law and Economic Regulation* (Europa Law Publishing 2009).

Ewick P and Silbey S, *The Common Place of Law: Stories from Everyday Life* (Univ Chicago Press 1998).

Farber DA and O'Connell AJ (eds), *Research Handbook on Public Choice and Public Law* (EE 2010).

Foster CD, *Privatization, Public Ownership and the Regulation of Natural Monopoly* (Blackwell 1992).

Fourcade M, *Economists and Societies: Discipline and Profession in the United States, Britain & France, 1890s to 1990s* (Princeton Univ Press 2009).

Friedman M, *The Methodology of Positive Economics, in Essays in Positive Economics* (Univ Chicago Press 1953).
Galligan DJ, *Discretionary Powers: A Legal Study of Official Discretion* (Clarendon Press 1990).
Géradin D (ed), *The Liberalisation of State Monopolies in the European Union and Beyond* (Kluwer Law International 1999).
Géradin D and Kerf M, *Controlling Market Power in Telecommunications: Antitrust vs Sector-Specific Regulation* (OUP 2003).
Géradin D, *Remedies in Network Industries: EC Competition Law vs Sector-Specific Regulation* (Intersentia 2004).
Ginsburg T and Kagan RA (eds), *Institutions and Public Law: Comparative Approaches* (Peter Lang Publishing 2005).
Gómez-Ibáñez JA, *Regulating Infrastructure: Monopoly, Contracts and Discretion* (Harvard Univ Press 2003).
Griffith JAG, *The Politics of the Judiciary* (5th edn, Fontana Press 1997).
Harrison J, Morgan T, and Verkuil P, *Regulation and Deregulation: Cases and Materials* (2nd edn, Thompson/West 2004).
Harlow C and Rawlings R, *Law and Administration* (3rd edn, CUP 2009).
Hawkins K, *Law as Last-Resort: Prosecution Decision-making in a Regulatory Agency* (OUP 2002).
Hood C and M Jackson M, *Administrative Argument* (Dartmouth 1991).
Hume D, *A Treatise of Human Nature* (Dover Philosophical Classics 2003, first published in 1740).
Jasanoff S, *Science at the Bar: Law, Science and Technology in America* (Harvard Univ Press 1995).
Jordana J and Levi-Faur D (eds), *The Politics of Regulation: Institutions and Regulatory Reform for the Age of Governance* (EE 2004).
Kagan RA, *Adversarial Legalism: The American Way of Law* (Harvard Univ Press 2003).
Kahn AE, *The Economics of Regulation: Principles and Institutions* (MIT Press 1988).
King J, *Judging Social Rights* (CUP 2012).
Kohen J, *Between Truth and Power: The Legal Constructions of Informational Capitalism* (OUP 2019).
Komesar NK, *Imperfect Alternatives: Choosing Institutions in Law, Economics and Public Policy* (Univ Chicago Press 1994).
Laffont J-J and Tirole J, *Competition in Telecommunications* (MIT Press 2000)
Landis J, *The Administrative Process* (Yale Univ Press 1938).
Langenbucher K, *Economic Transplants: On Lawmaking for Corporations and Capital Markets* (CUP 2017).
Larouche P, *Competition Law and Regulation in European Telecommunications* (Hart 2000).
Legomsky S, *Specialised Justice* (Clarendon Press 1990).
Lehman D and Weisman D (eds), *The Telecommunications Act of 1996: The 'Costs' of Managed Competition* (Kluwer 2000).
Levi EH, *An Introduction to Legal Reasoning* (Univ Chicago Press 1949).
Lianos I and Kokkoris I (eds), *The Reform of EC Competition Law: New Challenges* (Kluwer Law International 2010).
Luhman N, *Law as a Social System* (OUP 2004).
McCraw TK, *Prophets of Regulation: Charles Francis Adams, Louis D Brandeis and Alfred E Kahn* (Harvard Univ Press 1984).
McCrudden C (ed), *Regulation and Deregulation: Policy and Practice in the Utilities and Financial Services Industries* (OUP 1999).
McGrew JH, *FERC: Federal Energy Regulatory Commission* (ABA, Section of Environment, Energy and Resources 2003).

Mirowsky P, *More Heat Than Light: Economic as Social Physics, Physics as Nature's Economics* (CUP 1989).
Moran M, *The British Regulatory State: High Modernism and Hyper-Innovation* (OUP 2003).
Niskanen WA, *Bureaucracy and Representative Government* (Atherton 1971).
Olson M, *The Logic of Collective Action: Public Goods and the Theory of Groups* (Harvard Univ Press 1971).
Parsons C, *How to Map Arguments in Political Science* (OUP 2007).
Pasquale F, *The Black Box Society: The Secret Algorithms that Control Money and Information* (Harvard Univ Press 2015).
Perry HW, *Deciding to Decide: Agenda Setting at the United States Supreme Court* (Harvard Univ Press 1991).
Popper K, *The Logic of Scientific Discovery* (Routledge 1959).
Posner R, *Antitrust Law* (Univ Chicago Press 2001).
Posner R, *How Judges Think* (Harvard Univ Press 2008).
Posner R, *Reflections on Judging* (Harvard Univ Press 2013).
Prosser T, Law *and the Regulators* (Clarendon Press 1997).
Prosser T, *The Regulatory Enterprise: Government, Regulation, and Legitimacy* (OUP 2010).
Putnam H, *The Collapse of the Fact/Value Dichotomy and Other Essays* (Harvard Univ Press 2002).
Rose-Ackerman S, *Rethinking the Progressive Agenda: The Reform of the American Regulatory State* (Free Press 1992).
Roth AE, *Laboratory Experimentation in Economics, and its Relation to Economic Theory. Scientific Inquiry in Philosophical Perspective* (University Press of America 1987).
Schmalensee R, *The Control of Natural Monopolies* (Lexington Books 1979).
Schwartz B, *Administrative Law* (3rd edn, Little, Brown and Company 1991).
Sen A, *Collective Choice and Social Welfare* (Harvard Univ Press 1970).
Shapiro M, *The Supreme Court and the Administrative Agencies* (Free Press 1968).
Shapiro M, *Who Guards the Guardians? Judicial Control of Administration* (Univ Georgia Press 1988).
Sibony Anne-Lise, *Le Juge et le Raisonnement Économique en Droit de la Concurrence* (LGDJ 2008).
Sunstein CR, *After the Rights Revolution: Reconceiving the Regulatory State* (Harvard Univ Press 1990).
Teubner G (ed), *Autopoietic Law: A New Approach to Law and Society* (de Gruyter 1988).
Thaler R and Sunstein C, *Nudge-Improving Decisions about Health, Wealth and Happiness* (Yale Univ Press 2008).
Twining W, *Karl Llewellyn and the Realist Movement* (Weidenfeld and Nicolson 1973).
Twining W, *Rethinking Evidence: Exploratory Essays* (2nd edn, CUP 2006).
Twining W and Miers D, *How to do Things with Rules* (4th edn, Butterworths 1999).
Vermeule A, *Judging Under Uncertainty: An Institutional Theory of Legal Interpretation* (Harvard Univ Press 2006).
Vermeule A, *Law and the Limits of Reason* (OUP 2009).
Vermeule A, *Law's Abnegation* (Harvard Univ Press 2016).
Vibert F, *The New Regulatory Space: Reframing Democratic Governance* (Edward Elgar 2014).
Vickers J and Yarrow G, *Privatisation: An Economic Analysis* (MIT Press 1998).
Viscusi KW (ed), *Regulation Through Litigation* (Brookings Institutions Press 2002).
Viscusi KW, Vernon J, and Harrington J, *Economics of Regulation and Antitrust* (4th edn, MIT Press 2005).
Wade HWR, *Administrative Law* (1st edn, Clarendon Press 1961).
Williamson O, *Markets and Hierarchies, Analysis and Antitrust Implications: A Study in the Economics of Internal Organisation* (Free Press 1975).

Wilks S, *In the Public Interest: Competition Policy and the Monopolies and Mergers Commission* (Manchester Univ Press 1999).
Yeung K, *Securing Compliance: A Principled Approach* (Hart 2004).

## 2. Contributions to Edited Books

Bellamy C, 'An EU Competition Court: The Continuing Debate' in Ioannis Lianos and Ioannis Kokkoris (eds), *The Reform of EC Competition Law: New Challenges* (Kluwer Law International 2010) 33–52
Black J and Muchlinski P, 'Introduction' in Julia Black, Peter Muchlinski, and Paul Walker (eds), *Commercial Regulation and Judicial Review* (Hart 1998) 1–7.
Cane P, 'Judicial Review and Merits Review: Comparing Administrative Adjudication by Courts and Tribunals' in Susan Rose-Ackerman and Peter Lindseth (eds), *Comparative Administrative Law* (Edward Elgar 2010) 426–448.
De Streel A, 'Remedies in the Electronic Communications Sector' in Damien Geradin (ed), *Remedies in Network Industries: EC Competition Law vs. Sector-Specific Regulation* (Intersentia 2004) 67–124.
Farber D and O'Connell AJ, 'Introduction: A Brief Trajectory of Public Choice and Public Law' in Daniel Farber and Anne Joseph O'Connell (eds), *Research Handbook in Public Choice and Public Law* (EE 2010) 1–16.
Ginsburg T and Kagan RA, 'Institutionalist Approaches to Courts as Political Actors' in Tom Ginsburg and Robert A Kagan (eds), *Institutions and Public Law-Comparative Approaches* (Peter Lang 2005) 1–18.
Hauge J and Sappington D, 'Pricing in Network Industries' in Robert Baldwin, Martin Cave, and Martin Lodge (eds), *Oxford Handbook of Regulation* (OUP 2010) 462–478.
Joskow P and Noll RG, 'Regulation in Theory and in Practice: An Overview' in Garry Fromm (ed), *Studies in Public Regulation* (MIT Press 1981) 1–78.
Kavanagh A, 'Deference or Defiance' in Grant Huscroft (ed), *Expounding the Constitution* (CUP 2008) 184–216.
Legal H, 'Standards of Proof and Standards of Judicial Review in EU Competition Law' in Barry Hawk (ed), *Annual Proceedings of the Fordham Corporate Law Institute* 2005, vol 32 (Juris Publishing 2005) 107–117.
Lianos I, 'Judging Economists': Economic Expertise in Competition Law Litigation: A European View' in Ioannis Lianos and Ioannis Kokkoris (eds), *The Reform of EC Competition Law: New Challenges* (Kluwer Law International 2010) 185–321.
Magill E, 'Step Two of *Chevron v Natural Resources Defense Council*' in John E Duffy and Michael Hertz (eds), *A Guide to Judicial and Political Review of Federal Agencies* (ABA 2005) 85–102.
Rossi J, 'Public Choice, Energy Regulation and Deregulation' in Daniel Farber and Anne Joseph O' Connell (eds), *Research Handbook in Public Choice and Public Law* (EE 2010) 419–449.
Sappington D, 'Price Regulation' in Martin Cave, Sumit Majumdar, and Ingo Vogelsang (eds) *Handbook of Telecommunications Economics- vol 1* (Elsevier 2002) 227–287.
Taggart M, 'Reinventing Administrative Law', in Nicholas Bamforth and Peter Leyland (eds), *Public Law in a Multi-Layered Constitution* (Hart 2003) 311–336.
Tapia J and Mantzari D, 'The Regulation/Competition Interaction' in Damien Géradin and Ioannis Lianos (eds), *Research Handbook in European Competition Law* (EE 2013) 588–628.
Veljanovski C, 'The Regulation Game' in Cento Veljanovski (ed), *Regulators and the Market* (The Institute of Economic Affairs 1991) 3–28.

## 3. Articles


Allen R and Pardo M, 'The Myth of the Law-Fact Distinction' (2003) 93 Northwestern Univ L Rev 1769.

Andoni M and others, 'Blockchain Technology in the Energy Sector: A Systematic Review of Challenges and Opportunities' (2019) 100 Renew and Sustain Energy Rev 143.

Ariely D, 'Controlling the Information Flow: Effects on Consumers' Decision Making and Preferences' (2000) 27 J Consum Res 233.

Arthur B, 'Complexity and the Economy' (1999) 284 Science 107.

Arthur B, 'Foundations of Complexity Economics' (2021) 3 Nat Rev Phys 136.

Averch H and Johnson L, 'The Behaviour of the Firm under Regulatory Constraint' (1962) 52 Am Econ Rev 1053.

Bailey D, 'The Scope of Judicial Review under Article 81 EC' (2004) 41 Common Mark L Rev 1327.

Bamberger K and Strauss PL, 'Chevron's Two Steps' (2009) 95 Virginia L Rev 611.

Baum L, 'What Judges Want: Judges' Goals and Judicial Behavior' (1994) 47 Pol Res Q 749.

Baum L, 'Probing the Effects of Judicial Specialisation' (2009) 58 Duke LJ 1667.

Baumol W and Sidak G, 'The Pricing of Inputs Sold to Competitors' (1994) 11 Yale J Reg 171.

Baye MR and Wright JD, 'Is Antitrust Too Complicated for Generalist Judges? The Impact of Economic Complexity and Judicial Training on Appeals' (2011) 54 J L Econ 1.

Bickey J, 'A Fair Return for Public Utilities' (1927) 3 J Land Public Util Econ 61.

Black J, 'Talking about Regulation' [1998] Public Law 77.

Brenner S and Spaeth HJ, 'Issue Specialisation in Majority Opinion Assignment on the Burger Court' (1986) 39 West Pol Q 520.

Bressman L, 'Chevron's Mistake' (2009) 58 Duke LJ 549.

Breyer S, 'Economics for Lawyers and Judges' (1983) 33 J Legal Educ 294.

Brewer S, 'Scientific Expert Testimony and Intellectual Due Process' (1998) 107 Yale LJ. 1535.

Breyer S, 'Judicial Review of Questions of Law and Policy' (1986) 38 Admin L Rev 363.

Breyer S, 'Economic Reasoning and Judicial Review' (2009) 119 Econ J 123.

Cass RA, 'Models of Administrative Action' (1986) 72 Virginia L Rev 363.

Cave M, Genakos C, and Valletti T, 'The European Framework for Regulating Telecommunications: A 25-year Appraisal' (2019) 55 Rev Ind Organ 47.

Cheng EK, 'The Myth of the Generalist Judge' (2008) 61 Stanford L Rev 519.

Clarke M and Cummins T, 'Judicial Review in the Energy Sector: The England and Wales Perspective' (2011) 6 IELR 244

Coen D and Thatcher M, 'The New Governance of Markets and Non-Majoritarian Institutions' (2005) 18 Governance 329.

Cooper JC and Kovacic W, 'Behavioral Economics: Implications for Regulatory Behavior' (2012) 41 J Regul Econ 41.

Craig P, 'Case Comment—Judicial Review, Appeal and Factual Error' [2004] Public L 788.

Crocioni P, 'Ofcom's Record as a Competition Authority: An Assessment of Decisions in Telecoms' (2021) 9 J Antitrust Enforce 505.

Cross F, 'The Judiciary and Public Choice' (1998) 50 Hastings LJ 355.

Daly P, 'Deference on Questions of Law' (2011) 74 Modern L Rev 694.

Dunne N, 'Recasting Competition Concurrency under the Enterprise and Regulatory Reform Act 2013' (2014) 77 Modern L Rev 254.

Economides N, 'The Telecommunications Act of 1996 and its Impact' (1999) 11 Jpn World Economy 455.

Economides N and White LJ, 'Access and Interconnection Pricing: How Efficient is the Efficient Component Pricing Rule?' (1995) XL Antitrust Bull 557.

Economides N and White LJ , 'The Inefficiency of the ECPR Yet Again: A Reply to Larson' (1998) XLIII Antitrust Bull 429.
Elhauge E, 'Does Interest Group Theory Justify More Intrusive Judicial Review?' (1991) 101 Yale LJ 31.
Elhauge E, 'Preference-Estimating Statutory Default Rules' (2002) 18 Colum L Rev 2027.
Fordham M, 'Common Law Proportionality' (2002) 7 Jud Rev 10.
Foster J, 'From Simplistic to Complex Systems in Economics' (2005) 29 Cambridge J Econ 873.
Friedman B, 'The Politics of Judicial Review' (2005) 84 Texas L Rev 257.
Fritzche A, 'Discretion, Scope of Judicial Review and Institutional Balance in European Union' (2010) 47 Common Mark L Rev 361.
Fuller L, 'The Forms and Limits of Adjudication' (1978) 93 Harvard L Rev 353.
Ginsburg DH and Wright JD, 'Antitrust Courts: Specialists versus Generalists' (2013) 36 Fordham Int LJ 788.
Golden JM, 'The Federal Circuit and the D.C. Circuit: Comparative Trials of Two Semi - Specialised Courts' (2010) 78 George Wash L Rev 553.
Haas P, 'Introduction: Epistemic Communities and International Policy Coordination' (1992) 46 Int Organ 1.
Hanson J and Kysar D, 'Taking Behavioralism Seriously: Some Evidence of Market Manipulation' (1999) 112 Harvard L Rev 1420.
Haw Allensworth R, 'Adversarial Economics in Antitrust Litigation: Losing Academic Consensus in The Battle of the Experts' (2012) 106 Northwestern Univ L Rev 1261.
Hemel DJ and Nielson AL, 'Chevron Step-One-and-a-Half' (2017) 84 Univ Chicago L Rev 757.
Hicks JR, 'The Foundations of Welfare Economics' (1939) 49 Econ J 696.
Horwitz P, 'Three Faces of Deference' (2008) 83 Notre Dame L Rev 1061.
Hovenkamp H, 'Technology, Politics and Regulated Monopoly: An American Historical Perspective' (1984) 62 Texas L Rev 1263.
Hovenkamp H, 'The Political Economy of Substantive Due Process' (1988) 40 Stanford L Rev 379.
Hviid M and Waddams Price C, 'Non-discrimination Clauses in the Retail Energy Sector' (2012) 122 Econ J 236.
Ioannidou M and Mantzari D, 'The UK Domestic Gas Electricity (Tariff Cap) Act: Re-regulating the Retail Energy Market' (2019) 82 Modern L Rev 488.
Ip EC, 'Taking a "Hard Look" at 'Irrationality': Substantive Review of Administrative Discretion in the US and UK Supreme Courts' (2014) 34 Oxford J Legal Stud 481.
Irvine Lord of Lairg, 'Judges and Decision-Makers: The Theory and Practice of Wednesbury Review' [1996] Public L 59.
Jaeger M, 'The Standard of Review in Competition Cases Involving Complex Economic Assessments: Towards the Marginalization of the Marginal Review?' (2011) 2 J Eur Compet L Pract 295.
Kaldor N, 'Welfare Propositions in Economics and Interpersonal Comparisons of Utility' (1939) 49 Econ J 549.
Kalintiri A, 'What's in a Name? The Marginal Standard of Review of "Complex Economic Evaluations" in EU Competition Enforcement' (2016) 53 Common Mark L Review 1283.
Kaplow L, 'An Economic Analysis of Legal Transitions' (1986) 99 Harvard L Rev 509.
Kaplow L, 'Rules versus Standards: An Economic Analysis' (1992) 42 Duke LJ 557.
Kearny JD and Merrill TW, 'The Great Transformation of Regulated Industries Law' (1998) 98 Colum L Rev 1323.
King J, 'Institutional Approaches to Judicial Restraint' (2008) 28 Oxf J Leg Stud 409.
King J, 'The Pervasiveness of Polycentricity' [2008] Public L 101.

Landes W and Posner R, 'The Independent Judiciary in an Interest-Group Perspective' (1975) 18 J L Econ 875.
Lang A, 'Governing 'As If': Global Subsidies Regulation and the Benchmark Problem' (2014) 67 Curr Leg Probl 135.
Larouche P, 'A Closer Look at Some Assumptions Underlying EC Regulation of Electronic Communications' (2002) 3 J Netw Ind 129.
Larouche P and De Visser M, 'The Triangular Relationship between the Commission, NRAs and National Courts Revisited' (2006) 64 Communications & Strategies 125.
Larson A, 'The Efficiency of the Efficient Component Pricing Rule: A Comment' (1996) 41 Antitrust Bull 429.
Lavrijssen R and de Visser M, 'Independent Administrative Authorities and the Standard of Judicial Review' (2006) 2 Utrecht L Rev 111.
Lavrijssen R and de Visser M, 'The Different Faces of Energy Consumers: Toward a Behavioral Economics Approach' (2014) 10 J Compet L Econ 257.
Levin R, 'The Anatomy of Chevron: Step Two Reconsidered' (1997) 72 Chicago-Kent L Rev 1253.
Levitt SD and List JA, 'What do Laboratory Experiments Measuring Social Preferences Reveal about the Real World?' (2007) 21 J Econ Perspect 153.
Lianos I, 'Lost in Translation? Towards a Theory of Economic Transplants' (2009) 62 Curr Leg Probl 364.
Lianos I, 'Polycentric Competition Law' (2018) 71 Curr Leg Probl 161.
Lianos I, 'Competition Law for a Complex Economy' (2019) 50 IIC Int Rev Intellect Prop Compet L 643.
Littlechild S, 'The Competition Assessment Framework for the Retail Energy Sector: Some Concerns about the Proposed Interpretation' (2014) 10(1) Eur Compet J 181.
Littlechild S, 'Promoting Competition and Protecting Customers? Regulation of the GB Retail Energy Market 2008–2016' (2019) 55 J Regul Econ 107.
Livingstone S, Lunt P, and Miller L, 'Citizens, Consumers and the Citizen-Consumer: Articulating the Citizen Interest in Media and Communications Regulation' (2007) 1 Discourse Commun 85.
Lombard M, 'Les analyses économiques dans le contrôle juridictionnel des actes pris sur proposition des agences de régulation' (2005) 1 Droit Administratif 88.
Mantzari D, 'The Quest for Reasonable Retail Energy Prices in Europe: Positive and Normative Dimensions' (2017) 36 Yearb Eur L 599.
Magill EM, 'Agency Choice of Policymaking Form' (2004) 71 Univ Chicago L Rev 1383.
Mashaw Jl, 'Recovering American Administrative Law: Federalist Foundations, 1787-1801' (2006) 115 Yale LJ 1256.
McCubbins MD, Noll RG, and Weingast BR, 'The Political Origins of the Administrative Procedure Act' (1999) 15 J L Econ Org 180.
McFadden C, 'Free Markets and Fettered Consumers' (2006) 96 Am Econ Rev 3.
McGrath MJ, 'Convergence of the Substantial Evidence and Arbitrary and Capricious Standards of Review During Informal Rulemaking' (1986) 54 George Wash L Rev 541.
Nazzini R and Mantzari D, 'The Ruling of the UK Competition Appeal Tribunal in *Ping v Competition and Markets Authority*' (2018) 6 J Antitrust Enforc 281.
Nelkin D, 'The Political Impact of Technical Expertise' (1975) 5 Soc Stud Sci 35.
North DC, 'Institutions' (1991) 5 J Econ Perspect 97.
Oldfather CM, 'Error Correction' (2010) 85 Ind LJ 49.
Olson SM, 'Interest Group Litigation in Federal District Courts: Beyond the Political Disadvantage Theory' (1990) 52 J Pol 854.

Oster J, 'The Scope of Judicial Review in the German and U.S. Administrative Legal System' (2008) 9 German LJ 1267.
Pierce RJ, Jr, 'The Choice between Rulemaking and Adjudication for Formulating and Implementing Energy Policy' (1979) 30 Hastings LJ 1.
Pierce RJ, Jr, 'Reconstituting the Natural Gas Industry from Wellhead to Burner Tip' (1988) 9 Energy LJ 12.
Pierce RJ, Jr, 'The Unintended Effects of Judicial Review of the Agency Rules: How Federal Courts Have Contributed to the Federal Crisis of the 1990s' (1991) 43 Admin L Rev 7.
Pierce RJ, Jr, 'The State of the Transition to Competitive Markets in Natural Gas and Electricity' (1994) 15 Energy LJ 323.
Pierce RJ, Jr, 'The Evolution of Natural Gas Regulatory Policy' (1995) 10 Environ Nat Resour 53.
Pierce RJ, Jr, 'The Special Contributions of the D.C. Circuit to Administrative Law' (2002) 90 Georgetown LJ 779.
Posner RA, 'What do Judges Maximize? The Same Thing as Everyone Else' (1993) 3 S Ct Econ Rev 1.
Posner RA, 'The Law and Economics of the Economic Expert Witness' (1999) 13 J Econ Perspect 91.
Pound R, 'Mechanical Jurisprudence' (1908) 8 Colum L Rev 605
Pound R, 'The Scope and Purpose of Sociological Jurisprudence' (1911) 24 Harvard L Rev 591.
Priest G, 'Major Public Utility Decisions in Perspective' (1960) 46 Virginia L Rev 1327.
Rawlings R, 'Modelling Judicial Review' (2008) 61 Current Leg Probl 95.
Revesz R, 'Specialised Courts in Administrative Law-Making System' (1990) 138 Univ Pennsylvania L Rev 1111
Roberts JG, 'Lecture: What Makes the DC Circuit Different? A Historical View' (2006) 92 Virginia L Rev 375.
Rossi J, 'Redeeming Judicial Review: The Hard Look Doctrine and Federal Regulatory Efforts to Restructure the Electric Utility Industry' (1994) 1994(4) Wisconsin L Rev 763.
Rossi J, 'Lowering the Filed Tariff Shield: Judicial Enforcement for a Deregulatory Era' (2003) 56 Virginia L Rev 1591.
Scalia A, 'Vermont Yankee: The APA, the D.C. Circuit, and the Supreme Court' (1978) 1978 Sup Ct Rev 345.
Scalia A, 'Judicial Deference to Administrative Interpretations of Law' (1989) 1989 Duke LJ 511.
Schiller RE, 'Rulemaking's Promise: Administrative Law and Legal Culture in the 1960s and the 1970s' (2001) 53 Admin L Rev 1139.
Schiller RE, 'The Era of Deference: Courts, Expertise, and the Emergence of New Deal Administrative Law' (2007) 106 Michigan L Rev 399.
Schram A, 'Artificiality: The Tension between Internal and External Validity in Economic Experiments' (2005) 12 J Econ Methodol 225.
Schwartz B, 'Mixed Questions of Law and Fact and the Administrative Procedure Act' (1950) 19 Fordham L Rev 73.
Sen A, 'The Nature and Classes of Prescriptive Judgements'(1967) 17 Philos Q 46.
Shapiro M, 'Appeal' (1980) 14 L Soc Rev 629.
Shapiro M, 'Administrative Discretion: The Next Stage' (1983) 92 Yale LJ 1487.
Shapiro M, 'APA: Past, Present, Future' (1986) 72 Virginia L Rev 447.
Shavell S, 'The Appeals Process as a Means of Error Correction' (1995) 24 J Leg Stud 379.
Sidak G, 'Court-Appointed Neutral Economic Experts' (2013) 9 J Compet L Econ 359
Sidak G and Baumol W, 'Stranded Costs' (1995) 18 Harvard J L Public Policy 835.
Sidak G and Spulber DF, 'Deregulatory Takings and Breach of the Regulatory Contract' (1996) 71 NY Univ L Rev 851.

Sidak G and Spulber DF, 'Deregulation and Managed Competition in Network Industries' (1998) 15 Yale J Reg 117.
Songer D and Sheelan R, 'Who Wins on Appeal: Upperdogs and Underdogs in the United States Courts of Appeals' (1992) 36 Am J Pol Sci 235.
Steyn Lord, 'Deference: A Tangled Story' [2005] Sum Public L 359.
Stephenson MC and Vermeule A, 'Chevron Has Only One Ste' (2009) 95 Virginia L Rev 597.
Stewart RB, 'The Reformation of American Administrative Law' (1975) 88 Harvard L Rev 1667.
Stigler G, 'Do Economists Matter? (1976) 42 Southern Econ J 347
Stigler G, 'What Does an Economist Know? (1983) 33 J Leg Stud 311
Stigler G, 'Perfect Competition, Historically Contemplated' (1957) 65 J Pol Econ 1.
Stigler G and Friedland C, 'What Can Regulators Regulate?' The Case of Electricity' (1962) 5 J L Econ 1.
Strauss PL, 'The Place of Agencies in Government: Separation of Powers and the Fourth Branch' (1984) 84 Colum L Rev 573.
Strauss PL, 'Considering Political Alternatives to "Hard Look" Review' (1989) 1989(3) Duke LJ 538.
Strauss PL, 'Revisiting Overton Park: Political and Judicial Controls Over Administrative Actions Affecting the Community' (1992) 39 UCLA L Rev 1251.
Strauss PL, 'Overseers or "Deciders"—The Courts in Administrative Law' (2008) 75 U Chicago L Rev 815.
Strauss PL and Sunstein C, 'The Senate, the Constitution, and the Confirmation Process' (1992) 100 Yale LJ 1491.
Sunstein CR, 'Interest Groups in American Public Law' (1985) 38 Stanford L Rev 29.
Sunstein CR, 'Constitutionalism after the New Deal' (1987) 101 Harv L Rev 421.
Sunstein CR, 'On the Costs and Benefits of Aggressive Judicial Review of Agency Action' (1989) 3 Duke LJ 522.
Sunstein CR, 'Interpreting Statutes in the Regulatory State' (1989) 103 Harv L Rev 405.
Sunstein CR, 'Law and Administration after "Chevron"' (1990) 90 Colum L Rev 2071.
Sunstein CR, 'Chevron Step Zero' (2006) 92 Virginia L Rev 187.
Sunstein CR, Jolls C, and Thaler R, 'A Behavioral Approach to Law and Economics' 50 (1998) Stanford L Rev 1471.
Sunstein CR and Vermeule A, 'Institutions and Interpretation' (2003) 101 Michigan L Rev 885.
Tversky A and Kahneman D, 'Judgment Under Uncertainty: Heuristics and Biases' (1974) 185 Science 1124.
Tversky A and Kahneman, D, 'The Framing of Decisions and the Psychology of Choice' (1981) 211(4481) Science 453
Waddams Price C and Zhu M, 'Empirical Evidence of Consumer Response in Regulated Markets' (2016) 12 J Compet L Econ 113.
Wald PM, 'The Contribution of the D.C. Circuit to Administrative Law' (1988) 40 Admin L Rev 507.
Weingast BR and Moran MJ, 'Bureaucratic Discretion or Congressional Control? Regulatory Policymaking by the Federal Trade Commission' (1983) 91 J Pol Econ 765.
Williamson O, 'Deregulatory Takings and Breach of the Regulatory Contract: Some Precautions' (1996) 71(4) NY Univ L Rev 1007.
Wood DP, 'Generalist Judges in a Specialised World' (1997) 50 SMU L Rev 1755.
Wright J and Diveley A, 'Do Expert Agencies Outperform Generalist Judges? Some Preliminary Evidence from the Federal Trade Commission' (2013) 1(1) J Antitrust Enforce 82
Wright JS, 'The Courts and the Rulemaking Process: The Limits of Judicial Review' (1974) 59 Cornell L Rev 375.

Yackee JW and Yackee SW, 'Administrative Procedures and Bureaucratic Performance: Is Federal Rulemaking "Ossified"?' (2010) 20 J Public Adm Res Theory 261.

Yackee SW, 'Sweet-Talking the Fourth Branch: The influence of Interest Groups Comments on Federal Agency Rulemaking' (2006) 16 J Public Adm Res Theory 103.

## 4. Electronic Sources

Rose V, 'Margins of Appreciation: Changing Contours in Community and Domestic Case Law' (April 2009) 5 Compet Policy Int.

## 5. Working Papers

Oguz F, 'Complexity of Electricity Markets and their Regulation: Insights from the Turkish Experience' (2020) MPRA paper 99261, University Library of Munich, Germany, available at: https://mpra.ub.uni-muenchen.de/99261/1/MPRA_paper_99261.pdf accessed 6 June 2022.

Pollitt, M and Shaorshadze, I, 'The Role of Behavioral Economics in Energy and Climate Policy', ESRC Electricity Policy Research Group (Cambridge 2011).

Waddams Price C and Zhu M, 'Prices and Consumer Switching in the British Retail Electricity Market', Working Paper 13-12 (Centre for Competition Policy 2013).

## 6. Reports

Cave M, 'Independent Review of Competition and Innovation in Water Markets – Final Report', April 2009, available at: <https://assets.publishing.service.gov.uk/government/uploads/system/uploads/attachment_data/file/69462/cave-review-final-report.pdf> accessed 6 June 2022.

Taylor RC, *Embedding Evidence Based Policy Making in Regulatory Organisation: A Case Study of the UK Office of Communications—OFCOM* (PhD thesis, University of Oxford 2009).

Littlechild SC, *Regulation of British Telecommunications' Profitability* (London: Department of Industry 1983).

Lord Woolf, Access to Justice, Final report to the Lord Chancellor on the civil justice system in England and Wales, June 1996, ch 13, available at: https://webarchive.nationalarchives.gov.uk/ukgwa/+/http:/www.dca.gov.uk/civil/final/contents.htm accessed 6 June 2022.

# Index

*For the benefit of digital users, indexed terms that span two pages (e.g., 52–53) may, on occasion, appear on only one of those pages.*

Tables and figures are indicated by *t* and *f* following the page number